New China's Population

New China's Population

DISCARDED

**China Financial & Economic
Publishing House**

MACMILLAN PUBLISHING COMPANY
NEW YORK

Collier Macmillan Publishers
LONDON

Macmillan Publishing Company
866 Third Avenue, New York, NY 10022

Collier Macmillan Canada, Inc.

Library of Congress Catalog Card No.: 87-26119

Printed in the United States of America

printing number
1   2   3   4   5   6   7   8   9   10

Library of Congress Cataloging-in-Publication Data

New China's population/China Financial and Economic Publishing
    House.
        p.   cm.
    ISBN 0-02-905471-0
    1. China—Population.   2. China—Census, 1982.   I. Chung-kuo
ts' ai cheng ching chi ch' u pan she.
HB3654.A3N48 1987
304.6'0951—dc19   87-26119
                                                                 CIP

CONTENTS

LIST OF TABLES

LIST OF CHARTS

            Ningxia (1982)   127

Chart 9-1. Marital Status of Chinese Population (1982)   133

Chart 11-1. Changes in the Total Fertility Rate of Minority and Han
            Women   186

     11-2. Changes in Total Fertility Rate Among Rural and Urban
            Minority Women (1964–1981)   186

     11-3. Fertility Rate of Han and Minority Women of Different
            Age Groups (1981)   188

     11-4. Fertility Rate of Women of Different Age Groups in Five
            Minority Areas (1981)   189

     11-5. Fertility Rate of Women of Different Age Groups in Five
            Minority Areas (1981)   189

     11-6. Fertility Rate of Women of Different Age Groups in Six
            Minority Areas (1981)   190

     11-7. Population Pyramids of Some Minority Regions   206

Chart 12-1. Changes in China's Total Fertility Rate (1970–1983)   224

     12-2. Changes in the Average Age of Marriage for Women
            Since 1970   225

LIST OF CONTRIBUTORS

Gu Jiantang   (Chapters 9 and 10)
   Lecturer
   Institute of Population Economics
   Beijing College of Economics

Li Muzhen   (Chapters 1 and 7)
   Associate Professor
   Institute of Population Economics
   Beijing College of Economics
   Deputy Chief Editor
   China's Population Series

Sun Jinxin   (Chapter 2)
   Director of Demographic Department
   State Statistical Bureau

Wang Weizhi   (Chapter 4)
   Associate Research Fellow
   Director, Institute of Demography
   Chinese Academy of Social Sciences

Wei Jinsheng   (Chapters 5 and 6)
   Associate Professor
   Institute of Population Economics
   Beijing College of Economics
   Deputy Chief Editor
   Population and Economics

Xiao Zhenyu   (Chapter 12)
   Director
   Statistics Office
   China Population Information Center

Xu Shaoyu   (Chapters 3 and 8)
   Associate Professor
   Institute of Population Economics
   Beijing College of Economics

Zhang Tianlu   (Chapter 11)
   Associate Professor
   Institute of Population Economics
   Beijing College of Economics

FOREWORD

The People's Republic of China has over one-fifth of the earth's total population living within its borders. Because the number of people in China looms so large, we need to understand what is happening to China's population size and growth, births and deaths, employment and economy, if we hope to know how the world is coping with its population problems. Yet for decades, until just a few years ago, detailed China population statistics collected by the Chinese government were not available to those of us who tried to fathom China's demographic situation.

This closed situation has been transformed in recent years since the Chinese government started to follow more open policies. This volume, *New China's Population*, provides a sample of the wealth of demographic information now made available to the world. In particular, it is full of detailed data in easily accessible form from China's high-quality 1982 census and 1982 nationwide fertility survey.

Today the government of China disseminates great quantities of important population data and allows its own demographers to analyze the statistics. Some of China's well-known population specialists have contributed chapters to this book. These authors organize and take part in the population research efforts of the Chinese government's State Statistical Bureau, State Family Planning Commission, Chinese Academy of Social Sciences, and leading academic institutions such as the Beijing College of Economics. They are influential in the making of population policy in the world's most populous country.

This book includes broad overviews of population conditions in China, as well as demographic details of importance to the specialist. Foreign observers of China will be especially interested in the sections on China's family planning policies, fertility trends, and dynamics of population growth. Several of the authors discuss the determinants of China's high birth rate in the past and causes of the recent fertility decline. Fertility differentials within the country are also pointed out. For instance, one author highlights the significant difference between the low fertility of China's majority Han population and the much higher number of births to women in minority groups.

Especially noteworthy is the skilled, comprehensive analysis of changes in the sex composition and age structure of China's population over time. Variations in these population characteristics from place to place are also tabulated and well explained. One author also traces the rise in age at marriage over time and shows that the proportion of men and women who marry is still very high in China today.

The book describes China's impressive mortality decline of recent decades. It also documents the unusually high proportion of China's population that is employed, and presents 1982 census data on the occupations of China's workers. Maps and tables show the extreme unevenness of the country's population distribution and density. The section on population migration is especially interesting, in spite of severe data problems we all face on this topic. *New China's Population* includes some useful statistics never before released, such as figures on China's urbanization trends by province.

Following this book, a series of thirty-two China Population Monographs will be produced under the direction of China's State Education Commission. China specialists eagerly await the publication of the series, which is to provide them with much more detailed information and analysis at both the national and the provincial levels.

Judith Banister
Chief, China Branch
Center for International Research
U.S. Bureau of the Census

PREFACE

China is the most populous country in the world. People have waited for a long time to see works written by Chinese scholars on the population of new China. Now, *New China's Population,* a book written by eight Chinese population experts, will be published in English by Macmillan Publishing Company. This is no doubt an event that deserves congratulations.

The book is based mainly on data collected in the 1953, 1964, and 1982 censuses, as well as on data from the one-per-thousand-population fertility sample survey in 1982. The reliability of the data has been acknowledged by both Chinese and foreign scholars. As to the reliability of data quoted from statistics based on residence registrations and other sources, explanations are given in relevant sections. The authors have discussed China's population conditions by proceeding from the country's reality and by employing scientific methods, including some useful methods and techniques used abroad. They have made an effort to search for the underlying law of China's population development, and have made a certain amount of progress in this regard.

The population phenomena of a given country are linked not only to its historical and geographical but also to its economic and social conditions. China's three censuses show that the country's population phenomena are unique in many respects. In demographic terms, over the past three decades or more China's population reproduction has gone through the stage of high birth and high mortality rates, high birth and low mortality rates, and low birth and low mortality rates. The population quality has markedly improved by a doubled life expectancy, a greatly reduced infant mortality rate, and a gradually rising literacy rate among adults. Although these changes have taken place after quite a few twists and turns, generally speaking, New China has made a great improvement in the population features as they were determined by the economic and social conditions of old China. The changes have also distinguished the country in many respects from some developing nations whose per capita GNP roughly stands on a par with that of China. Some indices (such as average life expectancy) are approaching the level of the developed nations. All these changes have taken place in the short period since 1949. These phenomena have rarely been observed in the world's population.

In such a populous country as China, these changes are not accidental. They were not and could not possibly have been decided by a small number of people. They grew out of China's unique economic and social conditions, and are inseparable from the establishment of socialist public ownership, the development of a national economy, the fair distribution of social wealth, and the initial improvement of living standards for the people. At the same time, the changes in population were determined by a large population base, the great pressure on society caused by the loss of control over population growth for a time during the 1960s, and the population policy adopted in view of these facts.

With regard to economic characteristics, China has a high proportion of employment but a fairly low labor productivity; a very high proportion of people engaged in agriculture and quite a small proportion employed in nonagricultural departments, especially those in service trades; a large rural and a small urban population. These factors are characteristic of most developing countries, but some are more pronounced in China. These characteristics also stem from China's economic and social conditions, and cannot be separated from the still backward level of China's economic development and from the semi-ossified economic management and labor systems that lacked vitality for a long time.

The analysis of a population as large as 1 billion belonging to fifty-six different ethnic groups is a very complicated project. It is very difficult to acquire a clear understanding of its true situation and law of development. It needs painstaking study and the work of many people. *New China's Population* is one of the first books on this subject. Because of limited space this book does not discuss all problems nor does it include all views on the subject. Many questions require further study and discussion, and different opinions will make the study develop in depth.

Although the book will receive different evaluations from its readers, I believe that the contents of the book will interest most of the readership. The Chinese government has decided to conduct a national population census every ten years in the future; the fourth census will be held in 1990. It will also undertake a national one-percent population sample survey between censuses; the last survey took place on July 1, 1987. These more frequent surveys will raise the study of China's population to a higher level.

Li Chengrui
Vice-President, International Statistical Institute
President, National Statistical Society of China

CHAPTER ONE

INTRODUCTION

Located in the eastern part of the continent of Asia and bordering on the western Pacific, the People's Republic of China covers an area of 9.6 million square kilometers (3.7 million square miles), accounting for 7% of the total landmass of the earth and ranking third after the Soviet Union and Canada.

China is divided into 30 administrative areas at the provincial level, with 3 municipalities directly under the Central Government, 5 national autonomous regions, and 22 provinces including Taiwan. At the end of 1984, the 29 provinces, municipalities, and autonomous regions on the mainland had under their jurisdiction 297 cities, 2,069 counties, and 595 city-administered districts, with a total population of 1,034.75 million. Before making an analysis and study of the various phenomena of China's population, it is necessary to deal briefly with the natural environment in which the Chinese people live and with their socioeconomic background.

GEOGRAPHICAL ENVIRONMENT AND NATURAL RESOURCES

China is a mountainous country. Of its 9.6 million square kilometers of territory, mountainous areas account for about 33%, plateaus 26%, basins 19%, hilly land 10%, and plains only 12%, with the mountains and plateaus making up more than half of the country's total area. About 25% is more than 3,000 meters, 32% is from 1,000 to 3,000 meters, 18% is from 500 to 1,000 meters above sea level, and only 25% is less than 500 meters above sea level. These basic topographical features not only affect the country's economic development but also have a direct bearing on the distribution of its population.

The general topography is that the land slopes down from west to east in the form of a staircase. The Qinghai-Tibet Plateau in the westernmost part of the country is one of the largest plateaus in the world. The greater part of this plateau rises about 4,000 meters above sea level and is known as the "Roof of the World." Being a high-altitude, frigid area, the region is hardly accessible and is to this day sparsely populated. Highlands and basins with an altitude of 1,000 to 2,000 meters above sea level surround the Qinghai-Tibet Plateau. These mainly include the Yunnan-Guizhou Plateau, the Loess Plateau, the Inner Mongolian Plateau, the Junggar Basin, and the Tarim Basin. As most of China's sandy and pebbly wastes and deserts are located here, this region is also sparsely populated. To the east are mountains, hills, and basins about 1,000 meters above sea level. They include the Greater and Lesser Hingan Mountains, the Yanshan and the Taihang Mountain Ranges, the Qinling and the Daba Mountains, and the hilly areas along the east coast. The comparatively large basins here include the Sichuan Basin and the Hanzhong Basin, which are all densely populated. On the east coast are hilly areas and rolling plains less than 500 meters above sea level. The larger ones include the North China Plain, the Northeast China Plain, the plains on the middle and lower reaches of the Yangtze River, as well as deltas, mountain basins, and river valleys. As these plains, basins, and valleys are fertile and endowed with abundant water resources and a favorable climate, two-thirds of China's cultivated land are found in these regions, which are also the most densely populated. Off the coast the continental shelf extends over a vast area, and China's territorial waters stretch from the Bohai Bay and the Yellow Sea in the north to the East China Sea and the South China Sea in the south. The vast sea areas and numerous islands not only provide excellent fishing grounds but are also a treasure house of petroleum and other resources.

COMPLEX WEATHER CONDITIONS

China's vast territory comprises different climatic regions with widely diverse weather conditions. In the south are the tropical and subtropical areas, and as we move northward we come to the warm-temperate and temperate regions, and then the temperate-frigid areas. The subtropical, warm-temperate, and temperate regions make up more than 70% of China's total area, and it is these regions with abundant sunshine and a favorable climate that provide an excellent environment for the people to live and various kinds of crops to thrive.

Washed by the waters of the western Pacific, China has a long zigzag coastline. In summer, when the southeast monsoon blows, there is abundant rainfall, which, combined with an adequate amount of warmth, is conducive to agricultural production. However, owing to the complicated topography and the varied distance from the sea, the amount of rainfall in different places is very uneven, with a gradual decrease from the coast to the hinterland. This is why large areas in the interior have little or no rain throughout the year. If we draw a straight line from the Greater Hingan Mountains down through Zhangjiakou, Yulin, Lanzhou, and Qamdu, thereby dividing China into two halves, rainfall in the southeastern half is about 400–2,000 mm a year, placing it in the humid and semihumid zones. The humid zone (with aridity less than 1), which accounts for 32% of the country's total area, includes mainly areas along the southeastern coast. The semihumid zone (with aridity ranging from 1.0 to 1.5), which accounts for about 15% of the country's total area, comprises mainly the North China Plain and the Northeast China Plain. These humid and semihumid areas, with the right amount of water and warmth, provide the Chinese people with favorable production and living conditions. The northwestern parts, with an annual rainfall of less than (400 mm), are arid and semiarid. The arid areas (with aridity greater than 2), which account for 31% of the nation's total area, are mainly in the vast region to the west of Lanzhou. As most areas are deserts and pebbly wastes and annual rainfall is low, people engage in agricultural production only in the "oases" irrigated by water from melted snow. The semiarid areas (with aridity ranging from 1.5–2), which account for about 22% of the country's total area, lie between the semihumid and the arid zones. Here we find China's major grasslands, which, compared with the southwestern parts of the country, are sparsely inhabited. The southwest monsoon also brings abundant rainfall, making many places in China's southwestern provinces and regions humid or semihumid. The climate and distribution of rainfall affect agricultural production in different parts of China and exert a big influence on people's activities in various spheres.

ABUNDANT NATURAL RESOURCES

Water Resources.   China abounds in water resources. Its numerous rivers total 420,000 km in length, and the basins of 79 of these rivers are each no smaller than 10,000 square kilometers. The nation's long rivers include the Yangtze, the Yellow, the Heilong, the Pearl, Liaohe, Haihe, Huai, Yarlung Zangbo, and Nujiang rivers. There are many lakes as well, 13 of which are large freshwater lakes with an area of more than 1,000 square kilometers each. These include the Poyang, Xingkai, Dongting, Hongze, Taihu, Hulun Nur, and Namco lakes, which are all rich in aquatic products.

However, the geographical distribution of China's water resources is very uneven. The rivers' surface runoff totals 2,700 billion cubic meters and their ground-water runoff amounts to approximately 1,000 billion cubic meters. But the Yangtze and Pearl rivers, whose basins make up one-fourth of the nation's total, account for half of the nation's total surface runoff and more than two-thirds of the total ground-water runoff. By contrast, the Yellow, Huai, and Haihe rivers, whose basins make up one-seventh of the nation's total, account for only one-twenty-fifth of the country's total surface runoff and one-fortieth of the total ground-water runoff. In China's vast northwest, where rainfall is scarce, the surface and ground-water runoffs are negligible, and glaciers and melted snow are the only sources of water supply there.

China is also rich in water power resources. Of the estimated total reserve of about 680 million kw, 370 million kw can be tapped, but so far only 4.3% of these resources have been developed. This shows that China has a big potential in hydroelectric power generation.

Land Resources.   Vast as China's territory is, arable land makes up only 10.3% of the nation's total area, with little land left that can be reclaimed. Grasslands account for 33% of the nation's total landmass, but most lack adequate supplies of water. This has limited the development of animal husbandry. Forests are few and far between, and they cover only 12.7% of China's total territory. Deserts and barren hills and mountains take up much of the land, which to a certain extent circumscribes the growth of the Chinese population.

But China's land resources have the potential for further development. The hitherto desolate mountains and unreclaimed land can be planted with trees, and the vast inland rivers and lakes and beaches along the coast may be utilized to develop a

Table 1-1 Types of Land Resources in China

TYPE	SIZE		PERCENTAGE IN NATIONAL TERRITORY (%)
	SQUARE KM	HECTARES (UNIT: 1 MILLION)	
Total	9.6 million	960	100
Cultivated land	993,000	99.333	10.4
Mulberry and tea plantations and orchards	33,000	3.333	0.3
Grasslands	3.167 million	316.667	33.0
Forests	1.22 million	122	12.7
Inland water surfaces	267,000	26.66	2.8
Coastal beaches	20,000	2	0.9
Barren hills and wasteland that can be planted with trees	779,000	78	8.1
Wasteland that can be reclaimed for farming	333,000	33.333	3.5
Land taken up by urban factories, mines, and transportation facilities	670,000	66.667	7.0
Other types	2.118 million	212	22.0

Source: *Economic Yearbook of China,* China Statistics Publishing House, 1984.

diversified economy. Available statistics show that China has 20,000 square kilometers of beachfront, of which roughly one-fourth is suitable for aquiculture. Of the 4.9 million square kilometers of sea area, 430,000 square kilometers of the shallow seas can be used to develop aquatic products. Moreover, most of the lakes and reservoirs can be used for fish-farming, and the hills and hillocks can be afforested and turned into timberland. The development of a diversified economy will not only help raise the land utility rate but also improve the food composition.

Land, of course, is the primary means of production for agriculture. In China the various kinds of land resources are unevenly distributed. Over 90% of the cultivated land, forests, and water surfaces are located in the humid and semihumid regions in the southeastern half of the country, while most of the grasslands and sandy wastes are in the arid and semi-arid areas of the northwestern half. The result is different agricultural setups and economic levels in different parts of the country, with their full impact on population composition and development. The fact that the Chinese population is concentrated mostly in the southeastern half of the country closely relates to the geographical distribution of various kinds of natural resources.

Mineral Resources. China is a country rich in mineral resources. Verified coal deposits are estimated at 600 billion tons, and annual output today is over 600 million tons, ranking third in the world. The nation's petroleum industry has bright prospects, as oil has been discovered both in continental sedimentary deposits and on offshore continental shelves.

Iron-ore deposits are estimated at more than 4.4 billion tons, and the country's deposits of nonferrous metals such as wolfram, tin, antimony, zinc, titanium, molybdenum, manganese, copper, and rare-earth elements are important resources in the world. There are also large deposits of many kinds of nonmetallic minerals, notably gypsum, barite, asbestos, and mica. Work has begun on tapping the rich resources of natural gas. Salt production in China is marked by its large output and great variety including sea salt, lake salt, well salt, and halite. The plenteous mineral resources are a material guarantee for the nation's economic development.

Judging from its vast landmass and rich resources, China is indeed a big country. But because of its large population, which accounts for one-fifth of the world's total, the amount of resources per person is lower than the world's average. Land for each person is less than 1 hectare (2.47 acres), which is only 30% of the world's average. Per capita cultivated land averages 0.1 hectare, or 33% of the world's average; per capita forest area stands at an average of 0.12 hectare, or 12% of the world's average; per capita grassland averages 0.3 hectare, or 40% of the world's average; and per capita river run-off averages 2,700 cubic meters, which is only 25% of the world's average. The amount of metallic and nonmetallic minerals for each person is also well below the world's average level.

China has made tremendous achievements in the building of water conservancy projects, in tree planting, and in the prevention of natural disasters since the founding of the People's Republic. But increased human activities as a result of the sharp rise in population have adversely affected the natural environment and ecological balance. An example is the irrational way land was opened up for farming in the past, with the result that 1.2 million square kilometers of land are under the constant menace of soil erosion. Surveys show that deserts are expanding, they have increased by 70,000 square kilometers in the last two decades. Forest cover, on the other hand, is diminishing with each passing day, and the amount of cut timber now exceeds that of new growth by almost 35%. There are many other problems, such as the reduction of cultivated land as a result of urban construction, environmental pollution, the deterioration of grasslands, the drop in the amount of offshore aquatic products, and the excessive use of ground water, all of which have an important bearing on the growth of population.

To lead the one billion Chinese people step by step on to the road of prosperity, apart from making the best use of the natural resources to develop production and protecting the natural environment, it is imperative to practice family planning so as to effectively keep population growth under control. This is a major policy decision of strategic importance made in the light of China's actual conditions.

NATIONAL ECONOMIC AND SOCIAL DEVELOPMENT

Before 1949, China was a semifeudal and semicolonial country with an extremely backward economy and culture. After more than 30 years of hard work since the founding of the People's Republic, China has made tremendous achievements both in economic construction and in social development.

Through the socialist transformation of the ownership of the means of production, China has established an economic system predominated by socialist ownership on the basis of which the nation has instituted a planned economy and the distribution system of "to each according to his work." This is a socioeconomic reform of far-reaching significance in Chinese history, and it has opened up vast vistas for the development of the national economy. Under the socialist system, industrial production has developed rapidly, and many industrial branches have been set up practically from scratch, gradually expanding to become comparatively complete systems. With this as the foundation, great changes have taken place in the conditions of agricultural production, resulting in a big boost to the level of production. From 1949 to 1984, China's total output value of

society increased from 55.7 billion yuan to 1,300.4 billion yuan, a 22.4-fold increase, of which the total output value of industry went up from 14 billion yuan to 704.2 billion yuan, a 49.3-fold increase. During the same period, the total value of fixed assets of publicly owned industrial enterprises went up from 14.88 billion yuan to 476.78 billion yuan, a more than 3.1-fold increase.* Compared with 1952, China's grain output multiplied almost three times to reach 86.35 million tons in 1984, and cotton output increased 3.8-fold to reach 6.258 million metric tons, both sufficient to feed and clothe its population. Commerce and foreign trade also made much headway. The country's total value of retail sales increased from 27.68 billion yuan in 1952 to 337.64 billion yuan in 1984, an 11.2-fold increase.

Adhering to the principles of equality and mutual benefit, China has established trade ties with more than 140 countries and regions the world over. Total import and export value increased from 6.46 billion yuan in 1952 to 120.1 billion yuan in 1984, a 17.6-fold increase. Along with economic development, communications and transportation have also improved considerably. Railway mileage increased from 22,000 kilometers in 1949 to 52,000 kilometers in 1984. In the same period, highway mileage went up from 81,000 kilometers to 927,000 kilometers, inland waterways open to navigation increased from 74,000 kilometers to 109,000 kilometers, and air service mileage from 11,000 kilometers to 260,000 kilometers. In addition, there were considerable increases in the means of transportation and in the shipment of both passengers and goods. The material and cultural well-being of urban and rural residents have improved steadily. Remarkable increases have been registered in their real income, living space, living standards, and savings deposits in the banks.

Economic growth has further consolidated the socialist system. Especially since the convening of the Third Plenary Session of the 11th Central Committee of the Chinese Communist Party, toward the end of 1978, "leftist" thinking has been repudiated, and with the institution and perfection of the legal system, the people's basic rights and interests are guaranteed and society has become more stable than ever before. At the same time, various public undertakings have made great progress. Education, culture, and science have advanced rapidly. In 1984, China had 185.576 million students in the primary and secondary schools and colleges (not including

* In early 1987, 100 yuan was roughly $27.

special schools for adults and technical schools). This was a 2.4-fold increase over 1952. That year, there were in China 902 colleges and universities with 1.396 million students; 97,015 secondary schools with 48.70 million students (of which 3,301 were secondary vocational schools having 1.322 million students); and 854,000 primary schools with 135.57 million pupils. Over the past 30-odd years, these colleges and universities and secondary vocational schools have trained 11.33 million competent professionals who have all been given employment. In 1984, China had 7.466 million scientists and technicians, which meant 72.5 for every 10,000 Chinese or 864.4 for every 10,000 industrial and service workers. Though the number was comparatively small, it was more than 16 times that of 1952. Medical and health work has also developed steadily. By the end of 1984, there were in China 67,000 hospitals with a total of 2.166 million beds; 117,000 clinics; more than 6,055 health and epidemic prevention stations as well as maternity and childcare centers; and 301 medical research institutes. There were 4.214 million doctors throughout the country, that is, 1.3 for every 1,000 people, which was more than double the figure for 1949. In addition, social welfare undertakings of various kinds have developed vigorously in both the cities and countryside, and the elderly, the disabled, and children are all well taken care of by the entire society.

Since the founding of New China, in 1949, there has been a big upswing in its economic and social development, which has made a notable impact on the changes in China's population.

POPULATION AND ITS CHARACTERISTICS

China is the most populous country in the world. According to the third national census (with 00:00 hour July 1, 1982 as the standard time), the mainland of China had a population of 1,008.18 million, or 21% of the world's total. The 29 provinces, municipalities, and autonomous regions had a total population of 1,034.75 million by the end of 1984. The main characteristics of China's population follow.

LARGE BASE, FAST GROWTH, CHECKED MOMENTUM

One of the most outstanding features of the Chinese population is the huge cardinal number of one billion people. This means that at the present birth and mortality rate, there are at least 52,000 newborn babies and about 20,000 deaths every day, and that the annual average growth rate is close to 10 million, which is about the population of a not too small country. The population showed the tendency to grow rapidly after the founding of New China in 1949, as illustrated in the three national censuses taken in 1953, 1964, and 1982. In 1953, when the first census was taken, the population in the 29 provinces, municipalities, and autonomous regions (not including Taiwan Province) was 582.6 million; this was a 7.19% increase over the 1949 year-end figure of 541.67 million, and the average annual rate of growth was 2%. The second census, in 1964, showed that the population had increased to 694.58 million; this was a 19.63% increase over 1953, and the average annual growth rate was 1.64%. At the third census, in 1982, the tally registered a sharp rise of 45.24% to reach 1.0818 billion. The average annual growth rate had jumped to 2.1%, which was higher than the average annual growth rate of 1.97% for the world population in the corresponding period and also higher than the average annual growth rate of 0.25% in China in the 100-odd years from 1840 to 1949.

This fast growth of China's population in the last 30-odd years was mainly the result of natural population growth (see Table 1-2). To make population growth compatible with the national economic development, the Chinese government has adopted effective family planning measures, the emphasis being on controlling the birthrate. Encouraging results have been obtained. Since the 1970s, the increase in population has basically been brought under control.

FAST-CHANGING YOUNG AGE COMPOSITION

At present the Chinese population is still young; 60% of the people were born after 1949 and most are now in their prime. According to the third national census, in 1982, people of 14 and under accounted for 33.6%, those between 15 and 64 accounted for 61.5%, and people of 65 and over accounted for 4.9%; the age median was 22.9 and the ratio of the number of elderly persons to the number of children was 14.6%. Thus the age composition of the Chinese population falls basically under the category in which the people are in transition from the young to adult period. A comparison and analysis of the statistics available in the three national censuses reveal marked changes (see Table 1-3).

Table 1-3 shows that in 1982 the proportion of 14-year-olds and under dropped by a big margin

Table 1-2   Natural Changes in China's Population (1949–1984)

YEAR	POPULATION (10,000)	BIRTHRATE (%)	MORTALITY RATE (%)	NATURAL GROWTH RATE (%)
1949	54,167	36.00	20.00	16.00
1950	55,196	37.80	18.00	19.00
1951	56,300	37.80	17.80	20.00
1952	57,482	37.00	17.00	20.00
1953	58,796	37.00	14.00	23.00
1954	60,266	37.97	13.18	24.79
1955	61,465	32.60	12.28	20.32
1956	62,828	31.90	11.40	20.50
1957	64,653	34.03	10.80	23.23
1958	65,994	29.22	11.98	17.24
1959	67,207	24.78	14.59	10.19
1960	66,207	20.86	25.43	−4.57
1961	65,859	18.02	14.24	3.78
1962	67,295	37.01	10.02	26.99
1963	69,127	43.37	10.04	33.33
1964	70,499	39.14	11.50	27.64
1965	72,538	37.88	9.50	28.38
1966	74,542	35.05	8.83	26.22
1967	76,368	33.96	8.43	25.53
1968	78,534	35.59	8.21	27.38
1969	80,671	34.11	8.03	26.08
1970	82,992	33.43	7.60	25.83
1971	85,229	30.65	7.32	23.33
1972	87,117	29.77	7.61	22.16
1973	89,211	27.93	7.04	20.89
1974	90,859	24.82	7.34	17.48
1975	92,420	23.01	7.32	15.69
1976	93,717	19.91	7.25	12.66
1977	94,974	18.93	6.87	12.06
1978	96,259	18.25	6.25	12.00
1979	97,542	17.82	6.21	11.61
1980	98,705	18.21	6.34	11.87
1981	100,072	20.91	6.36	14.55
1982	101,541	20.09	6.60	14.49
1983	102,495	18.62	7.08	11.54
1984	103,475	17.50	6.69	10.81

Source: *Statistics Yearbook of China*, China Statistics Publishing House, 1984.

since the previous census, while that of people of 65 and older increased. This demonstrates that the Chinese population is on the threshhold of becoming old. The characteristics of the age composition of the Chinese population give rise to three questions. First, the big proportion of working-age people

Table 1-3   Age Composition in the Three Censuses (%)*

YEAR	AGE GROUP		
	0–14	15–64	65+
1953	36.3	59.3	4.4
1964	40.7	55.7	3.6
1982	33.6	61.5	4.9

* Servicemen not included.
Source: The three national censuses of 1953, 1964, and 1982.

means that through the end of the century China has rich labor power resources, but at the same time it will have to tackle the thorny problem of finding jobs for them. Second, the proportion of people of child-bearing age has increased. In 1982 Chinese women of childbearing age accounted for 24.7% of the total population. In other words, close to 250 million women were married or about to get married and have children; this means the birthrate will go up again. Third, due to the fast change in age composition, in another 20 or 30 years the aging problem of the Chinese population will become very acute. Actually, this problem has already cropped up in the three municipalities of Beijing, Tianjin, and Shanghai, as well as in some other big cities, to the great concern of the central government and the departments involved.

UNEVEN POPULATION DISTRIBUTION

The extremely uneven distribution of the Chinese population finds expression, first and foremost, in the vast difference in the size of the population in different parts of the country. Most of the Chinese people live in the southeastern half of the country (that is, east of the line from the Greater Hingan Mountains in the north down through Zhangjiakou and Lanzhou to Qamdu). This half covers 47% of the total area of China but is inhabited by more than 90% of the population. The northwestern half covers 53% of the total area but is inhabited by only 10% of the population. If we divide the country into the coastal areas and the interior, then the 11 provinces, municipalities, and autonomous regions along the coast, covering only 14% of the total area, are inhabited by 43% of the Chinese population, while the remaining 18 provinces and autonomous regions in the interior, covering 86% of the total area, have only 57% of the population.

Population density also differs greatly in different places. According to 1983 demographic statistics, the population density in China averaged 107 people per square kilometer, or more than three times the world average of 34 people per square kilometer. There are great differences in population density between the various provinces, municipalities, and autonomous regions. In the 18 provinces and autonomous regions in the interior, the density is 71 people per square kilometer on the average; but it is 1.6 people per square kilometer in Tibet, 5.4 people per square kilometer in Qinghai, 8.2 people per square kilometer in Xinjiang, and 17 people per square kilometer in Inner Mongolia. In the 11 provinces, municipalities, and autonomous regions along the coast, the average population density is 312 people per square kilometer; but it is 598 people per square kilometer in Jiangsu, 494 people per square kilometer in Shandong, and 455 people per square kilometer in Henan. The density in these provinces is higher than that of the most densely populated countries elsewhere in the world, such as the Netherlands (346 people per square kilometer), Belgium (323 people), and Japan (316 people).

LOW URBANIZATION LEVEL AND LARGE RURAL POPULATION

As the industrial foundation of old China was very poor, the number of people living in the cities and towns was comparatively small. In 1949 people living in cities and towns accounted for only 10.6% of the total population. Although the proportion had risen to 18.4% in 1964 and 20.6% in 1982, it was still lower than the world's average level of 37% for the corresponding period. With the development of social productive forces, especially the flourishing of the rural economy, surplus labor gradually increased in the countryside. The inevitable result will be the urbanization of the Chinese population.

Since 1983 small towns have developed rapidly, and this has led to a rapid increase in the population of cities and towns throughout China. As there is as yet no standard classification, there is still a large percentage of rural population in the towns and cities. Therefore, the present total population of the cities and towns does not fully reflect the actual level of urbanization in China.

COMPLEX SOCIAL COMPOSITION

China is a unified multinational country with 56 nationalities. According to the third census, in 1982, people of Han nationality in the 29 provinces, municipalities, and autonomous regions on the mainland numbered 936.7 million, that is, 93.3% of the total population, while people of the 55 minority nationalities numbered 67.23 million, or 6.7% of the total. This was a 68.4% increase over the number at the second census, in 1964, a higher growth rate than that for the Han people.

The employment rate of the Chinese people is high. According to figures obtained at the third census, in 1982, the number of employed in that year totalled 521.506 million, or 51.9% of the total population. This was higher than the 44% in the United States, 47.4% in Japan, and 44.3% in Britain. While this showed that people between 15 and 64 occupied a large proportion in China and that the employment problem was comparatively well solved, it also showed that the cultural and educational level in China was comparatively backward and that enrollment in the schools, especially enrollment in the institutes of higher learning, was low. According to census figures available in 1982, out of every 10,000 people in China, there were only 662 people with a senior middle school and higher education, and only 60 of them had a college education; the number of college educated in China was much lower than in the United States (1,492), Canada (1,198), Japan (637), and the Soviet Union (450). The level of education has a direct bearing on the proportion of manual laborers to skilled workers.

In China today, 94.6% of the employed work in material-production departments and only 5.4% in the science, education, and other nonproduction departments.

With regard to marriage, the situation is quite stable in China. Marriage is almost universal in the population, and the divorce rate is below 0.5%. The proportion of single at age group 30 – 34 was 8.9% for men, and only 0.7% for women. The overwhelming majority of young people between 25 and 29 are married.

Population is one of the decisive factors in deter-mining whether China can achieve the magnificent goal of the four modernizations — agriculture, industry, national defense, and science and technology — by the end of the century. As China's population is about one-fifth of the world's total, it is therefore a question of world significance. The study of modern China's population question is an important task both in China and internationally. The following chapters of this book will give a detailed account and analysis of New China's population.

CHAPTER TWO

THE CHINESE POPULATION: ITS SIZE AND GROWTH

The size of a country's population, that is, the total number of people of the whole country at a particular time, is the basic feature of that country's population, whose size, big or small, reflects the amount of work resources of that country. In countries with a planned economy the degree of change in the population size during different periods has a direct bearing on the economic planning of the country. To a certain extent, the rate of population change determines the scale of material production under certain conditions and the market in which commodities are sold. Naturally, it also directly affects the reproduction of population itself.

China has a history of several thousand years, and the Chinese civilization is one of the oldest in the world. Its population has undergone a long period of development, and numerous new features and changes have emerged, particularly after the founding of New China. This chapter deals mainly with the size and historical development of the Chinese population and its growth in the last 30-odd years, and tentatively analyzes the factors affecting the changes in the size of New China's population.

THE PAST AND PRESENT SIZE OF CHINA'S POPULATION

To make a historical comparison it is necessary to recapitulate the history of the development of China's population prior to the establishment of the People's Republic. The country had gone through primitive society, slave society, feudal society, and semicolonial and semifeudal society. In China's recorded history of more than 4,000 years, the first datum on the population can be traced back to 2140 B.C. during the early Xia Dynasty, which saw the beginning of slave society in China. According to esti-

mates made by Huangpu Mi (215–282) of the Jin Dynasty in his *Chronicle of Emperors and Kings*, China at that time had a population of 13,553,923.* This figure is of reference value although it is hard to determine its accuracy, the way it was obtained, and the extent of areas it covered. The fact that, during the 600,000 years from the Yuanmou Man to the founding of the Xia Dynasty, China had only a little more than 10 million people shows that the productive forces at that time were of a very low level, and although the birthrate was high, an equally high mortality rate slowed the population growth, sometimes to a standstill.

During the time of slave society, cruel exploitation and suppression by slave-owners deprived the slaves of the freedom to marry and give birth to children. Frequent feuds and wars between slave-owners resulted in the death of large numbers of slaves, and when a slave-owner died, large numbers of slaves were buried alive with him. This explains why population growth was slow in slave society, although the productive forces of this period were more developed than in primitive society. Statistics were lacking about the population size during the middle and late Spring and Autumn Period (770–475 B.C), when slave society came to an end. According to estimates made by Hu Huanyong and Zhang Shanyu, the number of people must have been at least equal to the peak figure of the most prosperous years of the Western Zhou Dynasty (c. eleventh century B.C. to 771 B.C.), that is, about 20 million.† According to this estimate, the average annual growth

---

* Huangpu Mi: *Chronicle of Emperors and Kings,* Commercial Press, 1950 edition, p. 48.
† Hu Huanyong and Zhang Shanyu: *China's Demographic Geography,* Book One, East China Normal University Press, 1984, pp. 5–6.

rate of the population during the entire slave society in China was approximately 0.25%.

China's feudal society lasted more than 2,000 years from the Warring States Period (475–221 B.C.) to the outbreak of the 1840 Opium War. Under the feudal system, the basic means of production, that is, land, belonged to the feudal lords, while the peasants who had their own farm implements could barely manage to provide for their families after paying the rent. Under the feudal system large families were an advantage, and this resulted in the popular concepts that "more children means greater fortune" and that "the family name should be carried down from generation to generation." Thus the people were imbued with the idea "the more children, the better," which to a certain extent promoted the growth of the population.

But the sharp contradictions within the feudal landlord class unavoidably led to large-scale wars between the ruling cliques, and the irreconcilable class contradictions between the landlords and the peasants also often sparked peasant rebellions. The frequent wars, coupled with natural disasters and epidemics, took a heavy toll of lives. Generally speaking, the early days of every feudal dynasty were marked by a sharp decrease in population as a result of wars that brought about a change of regime, and the population began to increase considerably again during the dynasty's heyday when political stability and economic development reigned. Toward the final stage of the dynasty, the population began to decrease again as a result of natural disasters and wars.

Because of social and political upheavals and people's inability to combat nature, the population grew very slowly under feudalism. During the Warring States Period, the population reached an all-time high of 30 million.* By the time of the Western Han Dynasty 350 years later, the population reached 60 million.† The average annual growth rate was about 2‰ (0.2%) during this period. From the heyday (A.D. 6) of the Western Han Dynasty to the heyday of the Tang Dynasty, around A.D. 752, the population had increased to 80 million,‡ the annual growth rate averaged about 0.6‰ (0.06%). The population registered a considerable growth during the Ming (1368–

1644) and Qing (1644–1911) Dynasties, reaching 412.81 million in 1840, or the twentieth year of the reign of Emperor Xuan Zong, according to the *Historical Records of the Reign of Emperor Xuan Zong.*

During the entire feudal period in China (from 475 B.C. to 1840), the population increased from 30 million to 412.81 million, the average annual growth rate being 1.1‰.

China became a semifeudal, semicolonial society after the 1840 Opium War as a result of the aggression by foreign capitalist powers. In the 109 years from the Opium War to the founding of the People's Republic, in 1949, the Chinese population increased from 412.81 million to 541.67 million (by the end of 1949)—a net increase of 128.86 million and an annual growth rate of 2.5‰.

The history of the development of the Chinese population prior to the founding of the People's Republic of China was characterized by a high birthrate and mortality rate and a low natural growth rate. Due to frequent wars, natural disasters, and epidemic diseases, the population grew slowly with great ups and downs. Generally speaking, China's population grew faster in feudal society than in slave society, and even faster during the semicolonial, semifeudal society that followed.

The population started to grow fast after the founding of the People's Republic of China. This can be attributed to the fundamental changes in the country's social system and economy. The annual growth rate averaged as high as 18.7‰ from 1949 to the end of 1984. In the 4,000 years before the founding of the People's Republic, the population increased from 30 million to 541.67 million—a net increase of 510 million and an average increase of less than 130,000 each year. But during the 35 years from 1949 to 1984, the net increase of China's population was 493.08 million or an average annual net increase of 14.09 million. Therefore it can be said that the vast expansion and the enormous increase in the total population of China took place mainly in the years after the founding of the People's Republic, in 1949.

POPULATION GROWTH IN NEW CHINA

After the founding of the People's Republic, China's population increased from 541.67 million in 1949 to 1,034.75 million in 1984, with the growth rate toppling all previous records. Due to political, economic, social, and cultural changes in the 35 years after the founding of New China, the speed of popula-

---

* Hu Huanyong and Zhang Shanyu: *China's Demographic Geography*, Book One, East China Normal University Press, 1984, p. 12.
† Liang Fangzhong: *Statistical Data on Chinese Households, Land and Land Tax in Various Dynasties*, Shanghai People's Publishing House, 1980.
‡ Hu Huanyong and Zhang Shanyu: *Demographic Geography*, p. 33.

Table 2-1   China's Population (1949–1984)*

	(YEAR-END FIGURES)		
YEAR	TOTAL POPULATION (10,000)	YEAR	TOTAL POPULATION (10,000)
1949	54,167	1967	76,368
1950	55,196	1968	78,534
1951	56,300	1969	80,671
1952	57,482	1970	82,992
1953	58,796	1971	85,229
1954	60,266	1972	87,177
1955	61,465	1973	89,211
1956	62,828	1974	90,859
1957	64,653	1975	92,420
1958	65,994	1976	93,717
1959	67,207	1977	94,974
1960	66,207	1978	96,259
1961	65,859	1979	97,542
1962	67,295	1980	98,705
1963	69,172	1981	100,072
1964	70,499	1982	101,541
1965	72,538	1983	102,495
1966	74,542	1984	103,475

* Population figures for each year included the population of the 29 provinces, municipalities, and autonomous regions on China's mainland as well as servicemen.
Source: *Statistics Yearbook of China 1985*, China Statistics Publishing House, 1985, p. 185.

tion growth varied in the different stages (see Table 2-1).

The speed of population growth in the postliberation years may be calculated according to the time needed for the increase of every 100 million people (see Table 2-2). In doing so, it should be noted that the time needed for the increase of every 100 million people was subject to two factors: the fertility level of women and the base number of the population at that time. For example, Table 2-2 shows that the time needed for the increase of every 100 million people after 1976 was the longest (9.3 years), and the base number of the population then was also the largest.

Thus the population growth rate of this period was actually much slower than that shown in the table.

The speed of New China's population growth may be divided into five stages: the first peak period, low-ebb period, second peak period, third peak period, and period of decrease.

The first peak period was from early 1950 to the end of 1958. During this period, the total population increased from 541.67 million to 659.94 million, averaging an increase of 13.14 million a year, or an average annual growth rate of 22.2%.

The first few years of this stage—from the beginning of 1950 to the end of 1952—may be called an

Table 2-2   Population Growth in New China

YEAR	YEAR-END POPULATION (10,000)	INCREASE OVER PRECEDING YEAR IN TABLE (10,000)	TIME NEEDED FOR INCREASE OF EVERY 100 MILLION PEOPLE (YEARS)
1949	54,167	—	—
1957	64,653	10,486	7.6
1966	74,542	9,889	9.1
1971	85,229	10,687	4.7
1976	94,974	9,745	5.1
1985	104,639	9,665	9.3

Source: *Statistics Yearbook of China 1985*, China Statistics Publishing House, 1985.

"inertia" period. The birthrate in this period was not much different from that before the founding of New China, remaining at a little above the 37‰ level, and the death rate was reduced only from 20‰ in 1949 to 17‰ in 1952.

From the beginning of 1953 to the end of 1958, improvement in medical care and public health conditions facilitated the prevention and cure of many serious contagious and infectious diseases, and the death rate dropped greatly (from 17‰ in 1952 to 11.98‰ in 1958). The implementation of the First Five-Year Plan brought about a significant development of the productive forces and improvement in the people's living standards. This, together with the implementation of a new marriage law, resulted in a rise in birthrate. The average annual birthrate in this period was 33.79‰, and the average annual natural population growth rate was 21.51‰. The country's total population increased from 574.82 million in early 1953 to 659.94 million by the end of 1958, with an average annual increase of 14.19 million and an average annual growth rate of 23.3‰. During this period, both the birthrate and natural population growth rate in the cities were higher than in the countryside. In the 1954–58 period, the average annual birthrate in the urban areas was 39.80‰, while that of the rural areas was 32.34‰. The average annual natural population growth rate in the cities was 31.31‰, and that in the countryside was 20.00‰.

Population growth in the second stage (from the beginning of 1959 to the end of 1961) was at a low ebb. During this period, the mistakes made in the "Great Leap Forward" and the "anti-Rightist" movements, as well as the serious natural calamities in 1959–61, brought about a decline in birthrate and a rise in death rate, resulting in the lowest rate of population reproduction since the founding of the People's Republic. China's total population decreased from 659.94 million in early 1959 to 658.59 million at the end of 1961. Urban birthrate was 22–29‰ during this period, while that of the rural areas dropped to 17–24‰.

The third stage (from the beginning of 1962 to the end of 1967) was the second peak period in China's population growth. The total population increased from 658.59 million to 763.68 million, with an average annual increase of 17.52 million, or an average annual growth rate of 25.0‰.

During this period, as the state adopted the principle of "readjustment, consolidation, filling out and improvement of quality" for the national economy and a series of correct policies and resolute measures, the economy was quickly restored and continued to develop, and population growth became normal again. During the three difficult years from 1959 to 1961, most women stopped giving birth to babies, while the 1962–67 period witnessed a "compensatory" growth in fertility rate, resulting in a sharp rise in the birthrate. In 1963, the birthrate throughout the country was as high as 43.32‰, and the death rate dropped to 10.04‰. In this way, the natural population growth rate reached a record high since the founding of New China. By the end of 1963, China's total population topped 700 million.

But, the birthrate and natural population growth rate in the cities slowed down again beginning from 1964. By 1966, the birthrate plunged to 20.85‰, and the natural population growth rate went down to 15.26‰. In the countryside, however, the birthrate remained at over 36‰, and the natural growth rate at over 27‰. The main reason for this was that family planning work, which had started earlier, began to achieve tangible results in the cities. It should be stressed here that in the period from 1963 to 1967 the birthrate and natural population growth rate in China dropped year after year, reaching the lowest point by 1967. Had it not been for the "cultural revolution," China's natural population growth would have continued to decrease.

The fourth stage (from the beginning of 1968 to the end of 1973) was the third peak period in China's population growth. During this period, the country's population went up from 763.68 million to 892.11 million, with an average annual increase of 21.41 million, or an average annual growth rate of 26.2‰. Thus, the natural population growth rate, which had begun to go down, rose again, leading to another peak in population growth. This peak period (1968–73) differed from the 1962–67 one in terms of characteristics, scale, and causes. Whereas the earlier peak was "compensatory" in nature, this one was caused by an anarchic upswing in the birthrate resulting from the "cultural revolution."

The fifth stage (from the beginning of 1974 to the end of 1984) witnessed a decline in the population growth rate. During this period, China's population increased from 892.11 million to 1,034.75 million, with an average annual increase of 12.97 million, or an average annual growth rate of 13.6‰. The average annual birthrate was 19.92‰, and the average annual natural growth rate was 13.16‰. Thanks to the energetic promotion of the family planning policy by the Chinese government, the country's birthrate and natural population growth rate had dropped every year since 1974. By 1976 the birthrate was reduced to 19.91‰, and the natural growth rate was 12.66‰. According to a sample survey in China's 29 provinces, autonomous regions, and municipalities, 18.02 million babies were born in 1984, the birthrate being 17.50‰, and 6.89 million people died that year, the death rate being 6.69‰. The natural population increase was 11.13 million, the natural growth rate being 10.81‰.

In 1974, the natural population growth rate in the cities had already dropped to below 10‰. The average annual rate was 9.30‰ in the 1974–83 period. In the countryside, the average annual natural growth rate in those ten years also dropped to 14.04‰. This showed that remarkable progress had been made in the implementation of the family planning policy and the work to control population growth in both the cities and countryside.

AN ANALYSIS OF THE CAUSE OF CHANGES IN NEW CHINA'S POPULATION

As early as in 1957, Ma Yinchu, a well-known Chinese economist, analyzed the causes of the rapid increase in China's population at that time. He listed the following seven causes:*

- The increase of employment opportunities and improvement of economic conditions enabled the people to build their own families, and an increasing number of people got married.

- Infant mortality dropped as a result of maternity and child care provided by the government departments.

- The death rate among the aged also dropped, thanks to the government's concern for the old widows and widowers who had no one to support them.

- The number of people who died from accidents or mishaps decreased because of the unprecedented stability and social security in the country.

- Following the change of the social system, prostitution was abolished, and most nuns and monks became secular and got married.

- Many old people were still under the influence of old ideas, such as "a prosperous posterity" and

"sons and grandsons fill the hall." Of the three unfilial sins, not having a son is the worst. These and other feudal ideas still existed.

- The government offered awards and subsidies to mothers who gave birth to twins or more than two babies.

Ma Yinchu's analysis of the situation in the early and mid-1950s corresponded with the facts. However, after the basic completion of the socialist transformation of the ownership of the means of production in 1956, tremendous changes took place in various fields. Population continued to increase unchecked. During the period from the late 1950s to the early 1970s, few people were concerned about the population problem. It was not until the late 1970s and the early 1980s that attention was paid again to the study of China's population. Scholars began to study and investigate the causes of the increase of population and put forward their views. Some held that the rapid increase of population was mainly due to the following causes.*

BACKWARD ECONOMY

Although the social productive forces have developed to some extent following the change in the social system and the relations of production, the level of the productive forces in China is still low and the backwardness of its economy has not taken a fundamental turn for the better. The level of mechanization and automation in industrial production is not high, and farm production is by and large done by hand. Thus, in essence, China has not yet rid itself of the situation in which "poverty leads to a high birthrate." The concrete manifestations are as follows:

- The amount of labor force available still occupies an important place in production, particularly in agricultural production. Therefore, the income for rural families is mainly determined by the number of laborers, rather than by the quality of the work done. With the policy of "low wages and more employment opportunities" now in effect, the amount of income for each family is largely determined by the number of children earning wages. The basic situation in the countryside today is that more laborers means more income, and families with more able-bodied laborers become well-off faster than the others. It

* Ma Yinchu: *New Theory on Population*, Beijing Publishing House, 1979, pp. 2–3.

* Tian Xueyuan: *Theory of Population in the New Period*, Heilongjiang People's Publishing House, 1982, pp. 29–35.

stands to reason that many peasants want to have more children and as early as possible. They would rather tighten their belts for the time being so as to have more children and become well-off later. This is what they call "sweetness follows bitterness."

• The expenses for raising children are low. This mainly refers to the vast countryside. What is required for farm work is physical strength rather than high cultural standards or technical skills. The upbringing of a child is not a heavy burden for a rural family, whether in terms of living expenses or expenditures for acquiring an education.

• Owing to the low level of economic development, the standard of social welfare for people after retirement cannot be high. Most people in the countryside have to rely on their children when they grow old. This is the material basis and the reason why the ideology of "rearing children for support in old age" is so widespread in rural areas.

• Because of the low cultural level, particularly because of the high rate of illiteracy among the women in the countryside, many people do not understand the need for planned parenthood, and they lack the knowledge of birth control.

DEEP INFLUENCE OF FEUDAL IDEOLOGY

Feudal society lasted more than 2,000 years in China. Feudal ethics and morals are deep-rooted among the people and cannot be done away with within a short time. Even today some traditional ideas still exert strong influences on the society, such as "more sons means greater happiness" and "of the three unfilial pieties, not having a son is the greatest unfilial manifestation." On the question of childbearing, many people take into consideration their own family interests only, or hope to have several boys merely because of social pressure. This is especially so in the countryside. Such feudal ideology inevitably leads to a high birthrate.

ONE-SIDED VIEWS ON POPULATION THEORY AND MISTAKES IN WORKING OUT POPULATION POLICIES

In the early days after the founding of New China, the population problem was not given due attention. When the 1953 census showed a high birthrate and a high natural population growth rate, it drew the attention of the government and some far-sighted personages.

The government began to promote birth control. For instance, the revised law on birth control and abortion was approved by the Government Administration Council (the forerunner of today's State Council) in August 1953. In December 1954, the State Council ordered the department concerned to set up a birth-control group to study the problem. In September 1956, in his report on the Second Five-Year Plan for the Development of the National Economy, Premier Zhou Enlai stressed the need to adequately limit childbirth. The "National Programme for Agricultural Development (Draft)" also stated that family planning should be popularized and promoted in densely populated areas. At that time analysts also set forth their views on population questions and made proposals on limiting childbirth.

Unfortunately, in the mid- and late 1950s, the theories and views on population control, particularly the new theory of population put forth by Ma Yinchu, were subjected to severe criticism. A big population was wrongly regarded as a manifestation of the superiority of the socialist system and law of development, and the theory of ever increasing population was looked upon as the socialist orthodox theory. As a result, a series of policies encouraging population growth came into being. Such a situation lasted till the end of the 1960s and the early 1970s. During that period, as a result of the wrong theory and policies regarding population, China's population increased greatly, with serious consequences for the size of China's population and its growth for some years to come. This problem will be discussed in detail in the chapters that follow.

CHAPTER THREE

TRENDS AND DIFFERENCES IN CHINA'S FERTILITY RATE

Demographically speaking, three factors determine the growth of population: birth, death, and migration. Birth is a physiological phenomenon subject to the combined influences of social, economic, political, and cultural factors as well as customs, and the determinants of fertility are very complicated.

All things considered, the level of fertility in China has a direct bearing on whether its strategic goals for population growth can be realized. This is because fertility directly affects the control of the nation's total population, the improvement of the quality of the population, and the readjustment of the population composition. This chapter deals mainly with the question of fertility in China.

CHINA'S BIRTHRATE, PAST AND PRESENT

BIRTHRATE IN OLD CHINA

Data on the birthrate in old China were extremely inadequate. No accurate figures were available for the various periods, and there were only estimates based on sample investigations by some scholars and fragmentary materials released by the Kuomintang government. These data and materials could only approximately reflect the situation in old China.

According to an estimation based on data collected from sample surveys by the Chinese scholars Yan Xinzhe, Chen Da, Xu Shilian, and Sun Benwen, old China's birthrate averaged 35‰ and death rate about 25‰. The Kuomintang government also published some data, such as the birthrate in six major cities from 1931 to 1933 (see Table 3-1) and the birthrate in the various provinces and regions in 1936 (see Table 3-2).

As indicated by these two tables, the birthrate in old China was very high, and the birthrate in the rural areas was much higher than that of the cities.

BIRTHRATE IN NEW CHINA

Since its founding, in 1949, New China has established and gradually improved its statistics on births, which are not only richer in quantity but much higher in quality than those of old China.

Theoretically speaking, it is not difficult to collect statistical figures of newborn babies. In reality, however, the accuracy of these figures is often affected, sometimes to a great extent, by the social, economic, political, and cultural factors as well as the customs of different periods. That is why such data are, to varying degrees, not as accurate as people imagine. In old China, to evade draft and taxes,

Table 3-1   Birthrate in Six Major Cities (1931–1933)

	BIRTHRATE ‰						
YEAR	NANJING	SHANGHAI	BEIPING	HANGZHOU	HANKOU	GUANGZHOU	ANNUAL AVERAGE
1931	23.3	18.8	24.4	19.7	18.9	14.7	19.91
1932	16.9	12.2	29.8	18.5	15.1	13.9	17.73
1933	23.4	19.0	34.0	19.3	19.5	18.0	22.22
Average (1931–33)	21.2	16.7	29.3	19.2	17.8	15.5	—

Source: *Economic Yearbook of China 1935* (sequel), Ministry of Industry of the Kuomintang government, p. (B) 33.

Table 3-2   Birthrate in Selected Provinces and Regions (1936)

PROVINCE	NUMBER OF RURAL COUNTIES SURVEYED	BIRTHRATE (‰)
Hebei, Shandong, Shanxi, Shaanxi, Anhui	37	38.9
Suiyuan, Shanxi, Shaanxi	7	31.2
Guangdong, Fujian	6	37.8
Zhejiang, Jiangxi	4	38.5
Yunnan, Guizhou	3	53.4
Sichuan	15	44.1
Jiangsu, Anhui, Zhejiang Hubei	27	37.2
Sichuan, Yunnan	2	38.3
Whole country	101	38.9

Source: *Economic Yearbook of China 1936*, Ministry of Industry of the Kuomintang government, Book 3, p. (B) 29.

parents often deliberately withheld the truth about their children. Even today, with the institution of a strict household registration system, omissions or instances of overlapping in the registration of new-born babies are unavoidable for various reasons. Nevertheless, the accuracy of New China's statistical data in this regard is quite high.

According to the 1982 census, China's birthrate in 1981 was 20.91‰. A total of 20.69 million babies were born, that is, a baby was born every 1.5 seconds. This birthrate was considerably lower than that of the 1950s or 1960s. (In 1952, for example, the birthrate was 37‰.) This reflects the process of a gradual drop in China's birthrate along with its economic and social development and, in particular, the implementation of the policy of controlling the growth of population.

THE EVOLUTION OF NEW CHINA'S BIRTHRATE

In the years from 1950 to 1984, the evolution of China's birthrate can be roughly divided into two periods. The first period, from 1950 to 1970, was one of laissez-faire births, and the average annual birthrate was 33.70‰. In the second period, from 1971 to 1984, family planning was introduced and the average annual birthrate was 22.05‰, a more than one-third drop from the first period.

The first period of laissez-faire births was marked by a big fall and rise of birthrate. In 17 of the 21 years of that period, the birthrate was more than 30‰; of those 17 years, the birthrate in 6 years was 30–35‰, in 10 years was 35–40‰, and 1 year had a birthrate of more than 40‰. As for the remaining 4 years (1958–61) of this period, the birthrate was less than 30‰. The first period can again be subdivided into three stages:

• The first stage, from 1950 to 1958, saw a continued high birthrate hovering at an annual average of 34.95‰. In the years 1950 to 1952, the national economy was restored and land reform was carried out in rural areas. In addition, the promulgation of the Marriage Law, in 1950, created favorable conditions for laboring people to build happy families and lead a happy life. Widely improved living standards and the traditional concept that more children would bring more happiness contributed to the continued high birthrate of this stage. In the years 1953 to 1958, China carried out its First Five-Year Plan (1953–57) for the development of the national economy. Large-scale economic construction increased the demand for labor forces. In addition, the concept that "the more people we have, the easier it is to have things done" was widely accepted. As a result, the birthrate remained high, reaching 37.97‰ in 1957 (only slightly lower than the record high year of 1963). During that stage, the birthrate in both urban and rural areas exceeded 30‰, and that of the urban areas was higher than that of the rural areas. In three of the six years from 1953 to 1958, the birthrate was more than 40‰, and that of 1957 reached the record high of 44.5‰.

• The second stage—from 1959 to 1963—saw China's birthrate fall and rise dramatically. The average annual birthrate was 28.81‰, lower than that of the 1953–58 period by 17.6%. From 1959 to 1961, China's national economy suffered from serious natural calamities. Crop failure and strained supply of materials continued for three years running, causing a great change in China's population. The incidence of disease soared, and the death rate was the highest since 1949. Because of shortage of food and impaired health, many women of childbearing age suffered from such conditions as amenorrhea and uterine prolapse, resulting in a big drop in birthrate, which went down from 29.22‰ in 1958 to 24.78‰ in 1959 and 20.86‰ in 1960. Then, in 1961, the birthrate sank to the lowest postliberation point of 18.02‰.

After the three difficult years of 1959–61, the national economy began to take a turn for the better in 1962–63. Beginning in the second half of 1962, a "compensatory" baby boom emerged, which raised the birthrate that year to 37.01‰. The next year it rose further to 43.37‰, hitting an all-time high in the 30-odd years since liberation. That year nearly 30 million babies were born.

• The third stage was from 1964 to 1970. Following the implementation of the principle of "readjustment, consolidating, filling out and raising the quality," the national economy gradually embarked on the road of sound development. During this stage, the undeniable influence of population on the economic development drew the attention of the government. Policies and specific measures designed to control population growth were introduced in the cities on a trial basis and were scheduled to be spread promptly to the countryside. Unfortunately, what followed was the disastrous "cultural revolution," and although the slogan of family planning was not abandoned, anarchy prevailed. As a result, the birthrate remained high, with the average annual rate reaching as high as 35.59‰ in the years 1964 to 1970. Judging from this birthrate, the level for the years 1964–70 was approximately the same as that of 1950–58. In 1964 the birthrate in the cities dropped considerably, whereas the reduction in the countryside was only marginal. The urban birthrate decreased from 44.50‰ in 1963 to 20.85‰ in 1966, a 53% drop. In the countryside, however, the birthrate went down from 43.19‰ in 1963 to 36.71‰ in 1966, which was a drop of only 15%. The urban birthrate helped pull down the national birthrate in the late 1960s (see Table 3-3).

The second period was a period of family planning, characterized by the quick transition from a

Table 3-3.   China's Birthrate (1950–1970)

YEAR	BIRTHRATE (‰)	YEAR	BIRTHRATE (‰)
1950	37.00	1961	18.02
1951	37.80	1962	37.01
1952	37.00	1963	43.37
1953	37.00	1964	39.14
1954	37.97	1965	37.88
1955	32.60	1966	35.05
1956	31.90	1967	33.96
1957	34.03	1968	35.59
1958	29.22	1969	34.11
1959	24.78	1970	33.43
1960	20.86		

Source: *Statistics Yearbook of China, 1984*, compiled by the State Statistical Bureau and published by the China Statistics Publishing House, 1984, p. 83.

Table 3-4.   China's Birthrate (1971–1984)

YEAR	BIRTHRATE (‰)	YEAR	BIRTHRATE (‰)
1971	30.65	1978	18.25
1972	29.77	1979	17.82
1973	27.93	1980	18.21
1974	24.82	1981	20.91
1975	23.01	1982	21.09
1976	19.91	1983	18.62
1977	18.93	1984	17.50

Sources: *Statistics Yearbook of China, 1984*, compiled by the State Statistical Bureau and published by the China Statistics Publishing House, 1984, p. 83, and *Statistics Yearbook of China, 1985*, compiled by the State Statistical Bureau and published by the China Statistics Publishing House, 1985, p. 186.

high birthrate to a low birthrate (see Table 3-4). From 1971 onward, the birthrate began to drop relatively quickly. In the 11 years from 1970 to 1981, the birthrate for the whole country dropped by 37.45%, the average annual rate of decrease being 4.18%. The birthrate in 1982 was basically the same as in 1981, but in 1983 and 1984 it began to drop again.

The 14 years beginning in 1970 saw a drop in China's birthrate that has rarely been seen in other parts of the world. The most direct and most important reason for this rapid and continuous drop is, apart from social and economic factors, the energetic implementation of family planning both in the cities and in the countryside.

DIVERGENCES IN STATISTICAL DATA ON POPULATION

For one reason or another, statistics on a country's population are often complicated by overlaps or omissions. This is also the case with China. From the population of different age groups in the 1982 census we find that the number of new births in the regular statistics of some years tended to be too small. When the number of new births for 1981 was double-checked, it was found that the census did not tally with the data in the regular statistics. Generally speaking, China's statistics of new births in the past decade were lower than the actual number.

Results of the 1982 census showed that those aged from 0 to 8 (i.e., those born between July 1, 1973 and June 30, 1982) numbered 180.36 million, or 7.28 million more than the number of regular statistics for the corresponding years. If the number in the 1982 census for the 0–8 age group was accurate, it can be said with certainty that there were omissions in the regular statistics for those years. In addition, the 1982 census showed that the number of births in 1981 was different from the number of that year's regular statistics. The 1982 census showed that 1981's new births numbered 20.69 million, which was 3.24 million more than the number actually registered that year. In evaluating the results of the 1982 census, China's demographers generally agreed that the data in the census were more reliable than the data available from the regular household registrations.

CHINESE WOMEN'S FERTILITY RATE
GENERAL FERTILITY RATE OF CHINESE WOMEN

According to the results of the 1982 census, the general fertility rate of Chinese women in 1981 was 82.36‰, higher than that in some of the world's more developed countries for the corresponding year. (For example, it was 61.30‰ in the United States and 50.12‰ in Japan.) The proportion of Chinese women of childbearing age was 24.75‰ in 1981, which was close to that of the United States (25.94‰) and Japan (25.89‰) for that year. Similar comparisons based on the same data can also be made between China and other countries (see Table 3-5).

CHANGES IN THE TOTAL FERTILITY RATE OF CHINESE WOMEN

The total fertility rate is the sum total of the age-specific fertility rate of women. It is, in nature, both a

Table 3-5. Proportion of Women Aged 15 to 49 in the Total Population of Selected Countries in 1981 and General Fertility Rate

COUNTRY	PROPORTION OF WOMEN AGED 15 TO 49 IN THE TOTAL POPULATION (‰)	GENERAL FERTILITY RATE (‰)
Japan	25.89	50.1
Czechoslovakia	23.93	64.9
Federal Rep. Germany	24.83	40.8
Britain	23.45	54.6
Hungary	23.92	55.8
Norway	22.86	54.1
Poland	25.35	74.6
Sweden	23.05	49.0
Australia	25.08	63.0
China	24.75	82.4

Sources: Data on China are based on the *1982 Population Census of China,* and data on other countries are from the *U.N. Demographic Yearbook 1982.*

"standardized" index as well as a "signal" index. Therefore, it can be used to compare the general level of the fertility rate of women in different periods and different places, and it also serves as an indication of the general direction of development of the population in the future.

Data on the total fertility rate from 1964 to 1981 were obtained through a one-thousandth sample survey of China's birthrate conducted in 1982. Since the survey was of a retrospective nature, it was impossible to obtain the age-specific fertility rate of women aged 15 to 49 prior to 1964. For lack of figures from direct surveys, only estimations can be made to obtain an approximate number. Data for the 1950–63 period were obtained in this way. (See Table 3-6.)

Changes in the total fertility rate in China conformed with its birthrate, and can be divided into two periods in the 30-odd years since the founding of New China (similar to the two periods for birthrate). That is, the first period was from 1950 to 1970, marked by "a high-level fertility rate, with many ups and downs"; the second period was from 1971 to 1982, marked by "a rapid transition from a high to a low fertility level."

The first period can be subdivided into three stages:

• In the first stage, from 1950 to 1958, the average annual total fertility rate was 6.057 births per woman; the rate for the peak year (1952) was 6.472, and that of the lowest year (1958) was 5.679. The total fertility rate for this stage was relatively stable and of a high level.

• The total fertility rate in the second stage (from 1959 to 1963) was characterized by a big drop in the first three years and a big rise in the last two years. In 1961 it dropped to the lowest level of 3.287, and in 1963 it rose to the peak level of 7.502. The main reason for the big drop was natural calamity during those years; the factor contributing to the big rise was the national economy, which took a turn for the better. This was a stage of great fluctuations, with the average annual total fertility rate hovering around 5.026.

• The third stage was from 1964 to 1970, with the total fertility rate rising again to a high level but slightly lower than that of the first stage. (The average annual rate was 5.972.) The change in the total fertility rate of this stage had two characteristics: first, a slight drop from the high level; second, the total fertility rate in the cities and towns showed a steady drop from 1964 to 1967, while in the rural

Table 3-6. Total Fertility Rate of Women in China (1950–1970)

	1950	1951	1952	1953	1954	1955	1956	1957	1958	1959	
Total fertility rate	5.813	5.699	6.472	6.049	6.278	6.261	5.854	6.405	5.679	4.303	
	1960	1961	1962	1963	1964	1965	1966	1967	1968	1969	1970
Total fertility rate	4.015	3.287	6.023	7.502	6.176	6.076	6.259	5.313	6.448	5.723	5.812

Source: "Analysis on One-per-thousand-population Fertility Sampling Survey in China," *Population and Economy*, 1983, pp. 152–153.

areas it rose steadily from 1964 to 1966. There was a rise in both the cities and the countryside in 1968, and the rise in the countryside was higher than in the cities. This showed that the work of family planning in the cities had been effective.

During the second period, from 1971 to 1984, the total fertility rate of women in China dropped considerably (see Table 3-7). The average level was 3.264, which was 2.708 lower than the average level of 5.972 for the 1964–70 period, a drop of 45.3%. This big drop in the short period of 14 years was attributable to many factors, but the most important reason was the widespread and thorough-going implementation of family planning.

Table 3-7 also shows that the total fertility rate in 1981 and 1982 began to rise again. There were two reasons for this rise: First, the new Marriage Law promulgated in 1981 lowered the marriage age; second, with the reform of the economic structure in the countryside, the responsibility system in agricultural production was introduced, while the work of family planning was somewhat neglected, thus resulting in a laissez-faire attitude toward the birth of babies.

CHILDBEARING PATTERN OF CHINESE WOMEN

As mentioned previously, there was a rapid drop in the total fertility rate of Chinese women after the 1970s. This has resulted in an essential change in the childbearing pattern of Chinese women. That is, today there has been a shift from early, dense, and prolific births to late, sparse, and few births. This pattern of change has two distinctive features. First, the one-child rate has risen steadily, while the multi-child rate has plummeted. Second, the intervening period between the first and the second child has lengthened, and there has been a big change in the tradition of dense births.

Following is a brief account of the change in the childbearing pattern of women in China based on the results of a one-thousandth sample survey of the China's birthrate conducted in 1982.

CHANGE IN CHILDBEARING PATTERN

A study will first be made of the percentage distribution of the total fertility rate of Chinese women in different periods. This percentage distribution refers to the percentage of the age-specific fertility rate of different age groups of a certain year or period in the total fertility rate of that year or period. Such a study is of help in analyzing the change in the childbearing rate of women of different age groups.

The percentage distribution of the total fertility rate of Chinese women has undergone a considerable change since the 1950s. We shall here divide women of childbearing age into three age groups, that is, 15 to 19, 20 to 29, and 30 and above, and make a comparison between their percentage distribution in the different periods (see Table 3-8).

Table 3-7. Total Fertility Rate of Women in China (1971–1984)

YEAR	1971	1972	1973	1974	1975	1976	1977
Total fertility rate	5.442	4.984	4.539	4.170	3.571	3.235	2.844
YEAR	1978	1979	1980	1981	1982	1983	1984
Total fertility rate	2.716	2.745	2.238	2.631	2.480	2.070	2.030

Source: "Analysis on One-per-thousand-population Fertility Sampling Survey in China," *Population and Economy*, 1983, pp. 153–154, 161, 164.

Table 3-8.   Total Fertility Rate of Three Age Groups in Different Periods (%)

PERIOD	TOTAL	FERTILITY		
		15–19	20–29	30–49
1950s	100.00	7.15	46.74	46.11
1960s	100.00	4.75	49.98	45.27
1970s	100.00	2.87	59.37	37.76
1980–84	100.00	2.28	76.76	20.96

Source: Based on the results of "One-per-thousand-population Fertility Sampling Survey in China."

From the change in the percentage distribution of the total fertility rate of Chinese women in different periods, one can clearly see the following three characteristics. First, from the 1950s to the present day, the percentage of the age-specific fertility rate of women in the 15–19 age group has steadily decreased. This indicates that among Chinese women aged 19 and under, there are fewer early marriages and early births. Second, the percentage of the age-specific fertility rate of women in the 20–29 age group, which is physiologically the most prolific group, is steadily increasing. This is the most striking characteristic in the change of the childbearing pattern among Chinese women. Third, the percentage of the age-specific fertility rate of women aged 30 and above in the total fertility rate of women in China has dropped considerably. This indicates that Chinese women, after passing through the prolific period, have exercised control over the birth of babies.

Of course, the change in the childbearing pattern of Chinese women in the past 30 years has not been a smooth or progressive process. In fact, the pattern remained much the same before the 1970s. It was not until the 1970s that a sharp change took place (see Table 3-9 and Chart 3-1). This change is manifested in the following aspects in a comparison between 1981 and 1970.

• Age-specific fertility rate. The age-specific fertility rate in all the childbearing age groups in 1981 was lower than that of 1970. The height of the curve that showed the age-specific fertility rate of women in various age groups descended in 1981, which meant that the percentage of one-child mothers of childbearing age in 1981 was much higher than the 1970 figure.

• Fertility age range. The curve at the 0.1 level of age-specific fertility in 1981 was 10 years, a big drop from the 1970 figure of 23 years, and at the 0.2 fertility level in 1981 it was a mere 5 years, compared to 15 years in 1970. This reflects the great achievements in family planning work in the 11 years from 1970 to 1981.

• Average childbearing age. The average childbearing age was 27.2 years old in 1981, 2.6 years less than the 1970 figure of 29.8. This shows that the number of comparatively old women giving birth to more than one baby had decreased.

• Ninety percent of childbearing was completed by age 39 in 1970 and by age 34 in 1981, much younger than in 1970.

DIFFERENCE BETWEEN CITIES AND COUNTRYSIDE IN CHILDBEARING PATTERN

A comparison between the childbearing pattern of women in the cities and rural areas in 1970 and that in 1981 (see Chart 3-2) shows that enormous differences existed in the process of change. In cities and towns the width of the 0.1 level of fertility rate dropped from 13 years in 1970 to 5 years in 1981, and the 0.2 level dropped from 7 years in 1970 to 3 years in 1981. In 1970, women in cities and towns giving birth to babies were mostly between 27 and 33 years old. But in 1981, most were between 24 and 28 years old, and particularly between 25 and 27 years old. In

Table 3-9.   Percent Distribution of Age-Specific Fertility Rates by Age of Mother in 1965, 1970, and 1981

AGE GROUP	1965		1970		1981	
	FERTILITY RATE (‰)	PROPORTION (%)	FERTILITY RATE (‰)	PROPORTION (%)	FERTILITY RATE (‰)	PROPORTION (%)
15–19	58.4	4.8	44.4	3.8	15.2	2.9
20–24	288.8	23.8	283.2	24.3	181.8	34.6
25–29	311.2	25.6	312.2	26.9	213.2	40.5
30–34	257.0	21.2	253.0	21.8	70.4	13.4
35–39	195.6	16.1	178.2	15.3	30.6	5.8
40–44	92.6	7.6	82.4	7.1	12.8	2.4
45–49	11.6	0.9	9.0	0.8	2.2	0.4
Total	1,215.2	100.0	1,162.4	100.0	526.2	100.0

Source: "Analysis on One-per-thousand-population Fertility Sampling Survey in China," *Population and Economy*, 1983, pp. 153, 164.

Chart 3-1.   Comparison Between Childbearing Patterns of Chinese Women (1965, 1970, 1981)

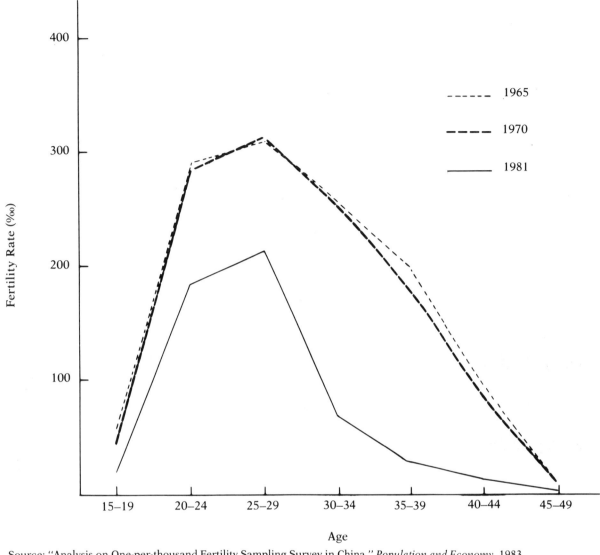

Source: "Analysis on One-per-thousand Fertility Sampling Survey in China," *Population and Economy*, 1983.

1970, 90% of the childbearing age was 35 years old, but in 1981 it was 30 years old, which means women aged 30 in cities and towns ended their prolific period.

In the countryside, the width of the 0.1 level of fertility rate dropped from 23 years in 1970 to 11 years in 1981, and the 0.2 level fell from 18 years in 1970 to 6 years in 1981. In 1970, most women in the rural areas giving birth to babies were between 19 and 43 years old, particularly between 27 and 37 years old. This shows the high age-specific fertility rate of rural women in many age groups in 1970. By 1981 childbearing women in the rural areas were

mostly between 20 and 30, particularly between 22 and 27 years old. In 1970, 90% of childbearing was completed by age 39 and by 34 in 1981.

In 1981, the pattern of control over the birth of babies was realized in the cities and towns of China. The total fertility rate of women had decreased from 3.267 in 1970 to 1.390 in 1981, much lower than the replacement level of population reproduction. On the other hand, the change of the childbearing pattern in the rural areas was very slow, and even when the birth-control pattern was taking shape there, it was of a low level and not stable at that. For instance, the total fertility rate of rural women in 1981 was still

Chart 3-2.   Change of Childbearing Pattern in the Cities and Countryside (1970, 1981)

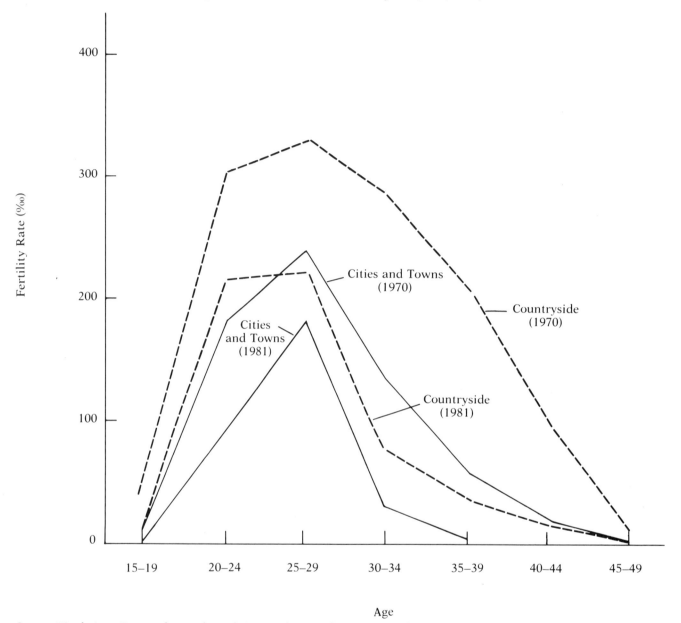

Source: "Analysis on One-per-thousand-population Fertility Sampling Survey in China," *Population and Economy*, 1983, pp. 156, 159, 165, 166.

as high as 2.910. Since 80% of the Chinese population live in the countryside, whether the traditional child-bearing pattern in China as a whole could change into one of birth control depends to a large extent on the countryside. Hence it is of strategic importance to step up family planning work in the rural areas.

COMPARISON WITH SELECTED COUNTRIES

Chart 3-3 makes a comparison between the child-bearing pattern of Chinese women in 1981 and the

different patterns of three other countries. The childbearing pattern curve of Chinese women in 1981 was more or less similar to that of Japan in 1980, but the age-specific fertility rate of Japanese women in different age brackets was lower than that of Chinese women. For example, that of Japanese women between 25 and 29 years old, the peak value age bracket, was 0.1757, while that of Chinese women of the same group was 0.2387.

The childbearing pattern of Chinese women is completely different from that of women in those

Chart 3-3.   Comparison of Childbearing Patterns Between China and
Selected Countries

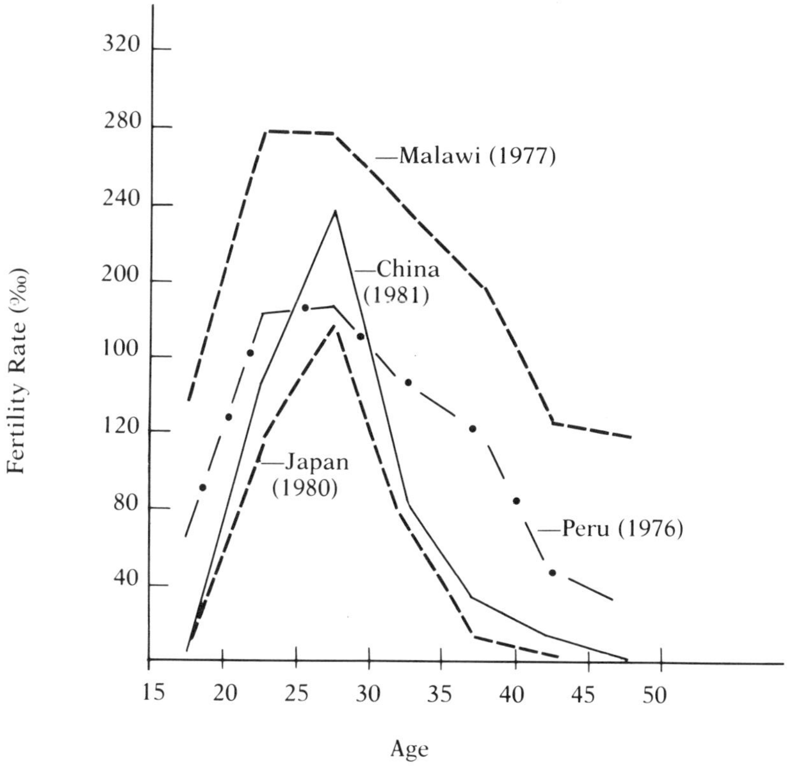

Sources: "Analysis on One-per-thousand-population Fertility Sampling Survey in
China," *Population and Economy*, 1983, p. 164; *U.N. Population Yearbook 1982.*

countries where early marriages, early childbirths, and high fertility rate among comparatively old women are prevalent. For instance, the curve of age-specific fertility rate for Malawian women of different age groups in 1977 was high and wide; that of the 15–19 age group was 0.1356, while that of the 45–49 group was also high, reaching 0.1181. Though the peak value age-specific fertility rate of Peruvian women was not high, their childbearing pattern was also of the wide type.

FACTORS AFFECTING WOMEN'S FERTILITY LEVEL

Changes in women's fertility level are attributable to many factors. In view of the actual conditions in China, however, the principal factors were and will continue to be the value of children's labor, the value of children providing support for their old parents, the cost of bringing up children, the mortality of infants and children, the average age of first marriages, educational level and jobs, and family planning policies.

THE VALUE OF CHILDREN'S LABOR

Numerous facts prove that the value of children's labor is closely related to the fertility rate. Generally speaking, the value of children's labor decreases in places where the level of urbanization and industrialization is comparatively high, primary education is fairly widespread, and the average per capita income is high. Conversely, the value of child labor will rise in places without these conditions. This is because the parents require their children to earn money in a direct or indirect way.

At present, great differences in the value of children's labor exist in China between the cities and countryside and between different rural areas. In the cities, since primary education is now universal, the value of children's labor no longer exists. In those rural areas where the economy is fairly developed, changes have also occurred in the outlook regarding childbearing and bringing up of children among the peasants, particularly the young peasants, many of them specializing in certain lines of farm work. These peasants often stress the importance of raising the quality of their children and do not use them as laborers. Consequently, they are willing to put in more money for the intellectual development of their children.

However, the value of children's labor is quite important for families in rural areas where the economy is comparatively backward. Primary education has not yet become universal in a considerable part of the vast countryside. Many school-age children, especially the girls, have not completed the required primary school education, and many junior middle school students in some towns and villages often drop out halfway to take up jobs or to work in the fields. It is not uncommon for enterprises to recruit school-age children in disregard of the regulations. Furthermore, there are parents who, because of immediate interests and temporary economic gain, refuse to send their children to school; instead, they send them to work in the fields, to tend cattle and sheep, to look after their younger sisters and brothers, or even to work as child laborers in township enterprises. To these parents, children are good laborers who can bring in money. As a result, they wish to have more children, especially boys. This childbearing outlook, if it is allowed to develop unchecked, will inevitably spur the rise of births in backward rural areas and worsen the already bad economic situation there.

THE VALUE OF CHILDREN PROVIDING SUPPORT FOR THEIR OLD PARENTS

It is a common concept in China's countryside that parents have children so that they will have someone to support them in their old age. At present, pension is only granted to retirees from state-owned and collectively owned enterprises, as the Chinese government is still financially unable to take care of the life and well-being of all old people. Although some economically well-developed towns in rural areas have instituted a pension system, they are very few in number. Therefore, it is only natural for peasants to think of bearing children for support in their old age. Peasants who wish to lead a secure life in their old age are often inclined to have more children so that the burden of support can be shared among more people. This outlook has a serious effect on the fertility rate in the countryside. Therefore it is essential to take steps to improve the welfare of the old people in rural areas, such as building homes of respect for the aged, with a view to reducing the influence of their traditional mentality regarding the bearing of children. The success of these efforts is dependent on the development of the rural and the national economy.

THE COST OF BRINGING UP CHILDREN

Here the cost means the expenses paid by the family to bring up children. This factor has a completely different influence on the childbearing rate in the cities and the countryside. Today, most couples in cities prefer small families, because of the high living expenses. More children implies a greater economic burden to the family. In the countryside, however, child rearing is comparatively inexpensive. Actually it has never been much of a problem to the peasants. As the saying goes: "One more child simply means an additional pair of chopsticks on the table and one more ladle of water in the pot."

According to estimates made by the Department of Demography of the Chinese People's University, to bring up and train a laborer costs 10,392 yuan in the cities and 4,615 yuan in the countryside. This cost refers to the total expenditure paid by the family and the society to cover the living expenses, education, medical care, and social services required by a child during the entire period from the mother's pregnancy to the age the youngster is fit to work. (Usually, the child is 18 years old when he or she graduates from the senior middle school in urban areas and 16 years old when he or she graduates from the junior middle school in rural areas.) The government has to spend another 8,500 yuan on training a college student.

THE MORTALITY OF INFANTS AND CHILDREN

Birthrate and mortality are interrelated. In places where infant mortality is high, parents tend to have more children, sometimes more than necessary. This was a common practice in old China's countryside where conditions were backward. As often as not, a peasant couple could be sure of keeping one boy alive only after three births. Since the founding of New China, death rates of infants and children have come down drastically, and this is an important reason that the childbearing rate has dropped. However, in some places (especially rural areas), people still want more children to play safe. Consequently, to improve maternity and child care and to bring up healthy children is essential to the reduction of the childbearing rate, especially in rural areas where conditions are backward and mortality is high.

AVERAGE AGE AT FIRST MARRIAGE

The younger a woman gets married, the more opportunities she will have to conceive. Besides, early marriages often result in early births and the concomitant reduction of the age gap between generations. The consequence is a rapid rise in birthrate. Therefore, changes in the average age of first marriages have a serious effect on the fertility rate. The average age for Chinese women to get married has been on the rise since the 1940s. For instance, the 1940s it was 18.5 years old; in the 1950s, 19.0 years old; in the 1960s, 19.8 years old; and in the 1970s, 21.6 years old. In 1980 it reached a record high — 23.1 years old. Then in 1981 it dropped to 22.8 years old, and in 1982 to 22.6 years old. It is estimated that because of this factor, the total fertility rate in 1980 was lower than that of 1970 by one-third. If a woman marrying three years later than the lawful age for marriage can be considered a late marriage, then there is still much room for promoting late marriages among women in the rural areas so as to raise further the average age of first marriages.

EDUCATIONAL LEVEL AND JOBS

Facts have abundantly proved that the higher the women's educational level is, the greater the proportion of women working in departments other than agriculture, forestry, animal husbandry, and fishery and the lower the childbearing rate becomes. Women's educational level and jobs are important social factors exerting a great influence on the changes in fertility rate of the cities and countryside. We will discuss this question in our next section.

POLICY FOR FAMILY PLANNING

China's family planning policy is winning increasing support and is accepted by millions upon millions of Chinese people. This policy has become the fundamental factor influencing China's birthrate. Chapter 12 describes in detail the process of the noticeable drop in the fertility rate of women in China following the promotion of family planning on an extensive scale. However, the effect of the government's family planning policy is different in different localities owing to the uneven economic, cultural, and social development in the cities, the countryside, and the areas inhabited by national minorities. Moreover, with regard to the population of the national minorities, the influence of China's policies toward the nationalities must be taken into consideration.

At present, the Chinese government is working for the further improvement of its family planning policy in the light of the actual situation in different localities (especially in rural areas), so that it is built on a reasonable basis and is supported by the masses and facilitates the work of the cadres. It can be expected that this policy will produce still better results in the future.

Different factors produce differences in the childbearing rate in China. Following is an analysis of these differences.

DIFFERENCE IN FERTILITY RATE
DIFFERENCE IN FERTILITY RATE BETWEEN WOMEN IN CITIES AND COUNTRYSIDE

Today, as the level of economic and social development in the cities and the rural areas varies greatly, there exists an enormous difference between the fertility rate of women in urban areas and that of women in the countryside, with that of the former about twice as low as that of the latter.

Since the founding of New China, the change in the difference between the total fertility rate of women in the cities and towns and that of women in the rural areas has roughly undergone the following process: approximating — widening — narrowing (see Table 3-10 and Chart 3-4).

The First Stage (1950–63). During this period, the total fertility rate of women both in the cities and in the rural areas remained at a high level, and the difference was comparatively small. This shows that women both in the cities and the countryside differed very little in their attitude toward childbearing and they all had many children. In this period (except 1963), the year with the highest total fertility rate was 1957 in the cities and towns, reaching 5.943, and it was 1952 in the rural areas, reaching 6.667.

The Second Stage (1964–74). During this period, the difference widened. Two phenomena that warranted attention emerged. First, after the "compensatory" fertility peak in 1963, the total fertility rate of women in the cities and towns began to drop in 1964 and continued going down in the ensuing years. In the rural areas, however, little change took place. For example, the total fertility rate of women in the cities and towns plummeted from 6.207 in 1963 to 3.104 in 1966. But in the rural areas it dropped only from 7.784 to 6.958 in the corresponding period. Second, in 1974 the rate dropped further in the cities and towns to 1.982, which was lower than the replacement level of population reproduction. In the rural areas it decreased to 4.642 in that year, an indication that the fertility rate of women in the countryside had begun to drop, too. Since then, whether in the cities and towns or in the rural areas, the total fertility rate of women has been below the 1974 level.

Table 3-10.   Total Fertility Rate of Women in the Whole Country and Urban and Rural Areas (1950–1982)

YEAR	WHOLE COUNTRY	URBAN AREAS	RURAL AREAS	YEAR	WHOLE COUNTRY	URBAN AREAS	RURAL AREAS
1950	5.813	5.001	5.963	1967	5.313	2.905	5.847
1951	5.699	4.719	5.904	1968	6.448	3.872	7.025
1952	6.472	5.521	6.667	1969	5.723	3.299	6.263
1953	6.049	5.402	6.183	1970	5.812	3.267	6.379
1954	6.278	5.723	6.390	1971	5.442	2.882	6.011
1955	6.261	5.665	6.391	1972	4.984	2.637	5.503
1956	5.854	5.333	5.974	1973	4.539	2.387	5.008
1957	6.405	5.943	6.504	1974	4.170	1.982	4.642
1958	5.679	5.253	5.775	1975	3.571	1.782	3.951
1959	4.303	4.172	4.323	1976	3.235	1.608	3.582
1960	4.015	4.057	3.996	1977	2.844	1.574	3.116
1961	3.287	2.982	3.349	1978	2.716	1.551	2.968
1962	6.023	4.789	6.303	1979	2.745	1.373	3.045
1963	7.502	6.207	7.784	1980	2.238	1.147	2.480
1964	6.176	4.395	6.567	1981	2.631	1.390	2.910
1965	6.076	3.749	6.597	1982	2.480	1.405	2.714
1966	6.259	3.104	6.958				

Source: "Analaysis on One-per-thousand-population Fertility Sampling Survey in China," *Population and Economy*, 1983, pp. 152–166.

The Third Stage (1975–82).   During this period, the total childbearing rate of women in the cities and towns continued to drop, and the rural areas also entered the stage of sustained decrease. Judging from absolute values, the difference between the cities and the rural areas was smaller than in the preceding stage. For example, the total fertility rate of women in the rural areas and in the cities in 1980 was 2.480 and 1.147, respectively, with a difference of 1.333 in absolute value, while the absolute value of difference between the two reached the highest point of 3.854 in 1966. Nonetheless, the difference between the total fertility rate of women in the cities and in the countryside was still relatively big, with that of the rural areas higher by about 100%.

In 1982, the total fertility rate of women in China was 2.4803 — 1.4052 for those in the cities and towns and 2.7143 for those in the rural areas, and the rate in

Chart 3-4.   Total Fertility Rate in China (1950–1982)

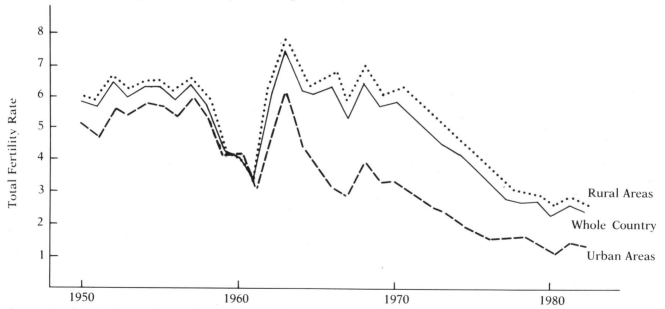

Source: "Analysis on One-per-thousand-population Fertility Sampling Survey in China," *Population and Economy*, 1983.

the rural areas was higher than that in the cities and towns in all the age groups (see Table 3-11). The childbearing peak age of women was 26 years old in the cities and towns and 25 years old in the countryside, and the age-specific fertility rate of urban women aged 26 was 0.2242, while that of rural women aged 25 was 0.2868, with the latter higher by 28% than the former. The width of the 0.1 level of fertility rate of women in the cities was five years, and it was ten years in the rural areas; the width of the 0.2 level of childbearing rate of women in the cities was three years, and it was five years in the rural areas (see Chart 3-5).

DIFFERENCE IN FERTILITY RATE BETWEEN WOMEN OF HAN NATIONALITY AND WOMEN OF MINORITY NATIONALITIES

Before liberation in 1949, the population of the minority nationalities in China increased very slowly, and their population reproduction was in an abnormal state. In the early postliberation years, the birthrate in some places inhabited by the minority nationalities was still relatively low. But around 1963, the population of the minority peoples rose sharply, as was the case with the people of Han nationality. The promotion of family planning, however, has had little impact on the minority nationalities, so the birthrate of most minority nationalities has gradually exceeded that of the Han people, and

the difference is steadily increasing. In 1965, the birthrate in some provinces and autonomous regions where the minority peoples are highly concentrated, such as Qinghai, Ningxia, Gansu, Yunnan, Guizhou, Guangxi, and Xinjiang, all surpassed the average level for the whole country. In 1981, the number of newborn babies of the minority nationalities, whose population makes up only 6.7% of the total population of China, accounted for 10.18% of the nation's total.

At present, the difference between the fertility rate of women of the minority nationalities and that of Han women is chiefly in the rural areas; there is practically no difference of this nature in the cities and towns. In 1981, the general fertility rate of minority women in the whole country was 129.75‰, and that of Han women was 81.45‰, the former being 48.30‰ higher than the latter. In the same year, however, the general fertility rate was 134.45‰ for minority women in the countryside, while that of Han women was 88.28‰, the former being 46.17‰ higher than the latter. In the cities, the general fertility rate was 50.27‰ for minority women and 49.68‰ for Han women, the two being almost equal.

In 1980 and 1981, such difference in the rural areas found expression mainly in the following aspects:

1. The Total Fertility Rate. The total fertility rate in the countryside in 1980 was 4.356 for minority

Table 3-11.   Age-Specific Fertility Rates of Urban and Rural Women (1982)

AGE	URBAN AREAS	RURAL AREAS	AGE	URBAN AREAS	RURAL AREAS
TOTAL	1.4052	2.7143	32	0.0195	0.0692
15	0.0000	0.0000	33	0.0211	0.0593
16	0.0008	0.0014	34	0.0118	0.0472
17	0.0007	0.0040	35	0.0045	0.0377
18	0.0012	0.0158	36	0.0048	0.0356
19	0.0010	0.0378	37	0.0039	0.0312
20	0.0127	0.0880	38	0.0013	0.0295
21	0.0307	0.1584	39	0.0028	0.0210
22	0.0679	0.1999	40	0.0012	0.0254
23	0.0843	0.2592	41	0.0012	0.0167
24	0.1693	0.2812	42	0.0000	0.0100
25	0.2036	0.2868	43	0.0000	0.0093
26	0.2242	0.2571	44	0.0000	0.0080
27	0.2030	0.2107	45	0.0000	0.0056
28	0.1378	0.1658	46	0.0000	0.0038
29	0.0913	0.1414	47	0.0000	0.0015
30	0.0612	0.1077	48	0.0000	0.0023
31	0.0434	0.0848	49	0.0000	0.0010
32	0.0195	0.0692			

Source: Zhao Xuan, "The Sampling Survey Report for First-Marriage Birth of China's Women in 1982," *Population and Economy*, No. 4, 1985, p. 27.

Chart 3-5.   Fertility Rates of Urban and Rural Women of Different Ages (1982)

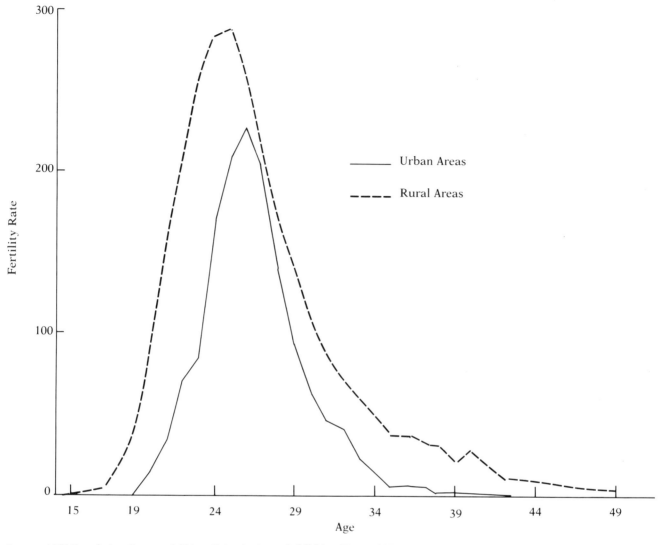

Source: *1982 Population Census of China*, China Statistics Publishing House, 1985.

women and 2.345 for Han women, the former being 85.8% higher than the latter. In 1981, the former was 5.049 and the latter was 2.758, a difference of 83.1%.

Take 1980, for example. The first-birth fertility rate and second-birth rate in the countryside were very close between minority women and Han women. But the difference of third and over birth fertility rate between the two was great (see Table 3-12). This shows that in the rural areas the number of minority women bearing more than two children was much greater than that of Han women.

2. Peak Fertility Age and Peak Fertility Rate.   The peak fertility age for both minority and Han women in the countryside was 25 years old in 1980 and 1981.

However, there were differences in the peak value childbearing rate which was 0.321 for minority women and 0.261 for Han women, respectively, with the former 23% higher than the latter. In 1981, it was 0.367 for minority women and 0.313 for Han women, with the former higher by 17%.

3. Peak Childbearing Period.   The peak childbearing period refers to the period during which the level of childbearing rate was over 0.2 for women of different ages. Minority women in the countryside have a longer peak period than Han women. In 1980, it was nine years for minority women (22–29 and 31) and five years for Han women (23–27). In 1981, the former was 13 years (21–33), and the latter was six

Table 3-12. Parity-Specific Total Fertility Rates for Rural Women of Han and Minority Nationalities (1980)

NATIONALITY	TOTAL FERTILITY RATE	1st-BIRTH FERTILITY RATE	2nd-BIRTH FERTILITY RATE	3rd-AND-OVER-BIRTH FERTILITY RATE
Minority	4.356	0.895	0.699	2.762
Han	2.343	0.890	0.623	0.830

Source: Based on "One-per-thousand-population Fertility Sampling Survey in China."

years (22–27). The difference in 1981 was greater than that of 1980.

4. Age-Specific Fertility Rate. A study of the age-specific fertility rate of women in different localities and different periods helps us to understand the age when the peak childbearing period ends and the circumstances surrounding early childbirths and late childbirths by women who are comparatively old. Table 3-13 describes the differences between minority women and Han women in this regard as in 1980 and 1981.

a. Most of the childbirths among Han women took place between 20 and 29. The fertility rate of women of these ages was a little over 75% of the total fertility rate, whereas that of minority women of the same age bracket was only 55%.
b. The level of early and late childbearing rate of minority women was much higher than that of Han women. The proportion of early (15–19) age-specific fertility rate in the total fertility rate was around 4% for minority women and around 3% for Han women. The proportion of late (30–49) age-specific fertility rate was 40% for minority women and 20% for Han women. Since late childbirths among comparatively old minority women occupied a large proportion of the total fertility rate, their third and over birth rate was therefore much higher than that of Han women. For in-

stance, in 1981, the third-and-over-birth rate of Han women in the countryside was 27.97%, while that of minority women was 58.25%.

DIFFERENCE IN FERTILITY RATE OF WOMEN WITH DIFFERENT EDUCATIONAL LEVELS

Educational level is playing an increasingly important role in influencing the level of childbirths. Generally speaking, it affects women's marriages and childbirths in three ways.

a. A longer period of education for women results in late marriages and late births.
b. The higher a woman's educational level is, the more time she devotes to her career. Consequently, she prefers a small family.
c. The higher a woman's educational level is, the better she will understand the use of contraceptives.

Since the founding of New China, more and more girls have had the opportunity to go to school, and an increasing number of them receive a higher or secondary education. This has a profound influence on the fertility rate of women. The higher their education level, the lower their average fertility rate. This has been proved by the 1982 census (see Table 3-14).

Table 3-13. Age-Specific Fertility Rate of Minority and Han Women in Rural Areas (1980 and 1981) (‰)

	1980		1981	
AGE GROUP	MINORITIES (‰)	HANS (‰)	MINORITIES (‰)	HANS (‰)
Total	100.00	100.00	100.00	100.00
15–19	4.20	2.69	3.94	2.86
20–24	24.43	34.84	23.89	38.00
25–29	30.28	41.45	29.67	39.16
30–34	19.31	13.22	21.86	12.47
35–39	14.14	5.25	12.64	5.15
40–44	6.47	2.00	6.87	2.07
45–49	1.17	0.55	1.13	0.29

Source: "Analysis on One-per-thousand-population Fertility Sampling Survey in China," *Population and Economy*, 1983, pp. 92–94.

Table 3-14.   Fertility Rate and Number of Births by Educational Level (1981)

EDUCATIONAL LEVEL	FERTILITY RATE (‰)	1-BIRTH RATE (%)	2-BIRTH RATE (%)	3-BIRTH RATE (%)	4-BIRTH RATE (%)	5-AND-MORE-BIRTH RATE (%)
Total	82.36	47.25	25.60	12.93	6.64	7.58
Educated	75.66	57.74	24.19	9.71	4.41	3.95
College	42.18	87.23	11.18	0.98	0.32	0.29
Senior middle school	63.88	81.83	14.78	2.47	0.57	0.35
Junior middle school	67.43	70.32	20.46	5.73	1.97	1.52
Primary school	86.25	44.33	28.76	13.85	6.80	6.26
Illiterate and semiilliterate	94.50	32.02	27.64	17.60	9.88	12.86

Source: *1982 Population Census of China*, China Statistics Publishing House, 1985.

Even without the influence of a family planning policy, educational level is still a decisive factor in determining the fertility rate. This has been proved by the one-per-thousand-population fertility sampling survey in China conducted in 1982, and amply illustrated by the results of investigation of women aged 50 that year, during whose period of fecundity China was without a comprehensive family planning program (see Table 3-15). Therefore, raising the educational level of the whole nation, especially that of women, is of vital importance to reducing the fertility rate. Only then will women consciously practice birth control.

DIFFERENCE IN FERTILITY RATE BETWEEN WOMEN OF DIFFERENT OCCUPATIONS

Socially speaking, the fertility rate of women is directly related to their employment level. The higher their employment rate in a country or region, the lower their fertility rate. However, in economically less developed countries and regions, the childbearing rate is also related to the departments in which women are employed.

Women's socioeconomic status was low in old China. This has undergone great changes in New China, as manifested in the increasing number of women taking part in social labor. The 1982 census shows that working women made up 46.63% of the total female population, and 43.69% of the total number of employees. Among women of childbearing age (15–49), 84.12% were employed. The rise in the proportion of working women indicated the expansion of women's rights in the family and society. This has also greatly affected their fertility rate.

Because of the nature of different jobs, the fertility rate of women in different occupations also varies. As relevant data in the 1982 census indicate, this difference is found mainly between women engaging in farming, afforestation, stock-breeding, and fishery and those in other occupations (see Table 3-16).

In present-day China, the level of fertility rate is directly connected with the proportion of women employed in farming, forestry, animal husbandry, and fishery in the total number of employed women.

At the end of 1983, there were 40.93 million salaried working women throughout China, or 8.3% of the total population of women. However, this figure represented less than 20% of the working-age (16–54) women. This shows that though women's employment has greatly improved compared with the situation in old China, the proportion of women with fixed income is still small. The greater part of working women are engaged in farming, forestry, animal husbandry, and fishery in the vast countryside. In

Table 3-15.   Average Number of Births by 50-Year-Old Women of Different Educational Levels (1982)

EDUCATIONAL LEVEL	COLLEGE	SENIOR MIDDLE SCHOOL	JUNIOR MIDDLE SCHOOL	PRIMARY SCHOOL	ILLITERATE
Average births	2.05	2.85	3.74	4.80	5.86

Source: "Analysis on One-per-thousand-population Fertility Sampling Survey in China," *Population and Economy*, 1983, p. 43.

Table 3-16. Births and Fertility Rate of Women in Different Occupations (1981)

OCCUPATION	FERTILITY RATE (‰)	1st BIRTH (%)	2nd BIRTH (%)	3rd BIRTH (%)	4th BIRTH (%)	5th AND MORE BIRTH (%)
Total	85.32	47.94	25.02	12.73	6.64	7.67
Professionals and technicians	67.78	81.50	14.96	2.24	0.67	0.63
Responsible members of state organs, political parties, people's organizations and enterprises	32.89	83.76	13.52	1.73	0.49	0.50
Clerks and other office workers	61.18	89.26	9.46	0.89	0.25	0.14
Employees in commercial establishments	64.85	82.25	13.57	2.55	0.90	0.73
Employees in service trades	50.97	83.64	12.58	2.24	0.81	0.73
Workers in farming, afforestation, stock-breeding, and fisheries	93.21	40.94	27.33	14.81	7.82	9.10
Industrial workers, transport workers, and other workers	58.93	82.83	13.30	2.53	0.81	0.53
Other laborers	49.32	81.39	13.44	3.03	1.23	0.91

Source: Based on the *1982 Population Census of China*. China Statistics Publishing House.

other words, this difference in occupations actually means the difference between the cities and the countryside.

This kind of difference is quite evident between the various provinces, municipalities, and autonomous regions. For instance, in 1983, salaried women workers and staff members made up about 50% of the total number of working-age women in the three municipalities of Beijing, Tianjin, and Shanghai.

Consequently, the fertility rate was low there. In contrast to this, in Guizhou and Yunnan provinces, where salaried working women made up only 10%, the fertility rate of women in these provinces was much higher than in the three municipalities. It goes without saying that an increase of job opportunities for women in departments other than farming, forestry, animal husbandry, and fishery will gradually reduce their fertility rate.

CHAPTER FOUR

TRENDS AND DIFFERENCES IN CHINA'S MORTALITY RATE

Before the founding of the People's Republic, in 1949, the traditional pattern of the reproduction of population in China was one of high birthrate, high death rate, and low growth rate. In old China the death rate was 25–33‰, infant mortality rate was 200–250‰, and life expectancy was on the average only 34 years old. In the more than 100 years from 1840 to 1949, the average annual population growth rate was only 2.6‰, basically a state of stagnation. The basic causes for this were: Old China was economically backward, the people led an impoverished life, the land was frequently hit by natural disasters and ravaged by wars and famines, and infectious diseases often ran rampant, taking a heavy toll on the people. It was after the founding of New China that a basic change was effected in bringing down the death rate.

CRUDE DEATH RATE AND NUMBER OF DEATHS

In the 35 years since the founding of the People's Republic, the death rate of China's population has dropped, but there have been fluctuations. The change in the death rate may be roughly divided into four stages:

• 1949–52 period. This was a period of restoration of China's economy, and the people who were politically liberated began to lead a stable life; medical and health services developed steadily and many malignant infectious diseases were gradually brought under control. In the short space of three years, the death rate plummeted (see Table 4-1) and the average annual death rate was 17.8‰.

• 1953–58. This was the period of China's First Five-Year Plan for economic construction, a period

Table 4-1.   Crude Death Rate (1949–1952)

YEAR	NUMBER OF DEATHS (10,000)	CDR (‰)
1949	1,080	20.00
1950	984	18.00
1951	948	17.00
1952	967	17.00

Source: *Statistics Yearbook of China*, China Statistics Publishing House, 1984, p. 83.

that saw comparatively rapid economic growth and improvement in the people's living standards. During this period, the death rate dropped from 17‰ to 11‰, and the average annual death rate was 12.1‰, a drop of about 33% in six years. This was a rapid change. It took dozens of years for the death rate to fall from 17‰ to 10–11‰ in many other countries, at least a dozen or so years at the fastest. In Sweden, it took 64 years (from 1881 to 1945) to achieve such a decrease in death rate; in Britain, 52 years from 1896 to 1948; and in Japan, 14 years from 1936 to 1950. But in China it took only five years (see Table 4-2).

It is clear from Table 4-2 that the death rate in 1958 rose again. This was because of the disproportionate development of China's economy at that time, which affected the people's livelihood.

Table 4-2.   Crude Death Rate (1953–1958)

YEAR	NUMBER OF DEATHS (10,000)	CDR (‰)
1953	814	14.00
1954	779	13.18
1955	745	12.28
1956	706	11.40
1957	633	10.80
1958	781	11.98

Source: *Statistics Yearbook of China*, China Statistics Publishing House, 1984, p. 83.

• 1959–61. As a result of the mistakes of the "great leap forward" movement and natural disasters, China experienced three years of serious difficulties. The economy basically stagnated, and there were crop failures and an acute shortage of the means of livelihood, which posed great difficulties for the state and the people. Cases of undernourishment, famine, and diseases increased, leading to a sharp rise in the death rate. Especially in 1960, the death rate rose to over 25‰, surpassing the level of the early postliberation years (see Table 4-3). The average death rate between 1959 and 1961 was 18.1‰.

• 1962–84. After the three-year difficult period, the death rate began to decrease from year to year (see Table 4-4). From 1962 to 1964 the death rate was still over 10‰, rising in 1964. This was because the birthrate was high; for example, in 1963 it was 43.4‰. The high birthrate was coupled with a high infant mortality rate, which was why the death rate in 1963 and 1964 rose again slightly. In the period between 1965 and 1969, however, the death rate began to fall again. In the seven years between 1970 and 1976, the death rate was stable, averaging 7.4‰ a year. The death rate after 1977 continued to drop to less than 7‰, the average annual death rate in the eight years being 6.6‰. In 1983, the death rate rose again, because the proportion of old people increased.

Over the past 35 years, 422.31 million people died throughout the country, and the death rate averaged 9.8‰ a year.

The figures show that the death rate after liberation has on the whole decreased gradually, resulting in a stable, low level at present.

The drop of the death rate has been faster in China that in many other countries. Japan, for instance, took more than 50 years (1920–74) for its death rate to drop from 20‰ to 7‰, over 20 years more than China did. Of course, the young age composition of China's population was also a factor contributing to its low death rate.

Table 4-3.   Crude Death Rate (1959–1961)

YEAR	NUMBER OF DEATHS (10,000)	CDR (‰)
1959	970	14.59
1960	1,693	25.43
1961	939	14.24

Source: *Statistics Yearbook of China*, China Statistics Publishing House, 1984, p. 83.

Table 4-4.   Crude Death Rate (1962–1984)

YEAR	NUMBER OF DEATHS (10,000)	CDR (‰)
1962	666	10.02
1963	684	10.04
1964	802	11.50
1965	678	9.50
1966	649	8.83
1967	636	8.43
1968	636	8.21
1969	639	8.03
1970	620	7.60
1971	613	7.32
1972	656	7.61
1973	622	7.04
1974	661	7.34
1975	671	7.32
1976	675	7.25
1977	648	6.87
1978	598	6.25
1979	602	6.21
1980	619	6.34
1981	629	6.36
1982	665	6.60
1983	722	7.08
1984	689	6.69

Source: *Statistics Yearbook of China*, China Statistics Publishing House, 1984.

Compared with developed countries, China's death rate, if calculated according to specific standards, would be higher than that of many countries. For instance, Japan's death rate was recently 6‰, approximately the same as China's; but if calculated in accordance with Japan's age composition, China's death rate would be 9.14‰. The death rate in the United States was 9‰, and if China's death rate was calculated in accordance with the U.S. age composition, it would be 11.07‰. Similarly, the Federal Republic of Germany's death rate was 12‰, and Sweden's was 11‰; if calculated in accordance with the age composition of these two countries, China's death rate would be 12.27‰ and 15.02‰, respectively.

AGE-SPECIFIC MORTALITY RATE

The death rate varies greatly at different ages. As the total death rate decreases, the death rate at different ages also changes. After liberation, China conducted 11 surveys of deaths at different ages and made an analysis of the changes in the death rate at different ages on the basis of the materials collected in five typical years (1957, 1963, 1975, 1978, and 1981).

Table 4-5. Age-Specific Mortality Rate and Crude Death Rate (‰)

AGE GROUP	1957	1963	1975	1978	1981
Crude death rate	10.80	10.04	7.32	6.25	6.36
0	58.02	84.27	27.51	22.58	38.80
1–4	20.27	14.62	5.91	6.27	4.20
5–9	4.04	2.92	1.52	1.58	1.17
10–14	1.91	1.30	0.77	0.77	0.72
15–19	1.82	1.15	0.95	0.78	0.99
20–24	2.25	1.59	1.23	1.27	1.32
25–29	2.54	2.03	1.54	1.40	1.47
30–34	3.30	2.49	1.91	1.61	1.72
35–39	4.09	3.23	2.71	2.32	2.30
40–44	5.26	5.53	3.79	3.23	3.23
45–49	7.36	6.99	5.74	5.59	4.82
50–54	9.59	10.54	9.18	7.66	7.73
55–59	14.19	16.83	15.50	13.32	12.33
60–64	21.79⎤	28.97	25.35	21.99	20.77
65–69	31.51⎦		39.66	33.89	32.34
70–74	49.74⎤	55.58	64.04	52.28	53.78
75–79	64.85⎦		95.50	74.76	81.50
80–84	104.33⎤	96.13	160.71	112.53	134.24
85–89	160.84⎦		239.61	176.10	191.98
90+	265.53	130.78	394.14	340.65	273.15

Source: *Population Yearbook of China*, China Statistics Publishing House, 1985.

AGE-SPECIFIC MORTALITY RATE AND TENDENCY OF CHANGE

The difference in crude death rate means that the age-specific death rate ages (particularly the death rate of children) is also different. The main causes of a high crude death rate is the high death rate of children.

It can be seen from Table 4-5 that the death rate of each age group under 60 in 1957 and 1963 was higher than that in the years after 1975. This was especially so in those age groups under 15. Conversely, the death rate of the age groups over 60 after 1975 was higher than that of 1957 and 1963. It can be said that the death rate of the low age groups was in direct ratio to the crude death rate, and the death rate of the advanced age groups was in inverse ratio to the crude death rate. This can be seen more clearly from

the proportion of deaths of the various age groups in the total number of deaths (see Table 4-6).

Among those who died in 1957 and 1963, children who died before reaching the age of 5 accounted for more than 40%, and half of the people who died in 1957 had not reached the age of 18. This was even more serious in 1963, when half of those who died that year had barely lived to 10. On the contrary, the proportion of those who died at or over 50 in the total number of deaths was only one-seventh and one-sixth in 1957 and 1963, respectively, whereas the proportion rose to over 65% after 1975. Of those who died in 1975, 1978, and 1981, half were over 60 years old. In the past, it was "rare for people to live to 70," as a Chinese saying goes, but now it is not strange for people to live to the age of 80. The raising of the age median of deaths shows that there

Table 4-6. Proportion of Total Deaths Occurring at Ages 0–4 and Over 50

YEAR	DEATHS IN THE 0–4 AGE GROUP (%)	DEATHS IN THE 50 AND ABOVE AGE GROUP (%)	MEDIAN AGE OF THE DEAD
1957	42.3	35.9	17.6
1963	46.1	34.8	9.7
1975	14.3	67.3	63.2
1978	13.6	65.6	61.6
1981	15.9	64.7	62.0

Source: *Population Yearbook of China*, China Statistics Publishing House, 1985.

Table 4-7.   Regional Death Rates in 0–4 and Over-50 Age Groups (1981)

REGION	CRUDE DEATH RATE (‰)	DEATHS IN THE 0–4 AGE GROUP (%)	DEATHS IN THE 50 AND ABOVE AGE (%)	MEDIAN AGE OF THE DEAD
Beijing	5.78	5.20	78.7	68.7
Tianjin	6.10	5.63	80.3	68.6
Liaoning	5.32	8.50	75.7	69.3
Shanghai	6.44	4.92	81.7	70.4
Fujian	5.87	11.71	66.9	62.0
Henan	6.01	10.00	72.1	65.3
Guangdong	5.54	12.57	68.9	64.4
Guizhou	8.48	34.23	45.3	40.7
Gansu	5.72	17.30	60.3	58.8
Ningxia	6.08	37.55	44.2	38.1

Source: *Ten Per Cent Sample Materials from China's 1982 Census*, China Statistics Publishing House, 1983, pp. 446–465.

are more deaths among old people in China than before.

Owing to the difference in the total death rate, there are similar cases between the different regions and between the city and countryside.

Table 4-7 shows the death rate of old people and children and the ages of those who died in 1981 in 10 provinces and cities including Beijing.

These six provinces, three municipalities, and one autonomous region may be divided into three categories. The first category includes Liaoning, Guangdong, Gansu, Fujian, and Henan, where the death rate was slightly lower than the national average, and the proportion of deaths among infants was fairly high, whereas the proportion of those who died at or above the age of 50 was low. The second category includes Ningxia and Guizhou, where the proportion of deaths among infants was quite high and the proportion of those who died at or above the age

of 50 was very low. The third category includes the three municipalities of Beijing, Tianjin, and Shanghai, where the proportion of deaths among infants was small, but the proportion of those who died at or above the age of 50 was very high. These facts show that the reproduction of population in the various provinces, municipalities, and autonomous regions in China is actually at different stages and belongs to different types.

Table 4-8 shows the proportion of deaths among old people and children in 1981 in China's cities, towns, and rural areas. Much as the crude death rate varies in different regions, the proportion of the number of deaths among old people and children is also different.

Compared with some other countries, the death rate among China's old people was high. The death rate of those in the 45 and above age groups, especially those over 65, was generally higher than that of

Table 4-8.   Deaths in 0–4 and Over-50 Age Groups in Different Regions (1981)

	DEATHS IN THE 0–4 AGE GROUP (%)	DEATHS IN THE 50 AND ABOVE AGE GROUP (%)	MEDIAN AGE OF THE DEAD
Whole country	15.9	64.7	62.04
Men	15.7	64.0	60.67
Women	16.3	65.4	63.86
City population	8.9	73.2	64.67
Men	8.6	71.1	63.10
Women	9.2	75.7	66.65
Town population	9.8	69.2	63.84
Men	9.4	67.5	61.39
Women	10.4	72.0	67.23
County population	17.3	63.2	61.47
Men	17.1	62.7	60.23
Women	17.5	63.8	62.95

Source: *1982 Population Census of China*, China Statistics Publishing House, 1985, pp. 320–351.

Table 4-9. Mortality Rates in the 45 and Over Age Groups in China and Selected Countries (Per 100,000 People)

AGE GROUP	MEN				WOMEN			
	USA	JAPAN	SWEDEN	CHINA	USA	JAPAN	SWEDEN	CHINA
45–49	648	457	432	535	356	243	230	488
50–54	1,018	634	703	876	537	368	374	660
55–59	1,579	1,039	1,134	1,519	807	570	557	1,070
60–64	2,496	1,681	1,815	2,443	1,231	902	921	1,712
65–69	3,586	2,834	3,000	3,833	1,713	1,557	1,480	2,685
70–74	5,435	5,010	5,001	6,375	2,856	2,970	2,720	4,584
75–79	8,263	8,056	8,078	9,720	4,851	5,460	5,058	7,079
80–84	11,521	13,241	12,831	15,749	7,633	10,050	9,172	12,405
85+	17,984	22,235	23,066	23,428	14,312	19,129	18,706	19,577

Note: 1981 figures are used for China and 1976 figures are used for the other countries.

Sources: *Levels and Trends of Mortality Since 1950*, United Nations, 1982, pp. 69, 70, 74. Figures for China are based on data from the *Statistics Yearbook of China*, China Statistics Publishing House.

the United States, Japan, and Sweden. This was especially true in the case of women (see Table 4-9). In the days to come, with the development of China's medical and health work, the death rate of China's old people may fall. However, due to the extension of people's life span and the increase in the proportion of old people, the total death rate may rise again.

INFANT MORTALITY RATE

The study of infant mortality is of special importance to the study of the mortality of a population. Before liberation, infant mortality rate in China was as high as 200‰, according to the results obtained from some data. A survey conducted in 1954 showed that

Table 4-10. Infant Mortality Rate (1954–1981)

YEAR	INFANT MORTALITY (‰)
1954	138.5
1956	81.1
1957	70.9
1958	80.8
Cities	50.8
Counties	89.1
1959	88.3
1963	83.6
1973–75	47.0
Male	50.1
Female	43.7
1975	27.1
1978	22.3
1981	34.7
Male	35.6
Female	33.7

Sources: Jiang Zhenghau et al., "Initial Study of the Life Expectancy of China's Population," *Population and Economy*, No. 3, 1984; p. 16, *Renmin Ribao*, March 25, 1984.

infant mortality was still as high as 138.5‰, but since then there has been a big drop in infant mortality (see Table 4-10).

Of course, the situation varies from place to place. In 1981, for example, the infant mortality rate differed vastly in 10 provinces, autonomous regions, and municipalities including Beijing (see Table 4-11).

Whether taking the country as a whole or the various provinces, municipalities, and autonomous regions separately, infant mortality in China has dropped to a low level. Such rapid reduction of infant mortality is closely connected with the state's efforts to strengthen maternity and child care, especially the popularization of modern obstetrics and improvement of prenatal health work. In the early postliberation years, deaths from tetanus made up a very big proportion of infant mortality because of infection resulting from the old methods of delivery. With the popularization of the new method of mid-

Table 4-11. Regional Infant Mortality Rate (1981)

	TOTAL (‰)	MALE (‰)	FEMALE (‰)
Beijing	14.37	14.96	13.67
Tianjin	16.23	17.03	15.38
Liaoning	18.04	19.31	16.68
Shanghai	15.20	16.83	13.49
Fujian	19.20	19.59	18.78
Henan	19.59	19.25	19.96
Guangdong	17.66	17.87	17.42
Guizhou	58.76	61.28	56.06
Gansu	34.26	36.08	32.32
Ningxia	54.81	59.89	48.54

Sources: *Major Figures from China's Third Census*, China Statistics Publishing House, 1982, p. 19; *Ten Per Cent Sample Materials from China's 1982 Census*, China Statistics Publishing House, 1983, pp. 446–465.

wifery, tetanus was quickly brought under control, and in only a few years infant mortality fell from 200‰ to 70–80‰. In the three difficult years (1959–61) many children suffered from pneumonia and measles, which was why infant mortality hardly decreased in the early 1960s.

At present, the main cause of infant mortality is premature births and congenital malformation. In 1981, China's infant mortality was higher than that of the developed countries. But with the popularization of eugenics and improvement in the quality of the population as a whole, China's infant mortality will continue to fall and is expected to drop to 20‰ by the end of this century.

LAW GOVERNING AGE-SPECIFIC MORTALITY RATE

The mortality rate in different age groups has its own law and is best illustrated by a U-shaped curve: In the first year after birth, the mortality rate is comparatively high because of the babies' low resistance, and the number of deaths accounts for 1/20th to 1/30th of the number of births. After the first year, the mortality rate decreases rapidly. Generally speaking, the mortality rate of children at about 8 years old begins to rise again, and the mortality rate of people around 70 is about the same as that of infants. Then with the increase of age, it rises higher and higher until it reaches the level of 100%.

For the convenience of analysis, the population of different ages can be divided into four groups according to the level of age-specific mortality— .0001, .001, .01, and .1 (see Chart 4-1). Generally speaking, the curve of mortality rate of different age groups begins from the infant mortality of .01 (when infant mortality is high, the curve starts at .1), but it quickly moves to the .001 group (at about the age of 2 to 3), and then returns to the .0001 group (at the age of 7 to 8). By 18 or 19 years old, it reverts to the .001 group, which continues for a fairly long period of time; then at the age of about 55, the mortality rate rises to the level of the .01 group. At the age of 80, the mortality rate climbs to the .1 group.

However, the time when the change takes place varies in different places because the crude death rate is different. For instance, in Beijing, Shanghai, and Liaoning, the mortality rate moves into the .0001 group at the age of 2 to 4, while in Gansu and Ningxia it takes place at the age of 7 to 8. In Guizhou Province, where the mortality rate is relatively high, the mortality rate skips over the .0001 group and moves directly into the .001 group. With the increase of age,

the mortality rate begins to rise, changing from the .0001 group to the .001 group. At that time, the mortality rate begins to rise earlier in regions where the crude death rate is high than in regions where the crude death rate is low. For instance, the mortality rate moves into the .001 group at the age of 3 in Guizhou, at 17 in Ningxia, at 19 in Liaoning, at 30 in Beijing, and at 34 in Shanghai; the difference is quite large in different places. There is, however, not much difference when the mortality rate changes from the .001 group, all taking place at around the age of 55. There is also not much difference in time when the high mortality rate changes from the .01 group to the .1 group, all taking place at about the age of 80 (see Chart 4-1).

DIFFERENCES IN MORTALITY
DIFFERENCE OF MORTALITY RATES OF MEN AND WOMEN

Just as it is necessary to analyze the sex ratio of the population, so it is necessary to analyze the sex ratio of the number of deaths. Usually, the mortality rate of males is higher than that of females. So, although the number of baby boys is greater than that of baby girls when they are born, the two gradually come into equilibrium. At old age, because the death rate of the male population is high, the number of females exceeds that of males. The life expectancy of the female population is generally higher, a characteristic also found in the process of the development of China's population (see Table 4-12).

The ratio between the deaths of different sexes is related to the crude death rate. From the death rate of different years in the past or in different regions in the same period, we see that when the crude death rate was high, the death rate of females was higher than that of males; conversely, when the crude death rate was low, the death rate of females was lower than that of males. For example, in 1957 and 1963, when the total death rate was high, the sex ratio of deaths was about 95 male deaths per 100 female deaths. When the crude death rate dropped to below 7‰ after 1975, male deaths exceeded female deaths in number.

In addition, the sex ratio of the death rate in different regions varies with the level of the crude death rate. For example, because the crude death rate in Guizhou Province was high, the death rate of females was higher than that of males (see Table 4-13).

Chart 4-1. Age-Specific Mortality Rate in Beijing and Other Places in China (1981)

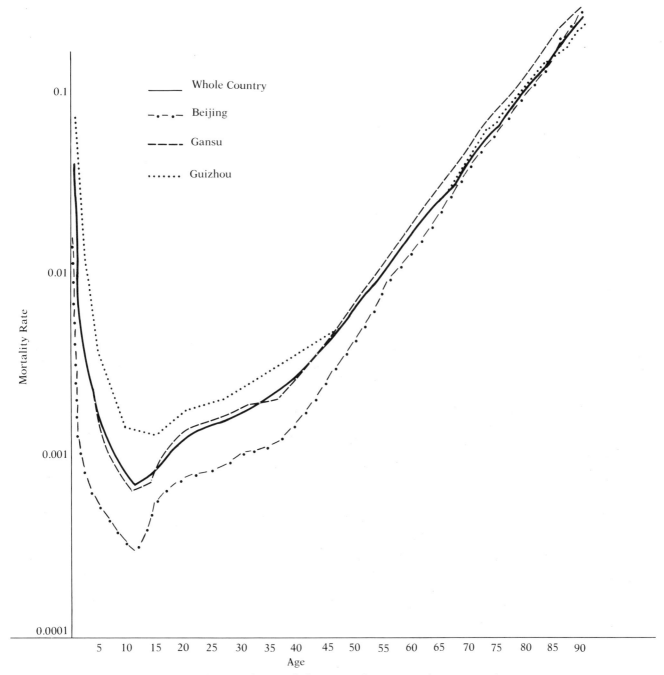

Source: Wang Weizhi, "Initial Analysis of the Death Rate of China's Population," *Population Research*, No. 5, 1984, p. 29.

The difference between the sexes in the number of deaths is quite noticeable in different age groups. With the exception of a few low age groups, the mortality rate of males is higher than that of females (see Table 4-14). In 1981, the mortality rate of boys under one year old was higher than that of girls; the mortal-ity rate of girls of the 1–4 age group was higher than that of boys in the same age group. (Perhaps this was because of the parents' subjective neglect of the girls.) In the 5–14 age group, the mortality rate of boys was higher than that of girls; in the 15–24 age group, the mortality rate was basically balanced, and

Table 4-12.   Sex Ratio of the Death Rate of China's Population (Female = 100)

YEAR	AVERAGE OF BOTH SEXES (‰)	MALE (‰)	FEMALE (‰)	SEX RATIO
Whole nation (1957)	10.63	10.39	10.89	95.4
City	8.19	7.55	8.94	84.5
County	10.93	10.75	11.11	96.8
Whole nation (1963)	9.96	9.81	10.12	96.9
City	7.09	6.90	7.29	94.7
Town	7.72	7.22	8.31	86.9
County	10.58	10.48	10.69	98.0
Whole nation (1975)	7.30	7.51	7.08	106.1
City	5.57	5.72	5.42	105.5
County	7.52	7.74	7.52	102.9
Whole nation (1978)	6.24	6.40	6.07	105.4
City	5.19	5.37	4.99	107.6
County	6.38	6.55	6.21	105.5
Whole nation (1981)	6.35	6.55	6.15	106.5
City	5.14	5.45	4.82	113.1
Town	4.63	4.81	4.44	108.3
County	6.71	6.89	6.51	105.8

Source: Wang Weizhi, "Initial Analysis of the Death Rate of China's Population," *Population Research*, No. 5, 1984, p. 27.

Table 4-13.   Sex Ratio of the Regional Death Rate (1981)
(Females = 100)

	TOTAL	CITY	TOWN	COUNTY
Whole nation	106.5	113.07	108.33	105.84
Beijing	111.80	111.04	100.58	119.58
Shanghai	108.91	104.72	98.70	116.09
Liaoning	117.90	119.30	114.49	118.03
Guizhou	93.30	98.90	109.37	92.23
Gansu	105.58	113.20	114.93	105.41
Ningxia	116.88	131.00	118.10	116.51

Source: Wang Weizhi, "Initial Analysis of the Death Rate of China's Population," *Population Research*, No. 5, 1984, p. 28.

Table 4-14.   Mortality Rate of Males and Females (1981)

AGE GROUP	MORTALITY RATE OF MALES (‰)	MORTALITY RATE OF FEMALES (‰)	SEX RATIO (FEMALES = 100)
0	39.65	37.42	105.82
1–4	3.99	4.32	92.36
5–9	1.28	1.05	121.90
10–14	0.79	0.65	121.54
15–19	1.01	0.92	109.78
20–24	1.42	1.34	105.97
25–29	1.46	1.48	98.65
30–34	1.76	1.68	104.76
35–39	2.43	2.16	112.50
40–44	3.51	2.91	120.62
45–49	5.35	4.21	127.08
50–54	8.74	6.60	132.42
55–59	14.31	10.18	140.57
60–64	24.43	17.13	142.62
65–69	38.37	26.85	142.91
70–74	63.75	45.84	139.07
75–79	97.20	70.94	137.02
80–84	157.49	121.17	129.97
85–89	222.56	178.32	124.80
90+	294.95	264.94	111.32

Source: Calculated on the basis of *1982 Population Census of China*, China Statistics Publishing House.

in the 25–29 age group, the mortality rate of females was higher than that of males, which was because women who died during lying-in made up a certain proportion. The difference in the mortality rate between men and women increased after 30 years old. In the 55–70 age group, the ratio of men to women was almost 1.5:1. The ratio gradually decreased after 70 years old.

REGIONAL DIFFERENCES IN CRUDE DEATH RATE

The natural conditions and the level of economic development differ greatly in the various regions, and there are also great differences in the occupations, culture, and health conditions of the people as well as in the living standards and age composition of the population. These factors all affect the death rate. In 1981, the nation's death rate was 6.36‰, the low-est being 4.95‰ in Heilongjiang and the highest being 9.92‰ in Tibet. The death rate was 5–6‰ in 9 provinces and autonomous regions, 6–7‰ in 10, and 7–8‰ in 5 (see Table 4-15).

Two factors account for the low death rate in Heilongjiang Province: Its industry is developed and the proportion of its urban population is large (40.5%); and its age composition is young and the proportion of the middle-aged population is large. A similar situation exists in Liaoning Province, where the death rate is relatively low. The reasons for the high death rate in Guizhou and Tibet are mainly because their economies are backward and their health conditions are poor. The average per capita output value of industry and agriculture in Guizhou Province is lower than half the nation's average level, and the average share of grain per peasant ranks last among the country's various provinces, municipal-

Table 4-15.   Crude Death Rate in Descending Order

	1954		1965		1975		1981	
	REGION	CDR (‰)	REGION	CDR (‰)	REGION	CDR (‰)	REGION	CDR (‰)
1	Tibet	18.90	Guizhou	15.2	Guizhou	10.53	Tibet	9.92
2	Hunan	17.52	Yunnan	13.0	Tibet	9.05	Yunnan	8.60
3	Yunnan	16.48	Shaanxi	13.0	Sichuan	8.86	Guizhou	8.48
4	Anhui	16.44	Gansu	12.3	Xinjiang	8.74	Xinjiang	8.41
5	Xinjiang	16.06	Sichuan	11.5	Yunnan	8.68	Qinghai	7.48
6	Hubei	15.95	Hunan	11.2	Hunan	8.34	Hubei	7.33
7	Sichuan	15.43	Xinjiang	11.1	Qinghai	8.24	Shaanxi	7.10
8	Guangxi	15.20	Shanxi	10.4	Shaanxi	8.16	Hunan	7.03
9	Shanxi	14.60	Shandong	10.2	Jiangxi	8.01	Sichuan	7.02
10	Jiangxi	14.22	Hubei	10.0	Hubei	7.88	Shanxi	6.54
11	Henan	13.19	Jilin	9.7	Shanxi	7.85	Jiangxi	6.54
12	Guangdong	12.72	Inner Mongolia	9.6	Ningxia	7.74	Shanghai	6.44
13	Guizhou	12.10	Jiangsu	9.5	Henan	7.66	Zhejiang	6.27
14	Jiangsu	12.06	Jiangxi	9.4	Shandong	7.53	Shandong	6.26
15	Shandong	11.70	Ningxia	9.3	Gansu	7.42	Tianjin	6.10
16	Zhejiang	11.47	Qinghai	9.1	Hebei	7.22	Jiangsu	6.10
17	Qinghai	11.43	Guangxi	9.0	Guangxi	6.77	Ningxia	6.08
18	Inner Mongolia	11.15	Henan	8.5	Jilin	6.74	Hebei	6.05
19	Gansu	11.10	Hebei	8.4	Tianjin	6.59	Henan	6.01
20	Shaanxi	11.05	Zhejiang	8.1	Fujian	6.54	Fujian	5.87
21	Fujian	10.72	Heilongjiang	8.0	Beijing	6.53	Beijing	5.78
22	Heilongjiang	10.54	Fujian	7.3	Jiangsu	6.46	Inner Mongolia	5.77
23	Jilin	10.38	Anhui	7.2	Zhejiang	6.31	Gansu	5.72
24	Hebei	10.19	Liaoning	7.1	Liaoning	6.16	Guangxi	5.61
25	Beijing	8.24	Guangdong	6.8	Guangdong	6.06	Guangdong	5.54
26	Liaoning	8.00	Beijing	6.7	Shanghai	6.01	Liaoning	5.32
27	Tianjian	7.82	Shanghai	5.7	Inner Mongolia	5.68	Jilin	5.32
28	Shanghai	7.12	Tianjin	4.9	Anhui	5.68	Anhui	5.20
29					Heilongjiang	5.43	Heilongjiang	4.95

Source: *Collection of Statistical Data on China's Population*, China Statistics Publishing House, 1986.

ities, and autonomous regions. In Tibet, which is on a plateau in the border region, the economy, communications, and health conditions are all far from developed.

Table 4-15 shows some changes in the order of death rate in the various provinces, municipalities, and autonomous regions in the years after 1954. In the various provinces and autonomous regions in southwest and northwest China, such as Tibet, Guizhou, Yunnan, Sichuan, Xinjiang, Hunan, Hubei, and Shanxi, the death rate always leads that of the other regions, while in some economically developed provinces and cities, such as the three provinces in the northeast, Beijing, Tianjin, Shanghai, Guangdong, Fujian, and other coastal provinces, the death rate is always relatively low. In 1981, some changes took place in the order of death rate in the various provinces and regions. The three municipalities directly under the central government—Beijing, Tianjin, and Shanghai—moved to the front in the order of death rate, which was the result of the increasing number of old people.

Death rate also varies between urban and rural areas. Over the last 35 years, the death rate of urban population has always been lower than that of rural population, and the death rate of urban population has decreased at a faster pace than that of rural population (see Table 4-16). In the 1954–58 period, the death rate of urban population fell to the low level of 10‰ a year. During the three difficult years of 1959–61, although the death rate rose a bit, it remained at a medium level (the highest being 13.74‰ in 1960). After 1965, it fell to below 7‰, and hit the lowest level of 4.96‰ in 1973. In 1976, when an earthquake hit Tangshan, the death rate of urban population rose to 6.6‰ again, but since then it has remained at the low level of less than 6‰.

The change in the death rate of the rural population was slightly different. In the 1954–58 period, it also dropped to a medium level, but during the three difficult years of 1959–61 it took a marked upturn and reached 28.58‰ in 1960, which was a rare case after liberation. In the 12 years, 1966–77, although the death rate of the rural population dropped, it still remained at over 7‰.

The difference between urban and rural death rate was mainly due to the vast difference in the level of economic, cultural, medical, and health development; in addition, it should also be attributed to the difference in the composition of their population. In cities and towns, the proportion of middle-aged people is fairly large and the proportion of old people and children is relatively low. The situation in rural

Table 4-16. Crude Death Rate of China's Urban and Rural Population Between 1954 and 1984 (‰)

YEAR	WHOLE NATION	CITY	COUNTY
1954	13.18	8.07	13.71
1955	12.28	9.30	12.60
1956	11.40	7.43	11.84
1957	10.80	8.47	11.07
1958	11.98	9.22	12.50
1959	14.59	10.92	14.61
1960	25.43	13.77	28.58
1961	14.24	11.39	14.58
1962	10.02	8.28	10.32
1963	10.04	7.13	10.49
1964	11.50	7.27	12.17
1965	9.50	5.69	10.06
1966	8.83	5.59	9.47
1971	7.32	5.35	7.57
1972	7.61	5.29	7.93
1973	7.04	4.96	7.33
1974	7.34	5.24	7.63
1975	7.32	5.39	7.59
1976	7.25	6.60	7.35
1977	6.87	5.51	7.06
1978	6.25	5.12	6.42
1979	6.21	5.07	6.39
1980	6.34	5.48	6.47
1981	6.36	5.14	6.53
1982	6.60	5.28	7.00
1983	7.08	5.92	7.69
1984	6.69	5.86	6.73

Source: *Statistics Yearbook of China*, China Statistics Publishing House, 1984, p. 83.

areas is just the opposite. For example, the 1982 census showed that the proportion of the population under 5 years old was 7.5% in the cities, 8.1% in the towns, and 9.9% in the countryside (9.4% in the whole country); the proportion of the population from 18 to 55 years old was 57.9% in the cities, 55.9% in the towns, and 46.7% in the rural areas (48.1% in the whole country); the proportion of people aged 60 and above was 4.7% in the cities, 4.2% in the towns, and 5.0% in the rural areas (4.9% in the whole country).

Table 4-17 shows that the death rate in rural areas of those six regions was generally higher than in the cities and towns. At the same time it showed that the death rate of the town population was lower than that of the city population, which was something that warranted attention. Economic and cultural factors and age composition could not fully explain this phenomenon. There seemed to be another reason: Many grown men worked and lived in towns while their families still lived and were registered in the countryside, so when there were deaths or births in their families, they did not have this registered in

Table 4-17. Regional Differences in Crude Death Rate of Urban and Rural Populations (‰)

	TOTAL	CITY (NOT INCLUDING COUNTY)	TOWN	COUNTY (NOT INCLUDING TOWN)
Beijing	5.78	4.89	3.48	7.23
Shanghai	6.44	6.51	5.40	6.23
Liaoning	5.32	4.72	3.79	5.87
Guizhou	8.48	7.19	5.42	8.90
Gansu	5.72	3.81	3.63	6.08
Ningxia	6.08	3.65	3.46	6.76

Source: Wang Weizhi, "Initial Analysis of the Death Rate of China's Population," *Population Research*, No. 5, 1984, p. 28.

the towns. This can be seen from the sex ratio of the population (especially the middle-aged population) in the cities, towns, and countries (see Table 4-18).

DIFFERENCE OF CRUDE DEATH RATE BETWEEN VARIOUS NATIONALITIES

At the time of the 1982 census, there were 55 minority nationalities in China with a population of 67.23 million, accounting for 6.7% of the total population of the country. On the whole, the various minority nationalities (except for a few nationalities) were economically and culturally less developed, their medical and health conditions were poor, and reproduction of population was mostly of a high birthrate and high mortality type. According to a survey conducted in 1982, in regions where the minority nationalities lived in compact communities, such as Tibet, Yunnan, Guizhou, and Xinjiang, the death rate was higher than the nation's average level of 6.36‰ (see Table 4-15).

Before the founding of New China, the death rate of the minority peoples was shockingly high. For instance, the death rate of the Mongolian nationality in the Hingan region in Inner Mongolia during the first half of the twentieth century was as high as 56‰, and the death rate of the Miao People in Xuyong County of Sichuan Province in 1943 was 50.6‰. Be-

cause of the high death rate, the population of the minority nationalities grew slowly and even decreased in some cases. For instance, the population of the Mongolian people in Inner Mongolia was 1.18 million when Emperor Jia Qing of the Qing Dynasty reigned, from 1796 to 1820. But the population had dropped to 830,000 in 1947 when the Inner Mongolian Autonomous Region was established. Again, for example, the Hezhen people had a population of 12,000 in 1661, but in 1945, when Japan surrendered, there were only 300. Tibet had a population of 5–6 million in the latter half of the eighth century, but the census conducted in 1953 showed that it had only 2.77 million people.

Since the founding of New China, the economy in the various minority nationality regions has developed and the living standards of the people have improved. The government has paid special attention to the prevention and treatment of diseases in these regions and many infectious diseases were quickly brought under control. As a result, the death rate fell rapidly. In Tibet, for instance, the death rate in 1954 was 18.9‰, but it dropped to 11.77‰ in 1967 and further to 9.92‰ in 1981.

Although the death rate in Tibet was still higher than in other provinces and regions in China, it was reduced by half in the 27 years between 1954 and 1981. A survey of some other minority nationality regions shows an almost similar situation (see Table 4-19).

Table 4-20 shows the death rate of areas where the minority groups are concentrated. The population of the minority nationalities so surveyed mostly accounted for a considerable proportion of the population of the nationality concerned. Those with a comparatively large proportion included the Uygurs, Moinbas, Lis, Tibetans, Bais, and Salas, all over 70%, and those with the smallest proportion, such as the Hui people, made up 13%. Therefore, the results of the calculations so made could be said to be typical. With the exception of the Li, Mongolian, and Korean nationalities, the death rates of other minority na-

Table 4-18. Sex Ratio of the Population Between 20 and 54 in the Cities, Towns, and Counties (1982) (Females = 100)

AGE	CITY	TOWN	COUNTY
20–24	107.16	107.77	102.77
25–29	107.60	113.84	105.79
30–34	111.63	126.80	105.91
35–39	113.09	140.03	108.56
40–44	109.11	135.32	113.44
45–49	112.99	138.42	109.85
50–54	119.63	145.91	107.72

Source: *1982 Population Census of China*, China Statistics Publishing House, 1985, pp. 272–345.

Table 4-19.   Crude Death Rate Among Minority Nationalities (‰)

	MONGOLIAN	SALA	MAONAN	MINORITY PEOPLES IN XINJIANG
1950s	17.9		14.7	19.4
1960s	12.7	20.4	13.9	9.4
1970s	5.9	12.9	11.5	8.3
1980s	3.8	6.9	7.1	10.8

Source: *Selection of Essays on the Population of China's Minority Nationalities,* Nationalities Publishing House, 1982.

tionalities were all higher than the average national level. The death rate for most minority nationality areas exceeds that for the total population. Of the 298 counties where the sample survey of the death rate of minority nationalities was conducted, the death rate of 119 counties exceeded 10‰, and in five of these counties the death rate exceeded 20‰. These five counties were: Qinghai's Dari County (24.3‰ for the Tibetans), Yunnan's Menghai County (23.9‰ for the Lahus), Xinjiang's Shache County (21‰ for the Uygurs), and Sichuan's Jinyang and Zhaojue Counties (20.9‰ for the Yis). The death rate in these counties was equivalent to the nation's average level at the time of liberation. The main reasons for such high death rates were that these counties were located mostly in remote mountainous areas, where

Table 4-20.   Crude Death Rate for Selected Minority Nationalities

NATIONAL MINORITY	TOTAL POPULATION IN AREA	AMONG WHICH		NO. OF DEATHS	CRUDE DEATH RATE IN AREA ‰	% OF MINORITY POPULATION OF ITS NATIONAL TOTAL
		NATIONAL MINORITY POPULATION	% OF TOTAL POPULATION IN AREA			
Mongolian	1,383,917	743,274	53.7	8,420	6.08	21.8
Hui	1,428,116	938,977	65.7	12,075	8.46	13.0
Tibetan	3,303,903	2,944,707	89.1	34,284	10.38	76.1
Uygur	5,956,623	5,233,063	87.9	75,212	12.63	87.9
Miao	1,911,893	1,145,742	59.9	15,775	8.25	22.8
Yi	2,361,102	1,438,610	60.9	28,871	12.22	26.4
Zhuang	11,784,012	9,274,914	78.7	76,459	6.48	69.3
Bouyei	2,037,636	1,033,705	50.7	21,184	10.39	48.8
Korean	972,106	588,641	60.6	5,841	6.00	33.4
Dong	1,228,679	701,973	57.1	10,432	8.49	49.3
Bai	1,189,517	800,448	67.3	10,300	8.65	70.8
Tu	3,229,336	1,685,301	52.2	24,904	7.71	59.5
Hani	1,230,907	729,152	59.2	13,502	10.96	68.4
Kazak	409,275	229,676	56.1	2,823	6.89	25.3
Li	1,458,433	633,679	43.5	7,120	4.88	77.5
Lisu	310,153	182,207	58.8	4,125	13.29	37.9
Va	124,207	104,766	84.4	2,035	16.38	35.1
Lahu	610,068	212,176	34.8	10,045	16.46	69.8
Shui	231,842	140,600	60.6	2,234	9.63	49.1
Dongxiang	187,309	132,760	70.9	1,328	7.08	47.5
Naxi	291,940	167,066	57.2	2,302	7.88	68.2
Kirgiz	55,300	42,600	77.0	707	12.78	37.4
Qiang	79,208	62,247	78.6	727	9.17	60.6
Sala	83,614	48,400	57.9	728	8.70	70.0
Maonan	24,269	19,330	79.60	223	9.18	50.7
Tajik	20,153	16,337	81.6	181	8.98	61.6
Moinba	7,642	5,099	66.7	61	7.98	81.60

Source: Based on statistical data from 1982 *Population Census of China.*

economic development was backward, health conditions were poor, and doctors and medicines scarce.

ANALYSIS OF THE CAUSES OF DEATH

The causes of death are usually diseases, war, famine, unexpected disasters, and accidents. Since liberation, China basically has enjoyed a peaceful environment. With the exception of individual wars, such as the war in Korea, not many people died in war. Natural disasters, though occurring now and then, are exceptional and uncertain factors, which do not have much significant influence. Deaths from other factors, such as poisoning, flood, fire, and other unfortunate disasters, are even less significant. Thus we see that diseases are now the main cause of deaths in China.

DISEASE—THE MAJOR CAUSE OF DEATHS

According to statistics provided by public health departments, 10 major causes account for more than 80% of the deaths in China today. The diseases differ slightly between the cities and the countryside (see Table 4-21). In 1982, the number of urban people who died from 10 major causes — cerebral diseases, heart disease, malignant tumor, diseases of the respiratory system, diseases of the digestive system,

trauma, poisoning, tuberculosis of the lung, newborn baby diseases, and urinary diseases — accounted for 87.5% of the total number of deaths in the cities; of this number, those who died from cerebral diseases, heart disease, and malignant tumor made up more than 60%. The situation was by and large the same in the countryside where 10 major causes of death — heart disease, cerebral diseases, malignant tumor, diseases of the respiratory system, diseases of the digestive system, poisoning, tuberculosis of the lung, trauma, infectious diseases (not including tuberculosis), and newborn baby disease — took a heavy toll of 87.2% of the total number of deaths in rural areas. According to surveys of the causes of deaths conducted between 1973 and 1975, heart disease was the primary cause of death, with a death rate of 129.11 per 100,000 people, accounting for 17.2% of the total number of deaths. Diseases of the respiratory system ranked second, accounting for 15.7%; malignant tumor ranked third, accounting for 10.28%; fourth came accidental casualties, which made up 9.4%; and diseases of the digestive system ranked fifth, accounting for 8.89%. These five causes together claimed 61.47% of the total number of deaths.

Since liberation, China's mortality rate has dropped quickly. The reasons are many, but the major ones are: decrease in the number of patients and, in particular, sharp reduction in the incidence

Table 4-21. Deaths Caused by 10 Major Diseases in Cities and Countryside (1982)

DISEASE	CITIES CDR (EVERY 100,000 PEOPLE)	PERCENTAGE OF TOTAL NUMBER OF DEATHS	COUNTRYSIDE CAUSE OF DEATH	CDR (EVERY 100,000 PEOPLE)	PERCENTAGE OF TOTAL NUMBER OF DEATHS
Cerebral diseases	124.44	22.26	Heart disease	159.32	23.70
Heart disease	117.70	21.05	Cerebral diseases	103.52	15.40
Malignant tumor	115.15	20.60	Malignant tumor	102.97	15.32
Respiratory system diseases	48.50	8.67	Respiratory system diseases	77.27	11.49
Digestive system diseases	24.44	4.34	Digestive system diseases	38.25	5.69
Trauma	18.14	3.25	Poisoning	28.48	4.24
Poisoning	11.55	2.07	TB	28.30	4.21
Tuberculosis	11.34	2.03	Trauma	19.96	2.97
Newborn baby disease*	514.41	1.63	Infectious disease (not including TB)	16.83	2.50
Urinary disease	9.03	1.61	Newborn baby disease*	655.37	1.65
Total		87.54	Total		87.17

* For every 10,000 babies born.
Source: *Health Yearbook of China 1982*, People's Health Publishing House, 1983, p. 67.

of acute infectious diseases. Before liberation, many acute infectious diseases ran rampant, and both the incidence of diseases and the mortality rate were high, seriously endangering the health and life of the people. According to surveys conducted in Chenggong County in Yunnan Province in 1940–44, people who died from infectious diseases accounted for 41.6% of the total number of deaths; of this number, those who died from cholera accounted for 11.9%. In the early postliberation years, infectious diseases were still rife, and the mortality rate, especially that of women and children, remained very high. Thanks to the efforts made by the government to strengthen medical and health work, some virulent infectious diseases, which seriously endangered people's health and caused a high mortality rate, were brought under control. The proportion of those who died from infectious diseases was reduced, and the crude death rate dropped. In 1982, the 10 major diseases causing deaths among urban people did not even include infectious diseases; in other words, the proportion of people who died from infectious diseases dropped by a big margin (see Table 4-22).

In the countryside, infectious diseases ranked ninth among the 10 major diseases in 1982, whereas they ranked second in the 1950s.

At present, the number of deaths from chronic diseases and old age diseases, such as cerebral and heart diseases, and their proportion tend to rise, but both the incidence of these diseases and the rate of deaths resulting from them are lower than those of the acute infectious diseases. That is why the death rate of China's population has remained at less than 7‰ since the 1970s.

DEATHS FROM NATURAL DISASTERS

Apart from diseases, natural disasters have a relatively big influence on the death rate of a population.

Table 4-22.   Deaths from Acute Infectious Diseases in 20 Cities Including Beijing

YEAR	DEATH RATE (PERSONS PER 100,000)	PERCENTAGE
1954	89.90	10.60
1957	56.60	7.93
1960	41.99	5.50
1963	21.24	3.96
1975	13.17	2.23
1978	9.43	1.60
1980	8.49	1.46
1982	8.82	1.17

Source: *Health Yearbook of China 1983*, People's Health Publishing House, 1983, pp. 66–67.

The biggest natural disaster after liberation was the earthquake in Tangshan, in 1976. According to rough estimates, the quake took a heavy toll of 240,000 people. Of this number, 142,000 died in Tangshan proper. As a result, the death rate of Tangshan was as high as 142.4‰ in 1976, and the net reduction of its population that year was 130,000 people. The Tangshan earthquake directly affected the death rate and natural growth rate of the population in north China and in cities across the country. In this big quake, 100,000 rural people died, which affected the rate of population change in the rural areas. The number of deaths and the death rate in the rural areas of Hebei Province in 1976 were both higher than in 1975 and 1977, whereas the natural population growth rate there was lower than that of 1975 and 1977.

DEATHS CAUSED BY FAMINE AND ACCIDENTS

Generally speaking, the phenomenon of death from famine on a large scale has been practically nonexistent since the founding of New China. During the three difficult years of 1959–61, the number of deaths in the country was three to four times that of normal years, and a good number of people (especially the elderly and children) died from diseases resulting from undernourishment and malnutrition. There were five provinces and autonomous regions where the death rate in 1960 exceeded 40‰. The death rate in a few counties in Henan and Guizhou Provinces was even more shocking, and the highest death rate exceeded 100‰. At the same time, difficulties in making ends meet, undernourishment, and diseases forced many women to stop giving birth to children. As a result, China's population decreased by 10 million in 1960–61.

Accidents mainly include drowning, death by fire or poisoning, industrial accidents, suicide, and murder. According to 1984 statistics, the number of people who died from accidents accounted for about 13% of the total number of deaths. Other surveys showed that the number of people drowned in floods or killed in industrial accidents each made up about 3%; deaths caused by fire and traffic accidents each accounted for 1%; and deaths due to other causes accounted for about 5%.

AVERAGE LIFE EXPECTANCY

The average life expectancy of a population reflects the high or low mortality rate of that population. In 1981, the average life expectancy of the Chinese people was 67.8 years old (66.3 for men and 69.2 for women). This was of a medium level compared with other countries. Close to China's level were many other countries including Mauritius, Brunei, Surinam, Chile, Panama, Albania, and Yugoslavia.

RISE IN AVERAGE LIFE EXPECTANCY

According to estimates of a 1931 survey, the life expectancy of people in old China was only 34 years. This rose gradually after liberation (see Table 4-23).

Calculated according to data obtained from a survey conducted among 52.25 million people in 1957, the average life span was 60 years old, much higher than the preliberation average of 34 years old. In 1957, the last year of China's First Five-Year Plan period, work in every field had progressed rapidly, the people's living standards had greatly improved, and medical and health work had made remarkable achievements. As a result, the death rate dropped to 10.8‰ and infant mortality also fell to 70‰. These achievements naturally boosted the average life expectancy of the Chinese people.

Calculations made on the basis of data collected from a survey conducted in 1963 among 198.33 million people showed that the average life span was 61.8 years old. Owing to the hardships of the three difficult years of 1959–61, the death rate in 1963 was comparatively high, and the average life expectancy that year was only slightly higher than that of 1957.

After checking and calculating the figures obtained from a survey conducted among 99.58 million people in 1975, it was found that the average life span of the Chinese people was 66.2 years old, which was four years higher than that of 1963, rising one year in every three years on the average. The Chinese Academy of Medical Science conducted surveys in 1973–75 and found that the life expectancy of men was 63.6 years and that of women was 66.3 years, the two being very close to each other.

In 1978, the average life expectancy was estimated at 68.2 years. This figure was on the high side, because most of the regions surveyed in 1978 were cities and rural areas where the economy was fairly developed and communications were convenient.

During the 1982 census, an investigation of those who died in 1981 was made, the first of its kind ever conducted on a nationwide scale in the history of China. The average life expectancy of 12 different nationalities was calculated on the basis of the data on the age at death throughout the country. The results showed that the average life expectancy of the Chinese people was 67.8 years, an increase of six years in the 18 years from 1963 to 1981, or an increase of one year in every three years on the average. Similar calculations were made nationwide, in the provinces, autonomous regions, and municipalities, as well as in the comparatively important cities, counties, and prefectures. More than 3,500 life tables were worked out nationwide. The results showed

Table 4-23. Average Life Expectancy of the Chinese People

YEAR	AVERAGE FOR MEN AND WOMEN	MALE	FEMALE
Whole nation (1957)	60.04	59.78	60.22
City	63.47	63.60	63.13
County	59.54	59.23	59.76
Whole nation (1963)	61.81	61.63	61.95
City	65.82	65.64	65.99
Town	64.73	64.40	64.90
County	60.89	60.68	60.98
Whole nation (1975)	66.17	65.34	67.08
City	69.61	68.31	70.95
County	65.80	65.02	66.69
Whole nation (1978)	68.24	66.96	69.63
City	71.27	69.55	73.09
County	67.99	66.66	69.34
Whole nation (1981)	67.77	66.28	69.27
City	70.77	69.06	72.60
Town	71.50	69.61	73.51
County	67.03	65.63	68.42

Source: Collection of Papers Read at China's Fourth Population Science Symposium.

Table 4-24.   Average Life Expectancy in Beijing and Five Other Regions (1981)

	BEIJING	SHANGHAI	LIAONING	GUIZHOU	GANSU	NINGXIA
Total population	71.92	72.92	70.69	61.35	65.75	65.51
Male	70.48	70.54	69.66	61.07	65.05	64.74
Female	73.40	75.14	71.86	61.55	66.49	66.40
City population	73.51	73.84	71.84	63.75	69.96	70.70
Male	72.01	72.07	70.49	62.84	68.81	69.18
Female	74.98	75.56	73.36	64.64	71.23	72.54
Town population	73.31	73.57	72.73	69.44	70.71	71.50
Male	71.81	71.13	71.61	67.52	69.10	69.95
Female	74.80	76.05	74.04	71.44	72.61	72.20
County population	69.61	71.88	69.78	60.03	65.12	64.52
Male	68.27	68.69	68.95	60.54	64.47	63.98
Female	71.04	74.79	70.77	60.66	65.82	65.20

Source: Collection of Papers Read at China's Fourth Population Science Symposium.

that although there were great differences in various places, the average life expectancy of the Chinese people as a whole was on the rise.

REGIONAL DIFFERENCES IN AVERAGE LIFE EXPECTANCY

The average life expectancy of the Chinese people differs greatly from place to place. Generally speaking, it is relatively high in the big cities and economically developed provinces and autonomous regions, whereas in the remote frontier regions where the minority peoples live and in the economically less developed provinces and autonomous regions, it is comparatively low. Also, the average life expectancy

is higher in the cities and towns than in the rural areas (see Table 4-24).

DIFFERENCE OF AVERAGE LIFE EXPECTANCY OF MEN AND WOMEN

There has always been a striking difference in the average life expectancy between men and women in China. As a rule, women live longer than men. The difference is generally three years. Judging from the statistical data of different years and different regions, the difference in the average life expectancy between men and women is in direct ratio to their average life expectancy. The longer the average life expectancy is, the greater the difference will be, and

Table 4-25.   Sex Difference in the Average Life Expectancy of the Chinese People (1957–1981)

YEAR	MALE (1)	FEMALE (2)	FEMALE-MALE (2)–(1)	SEX RATIO (MALE = 100)
Whole nation (1957)	59.78	60.22	0.44	100.74
City	63.60	63.13	−0.47	99.28
County	59.23	59.76	0.53	100.89
Whole nation (1963)	61.63	61.95	0.32	100.52
City	65.64	65.99	0.35	100.53
Town	64.40	64.90	0.50	100.77
County	60.68	60.98	0.30	100.49
Whole nation (1975)	65.34	67.08	1.74	102.66
City	68.31	70.95	2.64	103.86
County	65.02	66.69	1.67	102.57
Whole nation (1978)	66.96	69.63	2.67	103.99
City	69.55	73.09	3.54	105.09
County	66.66	69.34	2.68	104.02
Whole nation (1981)	66.28	69.27	2.99	104.51
City	69.06	72.60	3.54	105.13
Town	69.61	73.51	3.90	105.60
County	65.63	68.42	2.79	104.25

Source: Collection of Papers Read at China's Fourth Population Science Symposium.

with the decrease of the average life expectancy, the difference will be small, and sometimes the average life expectancy of men may even be higher than that of women.

The method of determining the difference of the average life expectancy between the sexes, apart from calculating the absolute difference between the average life expectancy of men and women, is to calculate the ratio of men's average life expectancy to that of women (by taking men's average life expectancy as 100). The sex ratio for the various years was mostly between 103 and 105 (see Table 4-25). The sex ratio in 1957 and 1963 was comparatively low, being 100.7 and 100.5, respectively, with very little difference between men and women in their average life expectancy. The sex ratio in the average life expectancy of the town population in 1981 was 105.60; the difference between men's and women's average life expectancy was quite big.

"CONTRADICTORY PHENOMENON" IN THE LIFE TABLE

In the case of the first few ages of the life table, we see that with the increase in age, the average life expectancy increases instead of decreasing (see Tables 4-27 through 4-31). This is called a "contradictory phenomenon" in demography. This phenomenon can be found in China's life table every year, but there are differences in this phenomenon as the average life expectancy differs. The lower the average life expectancy, the longer the "contradictory period," and the higher the average life expectancy, the shorter the "contradictory period," which may even gradually disappear. Judging from China's annual life table and the life tables of various regions in 1981, this phenomenon was quite conspicuous when the average life expectancy was below 60 years old. Sometimes, the "contradictory period" extended to over 14 years old, but when the average life expectancy was over 65 years, the "contradictory period" was only one or two years old. According to the United Nations' model life table for the Far East Region, when men's average life expectancy is 67 years old, the life expectancy is 67.8 years at one year old and 64.3 years at two years old, and the "contradictory period" was one year. When women's average life expectancy is 69 years old, the life expectancy is 70.5 years at one year old and 67.1 years at two years old, and the "contradictory period" is also one year. The average life expectancy of the Chinese people in 1981 was 67.8 years old; the life expectancy was 69.3 years at one year old, 68.7 years at two years old, 68.0 years at three years old and 67.3 years at four years old, and the "contradictory period" was three years, which tallies in the main with the United Nations' model life table for the Far East.

The shortening of the "contradictory period" indicates that China's infant mortality has dropped to a relatively low level, and most of the Chinese people can live beyond their childhood, youth, and adulthood to reach old age. In light of China's present-day average life expectancy, the average life expectancy of the Chinese people will reach 72 years by the end of this century.

Table 4-26. Number of Deaths and Crude Death Rate in China

| YEAR | NATIONWIDE | | CITY | | COUNTY | |
	NO. OF DEATHS (10,000)	CRUDE DEATH RATE (‰)	NO. OF DEATHS (10,000)	CRUDE DEATH RATE (‰)	NO. OF DEATHS (10,000)	CRUDE DEATH RATE (‰)
1950	984	18.00	—	—	—	—
1954	779	13.18	45	8.07	734	13.71
1957	688	10.80	57	8.47	631	11.07
1960	1,693	25.43	180	13.77	1,513	28.58
1965	678	9.50	52	5.69	626	10.06
1970	622	7.60	52*	5.35*	561*	7.57*
1975	671	7.32	59	5.39	612	7.59
1980	619	6.34	70	5.48	549	6.47
1981	629	6.36	103	5.14	526	6.53
1984	689	6.69	114	5.86	575	6.73

* 1971 figures.

Source: *Statistics Yearbook of China 1985*, China Statistics Publishing House. The number of deaths is a calculated figure.

Table 4-27.   Mortality Rate of the Chinese
Population (1981)

Table 4-27.   *continued*

AGE	MORTALITY RATE (‰)			AGE	MORTALITY RATE (‰)		
	TOTAL	MALE	FEMALE		TOTAL	MALE	FEMALE
CDR	6.36	6.55	6.15	50	6.86	7.65	5.96
<1 (or 0)	38.80	39.85	37.67	51	6.76	7.57	5.86
1	7.03	6.72	7.37	52	7.71	8.81	6.50
2	4.61	4.27	4.97	53	8.30	9.43	7.05
3	3.17	2.99	3.37	54	9.29	10.60	7.84
4	2.19	2.15	2.24	55	10.32	11.85	8.67
5	1.72	1.78	1.65	56	11.09	12.90	9.15
6	1.40	1.52	1.27	57	11.98	14.00	9.85
7	1.09	1.21	0.98	58	14.18	16.66	11.60
8	0.94	1.08	0.80	59	14.62	17.07	12.08
9	0.82	0.94	0.69	60	18.20	21.23	15.08
10	0.76	0.85	0.66	61	17.69	20.89	14.45
11	0.71	0.79	0.62	62	21.68	25.56	17.85
12	0.68	0.73	0.62	63	23.07	27.09	19.13
13	0.71	0.75	0.68	64	24.41	29.06	19.99
14	0.76	0.81	0.71	65	26.89	31.96	22.13
15	0.79	0.85	0.72	66	30.03	35.54	24.89
16	0.91	0.96	0.85	67	31.46	37.35	26.06
17	1.02	1.11	0.93	68	36.67	43.58	30.48
18	1.08	1.16	0.99	69	39.29	46.60	32.86
19	1.26	1.34	1.19	70	46.58	54.83	39.49
20	1.44	1.50	1.37	71	48.03	56.97	40.67
21	1.22	1.27	1.16	72	55.18	65.74	46.86
22	1.41	1.44	1.37	73	59.24	70.45	50.59
23	1.35	1.40	1.30	74	64.14	76.41	54.97
24	1.49	1.49	1.49	75	68.36	81.99	58.66
25	1.49	1.48	1.51	76	76.12	91.13	65.67
26	1.42	1.41	1.43	77	81.30	96.91	70.79
27	1.46	1.46	1.47	78	93.51	111.05	82.67
28	1.52	1.51	1.54	79	96.15	114.26	84.75
29	1.46	1.46	1.46	80	116.81	137.22	104.41
30	1.67	1.68	1.66	81	124.55	146.33	111.86
31	1.54	1.56	1.52	82	142.99	168.14	128.83
32	1.78	1.82	1.74	83	149.94	176.66	135.49
33	1.78	1.85	1.70	84	162.66	186.74	150.03
34	1.89	1.94	1.83	85	173.91	202.53	159.47
35	2.10	2.16	2.03	86	189.84	220.61	175.40
36	2.19	2.29	2.08	87	199.47	323.64	184.60
37	2.25	2.36	2.13	88	227.06	264.09	211.61
38	2.51	2.66	2.34	89	215.67	236.05	206.94
39	2.54	2.75	2.29	90	278.88	317.55	263.97
40	2.90	3.11	2.65	91	273.25	306.79	260.85
41	2.91	3.17	2.62	92	292.47	324.03	281.43
42	3.20	3.47	2.88	93	313.67	320.84	311.12
43	3.44	3.75	3.09	94	287.20	274.89	291.95
44	3.73	4.09	3.32	95	306.75	268.67	322.98
45	4.06	4.48	3.59	96	344.27	315.34	355.09
46	4.39	4.89	3.84	97	296.26	233.30	325.82
47	4.79	5.33	4.18	98	282.91	225.77	310.67
48	5.31	5.91	4.63	99	500.00	545.73	482.79
49	5.65	6.28	4.95	100	475.94	570.40	434.21

Source: *China Population Yearbook 1984,* China Statistics Publishing House.

Table 4-28.   Sex Ratio of Deaths (1981)

Table 4-28.   *continued*

AGE	MALE	FEMALE	SEX RATIO FEMALE = 100	AGE	MALE	FEMALE	SEX RATIO FEMALE = 100
Total	3,315,913	2,958,027	112.1	50	33,342	22,754	146.5
0	363,504	318,548	114.1	51	33,916	23,394	145.0
1	63,760	65,065	98.0	52	36,186	24,172	149.7
2	43,346	47,230	91.8	53	39,323	26,651	147.5
3	28.654	30.409	94.2	54	39,663	26,631	148.9
4	21,527	21,097	102.0	55	42,979	28,985	148.3
5	18,758	16,357	114.7	56	47,555	31,400	151.4
6	17.017	13,422	126.8	57	49,335	32,993	149.5
7	14,915	11,363	131.2	58	52,123	34,811	149.7
8	13,884	9,773	142.1	59	54,371	37,052	146.7
9	12,147	8,408	144.5	60	62,398	43,478	143.5
10	11,983	8,713	137.5	61	60,924	41,533	146.7
11	10,781	7,982	135.1	62	64,345	45,560	141.2
12	10,591	8,527	124.2	63	65,666	47,302	138.8
13	9,489	8,024	118.3	64	69,646	50,472	138.0
14	9,441	7,797	121.1	65	71,086	52,477	135.5
15	11,218	8,983	124.9	66	73,434	55,163	133.1
16	12,048	10,063	119.7	67	78,390	59,629	131.5
17	14,064	11,530	122.0	68	76,303	59,557	128.1
18	15,827	13,623	116.2	69	73,831	59,156	124.8
19	10,321	9,395	109.9	70	81,361	68,199	119.3
20	7,989	7,366	103.5	71	79,023	68,551	115.3
21	9,275	8,120	114.2	72	84,184	76,094	110.6
22	10,626	9,456	112.4	73	76,922	71,619	107.4
23	14,205	12,126	117.1	74	73,622	71,058	103.6
24	14,595	13,530	107.9	75	72,934	73,274	99.5
25	13,686	13,106	104.4	76	68,185	70,599	96.6
26	14,309	13,722	104.2	77	64,259	69,710	92.2
27	13,938	13,237	105.3	78	62,964	71,301	88.3
28	13,568	13,078	103.7	79	54,602	64,319	84.9
29	13,019	12,304	105.8	80	53,629	67,200	79.8
30	12,684	11,736	108.1	81	42,678	55,986	76.2
31	12,488	11,049	113.0	82	36,775	50,024	73.5
32	12,498	10,937	114.2	83	32,694	46,346	70.5
33	12,176	10,175	119.7	84	26,534	40,725	65.2
34	12,624	10.787	117.0	85	21,615	34,727	62.2
35	12,733	10,923	116.6	86	17,721	30,023	59.0
36	12,755	10,430	122.3	87	13,449	23,900	56.3
37	12,838	10,240	125.4	88	10,525	20,133	52.3
38	13,712	10,637	128.9	89	7,865	16,240	48.4
39	14,690	10,836	135.6	90	6,024	12,971	46.4
40	16,654	10,337	161.1	91	4,077	9,381	43.5
41	15,846	11,510	137.7	92	2,821	6,993	40.3
42	17,447	12,705	137.3	93	1,849	5,150	35.9
43	19,326	13,757	140.5	94	1,327	3,607	36.8
44	20.908	14,928	140.0	95	947	2,704	35.0
45	22,961	16,370	140.2	96	696	2,013	34.6
46	23,987	16,962	141.4	97	468	1,404	33.3
47	26,757	18,656	143.4	98	353	984	35.9
48	29,483	20,540	143.5	99	175	559	31.3
49	28,594	20,094	142.3	100	184	403	45.6

Source: *Data of the 1982 Census,* China Statistics Publishing House.

Table 4-29. Annual Death Rates from 10 Major Diseases in Cities and Counties

#	1957-CITIES CAUSE OF DEATH	DEATH RATE 1/100,000	DEATH TOTAL %	1963-CITIES CAUSE OF DEATH	DEATH RATE 1/100,000	DEATH TOTAL %	1975-CITIES CAUSE OF DEATH	DEATH RATE 1/100,000	DEATH TOTAL %	1980-CITIES CAUSE OF DEATH	DEATH RATE 1/100,000	DEATH TOTAL %	1982-CITIES CAUSE OF DEATH	DEATH RATE 1/100,000	DEATH TOTAL %
1	Disease of respiratory system	120.3	16.86	Disease of respiratory system	64.57	12.03	Cerebral blood vessel disease	127.91	21.61	Cerebral blood vessel disease	135.35	23.36	Cerebral blood vessel disease	124.44	22.26
2	Acute contagious diseases	56.6	7.93	Cancer	46.12	8.59	Heart trouble	115.34	19.49	Heart trouble	132.51	22.87	Heart Trouble	117.70	21.05
3	Pulmonary tuberculosis	54.6	7.51	Cerebral apoplexy	36.87	6.87	Cancer	111.49	18.84	Cancer	113.41	19.57	Cancer	115.15	20.60
4	Disease of digestive system	52.1	7.31	Pulmonary tuberculosis	36.32	6.77	Disease of respiratory system	63.64	10.75	Disease of respiratory system	51.97	8.97	Disease of respiratory system	48.50	8.67
5	Heart trouble	47.2	6.61	Heart trouble	36.05	6.72	Diseases of digestive system	28.78	4.86	Diseases of digestive system	22.68	3.91	Disease of digestive system	24.44	4.37
6	Cerebral apoplexy	39.0	5.46	Disease of digestive system	31.35	5.84	Pulmonary tuberculosis	21.15	3.57	Injuries	18.75	3.24	Injuries	18.14	3.25
7	Cancer	36.9	5.17	Acute contagious diseases	21.24	3.96	Injuries	16.84	2.85	Pulmonary tuberculosis	12.15	2.10	Poisoning	11.57	2.07
8	Disease of nervous system	29.1	4.08	Injuries	16.19	3.02	Contagious disease (except pulmonary tuberculosis)	13.17	2.23	Poisoning	10.46	1.80	Pulmonary tuberculosis	11.34	2.03
9	Injuries and poisoning	19.0	2.66	Disease of nervous system	13.76	2.56	Diseases of urogenital system	11.63	1.97	Disease of urogenital system	9.28	1.60	Diseases of newborn*	514.41	1.63
10	Other tuberculosis	14.1	1.98	Blood and blood-making vessel	9.81	1.83	Poisoning	6.27	1.06	Contagious diseases (except pulmonary tuberculosis)	8.49	1.46	Diseases of urogenital system	9.03	1.61
	Total		65.57	Total		58.19	Total		87.23	Total		88.88	Total		87.54

Table 4-29. *continued*

#	1975-COUNTIES			1980-COUNTIES			1982-COUNTIES		
1	Heart trouble	123.18	18.02	Heart trouble	170.57	25.84	Heart trouble	159.32	23.70
2	Cancer	119.57	17.50	Cerebral blood vessel disease	113.06	17.13	Cerebral blood vessel disease	103.52	15.40
3	Cerebral blood vessel disease	92.31	13.51	Cancer	96.89	14.68	Cancer	102.97	15.32
4	Disease of respiratory system	88.15	12.90	Disease of respiratory system	79.14	11.99	Disease of respiratory system	77.27	11.49
5	Diseases of digestive system	46.30	6.78	Diseases of digestive system	34.82	5.28	Diseases of digestive system	38.25	5.69
6	Pulmonary tuberculosis	32.61	4.77	Pulmonary tuberculosis	21.36	3.24	Poisoning	28.48	4.24
7	Injuries	24.26	3.55	Injuries	18.40	2.79	Pulmonary tuberculosis	28.30	4.21
8	Contagious diseases (except pulmonary tuberculosis)	23.82	3.49	Contagious diseases (except pulmonary tuberculosis)	18.24	2.76	Injuries	19.96	2.97
9	Diseases of newborn*	1,194.81	2.65	Diseases of newborn*	720.41	1.59	Contagious diseases (except pulmonary tuberculosis)	16.83	2.50
10	Diseases of urogenital system	10.16	1.49	Poisoning	9.34	1.41	Diseases of newborn*	655.37	1.65
	Total		84.66	Total		86.71	Total		87.17

* Death rate of newborn is counted with 10,000 as denominator.

Source: *Health Yearbook of China 1983*, People's Health Publishing House, 1983.

Table 4-30.   Regional Crude Death Rate

AREA	CRUDE DEATH RATE (‰)	NO. OF DEATHS (10,000)
Total for whole country	6.36	629.0
North China		
Beijing Municipality	5.78	5.2
Tianjin Municipality	6.10	4.6
Hebei Province	6.05	31.6
Shanxi Province	6.54	16.3
Inner Mongolian Autonomous Region	5.77	10.9
Northeast China		
Liaoning Province	5.32	18.7
Jilin Province	5.32	11.8
Heilongjiang Province	4.95	15.9
East China		
Shanghai Municipality	6.44	7.4
Jiangsu Province	1.10	36.4
Zhejiang Province	6.27	24.1
Anhui Province	5.20	25.6
Fujian Province	5.87	14.9
Jiangxi Province	6.54	21.5
Shandong Province	6.26	46.0
Central South China		
Henan Province	6.01	44.1
Hubei Province	7.33	34.5
Hunan Province	7.03	37.4
Guangdong Province	5.54	32.3
Guangxi Zhuang Nationality Autonomous Region	5.61	20.1
Southwest China		
Sichuan Province	7.02	69.3
Guizhou Province	8.48	23.7
Yunnan Province	8.60	27.5
Tibet Autonomous Region	9.92	1.8
Northwest China		
Shaanxi Province	7.10	20.2
Gansu Province	5.72	11.0
Qinghai Province	7.48	2.8
Ningxia Hui Nationality Autonomous Region	6.08	2.3
Xinjiang Uygur Autonomous Region	8.41	10.9

Source: *Major Figures from China's Third Census*, China Statistics Publishing House, 1982.

Table 4-31. Average Life Expectancy in China

AREA	TOTAL	CITY	TOWN	COUNTY (NOT INCLUDING TOWN)
Whole country	67.88	70.87	71.40	67.17
Males	66.43	69.12	69.55	65.79
Females	69.35	72.69	73.40	68.56
Beijing	71.92	73.51	73.31	69.61
Males	70.48	72.01	71.81	68.27
Females	73.40	74.98	74.80	71.04
Shanghai	72.91	73.84	73.57	71.88
Males	70.54	72.07	71.13	68.69
Females	75.14	75.56	76.05	74.79
Liaoning	70.69	71.84	72.73	69.78
Males	69.69	70.49	71.61	68.95
Females	71.86	73.36	74.04	70.77
Guizhou	61.35	63.75	69.44	60.03
Males	61.07	62.84	67.52	60.54
Females	61.55	64.64	71.44	60.66
Gansu	65.75	69.96	70.71	65.12
Males	65.05	68.81	69.10	64.47
Females	66.49	71.23	72.61	65.82
Ningxia	65.51	70.70	71.50	64.52
Males	64.74	69.18	69.95	63.98
Females	66.40	72.54	72.20	65.20

Source: Based on statistical data from the 1982 census.

CHAPTER FIVE

INTERNAL MIGRATION

Migration is an important and complex population phenomenon with characteristics of its own. Unlike the phenomena of births and deaths, it is not practical to give a clear and all-inclusive definition to the phenomenon of population migration now under study. Because of the difference in the scope, purpose, and conditions of study, it is necessary to give a clear definition to each special topic of research before undertaking it. Compared with the phenomena of births and deaths, changes in the degree and scope of population migration are more liable to be influenced by various kinds of subjective and objective factors. In the course of study, it is therefore necessary to take into consideration the social, political, and economic changes in the different periods and give explanations for the various stages so as to get a clear understanding of the general trend.

DEFINITION OF INTERNAL MIGRATION

First, this study is based on the state statistics on the migration of population in most of the years after the founding of the People's Republic of China, in 1949. In this way full use can be made of the valuable data available in this field. The objects of this study therefore tally with those in the state statistics, that is to say, the study is focused on the population migration between the townships (rural people's communes), between the towns, between the towns and townships, between the cities, and betwen the townships and the cities, with the registration of permanent residences as the basis. In addition, migrations between mainland China and Hong Kong, Macao, and Taiwan and foreign countries are also included. Since international migration occupies a very small proportion in the migration of the Chinese people, it can be neglected in calculation. So, generally speaking, the migration mentioned above can be classified as internal migration, the migrants having gone

through all the procedures required by the state. (For the sake of convenience, this will henceforth be referred to as internal or domestic migration.) Under China's actual conditions, changes in the registration of permanent residences constitute a reasonable and easy way of discerning migration. Investigations show that the registered permanent residences of 97–98% of the population conform with the actual places where they live. In fact, the registration of permanent residences in China is the only source of comprehensive and continuous information on population migration. Of course, it should be mentioned here that a difference between check-ins and checkouts does exist, because sometimes a person who has moved out of his or her place of origin toward the end of a year may not have registered at the place of destination that same year; moreover, there may be errors and slips. But, generally speaking, this does not in any substantial way affect the study of the general trend of China's internal migration.

Second, this chapter will also make a study of another important migration phenomenon in China, that is, migration between the various provinces, autonomous regions, and municipalities, as shown by the changes in the registration of permanent residences. This will hereafter be referred to as interprovincial migration. In China, the provinces, autonomous regions, and municipalities are important administrative units by which the state administers social and economic affairs. A survey of interprovincial migration is not only necessary to get an understanding of the changes in their population but also helpful in analyzing the progress made in these areas. As statistics on interprovincial migration were lumped together with other migrations before the early 1980s and no separate figures are available, we can only use the method for estimation of migration (that is, while neglecting international migration, the net migration number of a certain province in a certain year is equal to the number obtained by subtracting the number of the province's natural population growth from the total increased population of that province that year) to get the actual number of the population increase or decrease of the various provinces, autonomous regions, and municipalities in the different years caused by interprovincial migration. Because this method is comparatively rough, plus the possible errors and slips in the calculation of population migration and natural population growth, there may be discrepancies in the net interprovincial migration figures so obtained. This difference, however, will not in any substantial way affect the study of the changes in the trend of interprovincial migration.

Although China's statistics on population migration do not give detailed information on the migrants' sex and age, special surveys on interprovincial migration in some areas in recent years do provide some valuable data in this respect. That is one of the reasons why this chapter devotes some space to the study of internal migration from the angle of interprovincial migration.

In the following sections we will analyze the trend of internal migration in the different periods and stages after the founding of the People's Republic in 1949.

TRENDS OF INTERNAL MIGRATION

Population migration is not, in essence, an expression of willful personal behavior on the part of the migrants; but, rather, it is an expression finally determined by certain social, economic, political, and natural factors that restrict such migration behavior. Chart 5-1 shows the changing proportion of domestic migrants in the total population during the 1954–84 period; in other words, it shows the trend of internal migration rate.* (Owing to lack of necessary data, this chapter does not include migrations from 1949, when New China was founded, to 1953. Migrations relating to Taiwan are also not included.) The chart shows that in those 30 years China's domestic migration experienced great fluctuations. Taking the 30 years as a whole, the proportion of internal migrants in the total population was the highest in 1960 when

---

* Since the number of international migrations is negligible in China, the total number of in-migration in the country should approximately be equal to that of out-migration. Calculations of domestic migrations and migration rates may be made according to the number of in-migrations or out-migrations. The figures given in this chapter are all derived from in-migrations.

it was 3.3 times that of the lowest year of 1983, while changes in the various periods showed that migrations sometimes rose and fell abruptly within one or two years. For instance, the proportion of migrants in the total population between 1954 and 1956 increased by 29%. In sharp contrast to this, the proportion plummeted by 41% between 1960 and 1961. These sharp rises and falls, however, are not unpredictable. Owing to the influence of social, economic, and political factors since the 1950s, domestic migration changes showed distinctive patterns for the various stages (see Table 5-1).

• The First Stage (1954–57). During this period, China began large-scale planned economic and cultural construction on the basis of the restoration of the national economy shortly after liberation, and tangible achievements were made. The average number of migrants during this stage was 26.27 million annually, and the average annual migration rate was 43‰, which was second only to the peak figures of the abnormal stage between 1958 and 1960. This showed that migrations were carried out on a large scale and with high intensity during this stage. This resulted from the great demand for laborers on construction sites in different localities. Besides, since China's economy had been restored and life became stable, many people returned home from all over the country (epiphenomenal, secondary migration characterized by seeking refuge with relatives and friends). Table 5-2 shows that the difference between the highest annual migration rate and the lowest during this stage was approximately 11‰. The range of changes in this stage was the second largest, and the rate of migrations kept rising by a fairly big margin. There was a drop after the mid-1950s, due to the smooth development of economic construction. However, too much investment in new industrial areas again brought in its wake a rapid increase in migration rates. But readjustments were soon made.

• The Second Stage (1958–60). During this period, China launched the "great leap forward" movement and people's communes were set up all over the countryside. Exorbitant targets were set for production, and large-scale construction became the order of the day. "With steel as the key link," one-sided emphasis was placed in the development of heavy industry at the expense of agricultural production. The result was the seriously disproportionate development of the national economy. Under such circumstances, domestic migrations increased in scale and intensity to attain the highest, but abnormal, level in the more than 30 years since the founding of

Chart 5-1.   Changes in the Migration Rate of Domestic Population (1954–1984)

Proportion (‰)

Year

Source: Wei Jinsheng and Zhang Qingwu, *General Trends in the Migration of China's Domestic Population Since the 1950s,* and *Population Yearbook 1985,* China Social Sciences Publishing House, 1986.

Table 5-1.   Internal Migration Size and Migration Rates in Stages (1954–1984)

STAGE (YEAR)	AVERAGE ANNUAL MIGRANTS (10,000)	AVERAGE ANNUAL MIGRATION RATE (‰)
1954–57	2,627	43.0
1958–60	3,213	49.0
1961–65	1,680	25.0
1966–69	797	20.8
1970–76	1,466	18.0
1977–79	1,906	20.0
1980–84	1,820	18.2
1954–84	1,833	26.0

Sources: Wei Jinsheng and Zhang Qingwu, *General Trends in the Migration of China's Domestic Population Since the 1950s,* and *Population Yearbook 1985,* China Social Sciences Publishing House, 1986.

Table 5-2.   Annual Internal Migration Rate (1954–1957)

YEAR	MIGRATION RATE (‰)
1954	37.8
1955	41.8
1956	48.6
1957	43.0

Sources: Wei Jinsheng and Zhang Qingwu, *General Trends in the Migration of China's Domestic Population Since the 1950s*, and *Population Yearbook 1985*, China Social Sciences Publishing House, 1986.

New China. The average number of migrants came to 32.13 million annually and the annual migration rate was 49‰, the highest in all the seven stages. This was a reflection of the huge, but to a great extent misleading, demands for the redistribution of the labor force during the "great leap forward."

Table 5-3 shows that this excessively high migration rate and scale continued for three years during the "great leap forward" movement. During this period, the highest annual migration rate was less than 3‰ more than that of the lowest rate. The upshot was that tens of millions of peasants left their land and moved into the cities, placing an unbearable burden on the nation.

• The Third Stage (1961–65). This was a period when the Chinese government took resolute measures to readjust the national economy and, after overcoming the serious difficulties of the previous stage, to enable the national economy to gradually embark once again on the road of normal development. During this period, the average annual number of migrants dropped to 16.8 million, which was only half that of the second stage and ranked fifth in

all the seven stages. The average annual migration rate dropped to 25‰, also nearly half of that of the second stage but ranking third in all the seven stages, and the yearly figures (see Table 5-4) showed that the difference between the highest and lowest year was over 13 per thousand points. The range of change was the largest of all the seven stages, marking a sudden drop of the migration rate. All these are reflections of the readjustment measures taken by the state during this period for industrial enterprises on the migration of population measures such as "closing down, suspending production, amalgamating with other enterprises, or switching to the manufacture of other products," as well as cutting down the number of workers and staff and reducing the urban population.

• The Fourth Stage (1966–69). The outbreak of the "cultural revolution" during this stage disrupted normal production and work order was disrupted, with the result that economic and other undertakings suffered severe setbacks and damage. At the same time, undue emphasis was placed on preparation against war and construction work in the interior in disregard of the actual conditions. Under such a situation, the average annual number of migrants in this period drastically dropped to 7.97 million, the lowest in all the seven stages. The average annual migration rate also dropped to 20.8‰, ranking fourth in all the seven stages. The yearly figures (see Table 5-5) showed that the difference between the highest and lowest year was 4.7 per thousand points, ranking sixth in all the seven stages.

Such small scale and extent of migration reflected, on the one hand, the retrogression and stagnation of the economy; on the other hand, it reflected that normal population migration was greatly limited or even stopped following the disruption of normal

Table 5-3.   Annual Internal Migration Rate (1958–1960)

YEAR	MIGRATION RATE (‰)
1958	49.2
1959	47.5
1960	50.1

Sources: Wei Jinsheng and Zhang Qingwu, *General Trends in the Migration of China's Domestic Population Since the 1950s*, and *Population Yearbook 1985*, China Social Sciences Publishing House, 1986.

Table 5-4.   Annual Internal Migration Rate (1961–1965)

YEAR	MIGRATION RATE (‰)
1961	29.4
1962	32.5
1963	19.3
1964	20.2
1965	22.6

Sources: Wei Jinsheng and Zhang Qingwu, *General Trends in the Migration of China's Domestic Population Since the 1950s*, and *Population Yearbook 1985*, China Social Sciences Publishing House, 1986.

Table 5-5. Annual Internal
Migration Rate (1966–1969)

YEAR	MIGRATION RATE (‰)
1966	20.2
1967	18.3
1968	21.9
1969	23.0

Sources: Wei Jinsheng and Zhang
Qingwu, *General Trends in the
Migration of China's Domestic Popu-
lation Since the 1950s*, and
Population Yearbook 1985, China
Social Sciences Publishing House,
1986.

Table 5-6. Annual Internal
Migration Rate (1970–1976)

YEAR	MIGRATION RATE (‰)
1970	21.2
1971	19.6
1972	18.6
1973	16.3
1974	15.1
1975	18.0
1976	17.5

Sources: Wei Jinsheng and Zhang
Qingwu, *General Trends in the
Migration of China's Domestic Popu-
lation Since the 1950s*, and
Population Yearbook 1985, China
Social Sciences Publishing House,
1986.

order. (For instance, because of the suspension of classes in the colleges and universities during the "cultural revolution," there were few students travelling to various cities for enrollment.) Thus, although there were at times sudden increases of migration activities in this period—such as large numbers of cadres going to settle in the countryside, educated youth returning to urban areas from the countryside, and the beginning of large-scale construction in the interior—such increases of migration rate were to a large extent offset.

• The Fifth Stage (1970–76). During this stage, although the people of the whole country urgently hoped that production would be pushed up, the turmoil caused by the "cultural revolution" continued and the entire national economy was still at a standstill and in a terrible plight. The average annual number of migrants increased, but the total was only 14.66 million, ranking sixth in all the seven stages. The annual average migration rate dropped to 18‰, the lowest in the seven stages. The yearly figures (see Table 5-6) showed a decrease, although there were fluctuations.

The difference between the highest and lowest year was 6‰, ranking fifth in all the seven stages. The low migration rate and small migration scale occurred because since the early seventies, the number of cadres and educated youth going to the countryside had dropped greatly, and many construction projects in the interior proceeded slowly, because they were divorced from the actual conditions. Moreover, beginning from this period, the above-mentioned category of migrants began to move back gradually, although the scale was not so large as that in the mid-1970s.

• The Sixth Stage (1977–79). After the "cultural revolution," which brought chaos to the whole na-

tion, was put to an end, industrial and agricultural production during this period quickly picked up and continued to develop as before. However, there still existed the tendency to hanker after excessively high targets and speed of development, which gave rise to the need of readjusting the national economy in 1979. In these circumstances, the average annual number of migrants and rate of migration in the country registered an increase as compared with the previous stage. The former reached 19.06 million, rising to the third highest for all the seven stages, while the latter was 20‰, ranking fifth in all the seven stages. The rising trend in population migration was quite obvious in this stage (see Table 5-7).

The difference between the migration rate of the highest year and that of the lowest year was 8 per thousand points, and ranked third in all the seven stages. While this rising trend was inevitable and advantageous because it represented a correction and remedy to the abnormal population migration in the past few years, excessively high recruitment of

Table 5-7. Annual Internal
Migration Rate (1977–1979)

YEAR	MIGRATION RATE (‰)
1977	16.6
1978	19.2
1979	24.2

Sources: Wei Jinsheng and Zhang
Qingwu, *General Trends in the
Migration of China's Domestic Popu-
lation Since the 1950s*, and
Population Yearbook 1985, China
Social Sciences Publishing House,
1986.

workers and population migration were bound to play a negative role.

• The Seventh Stage (1980–84). During this stage, further efforts were made throughout the country to readjust the economy and reduce the scale of capital construction. Along with the large-scale readjustment of industrial and agricultural production, more attention was paid to improving economic returns and to keeping economic growth at an appropriate and stable level. Thus the average annual number of migrants and rate of migration in this stage dropped to a certain extent. The number of migrants was 18.2 million, occupying the fourth place in all the seven stages, and the migration rate was 18.2‰, ranking sixth (see Table 5-8).

The difference between the migration rate of the highest year and that of the lowest was more than 6 per thousand points, occupying the fourth place in all the seven stages. Taken as a whole, internal migration decreased yearly prior to 1983, but it went up again, to some extent, after 1983. This change in scale and intensity showed that, on the one hand, the state drew lessons from the excessive population migration in the late 1970s and adopted appropriate measures to control and regulate it; on the other hand, the flow of educated youths and government employees back from the countryside to the cities had basically come to an end in the early 1980s, and the population migration caused by the retirement of old workers and their replacement by their sons and daughters was much smaller.

The fact that the migration rate began to rise again after 1983 reflected, to a certain degree, the impact of the state policy to enliven the domestic economy and other policies adopted in recent years for economic reforms. In particular, population migration resulting from the rational flow of trained professionals and reunion of family members living in different places has played a positive role in the economic and cultural development as well as social stability in general. Another factor that merits attention in the rise of migration rate was the return of people who had gone to the border regions to aid the construction there after the founding of New China in 1949.

DIFFERENT TYPES OF INTERNAL MIGRATION

Different methods are used to classify the types of population migration according to different purposes and different aspects of the question under review. Proceeding from China's actual conditions and the needs for a comparative study of migration in China and in other countries, we shall in this chapter classify migration of the Chinese population over the last three decades under five categories according to the causes of their migration.

MIGRATIONS FOR WORK

This refers to those who move from one place to another, either individually or collectively, in order to participate in labor services or to find work.

Collective migration refers to the migration of a definite number of people organized by the state to meet the needs of the country's social and economic development and is intended to achieve a rational distribution of the labor force in various places. Such migration can be subdivided into three types according to the nature of the work taken up by the migrants.

Migration for Industrial Development. Since the founding of New China, in 1949, the state and various localities have organized migrations for industrial purposes such as building factories, tapping mineral resources, and building highways as well as the moving of entire factories and industrial enterprises from one place to another. Such migrations, though on different scales during different periods, have been going on unabated over the last 30 years together with the development of the national economy, and the localities and scale of migrations involved differ with the size and characteristics of the industrial projects concerned. In the case of ordinary projects, migrations are organized within the provinces or autonomous regions. As for key state projects, inter-

Table 5-8. Annual Internal Migration Rate (1980–1984)

YEAR	MIGRATION RATE (‰)
1980	20.1
1981	21.2
1982	17.2
1983	15.0
1984	17.4

Sources: Wei Jinsheng and Zhang Qingwu, *General Trends in the Migration of China's Domestic Population Since the 1950s,* and *Population Yearbook 1985,* China Social Sciences Publishing House, 1986.

provincial migrations are organized, mainly from industrially developed coastal areas to the less developed provinces or autonomous regions in hinterland China. Migrants of this type are mostly city dwellers — workers, technicians, and managerial personnel, though during the "big leap forward" period, toward the end of the 1950s, a large section of the rural population was also involved.

Because most migrations for industrial purposes are well planned and organized, the migrants are mostly happy to settle in their new homes, playing an important part in the local economic development. But there are also a few cases in which migrations have been organized in disregard of the actual needs and possibilities or when the migrants are not mentally well prepared, with the result that many of these migrants have returned to their native places. This has brought poor social and economic results. Examples are the "big leap forward" toward the end of the 1950s, when migrations were organized in hasty efforts to develop industry in a big way, and migrations during the 1960s and 1970s, when large numbers of people went to widely scattered places in the vast hinterland to build factories for strategic purposes but with poor economic results.

Migrations for Agricultural Development. Since liberation, in 1949, the state and various localities have organized migrations of this type to develop agriculture, build reservoirs, set up farms, afforest the unwooded areas, and reclaim the land in remote regions. Most prominent are migrations intended to move residents away from places where reservoirs will be built. In the past 30-odd years, China has built 2,500 reservoirs of varying sizes, which submerged 1.5 million *mu* of cultivated land and necessitated the migration of 1.2 million people.* In building small and medium-sized reservoirs, migrants are often settled in places in their own provinces or autonomous regions where they can benefit from the projects built or are moved a short distance away so as to make room for the projects. But when a big reservoir is built, some people have to be moved to neighboring provinces or autonomous regions, where they can still benefit from this project. The migrants so involved are basically rural people. Migrations of this type, which have been carried out throughout the years, are the largest in scale for the purpose of agricultural development. Another type of agriculture-related migration is to organize the

people in the densely populated eastern parts of the country to reclaim the land and set up farms and forestry centers in the vast but sparsely populated provinces and autonomous regions in the northern and western parts of the country and to some places in the south. Migrants of this type are all peasants and number nearly 2 million; such migrations came to an end during the early 1960s. The state has also organized, chiefly in the 1950s, peasants in disaster-stricken areas to move to other provinces and autonomous regions to start life anew in various kinds of production. During the years of the restoration of the national economy and the early First Five-Year Plan period, for instance, some of the peasants in the flooded lower reaches of the Yellow River were moved to northeast China.

Migrations for Intellectual Development. Migrations of this type fall into two categories. First, large numbers of cadres were transferred during the early postliberation years from the long-liberated areas to the newly liberated areas to help with the consolidation of political power and other fields of work. Migrants of this type were mostly city dwellers (armymen are also considered part of the urban population), with cadres as the main body. They moved from the north to the southern parts of China where they have since lived and worked. The second category of migrants are scientists, engineers, technicians, educators, and other professionals from the eastern parts of the country who have settled, either temporarily or permanently, in the culturally underdeveloped border regions and inland provinces. Needless to say, they are city dwellers and most of them are intellectuals. At present, migrations for the cause of intellectual development are increasing, and indications are they will continue to increase in the future.

Among the job-motivated migrants are many individuals seeking jobs or taking on assigned work in other places. Unlike collective migrations, individual migrations are often scattered and quite frequent, and once the migrants reach the places where they find suitable work, they tend to settle there permanently. Individual migration can be subdivided into the following three types.

1. Migrations of employees recruited to work away from their native counties. These individuals are recruited by the state through certain official procedures to migrate and work in enterprises in places away from their home provinces. Such migrations often happen, and migrants in this category include both people in the cities and in the country-

* Li Rui, "How to Ensure Priority for the Development of Hydroelectric Power Station?" *Hongqi*, No. 19, 1983.

side. A considerable number of such migrants were from rural areas during the early postliberation years and the "big leap forward" period as well as several other periods. But with the rapid growth of the population and labor force after the 1970s, the needs of various cities and towns for workers and staff members from other places have been markedly reduced. However, certain trades such as mining, construction, and environmental protection, which have difficulty in recruiting enough local people, have to employ villagers from other parts of the country.

2. Migrations prompted by job assignments and transfers. The migrants are mostly city dwellers who leave their families for places in other provinces where they have been transferred or given jobs by the state according to normal procedures. During the chaotic period of the "cultural revolution" that started in the latter half of the 1960s, migrations of this type decreased drastically because of the suspension of classes in the universities and colleges across the country.

3. Migrations of individual job-hunters (including their family members) seeking better work and living conditions in other provinces. These were referred to as spontaneous migrations and involved mainly rural people in disaster-stricken areas or densely populated places where farmland was scarce. Their destinations were often places with fewer people or where more laborers were needed. Migrations of this type have long been in existence and the scale is quite large. In Xinjiang, for example, two-thirds* of its net in-migration population are former job-hunters or people from elsewhere in the country in search of better work and living conditions. The same is true of other provinces and autonomous regions such as Heilongjiang and Inner Mongolia where a good proportion of the population is composed of spontaneous migrants. Such spontaneous migrations have, on the one hand, alleviated the problem of overpopulation in the place of origin and made up for the labor shortage in the place of destination, thereby supplementing the needs of the state plan for deploying the country's labor force. But on the other hand, these spontaneous migrations have had negative effects on the places of their resettlement, destroying the natural resources and upsetting the ecological balance there. In some cases, the social order was also disrupted. Thus such migrations

* Chou Weizhi, "An Initial Study of Domestic Migration Since the Founding of the People's Republic," *Population and Economy*, No. 4, 1981.

should be carefully guided and brought under control. With the enlivening of the home economy and the improvement of the employment policy over the last few years, cities and towns have witnessed the influx of increasing numbers of workers and self-employed business people from other places, most of them being former peasants. They have become an important force in urban economic activities by making up for the shortage in the service trades and making production and daily life more convenient, thereby contributing to the prosperity of both urban and rural economy. This is notably a new phenomenon in the field of spontaneous migration.

Migration for work's sake, whether individual or collective, constitutes a basic and most important type of population migration in the various periods and stages in China. In postliberation Beijing, for example, of the annual influx of migrants from the rest of the country, 20 and sometimes 50% are migrants of this type. In fact, they make up the largest number of all the migrants to Beijing in most of the postliberation years. This shows that the economic factor is a constant and most important one circumscribing population migration.

MIGRATIONS RELATED TO PERSONAL LIFE

Migrations related to personal life can be subdivided into two types. The first type is people who migrate along with their family members to other places or join them some time later in order to live together with them. This is also called migration of a subordinate and dependent character. Migrants of this type include both urban and rural people, mostly women, children, and elderly people. They make up a major portion of migrants in China in the various periods, but with the passing of time, their number has gradually diminished. In the early postliberation days, most of these migrants went to seek financial support from their relatives and a few went to join their already migrated family members. For a time, increases in the number of able-bodied male migrants resulted in the concomitant increase in the number of their family members. Later, however, with more family members given employment and with the reduction of the size of families, migrants of this type have decreased in number. Of the in-migrants in Beijing, the proportion of those coming to join their family members increased from 30% in the early postliberation days to more than 40% in the mid-1950s; the proportion later gradually dropped and it was only 10% in 1983.

The second type is migration resulting from marriage. This refers to people who migrate in order to get married or to live together with their spouses. Naturally, most of such migrants are women, who move from villages to cities and from underdeveloped places to developed areas. This type of migration has been in existence since liberation and accounts for a large proportion of migrants from rural areas. Statistics show that of the total number of migrants from rural areas into Beijing during the 1980–82 period, 48.4% were migrants of this type.*

Migrations related to personal life are a major type of migration second only to migrations for work in New China. This shows that the social factor is also an important one in migration.

MIGRATIONS FOR ACADEMIC PURPOSES

Migrants for academic purposes are those who go to other places for cultural, scientific, and technical pursuits. Most of them are male urban dwellers. Migrations of this type showed a gradual increase prior to the "cultural revolution," a drastic drop during this movement, and a conspicuous increase after it. This faithfully reflects the many ups and downs in the 30-odd-year history of education in New China. In Beijing, for example, the percentage of people coming to the city for academic pursuits increased from 4% of all the in-migrants in the early postliberation years to more than 20% in the early 1960s; it dropped to 2% in 1966, when the "cultural revolution" started, and rose again to 20% in 1983.

MIGRATIONS FOR MILITARY REASONS

Migration by people when they are drafted for military service or demobilized and transferred to a civilian post are migrations for military reasons. It involves mainly the male population of military age both in urban and rural areas, notably the latter. It is therefore a major type of migration by the rural population. Such migrations have been in existence since liberation in 1949 and occupy quite a large proportion in some areas in some years. For example, the number of demobilized servicemen who moved into Beijing increased rapidly in 1983 and made up 42% of its total in-migrants that year. Of course, this was an isolated case, and the percentage in normal years is not so high.

* Ji Ping, Zhang Kaiti, and Liu Dawei, "A Brief Analysis of the Migration of Rural People on Beijing's Outskirts Resulting from Marriages," *China's Social Science*, No. 3, 1985.

MIGRATIONS OF OTHER TYPES

Population migration for reasons other than those mentioned previously is considered migrations of other types. Because of the strong influence of certain social and political factors, such migrations are very often unexpected and temporary in nature and, therefore, have their special characteristics. For example, the settlement of cadres and educated youth in the countryside during the "cultural revolution" and their return later to the cities were temporary population migrations involving millions of people. In Beijing, for instance, a large number of educated youth and cadres returned from the countryside in 1979, accounting for as high as 33% of the city's total in-migrants that year and making the percentage of other kinds of in-migrants almost insignificant. Such unexpected or sudden and temporary factors may upset the basic pattern of internal migration for a few years, but they are nevertheless transient and cannot change the basic pattern of China's internal migration for a long period of time.

SEX AND AGE COMPOSITION OF INTERPROVINCIAL MIGRANTS

Unlike birth and death, migration does not involve every member of a population. Only those who are, among other factors, socially and economically suitable for migration can be selected to become migrants. A study of this selectivity, especially the selection of sex and age, which are its two basic aspects, is of great importance to an understanding of the impact of migration on the process of population, social, and economic growth.

Though continuous and complete statistical data of the sex and age composition (especially age composition) of interprovincial migrants in China since the 1950s are not available, some basic patterns and changes in their sex and age composition over the past 30 years can be derived from the statistical data obtained through investigations in some provinces and autonomous regions. Though the materials and data selected for study here involve only Beijing, Tianjin, and Shanghai, the three municipalities directly under the jurisdiction of the central government, they are to a certain extent representative of the whole country. This is because most of the interprovincial migrations have happened either between urban and rural areas or between cities. Migrations from one rural area to another are on the whole insignificant, except for certain periods and a few areas.

Generally speaking, a country's internal migrants are mostly young people, with adults coming next; their ages are generally between 15 and 49. Most present-day demographers confirm this conclusion. However, this does not mean that internal migration of old people and children is insignificant, nor does it mean that there is only one migration pattern as far as age is concerned, irrespective of the actual conditions of different periods and different regions. In terms of sex, more women than men migrate internally in Western and Latin American countries, whereas in Asia and Africa men outnumber women. These phenomena should also be studied and analyzed in light of the actual conditions of different countries and regions.

SEX COMPOSITION OF MIGRANTS

Since the 1950s men have outnumbered women in China's interprovincial migrations; this is basically the same as the situation in most Asian and African countries. Judging from the situation in Beijing, Tianjin, and Shanghai, apart from a few postliberation periods when there were more women migrants, men have outnumbered women, both in urban in-migration and urban out-migration, and in the flow of agricultural and nonagricultural migrants into and from these cities. That is to say, male migrants into and out of these cities accounted for more than 50% of these cities' total migrants; in other words, the sex ratio of the migrants is more than 100. Sample surveys of 50,000 in-migrants of Yinchuan in the Ningxia Hui Autonomous Region in the years 1956 to 1983 showed that male in-migrants accounted for 55.9% of the total for those 27 years, so the sex ratio was 127.

Of course, in some periods and regions, such a male-dominated migration pattern might temporarily be changed because of certain stronger objective factors. For example, women outnumbered men in the in-migrations in the two cities of Beijing and Shanghai in 1954, so that the proportion of females was 52.6% in Beijing and 51.3% in Shanghai. This was because with the restoration of the economy and improvement and stability in living conditions after liberation, many rural residents moved to Beijing and Shanghai to live together with their relatives. That year the number of people who moved to Beijing for this reason accounted for 48% of the city's total in-migrants.

Second, in terms of migration direction, the percentage of male migrants from these cities is higher than that of male in-migrants in most of these years. Table 5-9 shows that the proportion of male migrants from Beijing and Tianjin was higher than that of male in-migrants in five and six of the seven representative years.

This difference was caused by the fact that more men than women were chosen to move from the comparatively well-developed coastal areas and big cities to the less-developed inland areas and small and medium-sized cities because of men's better adaptability. In contrast to this, in the case of migrations from the less-developed inland areas and small and medium-sized cities to the comparatively well-developed coastal areas and big cities where job opportunities and living and other conditions were better, the percentage of female in-migrants was comparatively higher than that of male in-migrants.

Of course, the percentage of male out-migrants exceeding that of male in-migrants as shown in Table 5-9 was not absolute. In specific periods and areas,

Table 5-9.   Proportion of Male Migrants in the Total Number of Migrants in Beijing and Tianjin

YEARS	BEIJING		TIANJIN	
	IN-MIGRANTS (‰)	OUT-MIGRANTS (‰)	IN-MIGRANTS (‰)	OUT-MIGRANTS (‰)
1950	60.7	56.8	59.6	59.8
1954	47.4	52.5	54.4	64.5
1959	68.3	72.9	62.8	72.0
1962	63.7	74.5	59.3	75.7
1969	64.5	58.4	63.8	61.5
1979	55.9	81.0	56.0	85.0
1983	74.6	76.3	68.4 (in 1982)	72.9 (in 1982)

Sources: Wei Jinsheng, *International Migration of Beijing, the Capital, Since the Founding of the People's Republic of China*, a paper for the International Symposium on Population and Development held in Beijing, December 1984, and *Population of Tianjin*, to be published soon by the China Financial and Economic Publishing House.

because of some much stronger objective factors, temporary changes did occur, that is, the percentage of male in-migrants exceeded that of male out-migrants. This was the case with Beijing and Tianjin in 1969. That year, the proportion of demobilized servicemen, mainly males, moving into these two cities increased rapidly to exceed that of any other group of in-migrants, in spite of the fact that large numbers of educated youth went to settle in the countryside at that time. Under such special conditions, the selectivity of sex was out of the question.

Third, the proportion of men exceeding that of women migrating from the nonagricultural population to the cities was greater than that from the agricultural population, as shown in Table 5-10 on the sex composition of migrants to Beijing over the years.

This situation was caused by the large number of females from the agricultural population who migrated to the cities for marriage, thus reducing the numerical supremacy of male agricultural migrants. This table also shows that the numerical superiority of male out-migrants from the agricultural population was higher than that of the nonagricultural population. This shows that the males enjoyed the special favor of agricultural and other production

sectors, such as mining, which recruited mainly agricultural population.

AGE COMPOSITION OF MIGRANTS

Since the 1950s more than half of interprovincial migrants have been between ages 15 and 59 (see Tables 5-11 and 5-12).

Beijing's statistics show that most of the migrants were young people of the 15–39 age group, accounting for more than 50% of the total number of migrants of all the age groups. This is because migrations for the sake of work and for academic pursuits, as mentioned above, have over the years remained the major reasons for migrations.

A closer study reveals that the proportion of migrants between 15 and 59 or between 15 and 39 in the total number of migrants has fluctuated year by year. This is an inevitable result of the social, economic, and political changes in various periods.

Second, of the interprovincial migrants, the proportion of children of 14 and under and old people of 60 and above was not high, but the difference for the various periods was not small. The cause for this lay in the difference in social environment. For example, Table 5-11 and Table 5-12 show a rise in the

Table 5-10.   Sex Composition of Migrants to Beijing* (%)

| | IN-MIGRANTS | | | | | |
| | TOTAL | | NON-AGRICULTURAL POPULATION | | AGRICULTURAL POPULATION | |
YEAR	M	F	M	F	M	F
1962	63.7	36.3	68.6	31.4	52	48
1969	64.5	35.5	68.3	31.7	58.6	
1979	55.9	44.1	57.6	42.4	37.3	62.7
1983	74.6	25.4	77.4	22.6	59.2	40.8

| | OUT-MIGRANTS | | | | | |
| | TOTAL | | NON-AGRICULTURAL POPULATION | | AGRICULTURAL POPULATION | |
YEAR	M	F	M	F	M	F
1962	74.5	25.5	74.8	25.2	65.5	34.5
1969	58.4	41.6	57.4	42.6	81.1	18.9
1979	81.0	19.0	80.9	19.1	81.6	18.4
1983	76.3	23.7	78.5	21.5	68.1	31.9

* Nonagricultural population refers to people living in the cities and their suburban areas, and agricultural population refers to people living in the outlying counties and areas.

Source: Wei Jinsheng, *International Migration of Beijing, the Capital, Since the Founding of the People's Republic of China*, a paper for the International Symposium on Population and Development held in Beijing, December 1984.

Table 5-11.   Age Composition of Nonagricultural Migrants in Beijing (%)

YEAR	14 YEARS OLD AND UNDER		15–39 YEARS OLD		40–59 YEARS OLD		15–59 YEARS OLD		60+ YEARS OLD	
	IN	OUT	IN	OUT	IN	OUT	IN	OUT	IN	OUT
1954	24	13	59	66	15	15	74	81	2	6
1959	16	13	70	47	7	20	77	67	7	20
1962	13	15	78	58	8	12	86	70	1	15
1969	9	3	86	92	4	3	90	95	1	2
1979	10	7	68	68	14	18	82	86	8	7
1983*	10	3	71	74	12	18	83	92	7	5

* Based on data obtained in January–June 1983.

Source: Wei Jinsheng, *International Migration of Beijing, the Capital, Since the Founding of the People's Republic of China*, a paper for the International Symposium on Population and Development held in Beijing, December 1984.

proportion of children migrating to the two cities of Beijing and Tianjin in the early 1950s, indicating that the recovery and development of the national economy in the early postliberation years led to the mass migration of workers' children to the two cities to live with their parents and relatives. Also, the increase in the proportion of old people moving out of the two cities by the end of the 1970s as shown in the two tables was the result of the implementation of the retirement system in this period.

Third, if we take a close look at the figures in Table 5-11 showing the number of nonagricultural migrants of Beijing and the figures in Table 5-12 showing the number of all the migrants of Tianjing, we may draw the following conclusions: In terms of age composition, nonagricultural people moving into the cities were mostly of the 15–59 working age group, as compared with agricultural people; only a few were of the 14 and under and 60 and above age groups. From the above two tables we can also see that the proportion of nonagricultural people between 15 and 59 moving into Beijing was between 82 and 90% in those years, while the proportion of all the migrants into Tianjin (including agricultural

people) of the same age group was between 54.3 and 84.3%, which was obviously smaller than the former. Contrary to this, the proportion of nonagricultural people aged 14 and under and those aged 60 and above who moved into Beijing was between 10 and 26%, while the proportion of those of the same age groups who moved into Tianjin, including agricultural population, was between 15.7 and 45.7%. This shows that the interprovincial nonagricultural migrants were mostly young people and adults who moved to the cities for the sake of work and academic pursuits, while the interprovincial agricultural migrants were mostly old people and children who moved to the cities to be together with their family members on whom they depended for a living.

EFFECTS OF INTERPROVINCIAL MIGRATIONS ON PROVINCIAL POPULATION CHANGES

Three factors bring about numerical changes in the population of the provinces and autonomous regions: natural changes in the population (i.e., the

Table 5-12.   Age Composition of Migrants in Tianjin (%)

YEAR	14 YEARS OLD AND UNDER		15–59 YEARS OLD		60+ YEARS OLD	
	IN	OUT	IN	OUT	IN	OUT
1953	13.8	12.7	84.3	85.5	1.9	2.1
1959	31.4	16.8	54.3	79.9	14.3	3.2
1964	33.3	9.9	61.1	86.5	5.6	3.6
1969	30.5	0.8	66.5	98.5	3.0	0.7
1979	13.8	2.4	82.7	90.6	3.5	7.0

Source: Population of Tianjin, to be published soon by the China Financial and Economic Publishing House.

difference between the number of births and deaths); changes resulting from interprovincial migrations (provided that international migrations are insignificant and not included in the calculations); and changes resulting from administrative redivisions with neighboring provinces or regions. The first two factors are constant, while the third one takes place only in certain periods in certain places. Therefore, the numerical changes of population are chiefly due to natural and migration changes. Further studies show that the influence of interprovincial migrations on the size of the population finds direct expression in the net migration (the difference between the number of in-migrants and out-migrants) and indirect expression in the natural changes in the population of provinces, municipalities, and autonomous regions. As mentioned above, interprovincial migrations in China involve chiefly young and able-bodied males. Therefore, the birthrate will go up and the mortality rate go down in provinces, municipalities, and autonomous regions where the in-migrants outnumber the out-migrants. As a result, there is a rise in the natural growth of the population. And the case is reversed in provinces, municipalities, and autonomous regions that have more out-migrants than in-migrants.

In order to give a detailed analysis of the influence of interprovincial migration on the size of the local population, it is necessary first of all to calculate the population growth rate (including the factor of administrative redivision, since the figures were given in accordance with the delineation of those years) of the mainland and 29 provinces, autonomous regions, and municipalities directly under the jurisdiction of the central government between the first census, in 1953, and the third census, in 1982. The results showed that provinces, municipalities, and autonomous regions exceeding the average growth rate of 72% on the mainland included Beijing, Inner Mongolia, Tianjin, Jilin, Heilongjiang, Qinghai, Ningxia, and Xinjiang (all of which increased by 100% and more), as well as Shanxi, Liaoning, Shanghai, Fujian, Jiangxi, Hubei, Guangxi, Guizhou, Yunnan, and Shaanxi (all of which increased by 72 to 100%). The difference between the total population growth of the mainland and 29 provinces, municipalities, and autonomous regions from 1954 to 1982 (figures for 1959–61 not available) and the natural growth indicated the net number of migrants of every province in each of these 26 years (including the factor of administrative redivision, since the figures were given in accordance with the delineation of those years). The result showed that 12 of the above-mentioned 18 provinces, municipalities, and autonomous regions (Beijing, Inner Mongolia, Jilin, Heilongjiang, Qinghai, Ningxia, Xinjiang, Shanxi, Jiangxi, Hubei, Guangxi, and Yunnan) had more in-migrants than out-migrants in at least 20 of those 26 years. Thus the influence of interprovincial migration on their rapid population growth was evident. In the case of the other six provinces and municipalities (Tianjin, Liaoning, Shanghai, Fujian, Guizhou, and Shaanxi), there were fewer years with net in-migrations than in the above-mentioned 12 provinces, municipalities, and autonomous regions, and their fairly rapid population growth was more or less related to changes in administrative delineation and natural growth.

This comparison illustrates the influence of interprovincial migrations on changes in the local population. However, owing to the limited data available, we are unable to list in detail the proportion of interprovincial migrations in the changes in the size of the population of the various provinces, municipalities, and autonomous regions. Nevertheless, rough estimates made from the 1950s to the present show that interprovincial migrations in China had little effect on the changes in the size of the local population. The reason for this is: Apart from the fact that this phenomenon is closely related to the scale and intensity of interprovincial migrations, there is also an important factor that deserves attention: that is, the direction of migrations in a number of municipalities, provinces, and autonomous regions underwent repeated changes and reversals following changes in the situation in various periods after liberation. For more than 30 years, the number of net out-migrations and net in-migrations offset each other, thereby limiting the scale of net migration. Completely different results of the effect of interprovincial migrations on the local population size would be obtained if we had examined year by year instead of taking the process of those 30-odd years as a whole. An example is Beijing, as shown in Table 5-13.

The small number and proportion of Beijing's net in-migration between 1950 and 1983 are indications of the influence of the 1960s. During this period, family planning was practically abandoned in the "cultural revolution," and birthrates hit a record high. Beijing's natural population growth came to 1.4 million in 1961–70. On the other hand, during the economic readjustment of the early 1960s, administrative setups were simplified and employees and their family members were sent back to the countryside to take part in agricultural production. During the tumultuous year of the "cultural revolu-

Table 5-13.   Sources of Beijing's Population Growth (1950–1983)

YEAR	TOTAL INCREASE (IN 10,000)	MIGRATION INCREASE		NATURAL INCREASE		INCREASE DUE TO ADMINISTRATIVE REDIVISION	
		NUMBER (IN 10,000)	% IN TOTAL INCREASE	NUMBER (IN 10,000)	% IN TOTAL INCREASE	NUMBER (IN 10,000)	% IN TOTAL INCREASE
1950–83	726.6	125.7	17.3	339.8	46.8	261.1	35.9
1950–60	525.4	157.8	30.0	107.4	20.5	260.2	49.5
1961–70	41.5	−100.4	−242.0	141.0	339.8	0.9	2.2
1971–78	79.1	34.7	43.9	44.4	56.1		
1979–83	80.6	33.6	41.7	47.0	58.3		

Source: *Prosperous Beijing—35 Years of Beijing's Economic and Social Development,* edited by the Beijing Bureau of Statistics, Beijing Publishing House, 1984.

tion," in the late 1960s, large numbers of cadres and young school-leavers went to settle in the country-side. The consequence of all this was that Beijing's net out-migration in the 1960s totalled about 1 million. Barring these extraordinary factors of the 1960s, the composition of Beijing's population growth can be clearly seen in Table 5-13. The proportion of migration increase in the city's total population growth was 30% in the years 1950–60, and it increased to over 40% during the 1970s and after. This was also the case with a number of provinces and autonomous regions. Take Hunan Province as an example. For more than 30 years, in-migrants were basically equivalent to out-migrants, and migration had little influence on population growth. However, when we make a year-by-year study, we find that the influence of interprovincial migration on Hunan's population growth was not insignificant but quite important. For instance, during the period between 1950 and 1982, in-migrants outnumbered out-migrants in 23 of those years, and in nine of these years the net increase of in-migration was more than 15% of the total annual increase of the population. The proportion in five other years exceeded 20%.

Again, take Liaoning Province as an example. In the years 1949–82, migrants into and out of the province almost equalled, and the aggregate number of in-migration was only 0.44 million, a little over 10,000 each year. But when we study the case year by year, we find that 14 of the 34 years had a net in-migration, while 20 showed net out-migration. But in-migration was much larger in number than out-migration, with the result that in-migrants still outnumbered out-migrants. All these changes are closely associated with the social and economic development of Liaoning Province.

In a word, the influence of interprovincial migration on population growth in the various provinces and autonomous regions should be studied not only in connection with the overall situation in the more than 30 postliberation years but also with due consideration to the changes in social and economic condition so as to analyze its influence in different periods and stages. We will then be able to deepen our understanding of the important effect of migration through different angles—population changes as well as social and economic development.

CHAPTER SIX

URBANIZATION

Rapid urbanization and increase in population are the two basic characteristics of the population question in the contemporary world. Since the founding of New China, in 1949, the government has taken measures to gradually control the overly rapid growth of population and to regulate by various means the increase of urban population and the level of urbanization. This chapter will deal with the pattern and characteristics of the urbanization of population in China since the 1950s and comparisons, whenever necessary, will be made with the situation in other parts of the world.

An explanation should first be given for the definition of urban population (the term is used in a broad sense in this book) and the statistical method used in China. There is as yet no internationally accepted standard in this regard. In China, there are three commonly used methods of compiling statistics for the urban population: (1) the total population of the cities and towns, i.e., the resident population (agricultural and nonagricultural population) of the organic cities (not including the counties under their jurisdiction) and towns; those residing in the cities (not including the counties under their jurisdiction) fall into the category of city population and those residing in the towns are classified as town population; (2) the nonagricultural population of the cities and towns (sometimes called the population of the cities and towns), i.e., the resident nonagricultural population of the organic cities (not including the counties under their jurisdiction) and towns; and (3) the nonagricultural population, i.e., the sum total of the nonagricultural population residing in the organic cities and towns and in areas other than these cities and towns. In this chapter, the first two methods are used, not only because they ensure maximum access to relevant materials but also because they complement each other, using as they do the areas under the jurisdiction of the cities and towns for the collection of the needed statistics.

GENERAL TREND OF THE GROWTH OF URBAN POPULATION AND URBANIZATION

Since the 1950s, the growth of urban population and the increase in the level of urbanization in China have undergone several stages of changes. On the whole, there has been a steady pace of change over the past 30 years, basically in conformity with the objective needs and prospects of social and economic development. But in certain periods, excessively big and rapid changes brought in their wake adverse effects. With the advent of the 1980s, urbanization has entered a new period of development along with the marked improvement of the nation's social and economic conditions. After making an analysis of Tables 6-1, 6-2, 6-3, and Chart 6-1 and other relevant materials, we find that the general trend and main characteristics are as follows:

1. The process of urbanization on a notable scale began quite late in China, and the level is still comparatively low at present. The level of modern urbanization in today's developed countries began to rise markedly in the middle of the last century, and after more than 100 years their urban population has increased from about 10% of the total population at that time to a little over 70% today, reaching a state of saturation. The process of marked urbanization in the developing countries started, by and large, in the 1920s, about 70 years later than in the developed countries. In 1920, their urban population accounted for about 10% of the total, but by 60 years later it had increased to over 30%. Though this proportion is 57% lower than that of the developed countries, it tends to increase at a faster speed. In China, urbanization on a notable scale began in the 1950s, a century later than in the developed countries and 30 years later than the average process in the developing countries. In 1950, China's urban population accounted for 11.2% of the total popula-

Table 6-1.   Total Population of the Cities and Towns in China and Growth Rate (1950–1983)

TOTAL POPULATION (MILLION)							
1950	1955	1960	1965	1970	1975	1980	1983
61.69	93.611	163.48	130.45	144.24	160.599	191.412	241.28
GROWTH RATE (%)							
1950–55	1955–60	1960–65	1965–70	1970–75	1975–80	1980–83	1950–83
8.7	11.8	−4.4	2.0	2.2	3.6	8.0	4.2

Source: Wei Jinsheng, "The General Trends of China's Urbanization Since the 1950s," *Population and Economics*, No. 6, 1985.

tion in the country; by 1983 it had increased to 23.5% (calculated according to the percentage of the population of the cities and towns in the total population of the nation) or 14.6% (calculated according to the percentage of the nonagricultural population of the cities and towns in the total population of the nation). Even calculated in terms of the higher percentage of the total population of the cities and towns, the level of urbanization in China is 67% lower than the present urbanization level in the above-mentioned developed countries and 24% lower than the average urbanization level in the developing countries. And if the lower percentage of the nonagricultural population of the cities and towns is taken for comparison, the urbanization level of China is 79% lower than the present level in the developed countries and 53% lower than the average level in the developing countries. Thus, the present urbanization level of China is still comparatively low in the world.

2. From the 1950s to the present time, the urban population of China has on the whole increased quite slowly and the level of urbanization has risen by only a small margin. During the years 1950–80 the total population in China's cities and towns increased at an annual average rate of 3.8% and their nonagricultural population at 2.6%, both being lower than the increased rate (4.3%) of the urban population in the developing countries as a whole in the corresponding period. The increase rate of the nonagricultural population of the cities and towns in China is even

lower than the increase rate (3.1%) of the urban population of the whole world, the developed countries included. Thus the level of urbanization in China over the past 30 years has risen by only a limited margin, as a result of the slow growth of its urban population. In 1980, the total population and the nonagricultural population of China's cities and towns accounted for 19.5% and 13.7% of the nation's total population, respectively, an increase of 74% and 22% as compared with those (both being 11.2%) of 1950. These increase rates were all lower than the increase rate (83%) of the urbanization level of the developing countries as a whole in the corresponding period, and the increase rate of the nonagricultural population of the cities and towns in China was even lower than those of the developed countries and the whole world (34 and 43%, respectively).

However, owing to the large base of the Chinese population, the accumulated absolute number and increased figure were quite large in spite of the slow growth rate and low level of urbanization over the past 30 years. In 1980 the total population and the nonagricultural population of the cities and towns in China reached 191.412 million and 134.13 million, accounting for 11% and 7.4%, respectively, of the urban population of the whole world that year and 20% and 14% of the urban population of the developing countries, thus making China one of the few big countries whose urban population topped the 100 million mark. In the 30 years from 1950 to 1980, the

Table 6-2.   Nonagricultural Population of the Cities and Towns in China and Growth Rate (1950–1983)

NONAGRICULTURAL POPULATION (MILLION)							
1950	1955	1960	1965	1970	1975	1980	1983
61.69	82.85	130.73	98.34	100.75	111.71	134.13	149.61
GROWTH RATE (%)							
1950–55	1955–60	1960–65	1965–70	1970–75	1975–80	1980–83	1950–83
6.1	9.5	−5.5	0.5	2.1	3.7	3.7	2.7

Source: Wei Jinsheng, "The General Trends of China's Urbanization Since the 1950s," *Population and Economics*, No. 6, 1985.

Table 6-3.   Level of Urbanization in China (1950–1983)

	1950	1955	1960	1965	1970	1975	1980	1983
Proportion of the total population of the cities and towns in the total population of the country (%)	11.2	15.2	24.7	18.0	17.4	17.5	19.5	23.5
Proportion of nonagricultural population of the cities and towns in the population of the country (%)	11.2	13.5	19.7	13.6	12.2	12.2	13.7	14.6

Source: Wei Jinsheng, "The General Trends of China's Urbanization Since the 1950s," *Population and Economics*, No. 6, 1985.

Chart 6-1.   The Urbanization Process in China, the Developing Countries as a Whole, the Developed Countries, and the World (1950–1980)

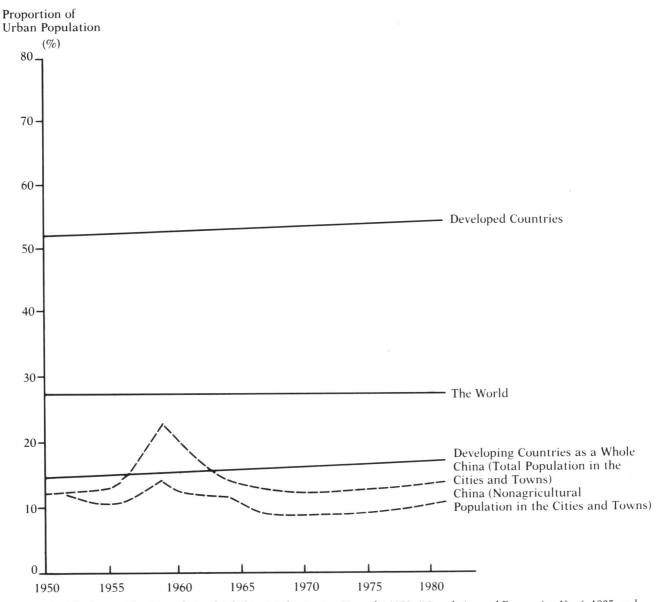

Sources: Wei Jinsheng, "The General Trends of China's Urbanization Since the 1950s," *Population and Economics*, No. 6, 1985, and United Nations, *World Population Trends and Policies, 1979 Monitoring Report*, Vol. I, and *1981 Monitoring Report*, Vol. I.

total population and the nonagricultural population of the cities and towns in China increased by 129.722 million and 72.44 million, respectively, accounting for 12% and 6.7%, respectively, of the increase in the world's urban population, and 18.6% and 10.4% of the increase in the urban population of the developing countries as a whole in the corresponding period. If we take the 1983 figure as the base, an increase of China's urban population by 1% means nearly 2.5 million and 1.5 million people will be added respectively to the total population and the nonagricultural population of the cities and towns. Obviously, such big increases are factors that cannot be overlooked for they will affect the scale of change in China's urban population and the proportionate social and economic development of the country.

3. The slow growth of the urban population and the low level of urbanization in China since the 1950s have not progressed in a straight line but have undergone curvilinear changes along with the social, political, and economic development in the country. The past 30 and more years may roughly be divided into five periods:

• The early and middle period of the 1950s. This was a period of rehabilitation of the national economy devastated by protracted wars and of large-scale economic reconstruction after the founding of New China. During this period, capital construction made big headway and a great number of large and medium-sized industrial projects were completed in and around the cities throughout the country. As a result, China's urban population increased quickly and its level of urbanization rose by a comparatively big margin and in a smooth and healthy way. From 1950 to 1955, the annual increase rate of the total population and the nonagricultural population of the cities and towns was 8.7% and 6.1%, respectively, or 2.3 times their average annual rate of increase in the years 1950–80. At the same time, the rise in the level of urbanization was also quite swift. The proportion of the population of the cities and towns in the total population of the country increased from 11.2% in 1950 to 15.2% in 1955, with an annual average growth of 0.8 percentage points. In the same period, the proportion of nonagricultural population in the cities and towns increased from 11.2% to 13.5%, with an annual average increase of 0.46 percentage points. This was a relatively swift growth in the process of urbanization over the past 30 years.

• The late 1950s. During this period, the "Big Leap Forward" movement was recklessly launched in China, which sought excessively high production

targets and large construction scales. Tens of millions of peasants came to the cities and towns to take part in running the industries and making steel. As a result, the total population of the cities and towns reached 160 million at the end of 1960 and registered a sharp increase of 70 million as compared with 1955, or an annual increase rate of 11.8%. In 1960, the proportion of the population of the cities and towns in the total population of the country jumped to 24.7%. All these hit in all-time high. Also in this period, the nonagricultural population of the cities and towns increased by more than 47 million, with an annual growth rate of 9.5%. In 1960 the proportion of nonagricultural population of the cities and towns in the total population of the country was 19.7%. While the urban population increased rapidly, the normal order of the national economy was thrown into disarray, and industrial and agricultural production suffered tremendous losses. Superficially, urbanization seemed to have developed swiftly in this period, but actually it went beyond the limit, bringing serious consequences.

• The first half of the 1960s. This was a period of economic readjustment. In 1961 the state began readjusting the national economy, which lasted for several years, in order to overcome the serious consequences of the previous period. One of the measures taken was to streamline the organizations and reduce the number of workers and staff members in the cities and towns with the aim of reinforcing the agricultural sector. From 1961 to June 1963, a total of 18.87 million workers and staff members and 26 million urban residents were reduced, and more than 20 million people returned to the agricultural production front. By 1965, the nonagricultural population of the cities and towns in China had been reduced from 130 million in 1960 to a little over 98 million, and its proportion in the total population of the country dropped from 19.7% to 13.6%, thereby reverting to the level of the mid-1950s. At the same time, the population of the cities and towns was also reduced from 160 million in 1960 to 130 million in 1965, and its proportion dropped from 24.7% to 18%, which was slightly higher than that of the mid-1950s. The reduction of the size of urban population and the degree of urbanization in this period, which were quite abnormal at that time, was conducive to overcoming the difficulties in the national economy and to creating conditions for future urbanization in a healthy way.

• The latter half of the 1960s to the mid-1970s. This was a period when the so-called cultural revolution was rashly launched. After readjustment, China's urban population could have grown again in a sound and healthy way along with the development of the national economy. Unfortunately, the "cultural revolution" did extremely grave damage to the national economy, and it was only through the joint efforts of the people and the cadres that production and construction were prevented from a total breakdown. Under these circumstances, the growth of urban population and urbanization in China first underwent a downturn and then began to pick up again slowly. The proportion of the population of the cities and towns dropped from 18% in 1965 (the proportion of nonagricultural population was 13.6%) to 17.4% in 1970 (the proportion of nonagricultural population fell to 12.2%), and then it began to increase slightly (the proportion of nonagricultural population remained unchanged). The annual growth rate in 1970–75 was 0.2 percentage points higher than that in 1965–70. (In the same period, the growth rate of nonagricultural population was 1.6 percentage points higher, but still lower than the average growth rate in the past 30-odd years).

• The latter half of the 1970s to the early 1980s. This was a period during which an end was put to the stagnation and retrogression of the national economy caused by the "cultural revolution," and readjustment of the national economy was vigorously carried out. In this period, China's urban population increased, and the annual increase rate of the population of the cities and towns in 1975–80 was 3.6%, or 1.4 percentage points higher than in the years 1970–75. The annual increase rate of the nonagricultural population was 1.6 percentage points. In 1980 the proportion of the total population and the nonagricultural population in the cities and towns were 19.5% and 13.7%, respectively, both being the highest level (excluding the period of abnormal development) ever attained since the 1950s, a level that reflected the actual, normal conditions at that time.

It should be noted here that while the proportion of the nonagricultural population in the cities and towns steadily increased to 14.6% by 1983, the proportion of the total population of the cities and towns had soared to 23.5%. Compared with 1980, the former had increased by only 0.9 percentage points, while the latter had increased by 4 points. The difference in the speed of growth was mainly due to the fact that the resident agricultural population in the cities and towns had steadily increased and the proportion raised with the expansion of the areas under the jurisdiction of the cities and towns as a result of redemarcation of the cities and towns since 1980. By 1983, the proportion of this agricultural population

accounted for 38.8% of the total population of the cities and towns; in the cities, in particular, it was as high as 42.5%, but toward the end of the 1970s, it was only around 30%. This led directly to the marked increase in the total population of the cities and towns and the swift rise of its proportion; but it had no effect, of course, on the increase of the nonagricultural population. Available statistics also showed that the average annual increase rate of the nonagricultural population of the cities and towns in 1980–83 was the same as that of 1975–80 (both being 3.7%), while the average annual growth rate of the total population of the cities and towns in 1980–83 was 8%, or 2.2 times that of 1975–80. Evidently, if no new stipulations are laid down for the statistics of urban population, the above-mentioned difference will be even greater. This also showed that the statistics of the total population and of the nonagricultural population must be used together to supplement each other in the study of the growth of China's urban population and the change of its level of urbanization.

REGIONAL DIFFERENCES IN GROWTH OF URBAN POPULATION AND LEVEL OF URBANIZATION

China is a vast and populous country in which the various regions differ in natural, social, economic, and historical conditions and in population. In order to get an overall, objective picture of the changes in the urban population and the process of urbanization in China, it is necessary to make an all-round study of the general trend and an in-depth analysis of the regional differences of this trend.

Taking into consideration the generality and particularity of the various areas in China and the availability of the necessary materials, this section will follow the common methods used, and by dividing the whole country into the major—coastal and inland—areas, make a comparative study of the regional differences and then analyze the changes in these differences. According to the general division, China's coastal area (not including Taiwan) consists of 12 provinces, municipalities, and autonomous regions: Liaoning, Tianjin, Beijing, Hebei, Shandong, Jiangsu, Shanghai, Anhui, Zhejiang, Fujian, Guangdong, and Guangxi. The inland area includes 17 provinces and autonomous regions: Heilongjiang, Jilin, Inner Mongolia, Shanxi, Jiangxi, Henan, Hubei, Hunan, Sichuan, Guizhou, Yunnan, Tibet, Shaanxi, Gansu, Qinghai, Ningxia, and Xinjiang.

Table 6-4. Total Population in the Whole Country and in the Cities and Towns of the Various Provinces, Municipalities, and Autonomous Regions and Their Growth Rate (1955–1983)

	TOTAL POPULATION OF THE CITIES AND TOWNS (MILLION)							ANNUAL GROWTH RATE OF THE TOTAL POPULATION OF THE CITIES AND TOWNS (%)						
	1955	1960	1965	1971	1975	1980	1983	1955–60	1960–65	1965–71	1971–75	1975–80	1980–83	1955–83
Whole country[1]	93.611	163.480	130.450	160.932	160.559	191.412	241.780	11.8	−4.4	1.8	2.6	3.6	8.0	3.4
Coastal area	52.642	81.974	66.866	70.099	77.595	89.601	118.020	9.3	−4.0	0.8	2.5	2.9	9.6	2.9
Liaoning	8.289	11.709	11.318	11.263	13.219	14.195	15.460	7.2	−0.7	−0.1	4.1	1.4	2.9	2.3
Tianjin	2.863	—	—	4.295	4.693	5.123	5.420	—	—	—	2.2	1.8	1.9	2.3
Beijing	3.210	5.100	5.047	4.791	5.108	5.719	6.170	9.3	0.1	−1.0	1.6	2.3	2.5	2.4
Hebei	4.236	10.613	8.758	4.984	5.594	6.707	8.440	20.2	−3.8	−9.0	2.9	3.7	8.0	2.5
Shandong	4.728	12.918	6.617	7.847	8.952	10.308	22.150	27.3	−12.6	2.9	3.3	2.8	29.1	5.7
Jiangsu	6.596	9.053	6.881	6.826	7.415	9.018	12.290	6.5	−5.3	−0.1	2.1	4.0	10.9	2.2
Shanghai	6.231	7.033	6.977	6.239	6.136	6.671	7.110	2.5	−0.2	−1.8	−0.4	1.7	2.1	0.5
Anhui	2.952	5.102	3.885	4.551	5.232	6.627	8.370	11.6	−5.3	2.7	3.5	4.8	8.1	3.8
Zhejiang	3.789	6.129	4.226	4.858	4.941	5.690	9.070	10.1	−7.2	2.3	0.4	2.9	16.8	3.2
Fujian	1.855	3.969	3.567	4.004	4.392	4.979	5.980	16.4	−2.1	2.0	2.4	2.5	6.3	4.3
Guangdong	6.099	8.043	7.175	7.691	8.764	10.691	13.000	5.7	−2.3	1.2	3.3	4.1	6.7	2.7
Guangxi	1.794	2.395	2.413	2.750	3.149	3.881	4.560	6.0	0.2	2.2	3.4	4.3	5.5	3.4
Inland area	40.969	81.506	63.584	70.333	78.464	97.311	119.000	14.7	−4.8	1.7	2.8	4.4	6.9	3.9
Heilongjiang	4.673	8.874	8.275	10.263	11.615	12.327	14.180	13.7	−1.4	3.7	3.2	1.2	4.8	4.0
Jilin	3.622	5.757	5.787	6.795	7.663	8.538	8.780	9.7	0.1	2.7	3.1	2.2	0.9	3.2
Inner Mongolia	1.223	4.758	3.614	2.359	2.637	5.349	5.700	31.2	−5.4	−6.9	2.8	15.2	2.1	5.7
Shanxi	2.451	5.213	2.762	3.856	4.385	5.027	7.120	16.3	−11.9	5.7	3.3	2.8	12.3	3.9
Jiangxi	2.042	4.843	3.726	5.163	4.914	6.146	7.090	18.9	−5.1	5.6	−1.2	4.6	4.9	4.5
Henan	3.960	11.405	5.758	6.829	7.925	8.948	11.750	23.6	−12.8	2.9	3.8	2.5	9.5	4.0
Hubei	3.459	5.739	4.850	5.659	6.382	7.865	13.950	10.6	−3.3	2.6	3.1	4.3	21.0	5.1
Hunan	3.390	4.885	4.056	4.709	5.318	6.711	8.750	7.6	−3.7	2.5	3.1	4.7	9.2	3.4
Sichuan	7.802	10.915	8.636	9.764	10.379	13.359	15.950	6.9	−4.6	2.1	1.6	5.2	6.1	2.6
Guizhou	1.393	3.034	2.253	2.718	2.983	5.432	5.510	16.8	−5.8	3.2	2.4	12.7	0.5	5.0
Yunnan	1.951	3.062	2.061	2.994	3.350	3.967	4.470	9.4	−3.2	2.4	2.8	3.4	3.0	3.0
Tibet	—	0.261	0.109	0.118	0.144	0.237	0.190	—	−16.0	1.3	5.1	10.5	−7.1	3.1[2]
Shaanxi	2.264	4.963	3.338	3.873	4.349	5.221	5.770	17.0	−7.6	2.5	2.9	3.7	3.4	3.4
Gansu	1.772	4.283	2.125	2.276	2.670	2.907	3.570	19.3	−13.1	1.2	4.1	1.7	7.1	2.5
Qinghai	0.250	0.904	0.426	0.544	0.630	0.747	0.770	29.3	−14.0	4.2	3.7	3.5	1.0	4.1
Ningxia	—	0.715	0.415	0.658	0.698	0.803	1.090	—	−10.3	8.0	1.5	2.8	10.7	5.5[2]
Xinjiang	0.717	1.895	1.494	1.755	2.425	3.727	4.360	21.5	−4.6	2.7	8.4	9.0	5.4	6.7

[1] The total population of the cities and towns in the whole country does not equal the sum of the total population of the cities and towns in both the coastal and inland areas, because the number of servicemen is only included in the total population of the whole country, and not in that of the coastal area, inland provinces, autonomous regions, and municipalities directly under the central government.

[2] Annual growth rate of the total population of the cities and towns in 1965–83.

Source: Calculated and compiled from the yearly forms of vital statistics submitted by institutions of population register and vital statistics.

The inland area accounts for 85% of the total area and 50% of the total population of China. It produces half of China's food grains and is endowed with most of China's mineral resources. Most parts of the area have secure and favorable conditions as far as national defense is concerned. However, owing to historical reasons and the limitations of various practical factors, the level of economic and social development in the inland provinces and regions lags far behind that of the southeastern coastal area, which has a strong technical foundation, rich managerial expertise, good conditions for production, and comparatively complete infrastructural facilities. Since the founding of New China, the state has adopted numerous measures to narrow the gap be-

tween the two areas, and tangible results have been achieved.

When the above-mentioned factors are manifested in the growth of urban population and the urbanization process, there emerge the regional differences of this process and the characteristics of their changes (Tables 6-4, 6-5, 6-6, 6-7, and Chart 6-2), which can be analyzed as follows:

1. The backwardness of the economy over a long period of time and the irrational distribution of production in old China resulted in the concentration of the limited urban population mostly in the southeastern coastal areas in the years immediately after the founding of the People's Republic in 1949. When the first census was taken in 1953, 57% of the

Table 6-5. Nonagricultural Population of the Whole Country and of the Cities and Towns in the Various Provinces, Municipalities, and Autonomous Regions and Their Growth Rate (1957–1983)

	POPULATION OF THE CITIES AND TOWNS (MILLION)					ANNUAL GROWTH RATE OF THE POPULATION OF THE CITIES AND TOWNS (%)				
	1957	1965	1972	1978	1983	1957–65	1965–72	1972–78	1978–83	1957–83
Whole country	99.49	98.34	106.24	119.94	149.61	−0.1	1.1	2.0	4.5	1.6
Coastal area	53.77	52.03	52.43	58.73	73.36	−0.4	0.1	1.9	4.5	1.2
Liaoning	8.64	9.45	9.22	10.10	12.65	1.1	−0.4	1.5	4.6	1.5
Tianjin	2.84	—	3.17	3.55	4.14	—	—	1.9	3.1	1.4
Beijing	3.42	4.32	4.05	4.40	5.24	3.0	−0.9	1.4	3.6	1.6
Hebei	4.89	6.40	3.14	4.25	5.28	3.4	−8.1	3.1	4.5	0.3
Shandong	4.80	3.73	4.23	4.94	6.58	−3.1	1.8	2.6	5.9	1.2
Jiangsu	6.48	5.56	5.28	6.07	7.93	−1.9	−0.7	2.4	5.5	0.8
Shanghai	6.34	6.89	6.11	6.05	6.99	1.0	−1.7	−0.1	2.9	0.4
Anhui	2.92	3.10	3.57	4.08	5.05	0.8	2.0	2.3	4.3	2.1
Zhejiang	3.62	2.98	3.10	3.39	4.40	−2.4	0.6	1.5	5.4	0.7
Fujian	2.77	2.35	2.41	2.76	3.30	−2.1	0.4	2.3	3.7	0.7
Guangdong	5.06	5.42	5.65	6.48	8.27	0.9	0.6	2.3	5.0	1.9
Guangxi	1.99	1.83	2.10	2.66	3.53	−1.1	2.0	4.0	5.8	2.2
Inland area	45.72	46.31	53.81	61.21	76.25	0.2	2.2	2.2	4.5	2.0
Heilongjiang	5.40	7.04	9.24	0.01	0.01	3.4	4.0	1.3	1.7	2.7
Jilin	3.72	4.63	5.40	6.14	6.95	2.8	2.2	2.2	2.5	2.4
Inner Mongolia	1.79	2.68	1.99	2.24	5.19	5.2	−4.2	2.0	18.3	4.2
Shanxi	2.61	2.22	2.66	3.01	3.81	−2.0	2.6	2.1	4.8	1.5
Jiangxi	2.35	2.50	2.78	3.33	4.21	0.8	1.5	3.0	4.8	2.3
Henan	4.72	3.55	4.17	4.81	6.39	−3.5	2.3	2.4	5.8	1.2
Hubei	4.21	4.09	4.64	5.53	6.91	−0.3	1.8	3.0	4.6	1.9
Hunan	3.20	3.31	3.78	4.38	5.59	0.4	1.9	2.5	5.0	2.2
Sichuan	7.49	6.64	7.63	8.24	9.84	−1.5	2.0	1.3	3.6	1.1
Guizhou	2.03	1.75	2.01	2.28	2.64	−1.8	2.0	2.1	3.0	1.0
Yunnan	1.93	1.78	2.03	2.43	2.89	−1.0	1.9	3.0	3.5	1.5
Tibet	0.16	0.11	0.10	0.16	0.16	−4.6	−1.4	8.2	0	0
Shaanxi	2.65	2.41	2.88	3.10	3.98	−1.2	2.6	1.2	5.1	1.6
Gansu	2.07	1.62	1.85	1.98	2.36	−3.0	1.9	1.1	3.5	0.5
Qinghai	0.41	0.34	0.48	0.58	0.66	−2.3	5.0	3.2	2.5	1.8
Ningxia	—	0.29	0.44	0.52	0.65	—	6.1	2.8	4.7	3.2[1]
Xinjiang	0.98	1.35	1.73	2.48	3.16	4.1	3.6	6.2	5.0	4.6

[1] The annual growth rate of the population of the cities and towns in 1965–83.

Source: Calculated and compiled from the yearly forms of vital statistics submitted by institutions of population register and vital statistics.

Table 6-6. Proportion of the Total Population of the Cities and Towns of the Country, the Provinces, and Regions in the Total Population of the Country (1955–1983) (%)

	1955	1960	1965	1971	1975	1980	1983
Whole Country	15.2	24.7	18.0	17.1	17.5	19.5	23.5
Coastal area	17.8	26.0	19.4	17.5	18.2	19.8	25.0
Liaoning	37.2	45.6	40.3	32.7	36.5	40.7	47.6
Tianjin	100.0	—	—	100.0	67.1	68.2	68.7
Beijing	100.0	68.4	65.0	61.2	67.1	64.5	66.1
Hebei	10.5	24.0	18.5	10.2	11.4	13.0	15.6
Shandong	9.1	24.8	11.6	11.9	12.8	14.1	29.3
Jiangsu	15.3	21.2	14.9	12.7	13.2	15.2	20.0
Shanghai	100.0	66.9	63.8	58.5	57.0	58.2	59.5
Anhui	9.2	16.5	11.8	11.1	11.6	13.5	16.6
Zhejiang	15.6	23.1	14.3	14.3	13.7	14.9	22.9
Fujian	13.5	24.9	20.3	19.0	19.0	19.8	22.7
Guangdong	16.7	20.1	17.0	15.5	16.4	18.5	21.4
Guangxi	9.7	12.2	9.9	9.5	9.8	11.0	12.2
Inland area	12.8	22.8	16.8	15.7	15.9	18.4	21.7
Heilongjiang	35.0	48.9	38.8	36.7	36.5	38.5	42.9
Jilin	29.9	41.0	35.3	31.0	32.3	38.6	38.7
Inner Mongolia	14.9	0.5	27.9	30.3	30.9	28.5	29.2
Shanxi	16.1	30.4	14.8	17.8	18.7	20.3	27.7
Jiangxi	11.5	24.0	16.9	19.5	16.6	18.8	21.0
Henan	8.5	23.5	11.0	11.0	11.7	12.3	15.5
Hubei	11.8	18.1	13.8	13.7	14.5	16.8	28.9
Hunan	9.8	13.6	10.4	10.2	10.7	12.7	15.9
Sichuan	11.3	15.9	12.1	11.4	11.0	13.6	15.8
Guizhou	8.7	18.2	12.4	12.0	11.8	19.5	19.0
Yunnan	10.8	16.0	12.0	11.5	11.6	12.5	13.5
Tibet	—	23.1	8.0	7.9	8.5	12.8	9.8
Shaanxi	13.2	25.4	15.6	15.5	16.2	18.4	19.7
Gansu	13.0	33.9	15.8	13.9	14.8	15.2	18.0
Qinghai	13.6	36.4	18.5	18.4	18.7	19.8	19.6
Ningxia	—	33.1	18.3	22.3	20.7	21.5	27.4
Xinjiang	13.7	26.9	18.9	17.4	21.0	29.0	33.1

Source: Calculated and compiled from the yearly forms of vital statistics submitted by institutions of population register and vital statistics.

total population (86.209 million) of the cities and towns were concentrated in the coastal areas and the remaining 43% were in the vast inland areas. In the process of large-scale and planned economic construction in the years that followed, the state carried out the policy of actively building new industrial areas in the inland provinces while rationally developing the old industrial areas along the coast. As a result, urban population in the inland areas increased at a faster rate than in the coastal regions, gradually leading to a more rational regional distribution of urban population in the country. The early 1970s witnessed a significant change: In 1971, the total population of the cities and towns in the inland areas increased to 70.333 million, surpassing for the first time in history the total population of 70.099 million in the coastal cities and towns. In the next year, the nonagricultural population (53.81 million) of the inland cities and towns also surpassed that

(52.43 million) of the coastal cities and towns. Since then, both the total population and the nonagricultural population of the inland cities and towns have been larger than those of the coastal cities and towns, and the tendency is that this gap will increase.

If the provinces and autonomous regions (the municipalities directly under the central government were not included because their conditions were different from those of the provinces and autonomous regions) were arranged in order according to the total population of their cities and towns in 1955, the first five would be Liaoning, Sichuan, Jiangsu, Guangdong, and Shandong, of which only Sichuan is in the interior. In 1980 the first five were Liaoning, Sichuan, Heilongjiang, Guangdong, and Shandong, with the inland province of Heilongjiang replacing the coastal province of Jiangsu. The above-mentioned situation reflected, on the one hand, the growth of the inland urban population in

Table 6-7. Proportion of the Nonagricultural Population of the Whole Country and of the Cities and Towns in the Various Provinces, Municipalities, and Autonomous Regions in the Total Population of the Country (1957–1983) (%)

	1957	1965	1972	1978	1983
Whole country	15.4	13.6	12.2	12.5	14.6
Coastal area	17.4	15.1	12.9	13.2	15.6
Liaoning	35.9	33.7	26.4	27.0	34.9
Tianjin	88.2	—	72.5	49.2	52.5
Beijing	85.3	55.7	51.1	51.8	56.1
Hebei	11.8	13.5	7.1	8.4	9.8
Shandong	8.9	6.5	6.3	6.9	8.7
Jiangsu	14.3	12.0	9.7	10.4	12.9
Shanghai	91.9	63.0	57.4	55.1	58.6
Anhui	8.7	9.4	8.5	8.7	10.0
Zhejiang	14.3	10.1	9.0	9.0	11.1
Fujian	18.9	13.4	11.2	11.3	12.5
Guangdong	13.3	12.8	11.2	11.6	13.6
Guangxi	10.3	7.5	7.5	7.8	9.4
Inland area	13.6	12.3	11.7	11.9	13.8
Heilongjiang	36.3	33.0	31.8	29.6	32.8
Jilin	29.6	28.2	24.0	24.8	30.6
Inner Mongolia	19.5	20.7	24.8	25.2	26.6
Shanxi	16.4	11.9	12.0	12.4	14.8
Jiangxi	12.6	11.3	10.2	10.5	12.4
Henan	9.7	6.8	6.6	6.8	8.4
Hubei	13.7	11.7	11.0	12.1	14.3
Hunan	8.8	8.5	8.0	8.5	10.1
Sichuan	10.4	9.3	8.7	8.5	9.8
Guizhou	12.0	9.6	8.7	8.5	9.1
Yunnan	10.1	8.2	7.6	7.9	8.7
Tibet	12.6	8.1	6.3	8.9	8.3
Shaanxi	14.6	11.2	11.3	11.2	13.6
Gansu	14.2	12.0	10.9	10.6	11.9
Qinghai	20.0	14.8	15.6	15.9	16.7
Ningxia	—	12.8	14.4	14.2	16.4
Xinjiang	17.4	17.1	16.4	20.1	24.0

Source: Calculated and compiled from the yearly forms of vital statistics submitted by institutions of population register and vital statistics.

this period, and, on the other hand, it showed that the comparatively large urban population of the economically more developed coastal provinces were determined by objective factors and could not be easily changed.

2. The steady growth of urban population in the inland areas and its overtaking that of the coastal regions obviously meant that the former has increased at a faster pace than the latter. In the period 1955–80, the average annual increase rate of the total population of the cities and towns in the country was 2.9%; the rate of increase in the coastal areas was only 2.1%, while in the inland areas it was 3.5%. What merits attention is that the gap between the growth rates of the inland and coastal areas did not widen in a straight line as time went by. In 1955–60, for example, the annual growth rate of the total popu-

lation of the inland cities and towns was 5.4 percentage points higher than that of the coastal cities and towns. But in 1975–80, the former was only 1.5 percentage points higher than the latter. In addition, although the growth rate of the inland urban population has been on the whole higher than that of the coastal urban population since the 1950s, there were exceptions, as in the years 1960–65 and 1980–83. In the case of the former period, the total population of the inland cities and towns increased more rapidly as a result of the "Big Leap Forward" movement, so when readjustments of the national economy were made later, then inland urban population was reduced by a greater margin than that in the coastal areas. In 1980–83, however, the growth rate of the population of the inland cities and towns was 6.9%, which was not slow. But, owing to the fact that the

Chart 6-2.   The Urbanization Process in the Coastal and
Inland Areas of China (1955–1980)

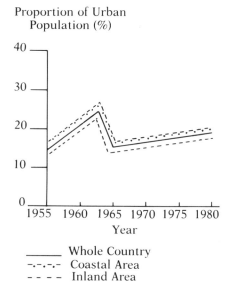

Proportion of Urban
Population (%)

Year

_____   Whole Country
–·–·–·–   Coastal Area
– – – –   Inland Area

Source: Calculated and compiled from the yearly forms of vital
statistics submitted by institutions of population register and
vital statistics.

population of the cities and towns in a few coastal
provinces and areas increased sharply in the short
span of two to three years, the growth rate of the
population of the coastal cities and towns as a whole
registered a tremendous upswing.

If the provinces and autonomous regions (excluding the municipalities directly under the central
government) were arranged according to the annual
increase rates of the total population of their cities
and towns, the first five would be the Xinjiang Uygur
Autonomous Region (6.8%), the Inner Mongolian
Autonomous Region (6.1%), Guizhou Province
(5.6%), Qinghai Province (4.5%), and Jiangxi Province (4.5%).

3. Owing to the higher growth rate of the population of the inland cities, the gap between their level
of urbanization and that of the coastal areas dropped
from 5 percentage points in 1955 (the proportion of
the population of the inland cities and towns at that
time was 12.8% and that of the population of the
coastal cities and towns was 17.8%) to 1.4 percentage
points in 1980 (the proportion of the population of
the inland cities and towns was 18.4% and that of the
population of the coastal cities was 19.8%. Of course,
the process of this change was not a consistent one,
but the basic trend over a long period showed that
the gap was gradually reduced.

If the increased rates in the proportion of the
population of the cities and towns in the provinces

and autonomous regions (again excluding the municipalities directly under the central government)
in 1955–80 were calculated and arranged in order,
the first five provinces and autonomous regions
were: the Xinjiang Uygur Autonomous Region (the
proportion of its urban population was raised from
13.7% to 29%, an increase of 15.3 percentage points),
the Inner Mongolian Autonomous Region (the proportion of its urban population was raised from
1.49% to 28.5%, an increase of 13.6 percentage
points), Guizhou (the proportion of its urban population was raised from 8.7% to 19.6%, an increase of
10.9 percentage points), Jilin (the proportion of its
urban population was raised from 29.9% to 38.6%, an
increase of 8.7 percentage points), and Jiangxi (the
proportion of its urban population was raised from
11.5% to 18.8%, an increase of 7.3 percentage
points). This showed, first, that the five provinces and
autonomous regions with the fastest pace of urbanization were all in the inland areas and were key areas
of economic construction. Second, with the exception of Jilin Province, the regions were also among
the above-mentioned areas with the fastest rate of
growth in their urban population. Though the
growth rate of the urban population of Jilin Province
was not among the fastest, it was relatively fast in
China (the annual growth rate of the urban population of Jilin Province was 3.5% in 1955–80). Third, in
the early 1950s, when urbanization was proceeding
rapidly, urbanization in most of these five provinces
and autonomous regions was of medium or below-
medium level as compared with the other parts of the
country. This showed that in a country with a comparatively low level of urbanization, the speed of
raising the urbanization level in the various regions
might have certain relationships with the level of
urbanization they had already achieved, when other
conditions are the same. This is a question worthy of
further exploration and study.

CHANGES IN THE COMPOSITION OF URBAN POPULATION AND ITS SEX AND AGE COMPOSITION
CHANGES IN THE COMPOSITION OF URBAN POPULATION

As far as the sources are concerned, changes in
China's urban population are attributable to the following three factors: 1) natural change, which is a
constant factor; 2) migration into or out of the cities,
which is an important factor to the changes in urban
population and especially to the changes in the pro-

portion of urban population. In a country like China, where international migration is minimal, such migration might be considered only as moving between the cities and the countryside; 3) a change of urban population resulting from the redemarcation of administrative areas under the jurisdiction of the cities or the redemarcation and redivision of the urban and rural areas. Although this is not a constant factor, it does have a significant effect on the increase or decrease of urban population when such a change takes place frequently or on a large scale. As this change reflects, in essence, the effect of the migration change of population, it is often considered together with migration change in analyzing the factors leading to the changes in the composition of urban population. This method is also followed in this book. In making an analysis of the factors leading to the changes in the composition of urban population in China, consideration is given to both the natural change of urban population and migration change or changes resulting from the redivision of the urban and rural areas.

Owing to the lack of comprehensive data in this respect, only the materials available now are used here to calculate the average annual growth rate and the average annual natural growth rate of the urban population of China in some periods. Then, the residual method is used to calculate the average annual growth rate of the population in these periods resulting from internal migration and from the changes in the redemarcation of administrative areas or redivision of the urban and rural areas, which is called the annual rate of urban population growth from internal migration and reclassification. From this we deduce the proportion of this growth rate in the total growth rate of the population in the cities and towns. This is how the figures in Table 6-8 are worked out. In using these figures, attention must be paid to the following two points: 1) the figures in the table can be regarded only as indicating certain trends, because of limitations in ascertaining the accuracy of the original data; 2) for the same reason, in Table 6-8 only the population of the cities (not including the counties under the jurisdiction of the cities) is calculated, which, of course, is not the same concept as the afore-mentioned total population of the cities and towns. But as the proportion of the population of the cities in the total population of the cities and towns is great (even when the population of the towns has rapidly increased in recent years, the proportion of the city population is still two-thirds or even three-fourths of the total population of the cities and towns), these figures are quite representative.

An analysis of the figures in Table 6-8 shows, first, that in the listed periods the proportion of population change resulting from migration and reclassification in the total change of urban population was at least around half and it was over 80% in most periods. This shows the great effect of this factor in all the periods. The only difference lay in the different direction of this effect in some periods. For example, the negative effect on the urban population in the whole country in 1962–66 brought about by migration (to the countryside) and redemarcation (some cities and areas under the cities were redemarcated as rural areas) was so great that even the natural growth of urban population in this period was far from being able to make up for the depletion. As a result, the population of the cities throughout the country dropped drastically in this period and the average annual rate of increase was negative (−3.7%), a rare phenomenon. The redemarcation of administrative areas and the redivision and classification of the urban and rural areas are here regarded

Table 6-8.   Source of City Growth in China in Selected Periods

PERIOD	ANNUAL GROWTH RATE OF CITY POPULATION (1)	ANNUAL RATE OF NATURAL INCREASE IN CITY POPULATION (2)	ANNUAL RATE OF CITY POPULATION GROWTH FROM INTERNAL MIGRATION AND RECLASSIFICATION (3) = (1) − (2)	PERCENTAGE OF CITY GROWTH FROM INTERNAL MIGRATION AND RECLASSIFICATION (4) = $\frac{(3)}{(1)}$
1955–59 (5 yrs.)	0.14000	0.02754	0.11246	80.3
1962–66 (5 yrs.)	−0.03700	0.02361	−0.06061	63.8
1971–75 (5 yrs.)	0.02500	0.01254	0.01246	49.8
1976–80 (5 yrs.)	0.04100	0.00827	0.03273	79.8
1981–83 (3 yrs.)	0.10400	0.01031	0.09369	90.1

Source: Wei Jinsheng, "The General Trends of China's Urbanization Since the 1950s," *Population and Economics*, No. 6, 1985.

as factors leading to the changes of urban population.

Second, the listed periods (with the exception of the period 1971–75) were periods when there were major changes in the migration of urban population and in the redivision of administrative areas in the cities and countryside in China and, consequently, the role played by the natural growth of the population was comparatively small. With regard to this, one should not draw general conclusions but should make concrete analyses. However, as far as these periods are concerned, the variations of internal migration and reclassification were factors of primary importance leading to changes in the composition of urban population in China. The proportion of such changes is quite great in comparison with the situation in many other countries (see Table 6-9).

As the above-mentioned changes were small in 1971–75, the proportion caused by changes from internal migration and reclassification in the changes of urban population dropped to 49.8%. From this fact and from the data in Tables 6-8 and 6-9, we may draw this conclusion: Of the factors leading to changes in the composition of urban population, internal migration and reclassification are the most active, and they change along with the changes in the social, political, and economic conditions. These factors deserve our attention in the study of the source of changes in the composition of urban population.

THE SEX AND AGE COMPOSITION OF URBAN POPULATION

As mentioned above, the increase of population due to internal migration occupies an important place among the sources of growth of urban population (urban-rural reclassification also reflects in essence the changes of population migration under normal conditions), and migration itself strongly manifests the selectivity of the sex and age of the migrants. As a result, under the long-term influence of frequent migration, the sex and age composition of urban population inevitably undergoes certain changes, differing from the rural population and even the total population.

Table 6-10 contains data on the proportion of people between the ages of 20 and 59 and their sex composition in the total population of the country, the total population in the cities, the total population in the towns, and the total population in the counties, processed and compiled from the third national census in 1982.

Table 6-9. Proportion of Growth of Urban Population Due to Internal Migration and Reclassification in the Total Increase of Urban Population During Intercensal Periods in Selected Countries (%)

COUNTRY	INTERCENSAL	PERCENTAGE
Africa		
Ghana	1960–70	42.8
Morocco	1960–71	37.0
Americas		
Canada	1961–71	35.9
Salvador	1961–71	22.1
Mexico	1960–70	31.7
Panama	1960–70	40.2
Puerto Rico	1960–70	64.2
USA	1950–60	35.4
	1960–70	29.2
Argentina	1947–60	50.8
Brazil	1950–60	49.6
	1960–70	44.9
Chile	1960–70	37.4
Paraguay	1962–72	34.9
Peru	1961–72	41.6
Uruguay	1963–75	7.3
Asia		
Bangladesh	1961–74	55.4
India	1951–61	30.1
	1961–71	32.3
Indonesia	1961–71	35.7
Iraq	1961–71	35.7
Japan	1955–65	64.6
Sri Lanka	1953–63	51.4
Turkey	1960–70	61.9
Europe		
Austria	1961–71	94.0
France	1962–68	55.9
Hungary	1960–70	87.7
Sweden	1960–70	49.5
Soviet Union	1959–70	61.1
Oceania		
Australia	1961–71	20.3

Source: United Nations, *World Population Trends and Policies, 1979, Monitoring Report*, Vol. I.

Among those migrating to the cities, the majority were young people, the middle-aged came next, while children and old people were comparatively few in number. This chapter deals with the situation since the 1950s, and the age limit used in the table is between 20 and 59. This reflects the effect not only of the ongoing migration to the cities but also of such migration over the past 30 years and more. In fact, from the data obtained from the third census, held in 1982, we can clearly see that the difference in the age and sex composition in the above-mentioned four groups of people is basically manifested in the 20–59 age group, and there is no remarkable difference in the other age groups, above or under this group. From this table it can be clearly seen that the propor-

Table 6-10.   Proportion of People Between the Ages of 20 and 59 and Their Sex Composition in the Total Populations of the Country, the Cities, the Towns, and the Counties

	PROPORTION OF PEOPLE BETWEEN THE AGES OF 20 AND 59 (%)			SEX COMPOSITION (FEMALE = 100)
	TOTAL	MALE	FEMALE	
Total population of the country	46.29	24.12	22.17	108.80
Total population in the cities	54.68	28.73	25.95	110.71
Total population in the towns	52.80	29.50	23.30	126.61
Total population in the counties	44.26	22.85	21.41	106.72

Source: "1982 Population Census of China (Results of Computers Tabulation)," China Statistics Publishing House, 1985.

tion of people between the ages of 20 and 59 in the total population of the cities and towns is higher not only than that in the total county population but also in the total population of the country. This is also the case with the sex composition. The proportion of the male population in the cities and towns in this age group is much higher than in the total population of the country and the total county population. This shows that in China, as in many Asian and African countries, the number of men migrating to the cities is greater than that of women. The opposite is the case with Europe and the Americas where a greater number of women migrate to the cities. What merits attention is that the data from China's third national census show that in the 20–59 age group, as well as in all other age groups, the difference in sex composition of the population of the cities and towns is greater than that of the total population of the whole country and the total population of the counties. The concrete figures are as follows: The sex differential of the total population of the cities is 107.61 for men (women being 100), that of the total population of the towns is 115.58, that of the total population of the counties is 104.33, and that of the population of the country, not including the military, is 105.45. The ratio for the total population is 106.27. As the sex composition of the under 20 and above 59 age groups in the population of the cities and towns shows no obvious difference from that of the county population and the total population, we may conclude that the greater number of men in the population of the cities and towns as a whole is basically the result of the greater number of men in the group between the ages of 20 and 59.

Table 6-10 also shows the relatively high proportion of people between 20 and 59 in the population of the cities and towns and the relatively high sex differential of this age group (even in the total population). These phenomena are more conspicuous in the town population than in the city population, an important

factor as this is the higher proportion of nonagricultural population in the town population. For instance, the proportion of nonagricultural population in the population of the towns throughout the country in 1982 was 73.7%, but in the city population it was only 66.9%. The relatively high proportion of the nonagricultural population often indicates the high proportion of migrants. This means that the selectivity of migration as regards sex and age has a greater influence on the town population than on the city population. Moreover, more dependents of the male population in the towns are left in the nearby rural areas than those of the male population in the cities.

CLASSIFICATION OF CITIES ACCORDING TO SIZE OF POPULATION AND THE TREND OF CHANGE

The cities are classified into different groups according to the size of the total city population or the size of the nonagricultural population of the cities. The former method is used here. This is for the purpose of studying and analyzing the distribution and changes of the urban population as well as the size of the cities. The classification of cities according to population may be done by two methods. One method is to stipulate the upper and lower limits of the population of the different city groups. According to this method, no stipulation is laid either for the upper limit of the population of those city groups with the greatest number of population of the lower limit, or for the lower limit of the population of those city groups with the smallest number of population of the upper limit. The second method is that there is only stipulation for the population of the lower limit but no stipulation for the population of the upper limit. When we use the latter method later in this book, we will indicate so by the words "classification without the upper limit." It is obvious that the relations between the city groups classified by these two methods are different. The relations between the different groups classified according to the first method are parallel and do not include each other, while the result of classification according to the second method is that the groups with a smaller population of the lower limit contain all other groups with a higher population of the lower limit.

An analysis of the data in Tables 6-11, 6-12, 6-13, 6-14, and Chart 6-3 gives a general picture of the classification of Chinese cities according to their population during the censuses held in 1953, 1964, and 1982. It also shows the general trend of changes during these three national censuses.

1. A greater number of the total population of the cities and towns in China have been concen-

trated in the cities since the early 1950s, especially in cities with a population of more than 100,000. And the trend is that the proportion of the population of these cities in the total population of the cities and towns continues to increase. During the 1982 national census, people residing in cities with a population of over 100,000 made up 69.7% of the total population of the cities and towns, an increase of 24.7% compared with the 1953 national census. (However, by the end of 1984, due to a great increase in the town population, China's city population was only 59% of the urban population.) People residing in cities with a population of less than 100,000 made up a very low proportion of the total population of the cities and towns in the early 1950s (only 4.9% in the 1953 census). It continued to drop, and by the time of the

Table 6-11.   Number of Cities, City Population, and Its Proportion in the Total Population of the Cities and Towns According to City Classification in the Three National Censuses

CITY CLASSIFICATION ACCORDING TO SIZE OF POPULATION (MILLION)	FIRST CENSUS 1953	SECOND CENSUS 1964	THIRD CENSUS 1982
Over 2 million			
Total population (million)	13.966	25.796	43.760
Number of cities	4	7	13
Proportion in the total population of the cities and towns (%)	16.2	19.8	21.2
1–1.99 million			
Total population (million)	7.053	12.968	31.622
Number of cities	5	9	25
Proportion in the total population of the cities and towns (%)	8.2	9.9	15.3
0.5–0.99 million			
Total population (million)	11.288	25.096	33.214
Number of cities	16	34	47
Proportion in the total population of the cities and towns (%)	13.1	19.2	16.1
0.3–0.49 million			
Total population (million)	3.958	11.961	18.515
Number of cities	10	30	48
Proportion in the total population of the cities and towns (%)	4.6	9.2	8.9
0.1–0.29 million			
Total population (million)	11.953	13.189	16.739
Number of cities	68	69	89
Proportion in the total population of the cities and towns (%)	13.9	10.1	8.1
Below 0.1 million			
Total population (million)	4.267	1.370	1.402
Number of cities	63	19	22
Proportion in the total population of the cities and towns (%)	4.9	1.1	0.68
All the cities			
Sum total of population (million)	52.486	90.380	145.253
Number of cities	166	168	244
Proportion in the total population of the cities and towns (%)	60.9	69.3	70.3

Source: Wei Jinsheng, "The General Trends of China's Urbanization Since the 1950s," *Population and Economics*, No. 6, 1985.

Table 6-12. Number of Cities, City Population, and Its Proportion in the Total Population of the Cities and Towns According to City Classification (Without the Upper Limit) in the Three National Censuses

CITY CLASSIFICATION (WITHOUT THE UPPER LIMIT) ACCORDING TO SIZE OF POPULATION (MILLION)	FIRST CENSUS 1953	SECOND CENSUS 1964	THIRD CENSUS 1982
Over 2 million			
Total population (million)	13.966	25.796	43.760
Number of cities	4	7	13
Proportion in the total population of the cities and towns (%)	16.2	19.8	21.2
Over 1 million			
Total population (million)	21.019	38.764	75.382
Number of cities	9	16	38
Proportion in the total population of the cities and towns (%)	24.4	29.7	36.5
Over 0.5 million			
Total population (million)	32.307	63.860	108.596
Number of cities	25	50	85
Proportion in the total population of the cities and towns (%)	37.5	48.9	52.6
Over 0.3 million			
Total population (million)	36.265	75.821	127.111
Number of cities	35	80	133
Proportion in the total population of the cities and towns (%)	42.1	58.1	61.6
Over 0.1 million			
Total population (million)	48.218	89.010	143.850
Number of cities	103	149	222
Proportion in the total population of the cities and towns (%)	55.9	68.2	69.7
All the cities			
Sum total of population (million)	52.486	90.38	145.253
Number of cities	166	168	244
Proportion in the total population of the cities and towns (%)	60.9	69.3	70.4

Source: Wei Jinsheng, "The General Trends of China's Urbanization Since the 1950s," *Population and Economics*, No. 6, 1985.

Table 6-13. Average Annual Increase Rate of the Population of the City Groups in the Period from the First Census in 1953 to the Third Census in 1982

CITY CLASSIFICATION ACCORDING TO SIZE OF POPULATION (MILLION)	AVERAGE ANNUAL GROWTH RATE OF THE CITY POPULATION FROM 1953 TO 1982 (%)
Over 2	4.0
1–199	5.3
0.5–0.99	3.8
0.3–0.49	5.5
0.1–0.29	1.2
Below 0.1	−3.8
All the cities	3.6

Source: Wei Jinsheng, "The General Trends of China's Urbanization Since the 1950s," *Population and Economics*, No. 6, 1985.

Table 6-14.   Average Annual Increase Rate of the Population of City Groups (Without the Upper Limit) from the First Census in 1953 to the Third Census in 1982

CITY CLASSIFICATION (WITHOUT THE UPPER LIMIT) ACCORDING TO SIZE OF POPULATION (MILLION)	AVERAGE ANNUAL GROWTH RATE OF THE CITY POPULATION BETWEEN 1953 AND 1982 (%)
Over 2	4.0
Over 1	4.5
Over 0.5	4.3
Over 0.3	4.4
Over 0.1	3.8
All the cities	3.6

Source: Wei Jinsheng, "The General Trends of China's Urbanization Since the 1950s," *Population and Economics*, No. 6, 1985.

1982 national census, the proportion had plummeted to 0.68%, and the absolute number was only 1.402 million.

2. Although more than half of the total population of the cities and towns live in cities with a population of over 100,000, their distribution differs conspicuously in cities with varying sizes of population. Twenty-one percent of the population of the cities and towns are concentrated in cities with a population of over 2 million. This was so in all three censuses, and this tendency is continuing. Then came the cities with a population of 0.5 million to 0.99 million and 1 million to 1.99 million. In the former case, the proportion of their population in the total population of all the cities and towns has been comparatively high all the time, and in the 1964 census it was as high as that of cities with a population of more than 2 million. But the proportion began to drop thenceforward. In the latter case, like cities with a population of over 2 million, the proportion of their population in the total population of all the cities and towns showed an increase in all three censuses. As regards cities with a population of 0.3–0.49 million and 0.1–0.29 million, there are altogether 137, but the population in these cities is not so big and the proportion of the population in these two groups of cities in the total population of all the cities and towns has decreased since the 1964 census.

3. Whether the proportion of the population of the various city groups is large or small the total population of all the cities and towns is related to the growth rate of the population of these cities, but the relation is not a simple, synchronous one. Table 6-13 shows that during the period between the first census in 1953 and the third census in 1982, the fastest growth rate of the city population had been achieved by those with a population of 0.3–0.49 million, the average annual rate of increase being as high as 5.5%.

But the proportion of the population of this group in the total population of the cities and towns was not high and, as mentioned before, had tended to decrease since the 1964 census. On the contrary, the growth rate of cities with a population of over 2 million was not remarkable, and their average annual growth rate was only 4%, ranking third among the various city groups. But the proportion of the population of these cities in the total population of the cities and towns had always topped all other city groups.

4. The data obtained in the third national census show that the regional distribution of the population of the various city groups in China is as follows: Of the 244 cities in China, 40% are located in the coastal areas and 60% are in the interior. This is on the whole quite reasonable and is a heartening achievement of the vigorous development of industries in the interior over the years. But, viewing from the regional distribution of the population of various city groups, there are still irrationalities. In 1982, of the 38 cities with a population of more than 1 million in China, 20, or more than half, are located in the coastal areas, and less than half are in the vast inland areas. In the same period, there were 22 small cities with a population of less than 0.1 million. All of them, with the exception of two coastal cities, are located in the inland areas.

CONTROL OF BIG CITIES AND DEVELOPMENT OF SMALL CITIES AND TOWNS

To control the big cities and develop the small cities and towns are the objective requirements of the social and economic development of China and also a basic state policy on city administration and plan-

Chart 6.3.   Changes in the Proportion of the Population of Various City Groups in the Total Population of the Cities and Towns in the Three Censuses

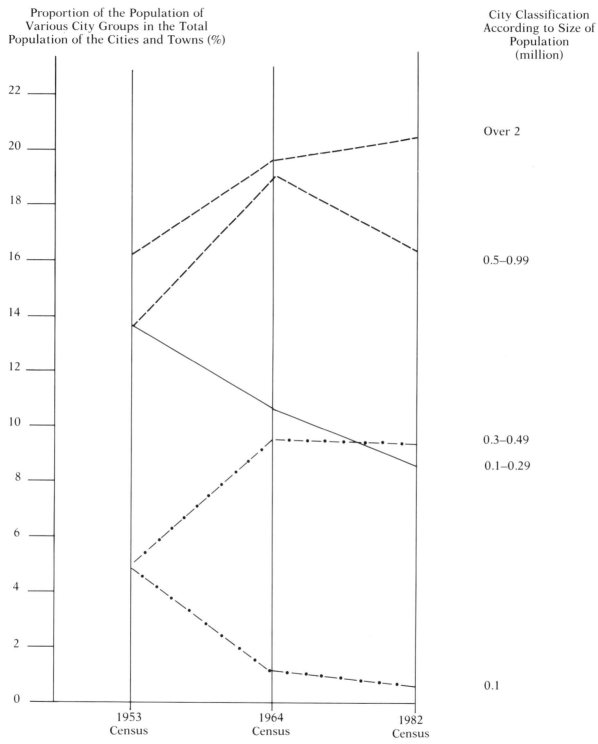

Proportion of the Population of
Various City Groups in the Total
Population of the Cities and Towns (%)

City Classification
According to Size of
Population
(million)

Source: Wei Jinsheng, "The General Trends of China's Urbanization Since the 1950s," *Population and Economics*, No. 6, 1985.

ning. The implementation of this policy has produced positive results on the growth of urban population and the process of urbanization in China.

CONTROL OF BIG CITIES

In China, big cities are those with a population of over 0.5 million, and those with a population of over 1 million are referred to as extremely big cities. According to the statistics of the first census, held in June 1953, the total population of the big cities was 32.307 million, accounting for 37.5% of the total population of the cities and towns of China at that time. The population of the extremely big cities was 21.019 million or 24.4% of the total population of the cities and towns throughout the country. In the years that followed, although restrictive measures were adopted to control the growth of the population of big cities, their population had increased to 93.905 million by the end of 1980, nearly three times the figure in the first census, and its proportion in the total population of all the cities and towns was raised to 49.1%. The population of the extremely big cities had increased to 68.471 million, more than three times the figure in the first census, and its proportion in the total urban population was raised to 35.8%. Taking the situation as a whole, the speedy growth of the population of the big cities, especially the extremely big cities with a population of over one million, has not been effectively controlled, and the excessive expansion of these cities has brought a series of problems to the society, the economy, and the people's livelihood. Of course, the important role of the big cities should not be underestimated, but must be brought into full play so as to help expedite the development of the whole country. But if China's social and economic development were to achieve the best and all-round results, the important role of the big cities should be brought into full play mainly through the technical transformation of existing key enterprises, the development of technique-intensive enterprises, and the raising of labor productivity so as to promote the industrial and agricultural development of the whole country and give support to other regions in the fields of culture, science, technology, and education. Thus, the development of the big cities in China does not require the simultaneous growth of their population. On the contrary, proceeding from the speedy growth of the population in the big cities, the momentum of such growth should be rationally adjusted and effectively controlled. Since the 1980s, the state has adopted a series of measures to reduce the natural growth rate of the population of big cities to the lowest level in the whole country. While carrying out the policy of rational migration to the big cities, strict control has been exercised on the recruitment of workers and staff members from the rural areas and the moving of people from other cities and towns to the big cities by way of transferring their work. While restricting the influx of people to the big cities, various means have been adopted to gradually transfer surplus technical workers, professional, managerial, and other personnel from the big cities to other areas (including the satellite towns of the big cities) where they are needed. In this way, the proportion of urban out-migration has been raised and the net inflow of people to the big cities reduced. Initial results have been achieved through these efforts. From 1980 to 1983, the proportion of the population of extremely big cities with a population of over 2 million in the total population of all the cities and towns was reduced from 21.7% to 18.4%, and the proportion of the extremely big cities with a population of over 1 million did not increase (in 1980 it was 35.8% and in 1983 it was 35.7%). At present, the problem is that the population of big cities with a population of 0.5 – 1 million continues to increase quite rapidly. As a result, the proportion of the population of all the big cities with a population of over 0.5 million in the total population of the cities and towns throughout the country rose from 49.1% in 1980 to 55.2% in 1983. Thus attention is now given to controlling the population of medium-sized and small cities so that not many of them will join the ranks of the big cities.

DEVELOPMENT OF SMALL CITIES AND TOWNS

In China, "small cities and towns" generally refers to those with a population of less than 0.3 million (sometimes 0.2 million). They are large in number and occupy a vast area, and they play an important role in enriching the economy both in the cities and rural areas, in helping a large portion of the agricultural population to become nonagricultural population, and in helping move a certain portion of the population from the big cities to the small cities and towns.

For a long time in the past, the small cities and towns underwent little development. During the first census, held in 1953, the proportion of the population of small cities and towns of the above-mentioned standard was 57.9% of the population of all the cities and towns in China. But the proportion dropped to 38.5% by the end of 1980. Since the 1980s, with the smooth progress of rural reforms, the rural economy has developed steadily. The rapidly developing enterprises of the towns and townships have absorbed an increasing amount of surplus labor force in the agricultural sector and enabled the vast rural areas and towns to revive and flourish. Since 1983 in particular, the state has adopted further measures, which have quickened the pace of development in the rural areas and towns. In this way, the number of organic towns increased from 2,874 in 1980 to 6,211 in 1984, and the proportion of the population of the towns in the total population of all the cities and towns in the country rose from 29.7% in 1980 to 41.1% in 1984, both hitting an all-time high.

However, continued efforts must be made to develop the small cities and towns. As a matter of fact, the proportion of the population of small cities with a population of less than 0.3 million in the total population of the cities and towns decreased from 8.7% to 7.4% in 1980–83, because the population of these small cities did not increase greatly. While these small cities must be actively developed on the basis of the speedy development of a great number of towns, attention should be paid to keeping the present size of their population under control so as to prevent a large number of them from becoming medium-sized or even big cities.

Since 1984 the population of all the towns in China has doubled. Economically, this means a large portion of agricultural population has become nonagricultural population (including those who are registered as engaged in farming but can no longer be regarded as agricultural population as far as their economic activities are concerned). However, the proportion of agricultural population in the population of all the towns in the country increased from 22.5% in 1980 to 61.1% in 1984. This proportion is of course too high. It means that the population of the towns inevitably includes a great portion of agricultural population. This is a question that involves the standards for organic towns and the method of collecting statistics in this field. It is also a question that merits attention in obtaining a correct understanding and appraising the trend of growth of urban population and urbanization in China in recent years.

CHAPTER SEVEN

DISTRIBUTION OF CHINESE POPULATION

A GENERAL SURVEY

China is an ancient country and one of the places of origin of the human species. On this land our ancestors lived and multiplied for hundreds of thousands of years. Throughout the ages, owing to natural, social, economic, and other factors, the Chinese people were mostly concentrated in the southeastern part of the country. Some Chinese scholars indicated before the birth of New China that if a straight line were drawn from Aihui (present-day city of Heihe) in northeast China's Heilongjiang Province to Tengchong in southwest China's Yunnan Province, thereby dividing the country into the southeastern and northwestern parts, then the former, covering an area of about 1.55 million square miles (4 million square kilometers) or 36% of the total territory, was inhabited by 440 million people, or 96% of China's total population at that time, while the northwestern half, which accounted for 64% of the total territory, was inhabited by 18 million people, or only 4% of the nation's population at that time.* This shows that the distribution of China's population was very uneven.

Since the founding of the People's Republic, herculean efforts have been made to boost economic development in the interior and build a number of new industrial areas. This has somewhat improved the distribution of population, but without any fundamental change. The uneven distribution of population remains a major problem in China today. According to the 1983 statistics, of the 29 provinces, municipalities, and autonomous regions on the Chinese mainland, seven provinces, three municipalities, and one autonomous region in the eastern coastal part make up only 13.5% of the nation's total territory but have 41.5% of the population; eight provinces and one autonomous region in the central

parts, which account for 29.8% of the territory, have 35.6% of the population; the remaining six provinces and three autonomous regions in western China make up 56.4% of the territory and have 22.9% of the population. This clearly points up the regional differences in the distribution of China's population (see Table 7-1).

POPULATION DISTRIBUTION ACCORDING TO PRESENT-DAY ADMINISTRATIVE REGIONS

Statistical data at the end of 1983 showed that Sichuan Province had the largest population in China, topping 100.76 million or 9.8% of the total, followed by Shandong and Henan Provinces, each with 75 million people, and Jiangsu and Guangdong Provinces, each with 60 million. Provinces with upward of 50 million people included Hunan, Hebei, and Anhui. The above eight provinces make up less than 20% of China's territory, but in 1983 more than half of China's population lived there. The remaining 21 provinces, municipalities, and autonomous regions, which occupy 82% of China's total territory, had only 48% of the population. The Tibet Autonomous Region had the smallest population, with only 1.93 million people, and the population of Qinghai Province and the Ningxia Hui Autonomous Region was less than 4 million each. (See Table 7-2.)

POPULATION DISTRIBUTION ACCORDING TO NATURAL ENVIRONMENT

Topography and climate are the two most important natural factors that, sometimes singly and sometimes in combination, affect the distribution of population.

The vertical distribution of China's population covers vast areas. For example, some Tibetan herdsmen live on plateaus 14,800 feet (4,800 meters)

---

* Hu Huangong, "Distribution of China's Population," *Geographical Journal*, No. 2, 1935.

Table 7-1.   Distribution of Population in Three Economic Regions in China

REGION	PROVINCES, MUNICIPALITIES, AND AUTONOMOUS REGIONS	PROPORTION OF AREAS (%)	PROPORTION OF POPULATION (%)	POPULATION DENSITY (PERSON/SQ. KM.)
Eastern	Liaoning, Beijing, Tianjin, Shanghai, Hebei, Shandong, Jiangsu, Zhejiang, Fujian, Guang- dong, Guangxi	13.5	41.5	325.1
Central	Heilongjiang, Jilin, Shanxi, Inner Mongolia, Anhui, Jiangxi, Henan, Hubei, Hunan	29.8	35.6	127.3
Western	Sichuan, Yunnan, Guizhou, Tibet, Shaanxi, Gansu, Qinghai, Ningxia, Xinjiang	56.4	22.9	43.4

Source: *Statistics Yearbook of China, 1984*, China Statistics Publishing House.

Table 7-2.   Distribution of China's Population (1983)

REGION	AREA (10,000 SQ. KM.)	PROPORTION OF AREA (%)	POPULATION (10,000)	PROPORTION OF POPULATION (%)	POPULATION DENSITY (PERSON/SQ. KM.)
China	960	100	102,495	100	107
Beijing	1.68	0.2	934	0.9	556
Tianjin	1.13	0.1	789	0.8	697
Hebei	18.77	2.0	5,420	5.3	289
Shanxi	15.63	1.6	2,572	2.5	165
Inner Mongolia	118.30	12.3	1,955	1.9	17
Liaoning	14.57	1.5	3,629	3.6	249
Jilin	18.74	2.0	2,270	2.2	121
Heilongjiang	46.90	4.9	3,306	3.2	70
Shanghai	0.62	0.1	1,194	1.2	1,926
Jiangsu	10.20	1.1	6,135	6.0	598
Zhejiang	10.18	1.1	3,963	3.9	389
Anhui	13.94	1.5	5,056	4.9	363
Fujian	12.12	1.3	2,640	2.6	218
Jiangxi	16.66	1.7	3,384	3.3	203
Shandong	15.33	1.6	7,564	7.4	494
Henan	16.70	1.7	7,591	7.4	455
Hubei	18.74	2.0	4,835	4.7	258
Hunan	21.00	2.2	5,509	5.4	262
Guangdong	21.20	2.2	6,075	6.0	287
Guangxi	23.63	2.5	3,733	3.7	162
Sichuan	56.70	5.9	10,076	9.8	178
Guizhou	17.64	1.8	2,901	2.8	165
Yunnan	39.40	4.1	3,319	3.3	84
Tibet	122.84	12.8	193	0.2	2
Shaanxi	20.56	2.1	2,931	2.9	143
Gansu	45.40	4.7	1,988	2.0	44
Qinghai	72.15	7.5	393	0.4	5
Ningxia	6.64	0.7	398	0.4	59
Xinjiang	160.00	16.7	1,318	1.3	8

Source: *Statistics Yearbook of China, 1984*, China Statistics Publishing House.

above sea level, while people of the Turpan Basin in Xinjiang live in places about 300 feet below sea level. Generally speaking, the land in the western parts of China is higher than in the east, and the higher the land elevation, the sparser the population. The plains are the most densely populated. In China, mountainous areas and plateaus over 3,000 meters above sea level make up about 25% of the territory but are inhabited by less than six million people, or a mere 0.6% of the total population. Highlands with an elevation of 500–3,000 meters account for 50% of the territory but are inhabited by less than 20% of the population. Plains and hilly areas less than 500 meters above sea level are mostly located in the eastern parts of China; they cover 25% of the territory but are inhabited by over 80% of the population.

Climatically, the eastern parts of China are blessed with favorable conditions. First and foremost, they have a temperate climate, and the accumulated temperature of 10°C and above in a year is generally between 3,500°C and 8,000°C, which is suitable for growing various kinds of crops. In the western parts of China, however, the accumulated temperature is only between 1,000°C and 3,500°C annually, which hampers the growth of certain crops. Second, the eastern parts have abundant rainfall, with an annual precipitation of 400–2,000 millimeters (mm). The rainfall is concentrated in the warm seasons, a boon to agricultural production. In contrast to this, the annual rainfall in most of the western parts is only 100–400 mm, and precipitation in some places is even less than 50 mm a year. Because of these reasons, the overwhelming majority of the Chinese people live in the eastern parts where the land elevation is not high and the climate is favorable.

Chart 7-1. Distribution of China's Population

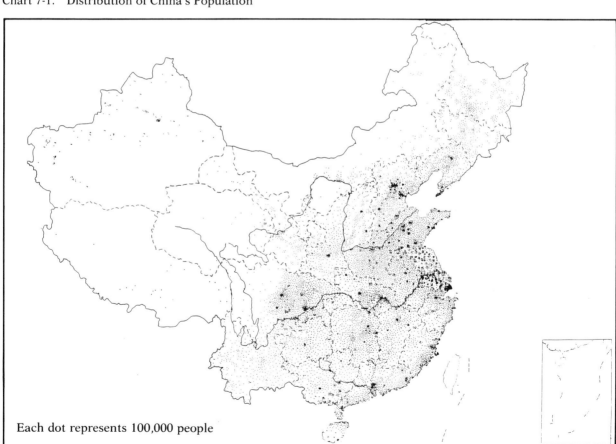

Each dot represents 100,000 people

The inset in the lower righthand corner represents the South China Sea Islands.

Source: Data from *Almanac of China's Economy '83*, Business Management Publishing House, 1984.

CHANGES IN THE DISTRIBUTION OF POPULATION

The concentration of China's population in the eastern coastal areas is the result of historical, natural, economic, and other factors throughout the centuries. It is particularly connected with the economic development of these areas, and is an indication of the uneven distribution of the productive forces in China. In terms of per capita mileage of highways, railways, and water transportation, output value of industry and agriculture, as well as personal income, the eastern parts outstrip the western parts and therefore attract more people to live there.

To change the concentration of the population in the coastal areas, the Chinese government adopted a series of measures after the founding of New China. In developing the national economy, the government has paid due attention to handling the relationships between the coastal areas and the interior, between the Han and the minority nationalities, and between large and medium-sized and small enterprises. At the same time it has allocated funds, materials, and manpower to assist in the construction of the hinterland and in opening up the border regions and to promote economic development in the western and northern parts of China. During the First Five-Year Plan period (1953–57), for example, the state stipulated that above-norm large enterprises should be built in the interior; large numbers of cadres, technical personnel, and their families working in the coastal cities were transferred to settle in the hinterland; and demobilized soldiers and urban educated youths were mobilized to set up state farms or stock-breeding centers in northeast and northwest China as well as in Inner Mongolia. These measures have not only given a boost to economic development in these regions but also improved the distribution of population. Meanwhile, the peasants in some places in east China have, of their own accord, migrated to northeast China, Inner Mongolia,

and northwest China as their ancestors had done before them, where most of them have settled down with the help of their relatives. In addition to this, the government has relaxed its policy on birth control in areas where the minority peoples live in compact communities, which is why the natural population growth rate in the western parts is generally higher than in east China.

All these measures have brought about changes in the distribution of population in various parts of China. The population growth rate in the populous eastern parts of China has dropped while that in the sparsely populated western parts has risen gradually (see Table 7-3).

Judging by the absolute number of increase in the population of the various provinces, municipalities, and autonomous regions, the increase in the 1953–82 period was the largest in Sichuan and Henan, topping 30 million, while in Guangdong, Shandong, Jiangsu, Heilongjiang, Hubei, and Hunan Provinces, the increase was over 20 million each. These large increases occurred because these provinces already had a large population base and their rapid economic construction had drawn an influx of people from the other provinces. The rate of population growth during the 1953–82 period was the smallest in Beijing, Tianjin, Shanghai, Qinghai, Ningxia, and Tibet; during those three decades, each of them except Tibet witnessed an increase of 2–5 million people. As the Tibet Autonomous Region had the smallest population base, the increase was only 720,000. As for the three municipalities of Beijing, Tianjin, and Shanghai, measures taken to check population growth and the work done to promote family planning played an important role in keeping down the population growth.

The relative increase in population also differed in various localities. Taking the data of the 1953 census as 100, then by the time of the 1982 census the population of Heilongjiang, Xinjiang, Ningxia,

Table 7-3.   Regional Changes in the Proportion of Population During China's Three Censuses

REGION	FIRST CENSUS 1953 (%)	SECOND CENSUS 1964 (%)	THIRD CENSUS 1982 (%)
National total	100	100	100
North China	11.0	11.8	11.1
Northeast China	7.4	8.9	8.8
East China	30.5	29.4	28.8
Central-South China	26.7	26.2	26.5
Southwest China	16.8	15.1	15.8
Northwest China	6.0	6.4	6.7
Taiwan, Hong Kong, and Macao	1.6	2.2	2.3

Source: Statistical data obtained during the three censuses.

Chart 7-2. Population Growth in the Various Provinces, Municipalities, and Autonomous Regions

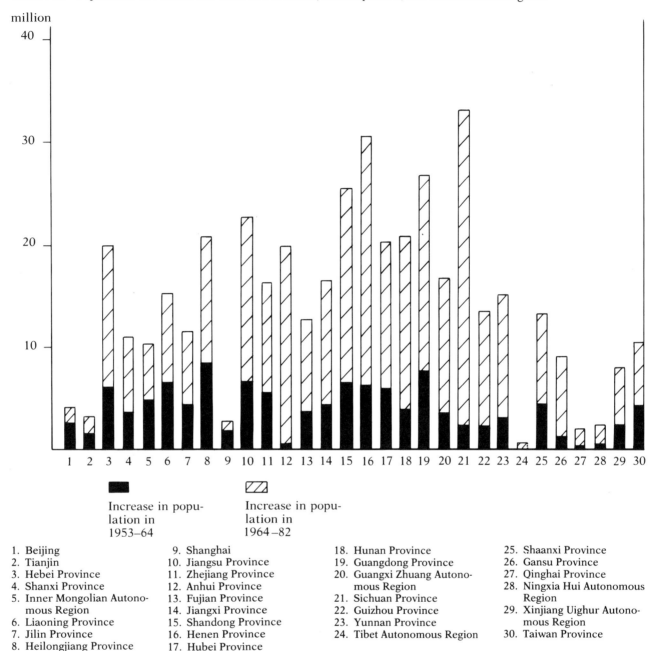

Increase in popu-
lation in
1953–64

Increase in popu-
lation in
1964–82

1. Beijing
2. Tianjin
3. Hebei Province
4. Shanxi Province
5. Inner Mongolian Autonomous Region
6. Liaoning Province
7. Jilin Province
8. Heilongjiang Province

9. Shanghai
10. Jiangsu Province
11. Zhejiang Province
12. Anhui Province
13. Fujian Province
14. Jiangxi Province
15. Shandong Province
16. Henan Province
17. Hubei Province

18. Hunan Province
19. Guangdong Province
20. Guangxi Zhuang Autono-
    mous Region
21. Sichuan Province
22. Guizhou Province
23. Yunnan Province
24. Tibet Autonomous Region

25. Shaanxi Province
26. Gansu Province
27. Qinghai Province
28. Ningxia Hui Autonomous
    Region
29. Xinjiang Uighur Autono-
    mous Region
30. Taiwan Province

Source: Data from 1953, 1964, and 1982 Population Censuses of China.

Qinghai, and Inner Mongolia had increased by 200%.
This was ample proof that the enormous efforts made
by the government in stepping up the construction of
the border areas and in changing the uneven distribution of the population had yielded tangible results.
Shanghai had the smallest increase during this period (130.8%). The population growth rate in the remaining 23 provinces, municipalities, and autonomous regions was between 150 and 200%.

DISTRIBUTION OF POPULATION DENSITY

According to the 1983 statistics, the average density
of China's population was 107 people per square
kilometer, almost three times the world's average.
Another characteristic of the population density in
China was the extreme unevenness in its distribution.

TENDENCY OF DISTRIBUTION OF POPULATION DENSITY

The tendency of distribution of the population density is basically identical with the distribution of the Chinese population, that is, the population density decreases gradually from southeast China to northwest China, or in other words, it increases gradually from the highlands to the plains. On the Chinese mainland, there are four grades of population density, with Shanghai, Jiangsu, Tianjin, and Beijing as the core areas. The population density in the core areas is over 500 people per square kilometer (the highest density being 1,926 people per square kilometer in Shanghai). Close to the four core areas are Shandong, Henan, Zhejiang, Hubei, Anhui, Guangdong, Hunan, Hebei, Liaoning, Fujian, and Jiangxi, which are the next most densely populated areas in China, with a density of 200–500 persons per square kilometer. The second-grade areas include Sichuan, Shanxi, Guangxi, Guizhou, Shaanxi, and Jilin, where the population density is 100–200 persons per square kilometer. The third-grade areas include Yunnan, Heilongjiang, Ningxia, Gansu, and Inner Mongolia, where the population density is 10–100 persons per square kilometer; and the fourth-grade areas include Tibet, Qinghai, and Xinjiang, which together cover an area of (3.55 million square kilometers) but have a population of only 19.04 million, the population density averaging no more than five persons per square kilometer (1.6 persons per square kilometer in Tibet).

Owing to the differences in the natural, economic, and other conditions, population density varies greatly from place to place. In Tibet, Xinjiang, and Qinghai, the population density as a whole is the lowest, but the density in the places where the people actually live is by no means low. In Qinghai, for example, about 90% of its population of 4 million live in the agricultural area in the eastern part, which accounts for only 5% of the total area of the province, and the population density is over 100 persons per square kilometer. Xinjiang has a population of more than 13 million, and almost all of them live in an oasis with an area of (100,000 square kilometers), where the population density is 100–200 persons per square kilometer. And the people of the Tibet Autonomous Region live mainly in the river valleys and at the foot of the mountains, whle the plateau, which covers an area of (430,000 square kilometers), is actually uninhabited. Such differences are also found in provinces and autonomous regions with a fairly high population density. For example, 80% of Sichuan's population of 100 million live on the Chengdu Plain and along the banks of the Changjiang (Yangtze) and Jialin Rivers of the Sichuan Basin. In this province, the Xindu County has the highest density of population, reaching over 1,000 people per square kilometer; counties with a population density of 800 people per square kilometer each include Guanghan, Pixian, Longchang, and Wenjiang, while the Shiqu, Seda, and Aba Counties have the lowest population density, averaging three persons per square kilometer. In Inner Mongolia, the banners and counties in the northern and western parts have an average population density of only one person per square kilometer, while the agricultural areas in the Hetao region in the southern parts have an average population density of more than 100 persons per square kilometer. The population density in Jiangsu Province is comparatively evenly distributed, yet the population density of some counties in southern Jiangsu is double that of counties in northern Jiangsu.

DENSELY POPULATED AREAS

Areas with the highest population density in China include:

• The Changjiang (Yangtze) Delta. This includes the Taihu Lake district, the Changjiang Delta, and the Qiantang Delta, which together form what is known as the Golden Triangle in China. In addition to several large cities such as Shanghai, Nanjing, and Hangzhou, the region is dotted with medium-sized and small cities and towns, and is economically developed and densely populated. The average population density in this region is 750 persons per square kilometer, and in some counties such as Taixing, Jingjiang, and Haimen the average is about 1,000 persons per square kilometer. The Chuansha County and Shanghai County, all under the jurisdiction of the Shanghai municipality, have a population density of 1,400 persons per square kilometer and may be classified as one of the most densely populated regions in the world.

• The Huang-Huai-Hai Plain. Formed by silt from the Huanghe (Yellow), Huai, and Haihe rivers, the low-lying plain is vast, covering an area of more than 500,000 square kilometers. It is inhabited by one-fourth of the nation's population, with a density of more than 500 persons per square kilometer. The population density in areas along the Beijing-Hankou railway line and some in suburban counties of Beijing and Tianjin is as high as 700 people per

Chart 7-3.   Distribution of Population Density in China

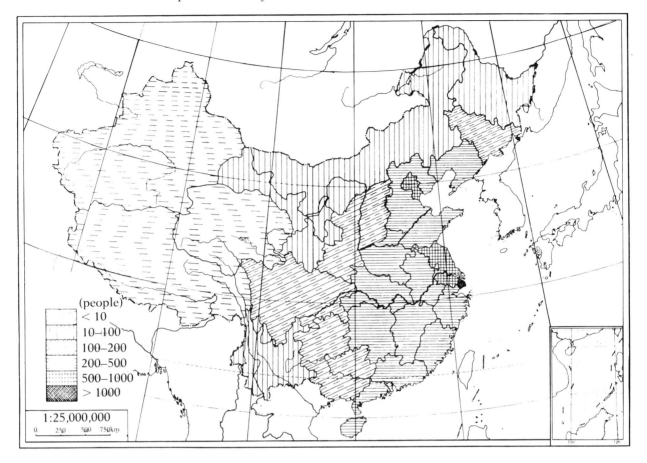

The inset in the lower righthand corner represents the South China Sea Islands.

Source: Based on Data from *Almanac of China's Economy '83*, Business Management Publishing House, 1984.

square kilometer, thus making the plain the largest densely populated area in China.

• The Liaohe Plain. Located in the central and southern parts of Liaoning Province in northeast China, it is an alluvial plain enriched by the soil washed down by the Liaohe River. Several large industrial cities are located here including Shenyang, Anshan, Fushun, and Benxi, making it one of the important industrial areas in China. Developed in economy and with good transport facilities, the plain has an average population density of 400 persons per square kilometer (over 500 people per square kilometer in some counties). It is one of the most densely populated areas in northeast China.

• The Zhujiang (Pearl River) Delta. This includes the land at the estuary of the Zhujiang River and the Hanjiang River in the Chaozhou prefecture in the coastal province of Guangdong. The average popula-

tion density here is 600 persons per square kilometer, the highest being over 1,700 persons per square kilometer in Chenghai County. Next to it are the Chaoyang, Jieyang, and Shunde Counties, where the population density is over 1,000 persons per square kilometer. All the other counties have a population density of over 500 persons per square kilometer. This makes it the most densely populated area in south China.

• The Guanzhong Plain. Extending for more than 300 kilometers from Tongguan in the east to Baoji in the west, this area was formed by the silt carried down by the Huanghe River and its tributaries. The land here is level and is rich in water resources. Known in ancient China as Qinchuan, the plain covers an area of over 30,000 square kilometers and has a population of 14 million, averaging over 470 persons per square kilometer. The density in some counties is over 600 persons per square kilometer. It was an economic, political, and cultural center of China in ancient times.

• The Sichuan Basin. The basin extends from Yibin in the south to Guangyuan in the north and from Wanxian in the east to the Chengdu Plain in the west. It covers a total area of about 150,000 square kilometers and is inhabited by over 80 million people. The population density is 530 persons per square kilometer (over 1,000 persons per square kilometer in some counties). Rich in natural resources and populous, it has been described as a "land of abundance" throughout the ages.

• The Middle-Lower Changjiang Plain and the Poyang-Dongting Area. These embrace the plain on the middle reaches of the Changjiang River (from Yichang to Wuhu) and the plain around the Poyang and Dongting Lakes. Known as a "land of fish and rice," this region is fairly densely populated, the average density being 350–400 persons per square kilometer (over 500 per square kilometer in some counties). When the Three Gorges Hydropower Station is completed in the future, the local economy will be further developed and the population and population density will increase too.

CHANGES IN THE DISTRIBUTION OF POPULATION DENSITY

Although the population density in various parts of China shows the general tendency of increase, the range of growth varies because of the different conditions in different places. Judging by the varied growth rate of population density in the coastal areas and in the interior, it can be seen that the population density of the 11 provinces, municipalities, and autonomous regions in the coastal areas rose from 232.7 persons per square kilometer in 1964 to 320.6 persons per square kilometer in 1982, an increase of 38%, while that of the 18 provinces and autonomous regions in the interior increased from 47.3 persons per square kilometer in 1964 to 71.4 persons per square kilometer in 1982, an increase of 51%. This shows that the population density in the interior areas had increased at a higher rate than in the coastal areas. If the population density in 1953 is taken as 100, the rate of increase in northeast China and northwest China by 1982 was the largest, reaching 109%; in southwest China and east China the increase was the smallest, reaching only 64–65%. Taking the 29 provinces, municipalities, and autonomous regions on the Chinese mainland as a whole,

then in 1982 Heilongjiang, Inner Mongolia, Xinjiang, Ningxia, and Qinghai registered a 150% increase over 1953. During the same period, Shanghai had the smallest increase rate in population density (only 31%), and the increase in the fairly populous provinces of Hebei, Jiangsu, Shandong, Hubei, and Sichuan was only 50%. This shows that there has been some improvement in the distribution of population density in China (see Table 7-4).

DISTRIBUTION OF POPULATION IN URBAN AND RURAL AREAS

There is no standard way of calculating urban and rural population among the different countries in the world today. In China the criteria for the demarcation of cities and towns are based on the decisions made by the State Council on three occasions. In 1955, the State Council stipulated the following conditions for setting up cities and towns:

a. Site of the people's council at or above the city or county (banner) level.

b. A place where permanent residents number more than 2,000, and 50% of them are nonagricultural population; or the site of industrial and mining enterprises, communication centers, schools, and scientific research organizations, where the permanent residents number over 1,000, of which 75% are nonagricultural population.

c. A health resort where the number of people who go for convalescence and rest every year exceeds half of the local permanent residents.

In 1963 the State Council made the following amendments:

a. When necessary, a town may be established in a place where industry and commerce or handicraft workshops are fairly concentrated and the population is over 3,000, of which over 70% are nonagricultural population, or the population is between 2,500 and 3,000, of which over 85% are nonagricultural population.

b. When necessary, a town may be established in a national minority area where industry and commerce and handicraft workshops are concentrated, though the population is less than 3,000 or the nonagricultural population is less than 70%; a town that has been set up but does not conform to these conditions should be annulled.

In 1984, the State Council issued a circular that modified the conditions for setting up towns:

Table 7-4. Changes in Population Density in the Various Provinces, Municipalities, and Autonomous Regions

REGION	POPULATION DENSITY (PERSON/SQ. KM.)			WITH POPULATION DENSITY IN 1953 AS 100	
	1953	1964	1982	1964	1982
National total	62	74	107	119	173
Beijing	278	425	549	163	201
Tianjin	405	553	687	137	170
Hebei	178	210	282	118	154
Shanxi	92	116	162	126	176
Inner Mongolia	6	10	16	167	267
Liaoning	141	185	245	131	174
Jilin	60	84	120	140	200
Heilongjiang	25	43	69	172	276
Shanghai	1,462	1,745	1,913	119	131
Jiangsu	371	434	590	117	159
Zhejiang	225	278	382	124	170
Anhui	220	224	356	102	162
Fujian	108	138	213	128	197
Jiangxi	101	126	199	125	197
Shandong	321	363	486	113	151
Henan	264	301	446	114	169
Hubei	149	180	255	121	151
Hunan	157	177	257	113	164
Guangdong	155	191	280	123	181
Guangxi	85	101	158	119	186
Sichuan	116	120	176	104	152
Guizhou	85	97	162	114	191
Yunnan	44	52	83	118	189
Tibet	1	1	1.6	100	160
Shaanxi	77	101	141	131	183
Gansu	25	28	43	112	172
Qinghai	2	3	5	150	250
Ningxia	23	32	59	139	257
Xinjiang	3	5	8	167	267
Taiwan	211	340	508	161	241
Macao, Hong Kong	2,000	3,000	5,379	150	269

Source: *Statistics Yearbook of China, 1983*, China Statistics Publishing House.

a. The site of local government organizations at the county level.

b. A township with a population of less than 20,000, the site of the township government with a nonagricultural population of more than 2,000; or a township with a population of more than 20,000, the site of the township government with a nonagricultural population that is over 10% of the total township population.

c. In a national minority area, a sparsely populated border area, mountainous area, and small industrial and mining area, small harbor district, scenic and tourist area, or border port, although the nonagricultural population is less than 2,000, a town may be set up when necessary.

d. A township may be changed into a town where conditions are ripe and the system of villages under the jurisdiction of the town concerned should be set up.

As the standards stipulated in the decisions made by the State Council on three occasions were not completely identical, they directly affected the statistical data on the population of the cities and towns. During China's third census, in 1982, the population of the cities and their suburban areas (not including the counties under the city jurisdiction) and the population of the towns were reckoned as the population of the cities and towns and, with this as the standard way of calculation, revisions of the population of the cities and towns were made. After the revision, the proportion of city and town population in the country's total population was 17.5% in 1969, 19.0% in 1979, 20.8% in 1982, 23.5% in 1983, and the proportion jumped to 31.6 and 36.3% in 1984 and 1985, respectively. This obviously was due to the modifications made with regard to the demarcation of city suburban areas and the establishment of towns. As a result, the total population of the cities and towns included a large number of people in the rural areas.

DISTRIBUTION OF URBAN AND RURAL POPULATION

Since the founding of New China, the population of the cities and towns has increased, but the rural population is still like an ocean encircling the cities and towns all over the country. With the exception of Beijing, Tianjin, and Shanghai—the three municipalities directly under the jurisdiction of the central government—the rural population accounts for the vast majority in all the provinces and autonomous regions. The 1983 statistics showed that the rural population totalled 783.69 million, or 76.5% of China's total population. As for the distribution of the rural population in the various provinces and autonomous regions, Sichuan Province topped the list with 84.81 million, followed by Henan and Shandong, with 64.16 million and 53.49 million, respectively. Hebei, Jiangsu, Anhui, Hunan, and Guangdong Provinces each had over 40 million, and the rural populations of the other provinces and autonomous regions were 20–30 million.

A major feature of the distribution of the city and town population in China is that the population is mainly concentrated in Beijing, Tianjin, and Shanghai, the northeast and the southeast coastal regions. According to the statistics at the end of 1983, for example, the total population of the three municipalities of Beijing, Tianjin, and Shanghai and their suburban areas was 23.53 million, or 9.8% of the total population of the nation's cities and towns. Next came the three northeastern provinces—Liaoning, Jilin, and Heilongjiang—with a total city and town population of 38.42 million, or 15.9% of the nation's total city and town population. These three provinces ranked first as far as urbanization was concerned. The total city and town population in the 11 provinces along the southeastern coast was 109.65 million or 45.5% of that of the nation's total city and town population. This was a region where such population was fairly concentrated. In comparison, the proportion of city and town population in Hebei and

Henan and in provinces in southwest China was quite small. These differences were closely connected with their industrial foundation and their original population.

Table 7-5 shows the distribution of China's urban and rural population at the end of 1983. However, it should be pointed out that the total city and town population listed in the table included the rural population in the suburban areas of the cities and within the town limits. According to statistics, in 1983 the nonagricultural population in the cities and towns accounted for 62% of the total city and town population, while the agricultural population made up 38%. Municipalities, provinces, and autonomous regions having the highest proportion of nonagricultural population included Beijing (84.9%), Tianjin (76.4%), Shanghai (98.3%), Inner Mongolia (91.1%), Liaoning (81.8%), Jilin (79.2%), Heilongjiang (76.6%), Qinghai (85.7%), and Tibet (84.0%). The following four provinces had the smallest nonagricultural population—Shandong (29.7%), Guizhou (47.9%), Zhejiang (48.5%), and Hubei (49.5%). In the other provinces and autonomous regions, the proportion of nonagricultural population in the cities and towns was around 50%. As a portion of the agricultural population are no longer engaged in farm production, it is therefore a very complicated problem to accurately and reasonably determine the distribution of China's urban and rural population.

In 1983, there were in China 271 cities with a total population of 174.71 million, constituting 72.4% of China's total city and town population. The distribution of China's city population was more or less the same as that of the population of China as a whole, that is, the people were mostly concentrated in the southeastern half of the country. Fifteen of the 20 metropolitan cities with a population of over one million each are in the eastern part. Most of the 28 large cities with a population of half a million to one million each are also in the southeastern half of the country. The distribution of medium-sized and small cities is comparatively even. There are 2,786 towns distributed all over China, and their total population accounted for 27.6% of the total city and town population in China. Of the town population, 72% were nonagricultural population, while agricultural population constituted the remaining 28%. Since 1983, the number of towns has increased rapidly, reaching 7,511 in 1985, with a total population of 166.33 million, but the proportion of nonagricultural population has dropped to 34.4%, the remaining 65.6% being agricultural population.

Table 7-5. Distribution of China's Urban and Rural Population (Year-End Figures, 1983)

REGION	TOTAL POPULATION (10,000)	TOTAL CITY AND TOWN POPULATION (10,000)	PERCENT URBAN	NON-AGRICULTURAL POPULATION IN CITIES AND TOWNS (10,000)	URBAN NON-AGRICULTURAL POPULATION, PERCENT OF TOTAL	TOTAL RURAL POPULATION (10,000)	RURAL PROPORTION OF TOTAL (%)	DENSITY OF CITY AND TOWN POPULATION (PERSON/SQ. KM.)
National total	102,459	24,126	23.5	14,967	14.6	78,369	76.5	21.6
Beijing	934	617	66.1	524	56.1	317	33.9	354.9
Tianjin	789	542	67.9	414	52.5	247	32.1	471.1
Hebei	5,420	844	15.6	528	9.7	4,576	84.4	39.4
Shanxi	2,572	712	27.7	381	14.8	1,860	72.3	34.7
Inner Mongolia	1,955	570	29.2	519	26.6	1,385	70.8	4.8
Liaoning	3,629	1,546	42.6	1,265	34.9	2,083	57.4	103.6
Jilin	2,270	818	38.7	695	30.6	1,392	61.3	47.7
Heilongjiang	3,306	1,418	42.9	1,086	32.8	1,888	57.1	27.8
Shanghai	1,194	711	59.6	699	58.5	483	40.4	1,132.6
Jiangsu	6,135	1,229	20.0	793	12.9	4,906	80.0	92.9
Zhejiang	3,963	907	22.9	440	11.1	3,056	77.1	98.2
Anhui	5,056	837	16.6	505	10.0	4,219	83.4	51.7
Fujian	2,640	598	22.7	330	12.5	2,042	77.3	45.2
Jiangxi	3,384	709	21.0	421	12.4	2,675	79.0	38.6
Shandong	7,564	2,215	29.2	658	8.7	5,349	70.8	93.9
Henan	7,591	1,175	15.5	639	8.4	6,416	84.5	61.4
Hubei	4,835	1,395	28.9	691	14.3	3,440	71.1	45.3
Hunan	5,509	875	15.9	559	10.2	4,634	84.1	39.0
Guangdong	6,075	1,300	21.4	827	13.6	4,775	78.6	52.7
Guangxi	3,733	456	12.2	353	9.5	3,277	87.8	21.3
Sichuan	10,076	1,595	15.8	984	9.8	8,481	84.2	25.0
Guizhou	2,901	551	19.0	264	9.1	2,350	81.0	30.7
Yunnan	3,319	447	13.5	289	8.7	2,872	86.5	10.4
Tibet	193	19	9.9	16	8.3	174	90.1	0.2
Shaanxi	2,931	577	19.7	398	13.6	2,354	80.3	26.6
Gansu	1,988	357	18.0	236	11.9	1,631	82.0	6.9
Qinghai	393	77	19.6	66	16.8	316	80.4	1.1
Ningxia	398	109	27.4	65	16.3	289	72.6	13.3
Xinjiang	1,318	436	33.1	316	24.0	882	66.9	2.3

Source: *Statistics Yearbook of China, 1984*, China Statistics Publishing House.

CHANGES IN DISTRIBUTION OF URBAN AND
RURAL POPULATION

In the years since the founding of New China, the
urban population has increased at a much faster
pace than the rural population. Beginning in 1983
the rural population has been declining. During the
1949–1983 period, the total city and town population increased from 57.65 million to 241.26 million,
or a 320% increase. The proportion of city and town
population in the nation's total population also increased from 10.6% to 23.5%. In the same period, the
rural population rose from 484.02 million to 783.69
million, or a mere 60% increase. The proportion of
rural population in the nation's total population
dropped from 89.4% to 75.5% (see Table 7-6). Since

1983, the tendency of city and town population to
increase has been even more evident than before.

The change in the distribution of city and town
population is also quite evident (see Table 7-7). According to the data collected during China's three
censuses, the increases of city and town population
in most of the provinces and autonomous regions
were around 200%. In some cases, the increase was
more than 300%, as in Inner Mongolia, Guizhou,
Qinghai, and Ningxia. And in Xinjiang the increase
was over 400%. This showed that the speed of increase of city and town population in some border
regions was faster than in the interior. This was partly
due to the attention paid by the state to the economic
construction of the border regions, resulting in the
emergence of a number of new cities and towns

Table 7-6. Changes in China's Urban and Rural Population Since 1949

YEAR	CHINA'S TOTAL POPULATION (10,000)	TOTAL CITY AND TOWN POPULATION (10,000)	PROPORTION IN NATION'S TOTAL POPULATION (%)	TOTAL RURAL POPULATION (10,000)	PROPORTION IN NATION'S TOTAL POPULATION (%)
1949	54,167	5,765	10.6	48,402	89.4
1950	55,169	6,169	11.2	49,027	88.8
1951	56,300	6,632	11.2	49,668	88.8
1952	57,482	7,163	12.5	50.319	87.5
1953	58,796	7,826	13.3	50,970	86.7
1954	60,266	8,249	13.7	52,017	86.3
1955	61,465	8,285	13.5	53,180	86.5
1956	62,828	9,185	14.6	53,643	85.4
1957	64,653	9,949	15.4	54,704	84.6
1958	65,994	10,721	16.3	55,273	83.7
1959	67,207	12,371	18.4	54,836	81.6
1960	66,207	13,073	19.8	53,134	80.2
1961	65,859	12,767	19.3	53,152	80.7
1962	67,295	11,659	17.3	55,636	82.7
1963	69,127	11,646	16.9	57,526	83.1
1964	70,499	12,950	18.4	57,549	81.6
1965	72,538	13,045	18.0	59,493	82.0
1966	74,542	13,313	17.9	61,229	82.1
1967	76,368	13,548	17.7	62,802	82.3
1968	78,534	13,838	17.6	64,691	82.4
1969	80,671	14,117	17.5	66,554	82.5
1970	82,999	14,424	17.4	58,568	82.6
1971	85,229	14,711	17.3	70,518	82.7
1972	87,117	14,935	17.1	72,242	82.9
1973	89,211	15,345	17.2	73,866	82.8
1974	90,859	15,595	17.2	75,264	82.8
1975	92,420	16,030	17.3	76,390	82.7
1976	93,717	16,341	17.4	77,376	82.6
1977	94,974	16,669	17.6	78,305	82.4
1978	96,259	17,245	17.9	79,014	82.1
1979	97,542	18,495	19.0	79,047	81.0
1980	98,705	19,140	19.4	79,505	80.6
1981	100,072	20.171	20.2	79,901	79.8
1982	101,541	21,154	20.8	80,387	79.2
1983	102,495	24,126	23.5	78,369	75.5

Source: *Statistics Yearbook of China, 1984*, China Statistics Publishing House.

Table 7-7.   Changes in the City and Town Population in China's Three Censuses

REGION	PROPORTION OF CITY AND TOWN POPULATION			RATE OF INCREASE OF CITY AND TOWN POPULATION, 1953–82 (%)
	1953	1964	1982	
National total	13.2	18.4	20.5	168
Beijing	49.3	62.0	64.7	141
Tianjin	62.4	55.2	68.7	86
Hebei	11.7	11.3	13.7	88
Shanxi	11.5	17.6	21.0	227
Inner Mongolia	15.3	24.3	28.9	389
Liaoning	29.1	40.1	42.4	152
Jilin	22.9	35.3	39.6	245
Heilongjing	30.5	39.9	40.5	260
Shanghai	75.5	64.0	59.0	2
Jiangsu	15.1	14.8	15.8	66
Zhejiang	13.0	15.9	25.7	220
Anhui	8.7	13.7	14.3	173
Fujian	18.5	20.4	21.2	125
Jiangxi	10.3	13.0	19.4	269
Shandong	8.1	12.9	19.1	259
Henan	8.3	11.6	14.5	178
Hubei	8.6	14.3	17.3	255
Hunan	8.8	11.4	14.4	180
Guangdong	17.6	17.8	18.7	92
Guangxi	8.5	10.2	11.8	171
Sichuan	9.1	13.9	14.3	138
Guizhou	7.3	11.9	19.7	393
Yunnan	9.0	11.5	12.9	160
Tibet	12.7	9.4	12.5	46
Shaanxi	11.4	15.4	19.0	201
Gansu	11.7	14.1	15.3	136
Qinghai	11.5	16.6	20.5	309
Ningxia	14.4	18.5	22.5	303
Xingjiang	14.9	17.0	28.5	414

Source: Based on the data from China's third census, in 1982.

there. Another reason was that the original population in these border provinces and autonomous regions was small, so that the increase in the proportion of city and town population was comparatively conspicuous. In some cities and provinces, the increase was less than 100%, such as Tianjin, Shanghai, Jiangsu, Guangdong, and Tibet. In Shanghai the increase was particularly small, because of its strict control over population growth and because of its aid in manpower to the economic construction of other cities and provinces.

FACTORS AFFECTING THE DISTRIBUTION OF POPULATION
NATURAL FACTORS

Natural environment is the material base for humanity's existence and the condition for the steady development of its productive forces. The influence of

natural factors on the distribution of population is not only important but many-sided. Following is an analysis of the influence of topography, climate, and resources on the distribution of population.

Influence of Topography. The elevation, undulation, and gradient of the land have a direct bearing on agricultural production and communications, and they exert a relatively big influence on the distribution of population. First of all, altitude restricts, to a certain extent, the scope of distribution of the population. This is because, with the altitude rising every 100 meters, the average temperature drops 0.5°C to 0.6°C, and the accumulated temperature at or above 10°C drops by 150°C to 200°C and lasts three to six days shorter. So at high altitudes not only do human beings have difficulty in adapting themselves to the environment but there are also many factors unfavorable for crops to grow. Hence the higher the altitude, the sparser the population. Second, the undulation of the land, or the relative difference in altitude, also affects the distribution of population, for it determines how much land can be cultivated, whether it is suitable for building water conservancy projects and for mechanizing farm work, and whether it is convenient to transportation. The people live mostly on the plains where the farmland extends for miles around, the conditions for building water conservancy projects and for the mechanization of agriculture are favorable, and convenient transportation facilities are easily available. On the other hand, the population is sparse in hilly and mountainous areas, for there the amount of arable land is limited and the supply of water and transportation facilities are inadequate. Third, the gradient of the land also affects the distribution of population, for it has a direct bearing on soil erosion, irrigation and drainage, and the fertility of the farmland. China's loess plateau in the northwest, for instance, is sparsely populated because of its steep gradient, serious soil erosion, and low level of agricultural production. In the eastern parts of the Huang-Huai-Hai plain, drained by the Huanghe, Heai, and Haihe rivers, the gradient is gentle (only one degree), but it is difficult for water to be drained off the farmland, thereby leading to water logging and alkalization. As a result, the population density here is lower than in the western parts of the plain.

Influence of Climate.   Sunlight, heat, and rainfall directly affect agricultural production and therefore play an important role in the distribution of population. China has relatively rich sunlight and heat resources, and its annual radiant energy amounts to 85 to 200 kilocalories per square centimeter. The sun shines for 1,800 to 3,300 hours a year, longer in the western parts and on the plateaus than in the eastern parts and on the plains. In terms of temperature distribution, the difference between the north and south is bigger than between the east and west; also their temperature difference is bigger in winter than in summer. For example, the absolute lowest temperature in January at the northern tip of northeast China's Greater Hinggan Mountains is on the average −40°C, while on Hainan Island in the southernmost part of China it is 10°C, a difference of more than 50°C. The average temperature in the hottest month of the year is 22.9°C in the north and 28.2°C in Guangzhou in the south, a difference of 5.3°C, while it is 27.1°C and 23.9°C in Shanghai in the east and Urumqi in the west, respectively, a difference of only 3.2°C. In terms of climate, the whole country can be

divided into four zones: the frigid-temperate zone in the northernmost part, which covers 25.9% of the country's total territory and has an average population density of 70 persons per square kilometer; the temperate zone, which accounts for 46% of the country's total area and has an average population density of more than 200 persons per square kilometer; the subtropical zone, which accounts for 26.1% of the country's total area and has an average population density of 230 persons per square kilometer; and the tropical zone, which makes up less than 2% of the country's total area and whose density of population averages 150 persons per square kilometer. The distribution of rainfall also determines, to a certain degree, the distribution of population. China's rainfall gradually decreases from the southeast to the northwest and so does its density of population. For example, the annual rainfall in coastal Jiangsu Province in the east is 800 to 1,200 mm and its density of population is 598 persons per square kilometer, while the Ruogiang (Qarkilik) area in the Xinjiang Uygur Autonomous Region in the west has an annual rainfall of only 10 mm and is actually a no-man's land except for a few well-irrigated oases. In addition, the areas along big rivers and around lakes have long been places where people live in large numbers. And the Huanghe (Yellow) River valley was the cradle of ancient Chinese civilization.

Influence of Resources.   Mineral resources exert a conspicuous influence on the distribution of population. For instance, with the opening up of the oilfields in northeast China's Heilongjiang Province, the city of Daqing with a population of 480,000 has emerged, and the development of the Panzhihua Iron Mine in Sichuan Province has given birth to the city of Dukou, which now has a population of 350,000. Most of the new industrial and mining cities in China today have emerged on the basis of developing and using local resources. Flora and fauna resources also have effects on the distribution of population. For example, the fishermen in the coastal areas, the herdsmen on the grasslands, and the Oroqen people in northeast China, whose main occupation is hunting, all have local animal and plant resources as the basis of their production and livelihood.

In short, the influence of natural factors on the distribution of population embodies the combined influence of topography, climate, and resources, and such influence is exerted through definite economic environment.

Table 7-8. Total Industrial and Agricultural Output Value of Different Regions and Their Population Density (1983)

REGION	TOTAL INDUSTRIAL AND AGRICULTURAL OUTPUT VALUE (100 MILLION YUAN)	TOTAL AGRICULTURAL OUTPUT VALUE (100 MILLION YUAN)	TOTAL INDUSTRIAL OUTPUT VALUE (100 MILLION YUAN)	AVERAGE PER-CAPITA OUTPUT VALUE (YUAN/PERSON)	POPULATION DENSITY PERSON/SQ. KM.	PERCENT URBAN
National total	9,046.25	2,881.84	6,164.41	882.6	107	23.5
Beijing	227.67	27.07	250.60	2,972.9	556	66.1
Tianjin	252.07	22.87	229.20	3,194.8	697	68.7
Hebei	411.03	158.61	252.69	758.4	289	16.2
Shanxi	218.68	66.81	151.87	850.2	165	27.7
Inner Mongolia	127.19	51.85	75.34	650.6	17	29.2
Liaoning	626.62	109.98	516.64	1,726.7	245	42.6
Jilin	242.17	77.10	165.07	1,066.8	121	38.7
Heilongjiang	400.48	111.98	288.50	1,211.4	70	42.9
Shanghai	719.38	40.80	678.58	6,025.0	1,926	59.6
Jiangsu	824.96	255.51	569.45	1,344.7	598	20.0
Zhejiang	409.57	141.46	268.11	1,033.5	389	22.9
Anhui	288.01	127.32	160.69	569.6	363	16.6
Fujian	162.60	66.79	95.81	615.9	218	22.7
Jiangxi	195.60	89.40	106.20	578.0	203	21.0
Shandong	666.28	260.70	405.58	880.9	494	29.3
Henan	440.56	203.92	236.64	580.4	455	15.5
Hubei	452.87	140.21	312.66	936.7	258	28.9
Hunan	362.08	156.22	205.86	657.3	262	15.9
Guangdong	455.23	149.29	305.94	732.9	287	21.4
Guangxi	180.47	85.59	94.88	483.5	162	12.2
Sichuan	593.53	253.56	399.97	589.1	178	15.8
Guizhou	114.20	51.97	62.23	393.7	165	19.0
Yunnan	158.64	69.48	89.16	478.0	84	13.5
Tibet	7.02	5.72	1.30	563.7	1.6	10
Shaanxi	192.53	63.08	129.45	656.9	143	19.7
Gansu	124.28	36.17	88.11	625.2	44	18.0
Qinghai	23.31	9.04	14.27	593.1	5.4	19.6
Ningxia	24.96	8.84	16.12	627.1	60	27.4
Xinjiang	93.99	40.50	53.49	713.1	8.2	33.1

Source: *Statistics Yearbook of China, 1984*, China Statistics Publishing House.

ECONOMIC FACTORS

Economy is the central link of the population question, and economic environment is a basic factor affecting the distribution of population. Since the various regions of China differ from each other in economic development and level of production, the distribution of population varies in the different provinces, municipalities, and autonomous regions.

First of all, the total industrial and agricultural output value has close connections with the density of population (see Table 7-8). For example, compared with the other provinces, municipalities, and autonomous regions, Jiangsu Province leads in industrial and agricultural output value, reaching 82.496 billion yuan, and its density of population is 598 persons per square kilometer, next only to Shanghai and Tianjin. In contrast, Qinghai and Tibet have the lowest industrial and agricultural output value and the lowest density of population as well (5.4 and 1.6 persons per square kilometer, respectively). This is because economically developed regions, which have a relatively high production level, attract more people to settle there. The phenomenon that China's population is overconcentrated in its southeastern part is, in the final analysis, a concrete demonstration of the uneven development of production between the different regions.

In addition, areas with different types of economy have great differences in the distribution of population. For example, in 1981, when the density of population in the Inner Mongolian Autonomous Region averaged 16 persons per square kilometer, the density of population in its 10 industrial cities averaged 298 persons per square kilometer, while that of its 32 agricultural banners and counties averaged 60 persons and its 18 semiagricultural and semipastoral banners and counties averaged 23 persons; the density of population in its four banners in the forestry area and 254 banners in the pastoral areas averaged 7 persons, respectively. All this is because the different labor productivity of the different economic sectors has different capacity for the population.

The conditions of transportation are also an important economic factor affecting the distribution of population. The construction of railways, highways, and harbors plays an important role in drawing an influx of migrants. In China, for example, the construction of railways and harbors has resulted in the development of a large number of communication hubs, such as Zhengzhou, Shijiazhuang, Xuzhou, Zhuzhou, Baoji, Yingtan, Wenzhou, Zhanjiang, Lianyungang, and Qinhuangdao. The construction of the Chengdu-Kunming and Sichuan-Yunnan railways has given rise to a rectangular region in southwest Sichuan into which people have moved. The density of population there today is more than 300 persons per square kilometer, and the region is dotted with rising cities and towns such as Dukou, Xichang, Miyi, Dechang, and Lugu.

SOCIAL FACTORS

Social factors influencing the distribution of China's population are the policies and principles adopted by the central government. For example, the policy of strictly controlling the population of big cities after the founding of New China in 1949 has enabled the population of big cities to grow at a steady pace and prevented overconcentration of population resulting from abnormal and unplanned development. Also, under the guidance of the policy of developing the economy of the inland provinces and frontier regions, many new economic projects have been built there and large numbers of people have been transferred from the coastal provinces and municipalities in aid of construction in those areas. This has caused the population of the inland provinces and frontier regions to grow at a faster pace than the coastal areas. Moreover, while advocating family planning throughout the country, the central government has adopted flexible policies for areas inhabited by the minority nationalities. All these have promoted the growth of population in the border regions and in places inhabited by the minority peoples, thereby greatly improving the uneven distribution of China's population.

In addition, traditional customs and habits also exert certain influences on the distribution of population. For example, the traditional concepts that men are superior to women and that more children will bring more happiness have resulted in a high birthrate and a high fertility and consequently a high population growth rate in some areas, especially in the rural areas. In particular, the birthrate in the rural areas of such provinces as Fujian, Guizhou, and Guangdong is around 20‰, which is why the proportion of their population in the nation's total has increased rapidly.

CHAPTER EIGHT

SEX AND AGE COMPOSITION OF CHINA'S POPULATION

Sex composition and age makeup are the basic features of a population, and they have a direct bearing on the production of materials and of population itself. They are, therefore, two major subjects of study in demography.

SEX COMPOSITION OF CHINA'S POPULATION

CHANGES AND CHARACTERISTICS

The sex composition of a population is closely and inseparably linked with the various population phenomena. For instance, the analysis and study of the sex ratio of a population are indispensable to an in-depth investigation and study of the births, deaths, and migrations of the population, as well as marriages, employment, educational level, and some other economic and social phenomena.

Sex Composition of Old China's Population. In old China, statistical data on the sex composition of the population were scarce and unreliable. Records of surveys made by related quarters showed that the sex ratio was very high. (The term sex ratio used here and hereafter means the ratio of the male population to the female population by taking the latter as 100.) Professor Chen Da, a well-known Chinese demographer and sociologist, said in his book *Population of Modern China:*

In the past, China's population reports often mentioned that the number of men far exceeded that of women. For instance, a report prepared in 1927 by the Ministry of Internal Affairs on the population in 12 provinces stated that the sex ratio was 124, the highest ever in population reports since the founding of the Republic of China in 1912. As the report was based on the reports and estimates

submitted by the civil affairs and public health departments and police organizations in various provinces, and not statistics collected in a population census, its reliability is open to question.*

Professor Chen Da also said, "Of the reports from modern censuses conducted between 1932 and 1939, seven included the population of entire counties and one included only part of the counties, and together they totalled 2,043,868 people. These reports showed that the average sex ratio was 112.17."† This ratio was much lower than that in the report prepared by the Ministry of Internal Affairs of the Kuomintang government in 1927.

In the 1930s, editors of the *Economic Yearbook of China*, basing their work on household registrations by civil affairs departments during the reign of Emperor Xuan Tong (1909–11) of the Qing Dynasty and revisions made by the Internal Affairs Ministry of the Republic of China in 1912, drew up household registration forms, after consulting other related materials. According to their calculations, the sex ratio of China's population was 121.7.‡

According to the statistics published in the *China Yearbook 1937*, the sex ratio of the country's population at that time was 118.7, with the male population totalling 237,903,962, and the female population 200,503,965. The ratio for various provinces and cities in 1937 is shown in Table 8-1.

In 1947, The Kuomintang government issued population statistics for 1946, which showed that the sex ratio was 109.6.§

---

* Chen Da, *Population of Modern China*, Tianjin People's Publishing House, 1981, p. 26.
† Ibid., p. 26.
‡ *Economic Yearbook of China* (1934), Vol. 1, Chap. 3 on population.
§ *Outline of Statistics of the Republic of China*, Finance and Statistics Bureau of the Kuomintang Government, 1947.

Table 8-1.   Sex Ratio in Various Provinces and Cities (1937) (Females = 100)

PROVINCE OR REGION	SEX RATIO	PROVINCE OR REGION	SEX RATIO
Jiangsu	107.6	Shanxi	120.9
Zhejiang	124.7	Shaanxi	119.1
Anhui	120.6	Gansu	120.3
Jiangxi	129.8	Qinghai	119.7
Fujian	135.6	Ningxia	122.2
Guangdong	117.3	Suiyuan	158.0
Guangxi	126.7	Chahar	136.0
Yunnan	106.9	Liaoning	123.6
Guizhou	102.3	Jilin	123.6
Hunan	122.4	Heilongjiang	123.6
Mongolia	108.1	Rehe	123.6
Hubei	116.6	Xinjiang	121.2
Sichuan	119.2	Nanjing	156.8
Xikang	95.4	Shanghai	135.9
Hebei	110.5	Peiping	159.1
Henan	116.9	Tianjin	142.8
Shandong	114.5	Tibet	107.6

Source: *China Yearbook 1937.*

Although the above statistics were not very complete and accurate, they nevertheless showed that the sex ratio in old China was very high. This was because, before the founding of New China, the Chinese people had long lived in poverty and, under the influence of feudal ideas that had existed for thousands of years, men were considered superior to women, resulting in a comparatively high death rate for women. Particularly in the years when infectious diseases ran rampant, the number of women who died in some places often far surpassed that of men. For instance, of the 641 people who died in the May–September period in 1942 in Zigong County of Yunnan Province, 281 were males and 360 were females, with the latter higher by 28%.* In Xiaogi Town of Jiangyin County in Jiangsu Province, the death rate for males was 38.3‰, while that for females was 39.2‰, and with regard to the mortality rate for babies under one year old, that of male babies was 283.6‰, and that of female, 392.0‰.†

Sex Composition of New China's Population.   Since the founding of the People's Republic of China in 1949, the mode of social production has changed, the social productive forces have grown, and, in particular, the age-old feudal ideas have been repudiated. As a result, a major change has taken place in the sex composition of China's population, compared with that of old China. Demographic work has been strengthened and the statistical data obtained in

these years are more accurate and comprehensive than before. New China has so far conducted three national censuses — in 1953, 1964, and 1982 — and a regular demographic system has been instituted.

The following is an analysis of the changes in the sex ratio of China's population based on the last three censuses.

1. Sex ratio as shown in the three censuses and regular demographic records. China's first census was conducted in 1953 (the standard time being 00:00 hour on July 1, 1953). The result of the census showed that China's population was 601,938,035. Of this number, 574,205,940 registered through direct surveys, and 27,732,095 were counted through other methods.* Of these 574,205,940, there were 297,553,518 males, accounting for 51.82%, and 276,652,422 females, accounting for 48.18%. The sex ratio was 107.56. This sex ratio did not include the 27,732,095 people who were counted through other methods.†

The second census was conducted in 1964 (the standard time being 00:00 hour on July 1, 1964). The results showed that China's population at that time was 723,070,269. The population of the 28 provinces, municipalities, and autonomous regions on the mainland. (Tianjin was under the jurisdiction of Hebei Province at that time), and the number of ser-

* Chen Da: *Population of Modern China*, Tianjin People's Publishing House, 1981, p. 154, Table 27.
† Ibid., p. 48.

* *Communiqué of the Statistical Bureau of the People's Republic of China on the Results of Registration During the First National Census* (November 1, 1954).
† "Some Major Statistical Data from the Second National Census," *Major Data from China's Third National Census*, Chinese edition, October 1982, Beijing, pp. 54–55.

vicemen together made up 694,581,759. Of this number, 356,517,011 were males, accounting for 51.33%, and 338,064,748 were females, accounting for 48.67%. The sex ratio was 105.46. The population on which the sex ratio was based did not include the 28,488,510 Chinese people in Taiwan Province, Hong Kong, Macao, and overseas.*

The third census was conducted in 1982 (with 00:00 hour on July 1, 1982 as the standard time). The census indicated that China's population was 1,031,887,961,† of which 1,008,152,137 (i.e., deducting the 28,601 people counted indirectly in the Tibet Autonomous Region from the 1,008,180,738 in the 29 provinces, municipalities, and autonomous regions on the mainland and men and women in active service in the People's Liberation Army) had clearly stated their sex: 519,406,895 were males, accounting for 51.52%, and 488,745,242 were females, accounting for 48.48%. The sex ratio was 106.27.

In China's three national censuses, the sex ratio of the entire population was calculated in roughly the same way and is therefore comparable.

A comparison between the results of the three national censuses and the regular population records of the corresponding years shows that the sex ratio of China's population from both sources was approximately the same (see Table 8-2 and Table 8-3).

2. Comparison with other countries. A comparison between the sex ratio of China's population in 1982 and that of some other countries and regions in

* Included: (1) Places in which election had not been conducted at basic level and those outlying areas that had poor transport facilities 8,397,477;
(2) Taiwan province 7,591,298;
(3) Overseas Chinese and foreign students, etc. 11,743,320.
† Included population of 29 provinces, municipalities, and autonomous regions of the mainland and Taiwan province, Hong Kong, and Macao.

1980 shows that the sex ratio in China was not only much higher than that of the developed countries but also higher than that of many developing nations (see Table 8-4).

3. Characteristics of the sex ratio in New China. From the foregoing, we see that the sex ratio of China's population had the following three salient features:

- The sex ratio showed a considerable reduction as compared with preliberation figures but was still higher than 105.
- Changes in the sex ratio can be divided into two phases: the period from the early postliberation days to 1969, during which time the sex ratio showed a decrease, and the period from 1970 to 1984, in which the population sex ratio started to grow slightly.
- The sex ratio of the Chinese population was among the highest in the world.

Factors Accounting for China's High Sex Ratio. The high sex ratio of China's population can be attributed to the following factors:

First, the sex ratio of those people who were born in old China and are still alive is rather high; they were mainly people of the 35–54 age group during the 1982 national census, numbering 190,878,404 and accounting for 19% of the total civilian population of 1,003,913,927 in the 29 provinces, autonomous regions, and municipalities. Of this number, 100,995,351 were male, accounting for 52.91%, and 89,883,053 were female, accounting for 47.09%. The sex ratio was 112.36. If these people were excluded from the total population, then the sex ratio would have been 103.89. The difference testifies to the big influence of people of this age group on the sex ratio of the Chinese population as a whole.

Table 8-2. Sex Ratio of China's Population (1949–1984)

YEAR	YEAR-END SEX RATIO	YEAR	YEAR-END SEX RATIO	YEAR	YEAR-END SEX RATIO	YEAR	YEAR-END SEX RATIO
1949	108.2	1958	107.5	1967	105.0	1976	106.2
1950	108.1	1959	108.0	1968	105.0	1977	106.2
1951	108.0	1960	107.4	1969	104.8	1978	106.2
1952	107.9	1961	105.9	1970	105.9	1979	106.0
1953	107.6	1962	105.3	1971	105.8	1980	106.0
1954	107.6	1963	105.6	1972	105.8	1981	106.1
1955	107.3	1964	105.2	1973	105.9	1982	106.3
1956	107.4	1965	104.9	1974	105.9	1983	106.5
1957	107.3	1966	105.1	1975	106.0	1984	106.7

Source: *Statistics Yearbook of China 1985*, China Statistics Publishing House, 1985, p. 185.

Table 8-3. Comparison of Sex Ratio of China's Population in
1953, 1964, and 1984 from National Censuses and Regular
Population Statistics

YEAR	NATIONAL CENSUS	REGULAR YEAR-END STATISTICS
1953	107.56	107.55
1964	105.46	105.20
1982	106.27	106.25

Sources: *Major Figures from China's Third Census*, China Statistics
Publishing House, 1982, pp. 2, 52, 54, and *Statistics Yearbook of China
1985*, China Statistics Publishing House, 1985.

Second, in the low age group, the mortality rate of girls was higher than that of boys—a factor that might cause a high sex ratio among the people of the higher-age groups.

Third, the sex ratio of China's newborn babies was higher than that of most countries in the world. According to the results of the 1982 census, the sex ratio of newborn babies in 1981 was 108.47.

But this high sex ratio as shown in the statistics might not wholly reflect the reality of the country. This is mainly because the people in some localities tended to cut back on the number of female infants in their demographic reports. The talk among some people abroad that female infanticide is one of the reasons for the high sex ratio of China's population is entirely groundless. With the social and economic development and the changes in people's ideology after the founding of New China, female infanticide, which is forbidden by law, has been wiped out.

DIFFERENCE IN SEX COMPOSITION BETWEEN
VARIOUS REGIONS
*Difference Between Provinces, Municipalities, and
Autonomous Regions on the Chinese Mainland.*   The
sex composition of China's population not only changes with the change of time but also differs to

varying degrees between the 29 provinces, municipalities, and autonomous regions on the mainland.

According to the 1982 census, the sex ratio of the total population of the 29 provinces, municipalities, and autonomous regions, not including servicemen, was 105.45. There were big differences between the highest, being 109.02 in Inner Mongolia, and the lowest, being 97.76 in Tibet (see Table 8-5). The first five provinces and one autonomous region in Table 8-5 had the highest sex ratio, all above 107. In fact, their sex ratio had always been high in the past. Since the founding of New China, their sex ratio has gradually dropped (see Table 8-6).

As for the sex ratio in the other provinces, municipalities, and autonomous regions, the general trend was that the difference between them had gradually been reduced from 1953 to 1982. The sex ratios in Beijing, Tianjin, and Shanghai had dropped from 136.53, 121.98, and 115.07 in 1953 to 102.43, 103.13, and 99.33 in 1982, respectively.

Of the 29 provinces, municipalities, and autonomous regions on the Chinese mainland, only the sex ratio in Shanghai and the Tibet Autonomous Region was below 100 in 1982. The sex ratio in Shanghai was 99.33, and in Tibet it was 97.76. But the reason for the low ratio was entirely different in the two places.

Table 8-4.   Comparison Between the Sex Ratio in China in 1982 and That of Selected Countries in 1980 (Females = 100)

COUNTRY OR REGION	SEX RATIO OF ENTIRE POPULATION	COUNTRY OR REGION	SEX RATIO OF ENTIRE POPULATION	COUNTRY OR REGION	SEX RATIO OF ENTIRE POPULATION
China	106.3	Afghanistan	104.4	Brazil	99.4
India	107.4	Algeria	98.6	Colombia	100.6
Pakistan	106.5	Hong Kong	105.1	Cuba	103.8
Libya	112.4	Albania	102.6	Egypt	102.2
Bangladesh	106.7	Argentina	99.6	Japan	97.2
France	96.2	United States	95.0	Britain	96.0
Democratic Germany	88.3	Soviet Union	87.7		

Source: All the figures except that on China are from United Nations Fund for Population Activities, *Population Facts at Hand*, 1981.

Table 8-5.   Sex Ratio of Total Population of 29 Provinces, Municipalities, and Autonomous Regions (1982 Census)

REGION	SEX RATIO	REGION	SEX RATIO	REGION	SEX RATIO	REGION	SEX RATIO	REGION	SEX RATIO
Chinese Mainland	105.45	Shaanxi	107.40	Qinghai	106.03	Heilongjiang	104.87	Tianjin	103.13
Inner Mongolia	109.02	Guangxi	107.30	Xinjiang	106.03	Hebei	104.81	Shandong	102.87
Shanxi	108.51	Gansu	107.18	Fujian	105.92	Guangdong	104.57	Yunnan	102.78
Hunan	108.07	Sichuan	106.58	Hubei	105.54	Liaoning	104.16	Beijing	102.43
Anhui	107.79	Jiangxi	106.49	Guizhou	105.24	Henan	104.05	Shanghai	99.33
Zhejiang	107.74	Ningxia	106.25	Jilin	104.99	Jiangsu	103.41	Tibet	97.76

Source: *Statistics Yearbook of China 1985*, China Statistics Publishing House, 1985, p. 194.

Shanghai, the biggest metropolis in China, leads the nation in social and economic development, and in culture and education, science and technology. In the early years after the founding of New China, the sex ratio in Shanghai was also high. It was 115.7 during the 1953 national census, but it dropped gradually, and by 1961 it was below 100. The main reasons for this were:

First, its administrative area was enlarged in 1956 to include 10 suburban counties where the sex ratio was relatively low. Hence the drop in the sex ratio of the total population of Shanghai.

Second, during the 1958–65 and 1966–76 periods, large numbers of workers and staff members as well as educated youth (including those waiting for jobs and middle school graduates) went to the border regions to support the construction there. The migration of such large numbers of people (more male than female) greatly affected the sex ratio of the Shanghai population.

Third, judging from the age composition, the proportion of old people gradually increased, and the sex ratio among the old people decreased with the increase of age. This was another factor accounting for the drop in the sex ratio.

Tibet, a pastoral area on a high plateau, has poor natural conditions; its population is sparse and traf-

fic inconvenient, and its economy and culture lag far behind Shanghai. The 1982 national census showed that the total population in the Tibet Autonomous Region was 1,863,623, of which 1,764,600 or 94.69% were Tibetans. In areas where Tibetans made up the overwhelming majority of the population, the sex ratio was particularly low. In Qamdo Prefecture, for instance, it was 96.15, in Loka Prefecture it was 96.84, in Xigaze Prefecture it was 97.21, and in Nagqu Prefecture it was 97.45. In 1982 Numu County had the lowest sex ratio in Tibet, being only 91.04. The low sex ratio in the Tibet Autonomous Region was due to the low sex ratio among the local Tibetans. The exact causes of this phenomenon remain to be investigated.

*Differences in Sex Composition in China's Cities, Towns, and Counties.** According to the administrative divisions at the time of the 1982 national census, there were 244 cities, 2,660 towns, and 2,133 counties of the 29 provinces, municipalities, and autonomous regions on the Chinese mainland. The total city population was 145,253,071 (14.47% of the

* City population does not include the population of the counties under the jurisdiction of the cities; and county population does not include the population of the towns under the jurisdiction of the counties.

Table 8-6.   Comparison of the Sex Ratio Between Six Regions (1953 and 1982)

REGION	1953	1982	DROP FROM 1953 TO 1982
Inner Mongolia	128.63	109.02	19.61
Shanxi	112.52	108.51	4.01
Hunan	109.59	108.07	1.52
Anhui	111.07	107.79	3.28
Zhejiang	110.82	107.74	3.08
Shaanxi	114.56	107.40	7.16

Source: Calculated according to the data collected during the 1953 and 1982 censuses.

total population on the mainland), of which 75,287,073 were males and 69,965,998 were females, giving a sex ratio of 107.61. The town population was 61,056,073 (6.08% of the total population on the mainland), of which 32,733,647 were males and 28,322,426 were females, with a sex ratio of 115.58. The county population was 797,604,783 (79.45% of the nation's total), of which 407,256,785 were males and 390,347,998 were females, with a sex ratio of 104.33.

Shanxi Province had the highest sex ratio (116.61) of the city population in 1982, and Shanghai had the lowest sex ratio (102.82). As for the sex ratio of the town population, Shanxi Province also had the highest ratio (144.94) and Heilongjiang Province had the lowest (102.59). As for the sex ratio of the county population, the Inner Mongolian Autonomous Region had the highest ratio (109.58) and Shanghai had the lowest (92.83).

From the sex composition of China's city, town, and county population, it can be seen that the town population had the highest sex ratio; next came the city population, and the county population had the lowest sex ratio. This showed that in China today the male population is chiefly concentrated in the cities and towns.

1. Sex composition of city population. In China there are old cities and new-rising cities; industrial and mining cities and cities of a comprehensive nature; big cities and medium-sized and small cities. The sex ratio of the city population differs with the different types of cities, and sometimes the differences are quite big.

China's 244 cities could be divided into seven groups according to the sex ratio of their population in 1982.

There were 5 cities whose sex ratio was less than 100; 150 cities had a sex ratio of between 100 and 109; 70 cities had a sex ratio of between 110 and 119; 9

cities had a sex ratio of between 120 and 129; 7 cities had a sex ratio of between 130 and 139; 1 city had a sex ratio of between 140 and 149; and 2 cities had a sex ratio of between 150 and 159. From this we can see that in most cities the sex ratio was between 100 and 119. Cities with a sex ratio of between 100 and 109 numbered 150, constituting 61.5% of the total number of cities in China, and cities with a sex ratio of between 110 and 119 numbered 70, constituting 28.7% of the total number of cities in the country. These two added up to 220 cities, making up 90.2% of the total in China.

On the mainland, Yima city, a coal-mining center in central China's Henan Province, had the highest sex ratio of 153.18 among China's cities, while Tumeng city in Jilin Province had the lowest sex ratio of 99.15.

Viewed from the development of the cities at the present stage, there is a close relation between the sex ratio and the size of the city population. Cities on the mainland can be divided into six groups according to the size of their population. Generally speaking, the bigger the size of the population, the lower the sex ratio is; otherwise, the opposite is the case (see Table 8-7).

The sex ratio of the city population is also related to the functions and types of economy of the cities concerned. For instance, in the extra large cities that are economic centers, such as Beijing, Shanghai, and Tianjin, the sex ratio is comparatively low. At the time of the 1982 census, the sex ratio was 103.47 in Beijing, 102.82 in Shanghai, and 103.62 in Tianjin. In comparison, the following industrial and mining cities with only a single function had a relatively high sex ratio.

• Coal cities. With only a few exceptions, the sex ratio in these cities is often high, since male workers are predominant there; many of them are single,

Table 8-7.   Sex Ratio in Cities of Different Sizes in Population

SIZE OF POPULATION	NUMBER OF CITIES	TOTAL POPULATION	MALE	FEMALE	SEX RATIO
Total	244	145,253,071	75,287,073	69,287,073	107.61
Over 4 million	4	21,064,749	10,696,491	10,368,258	103.17
2–4 million	9	22,695,533	11,683,006	11,012,527	106.09
1–2 million	25	31,622,467	16,380,778	15,241,689	107.47
0.5–1 million	47	33,214,313	17,305,326	15,908,987	108.78
0.1–0.5 million	137	35,254,314	18,476,370	16,777,944	110.12
Less than 0.1 million	22	1,401,695	745,102	656,593	113.48

Source: Based on Tables 17 and 21 in the *1982 Population Census of China*, China Statistics Publishing House, 1985, pp. 54–55 and pp. 64–85.

Table 8-8. Sex Ratio of Population in 29 Provinces, Municipalities, and Autonomous Regions (1982 Census)

PROVINCE/REGION	SEX RATIO OF CITY POPULATION	PROVINCE/REGION	SEX RATIO OF CITY POPULATION
29 Provinces, municipalities, and autonomous regions	107.61	Shanxi	116.61
Hebei	116.27	Gansu	115.86
Tibet	113.97	Anhui	113.63
Ningxia	112.35	Hunan	112.15
Shaanxi	111.07	Henan	110.56
Yunnan	110.47	Qinghai	110.21
Hubei	108.96	Jiangsu	108.75
Guangxi	108.72	Jiangxi	108.53
Guizhou	108.46	Sichuan	108.35
Zhejiang	107.51	Inner Mongolia	107.04
Fujian	106.65	Guangdong	106.08
Xinjiang	105.60	Shandong	104.81
Jilin	103.92	Tianjin	103.62
Beijing	103.47	Heilongjiang	103.37
Liaoning	103.23	Shanghai	102.82

Source: Based on Table 21 in the *1982 Population Census of China,* China Statistics Publishing House, 1985, pp. 64–85.

while others have their families living in the countryside. In 1982, the sex ratio of the population in Xuzhou was 118.60; in Tangshan it was 111.03; 116.71 in Datong; 128.79 in Yangquan; 133.47 in Pingdingshan; 153.18 in Yima; 135.88 in Huaibei; 114.13 in Huainan; 113.04 in Jiaozuo; 121.11 in Shizuishan; 117.62 in Hebi; and 112.9 in Qitaihe. The ratio is even higher in the mining areas of these coal cities. For instance, the sex ratio in Datong's coal-mining districts was 133.4; in Yangquan it was 185.9; and in Xuzhou, 240.4.

• Oil cities. The sex ratio in the oil cities is also high. For instance, in 1982 it was 115.19 in Jingmen; 118.03 in Yumen; 119.31 in Karamay; 110.47 in Maoming; and 111.73 in Nanyang.

• Steel cities. The sex ratio of the population in the old steel cities such as Anshan has now become normal, registering 103.34 in 1982. But that of new steel cities, such as Dukou, was high, reaching 141.45 in 1982.

• Small and medium-sized cities with metallurgical and mining centers. The sex ratio in these cities is currently high. The 1982 figure for Maanshan was 113.23; Lengshuijiang, 111.71; Jinchang, 122.89; Tongling, 124.49; Huangshi, 123.03; Jiayuguan, 132.71; Dongchuan, 110.63; and Gejiu, 108.46.

We now take Dukou of Sichuan Province as an illustration in our analysis of the causes of this phenomenon. Dukou is a new steel city, which has developed over the past 20 years. About 300,000 workers

and staff members, mostly males, have moved into Dukou from 22 provinces, municipalities, and autonomous regions across the country. Today its population has grown to 800,000. The number of workers employed in the city proper today is six times that of 1965. Of the working-age population of Dukou in 1982, the sex ratio was 148.71 in the 30–34 age bracket, and for every age in the 34–41 bracket it was over 200, the highest being 263. This meant the number of male workers was more than double that of female workers.

However, with the building of more facilities in various fields in the industrial and mining cities, along with the social and economic development of the country, jobs will be provided for more family members to move in, and the sex ratio of their population will come down step by step.

2. Sex composition of town population. The sex ratio of the town population in 1982 was 115.58. However, it varies greatly in different provinces, municipalities, and autonomous regions (see Table 8-9).

The highest sex ratio of the town population, 144.94, was in Shanxi Province, which abounds in coal deposits, and many of its coal towns have an especially high sex ratio. For instance, that of Xuangang was 322.05; Wangtaipu, 269.95; Liuwan, 256.39; Xiaoyu, 242,82; Zongzhen, 239.99; and Xinzhi, 204.22. Heilongjiang Province had the lowest town sex ratio (102.59) in the whole country, even lower than its county sex ratio. Of China's 2,660

Table 8-9.   Sex Ratio of Town Population in 29 Provinces, Municipalities, and Autonomous Regions (1982 Census)

PROVINCE/REGION	SEX RATIO OF TOWN POPULATION	PROVINCE/REGION	SEX RATIO OF TOWN POPULATION
29 Provinces, municipalities, and autonomous regions	115.58	Henan	117.13
Shanxi	144.94	Hebei	116.97
Shaanxi	132.40	Fujian	116.92
Sichuan	130.81	Anhui	116.71
Qinghai	127.44	Hubei	115.50
Tianjin	127.37	Jiangsu	115.12
Gansu	124.96	Guangdong	114.40
Beijing	123.75	Liaoning	113.05
Yunnan	121.85	Zhejiang	112.96
Ningxia	121.72	Guizhou	110.08
Guangxi	121.57	Shandong	109.58
Hunan	121.05	Inner Mongolia	108.42
Tibet	120.67	Xinjiang	107.86
Jiangxi	119.58	Jilin	105.40
Shanghai	117.97	Heilongjiang	102.59

Source: Based on Table 24 in the *1982 Population Census of China*, China Statistics Publishing House, 1985, pp. 90–150.

towns, 114, or 4.29%, had sex ratios below 100. In Hubei Province, 12.6% of its towns had a sex ratio of less than 100, representing the largest number of towns in a province with such a low ratio. The percentage in Jiangsu Province was 11.4%, and that of Zhejiang Province was 10.30%.

On the whole, the sex ratio of China's town population was comparatively high. This had something to do with the shift of surplus labor from the countryside to the towns under construction. Consequently, there were more male workers, especially in mining towns. But their families remained in the countryside, since it was only a short distance away from the towns and it was quite convenient for husband and wife to live a normal family life.

China's urbanization policy is: "Strict control over large cities, rational development of medium-sized cities, and energetic construction of small cities and towns." With the development of small cities and towns, more public facilities and service establishments will be built to provide jobs for female workers. In this way, the sex ratio of China's town population will be reduced.

3. Sex composition of county population. The sex ratio of the population of 2,133 counties in 1982 was 104.33, lower than the ratio of the city and town population. But there were great differences in the 29 provinces, municipalities, and autonomous regions (see Table 8-10).

The municipalities of Shanghai, Tianjin, and Beijing, as well as the Tibet Autonomous Region, had the lowest sex ratio. The developed economy of the three municipalities directly under central jurisdic-

tion had helped propel the development of their surrounding towns and counties. Large numbers of able-bodied male workers had moved from the countryside to the cities and towns and, as a consequence, there were more women than men in the counties. This was not the case with Tibet, whose low county sex ratio was because the sex ratio of the Tibetan population as a whole was low.

In some provinces, many counties had a low sex ratio because they were advanced in production and the people were comparatively well-off. Examples were Changhai County (sex ratio 98.90) of Dalian city in Liaoning Province; Haiyan County (99.51) of Jiaxing Prefecture in Zhejiang Province; Dangshan County (100.41) of Suxian Prefecture in Anhui Province; Nankang County (97.75) of Ganzhou Prefecture in Jiangxi Province; Changdao County (95.63) of Yantai Prefecture in Shandong Province; and Wenxian County (94.26) of Xinxiang Prefecture in Henan Province.* However, counties with a low sex ratio were not necessarily rich. Of China's 2,133 counties in 1982, 263 had a sex ratio of less than 100, and 56 of these counties were in the Tibet Autonomous Region and 18 in Qinghai Province. Quite a number of these 263 counties were economically underdeveloped. Counties located in the hilly and outlying regions, difficult of access because of poor communications with the outside world, usually had a high sex ratio. Examples were Yuxian County (sex ratio 123.38) of Zhangjiakou Prefecture in Hebei Province; Gaochun

* Hu Huanyong and Zhang Shanyu, *China's Demographic Geography*, East China Normal University Press, 1984, Vol. 1, p. 149.

Table 8-10.   Sex Ratio of County Population in 29 Provinces, Municipalities, and Autonomous Regions (1982 Census)

PROVINCE/REGION	SEX RATIO OF COUNTY POPULATION	PROVINCE/REGION	SEX RATIO OF COUNTY POPULATION
29 Provinces, municipalities, and autonomous regions	104.33	Qinghai	104.46
Inner Mongolia	109.58	Guizhou	104.41
Zhejiang	107.25	Hubei	104.40
Hunan	106.95	Ningxia	103.98
Anhui	106.71	Guangdong	103.59
Guangxi	106.43	Liaoning	103.36
Heilongjiang	106.07	Hebei	103.09
Xinjiang	105.94	Henan	102.65
Shaanxi	105.43	Jiangsu	102.11
Jilin	105.31	Shandong	102.01
Sichuan	105.28	Yunnan	101.06
Shanxi	105.25	Tianjin	100.43
Gansu	105.20	Beijing	98.52
Jiangxi	105.15	Tibet	95.94
Fujian	104.70	Shanghai	92.83

Source: Based on Tables 21, 24, 26 in the *1982 Population Census of China*, China Statistics Publishing House, 1985, pp. 64, 90, 154.

County (114.49) of Zhenjiang Prefecture in Jiangsu Province; Taishun County (123.37) of Wenjiang city in Zhejiang Province; Zherong County (128.93) of Ningde Prefecture in Fujian Province; Tonggu County (114.45) of Yichun Prefecture in Jiangxi Province; Shennongjia Forest Area (120.73) of Yunyang Prefecture in Hubei Province; and Barkam County (127.35) of the Ngawa Tibetan Autonomous Prefecture in Sichuan Province.

AGE COMPOSITION OF CHINA'S POPULATION

Like sex composition, age composition is also a basic feature of a nation's population. Its importance is being recognized by more and more research workers. Generally speaking, a person undergoes various periods in a lifetime—childhood, early youth, youth, middle age, and old age. The whole process, from birth to death, reflects a population's natural and social characteristics. People of different ages play different roles in society and have different demands, and child-rearing, education, marriage, childbirth, labor, and support of old people are all aspects of people's age. Consequently, the study of age composition is essential to mapping out development plans for the society, economy, defense, culture, education, science, technology, and service facilities of a country (or region), and to formulating population and related policies, and it provides a basis for forecasting the future of the population. In short, age composition has close connections with the production of materials and of population itself.

HISTORY OF STATISTICS ON POPULATION AGE

The collection and study of statistical data on the age of the population has been scant in Chinese history. Since ancient times, emphasis has always been on the registration of the number of households and their members while neglecting the sex and age composition of the population. Age was roughly divided into five periods—infancy, childhood, youth, middle age, and old age.* Moreover, the standards used in different periods varied greatly. The study and analysis of the age composition of the population was therefore out of the question. However, the situation improved slightly during the Qing Dynasty and more demographic statistics were compiled. After the founding of the Republic of China in 1912, academic institutions and scholars conducted limited investigations in this regard. In short, the investigation and study of the age composition of China's population was scarce in old China, and whatever data were collected were mostly unreliable.

The calculations of the Chinese sociologist Sun Benwen about the age composition of China's population during the 1930s are shown in Table 8-11.

Since the three censuses in 1953, 1964, and 1982, complete and accurate statistics on the sex and age composition of the population have been obtained. In addition, data for some years have also been obtained from calculations based on local investigations.

* "Population Investigation in Past Dynasties," *Selected Entries from Dictionary of Demography*, published in *Population Research*, No. 6, 1983, p. 46.

Table 8-11.   Age Composition of China's Population in the 1930s (Estimated Figures)

AGE GROUP	PERCENTAGE IN TOTAL POPULATION		
	WHOLE COUNTRY	RURAL AREAS	URBAN AREAS
0–14	33	35	30
15–49	52	51	53
50+	15	14	17
Total	100	100	100

Source: Liu Hongkang and Wu Zhongguan, comps., *Population Handbook* (revised edition), Chengdu Family Planning Publicity and Education Sub-Center, p. 181.

The 1953 census showed that China's population was 582,603,417 (not including the 19,334,618 people residing in Taiwan Province and in Hong Kong, Macao, and overseas). Of these, 567,446,758 had their age registered, representing 97.40% of the total counted in the census (see Table 8-12).

The 1964 census showed that China's population was 694,581,759 (not including the 28,488,510 living in Taiwan Province, Hong Kong, Macao, and overseas). Of this number, 689,705,152 or 99.30% had their age registered (see Table 8-13).

The Chinese population during the 1982 census was 1,008,180,738 of which 1,008,152,137 were counted directly in the census and 28,601 indirectly. People who had their age registered numbered 1,008,151,366 or 99.997% of the total number counted in the census (see Table 8-14). The 28,601 people counted indirectly did not give their age.

From the three censuses we see that the proportion of people who had their age registered increased with each census to reach 99.997% in 1982.

TENDENCY OF DEVELOPMENT IN THE AGE COMPOSITION OF CHINA'S POPULATION

Changes in the Age Composition of China's Population and Its Characteristics. Since the founding of New China, the changes in the age composition of China's population can be divided into two stages in terms of direction of development. In the first stage, from the early 1950s to the early 1970s, it changed in the direction of becoming younger; and in the second stage, from the early 1970s (especially from 1973) to the present day, the population has gradually become old. The change in the first stage resulted from the uncontrolled increase of the population, while the change in the second stage stemmed from efforts to control population growth, which conforms to the long-term interests of the nation's population growth.

After these changes the age composition of China's population has the following two characteristics.

First, the age composition of the Chinese popu-

Table 8-12.   Age Composition of the Two Sexes in China's Population (1953 Census)

AGE GROUP	TOTAL	MALE	FEMALE	SEX RATIO (FEMALE = 100)
Total	567,446,758	291,969,807	275,476,951	105.99
0–4	89,275,126	46,104,886	43,170,240	106.80
5–9	62,775,537	33,264,941	29,510,596	112.72
10–14	53,790,234	29,082,491	24,707,743	117.71
15–19	51,726,787	27,072,984	24,653,803	109.81
20–24	46,324,595	23,718,199	22,606,396	104.92
25–29	42,316,003	21,711,735	20,604,268	105.37
30–34	38,086,610	19,595,040	18,491,570	105.97
35–39	36,281,374	18,778,517	17,502,857	107.27
40–44	31,654,941	16,454,333	15,200,608	108.25
45–49	28,760,397	14,676,352	14,084,045	104.21
50–54	24,356,677	12,435,470	11,921,207	104.31
55–59	20,560,034	10,398,207	10,161,827	102.23
60–64	16,500,186	8,006,104	8,494,082	94.26
65–69	11,775,245	5,400,767	6,374,478	84.72
70–74	7,815,815	3,308,199	4,507,616	73.39
75–79	3,592,488	1,368,411	2,224,077	61.53
80+	1,854,709	593,171	1,261,538	47.02

Source: *Major Figures from China's Third Census*, China Statistics Publishing House, October 1982, p. 33.

Table 8-13. Age Composition of the Two Sexes in China's Population (1964 Census)

AGE GROUP	TOTAL	MALE	FEMALE	SEX RATIO (FEMALE = 100)
Total	694,581,759	356,517,011	338,064,748	105.46
0–4	100,141,956	51,461,891	48,680,065	105.71
5–9	94,177,434	49,283,349	44,894,085	109.78
10–14	86,351,645	45,005,259	41,346,386	108.85
15–19	62,115,488	32,356,349	29,759,139	108.73
20–24	50,820,751	26,483,045	24,337,706	108.81
25–29	50,395,408	26,798,450	23,596,958	113.57
30–34	46,706,090	24,719,798	21,986,292	112.43
35–39	41,169,912	21,591,224	19,578,688	110.28
40–44	35,645,215	18,438,348	17,206,867	107.16
45–49	30,852,836	15,710,681	15,142,155	103.75
50–54	26,505,382	13,292,133	13,213,249	100.60
55–59	22,568,247	10,749,195	11,819,052	90.95
60–64	17,671,454	8,125,730	9,545,724	85.12
65–69	11,635,116	5,109,214	6,525,902	78.29
70–74	7,378,249	3,002,343	4,375,906	68.61
75–79	3,757,366	1,377,689	2,379,677	57.89
80+	1,812,603	566,631	1,245,972	45.48
Age unclear	4,876,607	2,445,682	2,430,925	100.61

Source: *Major Figures from China's Third Census*, China Statistics Publishing House, October 1982, p. 36.

lation is still young at present, but it is already becoming manifest that it will gradually become older.

From Table 8-15 we see that great changes in the age composition of China's population have taken place. From 1953 to 1964, the proportion of people in the 0–14 age group rose, while that of people in the 15–64 and 65 and older groups dropped. However, a change in the reverse direction took place during the 1964–82 period. This indicates that efforts to control population growth yielded results, thereby changing the situation in which the age composition of the Chinese population tended to be too

Table 8-14. Age Composition of the Two Sexes in China's Population (1982 Census)

AGE GROUP	TOTAL	MALE	FEMALE	SEX RATIO (FEMALE = 100)
Total	1,008,152,137	519,406,895	488,745,242	106.27
0–4	94,704,361	48,983,813	45,720,548	107.14
5–9	110,735,871	57,026,296	53,709,575	106.18
10–14	131,810,957	67,837,932	63,973,025	106.04
15–19	125,997,658	64,420,607	61,577,051	104.62
20–24	76,848,044	40,300,907	36,547,137	110.27
25–29	93,142,891	48,310,132	44,832,759	107.76
30–34	73,187,245	38,153,148	35,034,097	108.90
35–39	54,327,790	28,669,005	25,658,785	111.73
40–44	48,490,741	25,878,901	22,611,840	114.45
45–49	47,454,949	25,123,395	22,331,554	112.50
50–54	40,856,112	21,568,644	19,287,468	111.83
55–59	33,932,129	17,530,819	16,401,310	106.89
60–64	27,387,702	13,733,702	13,653,367	100.59
65–69	21,260,370	10,171,973	11,088,397	91.74
70–74	14,348,045	6,434,731	7,913,314	81.32
75–79	8,617,043	3,496,703	5,120,340	68.29
80+	5,050,091	1,765,823	3,284,268	53.77
Age unclear	771	364	407	89.43

Note: This table includes servicemen. People aged 19 and under are included in the 15–19 age group and people aged 60 and over 60 are included in the 60–64 age group.

Sources: *1982 Population Census of China*, China Statistics Publishing House, 1985, p. 272; "Number of Servicemen During the 1982 Census," *Population Research*, No. 6, 1985, p. 6.

Table 8-15. Age Composition in China (During Three Censuses) and Selected Other Countries

		1953 CHINA	1964 CHINA	1982 CHINA	WORLD	1980 JAPAN	USA	HUNGARY	S. KOREA	COLOMBIA	BANGLADESH	KENYA
Proportion in total population (%)	Total	100.00	100.01	100.00	100.0	100.0	100.0	100.0	100.0	100.0	100.0	100.0
	0–14 Years	36.27	40.69	33.59	35.1	23.5	22.5	21.6	34.2	40.4	45.9	49.8
	15–64 Years	59.31	55.74	61.50	59.1	67.7	66.3	64.9	61.8	56.5	51.5	47.7
	65+	4.41	3.56	4.91	5.8	8.8	11.2	13.4	4.0	3.1	2.6	2.5
Median age (years old)		22.7	20.2	22.9	22.6	32.6	30.2	34.5	21.8	18.9	16.9	15.1
Old age dependency ratio (%)		7.44	6.39	7.98	9.81	13.00	16.89	20.65	6.47	5.49	5.05	5.24
Child dependency ratio (%)		61.16	73.01	54.62	59.39	34.71	33.94	33.28	55.34	71.50	89.13	104.40
Total dependency ratio (%)		68.60	79.40	62.60	69.20	47.71	50.83	53.93	61.81	76.99	94.18	109.64
Aged–child ratio (%)		12.16	8.76	14.62	16.52	37.45	49.78	62.04	11.70	7.67	5.66	5.02

Sources: *Major Figures from China's Third Census*, China Statistics Publishing House, October 1982; United Nations Fund for Population Activities, *Population Facts at Hand*, pp. 7, 21, 45, 53, 55, 84, 108, 117.

Table 8-16. Changes in the Population of Three Age Groups in the 1953–64 and 1964–82 Periods

	0–14		15–64		65+	
	1953–64	1964–82	1953–64	1964–82	1953–64	1964–82
Growth rate (%)	36.35	20.16	14.23	60.59	−1.82	100.4
Average annual growth rate (%)	2.86	1.03	1.22	2.67	−0.17	3.94
Proportion in net increases of population (%)	61.21	18.01	39.16	74.14	−0.39	7.85

Source: Calculated on the basis of Tables 8-12, 8-13, and 8-14.

young. The present situation, however, is that the age composition is still young, but China's long-term strategy of family planning has decided that the fertility rate of Chinese women will remain at a low level. Thus for a period of time to come, the age of the Chinese population will clearly increase, while the proportion of people aged 0–14 in the nation's total population will remain low.

Table 8-16 shows the changes in three different age groups. Comparing the second stage (1964–82) with the first stage (1953–64), the population growth rate of the 0–14 age group dropped by a big margin, while that of the 15–64 age group rose considerably, and the population of people at 65 and older doubled during the second stage. This was due to the fact that since the early 1970s both the fertility rate and mortality rate have been low.

During the years when the middle-aged population increased in large numbers, China had rich labor resources, but this also brought pressure on employment. Meanwhile, the number of women of childbearing age increased significantly too. From 1964 to 1982, the number of Chinese women of childbearing age 15–49 registered a net increase of nearly 100 million, 67% of them being young women aged 15–29 (see Table 8-17). This means that for a period of time in the future China still has to strictly control childbirths.

Second, there is great irregularity in the present age composition of the Chinese population; that is to say, the various neighboring age groups differ greatly in their respective proportion in the total population of the country. This is mainly caused by the abrupt change in the fertility rate. The irregularity found

Table 8-17. Increase of Women of Childbearing Age from 15 to 29 Years Old (1964–1982)

AGE GROUP	1964		1982	
	NUMBER OF WOMEN	PROPORTION IN TOTAL NUMBER OF WOMEN OF CHILDBEARING AGE (%)	NUMBER OF WOMEN	PROPORTION IN TOTAL NUMBER OF WOMEN OF CHILDBEARING AGE (%)
Total	77,693,803	51.24	142,862,293	57.49
15–19	29,759,139	19.63	61,561,763	24.77
20–24	24,337,706	16.05	36,482,906	14.68
25–29	23,596,958	15.56	44,817,624	18.04

INCREASE IN NUMBER OF WOMEN IN 1982 OVER 1964	INCREASE IN 1982 OVER 1964	
	INCREASE RATE (%)	AVERAGE ANNUAL INCREASE RATE (%)
65,168,490	83.88	3.44
31,802,624	106.87	4.12
12,145,200	49.90	2.27
21,220,666	89.93	3.63

Source: Calculated on the basis of Tables 8-12, 8-13, and 8-14.

Table 8-18.   Proportion of People of Various Age Groups in the Nation's Total Population in 1953, 1964, and 1982 (%)

AGE GROUP	1953 CENSUS	1964 CENSUS	1982 CENSUS
Total	100.00	100.00	100.00
0–4	15.73	14.42	9.43
5–9	11.06	13.56	11.03
10–14	9.48	12.43	13.13
15–19	9.12	8.94	12.49
20–24	8.16	7.32	7.41
25–29	7.46	7.26	9.22
30–34	6.71	6.72	7.27
35–39	6.39	5.93	5.40
40–44	5.58	5.13	4.82
45–49	5.07	4.44	4.72
50–54	4.29	3.82	4.07
55–59	3.62	3.25	3.38
60–64	2.91	2.54	2.73
65–69	2.08	1.68	2.12
70–74	1.38	1.06	1.43
75–79	0.63	0.54	0.86
80+	0.33	0.26	0.50

Source: Calculated on the basis of Tables 8-12, 8-13, and 8-14.

Chart 8-1.   Number of People from 0 to 34 Years Old in the 1982 Census

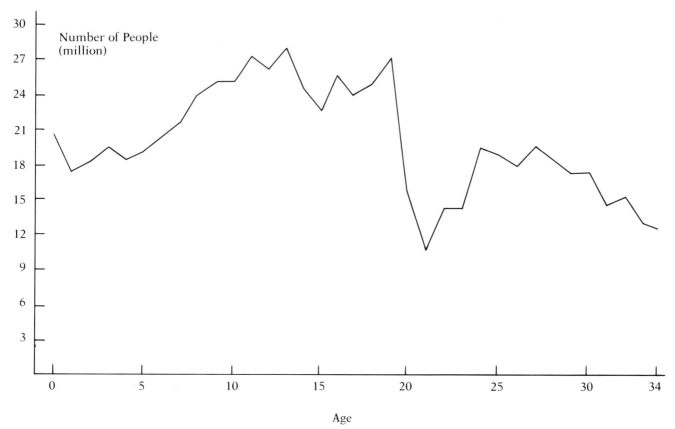

Age

Sources: *1982 Population Census of China*, China Statistics Publishing House, 1985, p. 272; "Number of Servicemen During the 1982 Census," *Population Research*, No. 6, 1985, p. 6.

concentrated expression in the various age groups between 0 and 34 years old in 1982 (see Table 8-18 and Chart 8-1).

Results of the 1953 and 1964 censuses showed that with regard to the proportion of people in each age group in the nation's total population, the tendency was the younger the age group, the bigger its proportion, as shown in Table 8-18, and there were no big fluctuations. But results of the 1982 census showed that the opposite was the case with the 0–4, 5–9, and 10–14 age groups, i.e., the younger the age group, the smaller its proportion in the nation's total population. However, the proportion of the 25–29 age group increased abruptly due to the sudden change in the fertility rate.

There were also great differences in the population of various neighboring ages, with many reversed phenomena, as between 0 and 1 year old in 1953; between 0 and 1 year old as well as between 4 and 5 years old in 1964; and between 17–18 years old and 19 years old and between 21 and 22 years old in 1982 (see Table 8-19).

Chart 8-2 is a comparison between the age composition of the Chinese population based on the 1982 census and the age composition of a stable population calculated according to the 1962–82 gross reproduction rate (GRR) and life table (or mortality table). The two curved lines in the chart may be divided into two parts. The first part turns to the right beginning from the 30–34 age group, where the two curves are fairly close to each other and move in basically the same direction. This shows the tendency of the age composition of people who were born in old China (when both the birthrate and mortality rate were high) and are still alive today. As the birthrate and mortality rate in old China were comparatively stable, the age composition of these people is basically identical with that of the stable population.

The second part turns to the left beginning from the 30–34 age group, indicating that the curve representing people born after the founding of New China and the stable population curve are comparatively far apart. The curve showing the age composition of the population in the 1982 census moves up and down irregularly: the 25–29 age group moves up, showing the high birthrate from 1952 to 1957; the 20–24 age group drops abruptly, indicating the fairly low birthrate from 1957 to 1962; then the 15–19 age group goes up again and the 10–14 age group continues to rise and reaches an apex. The people of these two age groups were born during the high birthrate years between 1962 and 1966 and between 1967 and 1971. Finally, the curve at the 5–9 age group goes down again and continues to descend at the 0–4 age group. This is due to the continued fall of the birthrate resulting from efforts to control population growth and promote family planning over the last 10 years.

The difference between the age composition of China's population in the 1982 census and that of the stable population was quite large. It should be affirmed that the descent of the curve at the 0–4 and 5–9 age groups was reasonable, but its upturn in some age groups revealed many unreasonable factors (mainly the result of lack of family planning).

It should be noted that such irregularities had brought difficulties to the arrangement of our plans. The reason was that in some age groups the number of people changed greatly in certain periods and, moreover, the changes occurred constantly. Hence the emergence of certain disproportionate though temporary phenomena. For instance, the drastic decrease in the number of school-age children created the situation in which the number of primary school teachers and teaching facilities exceeded what was actually needed. In some provinces and municipalities in China where the birthrate had dropped ear-

Table 8-19.   Changes in the Population of Some Neighboring Age Groups in 1953, 1964, and 1982

1953		1964		1982	
AGE	WITH 0 AGE AS 100	AGE	WITH 0 AGE AS 100	AGE	WITH 19 YEARS OLD AS 100
0	100.00	0	100.00	17	89.18
1	115.37	1	106.19	18	91.79
2	90.84	2	54.66	19	100.00
3	88.00	3	40.50	20	57.05
4	76.10	4	50.22	21	39.05
5	73.91	5	52.25	22	52.25

Source: Calculated on the basis of Tables 8-12, 8-13, and 8-14.

Chart 8-2.   Comparison Between the Age Composition of China's Population Based on the 1982 Census and the Age Composition of a Stable Population Calculated According to the 1964–82 GRR and Life Table (Divided into 5-Year Age Groups)

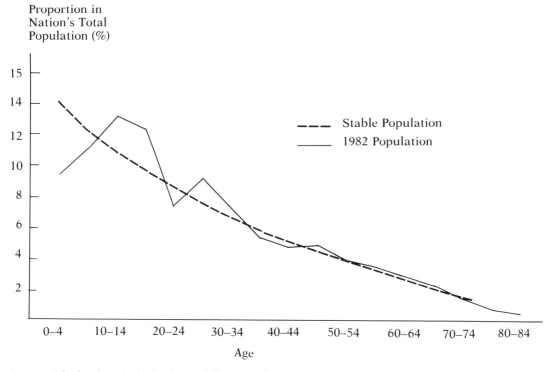

Source: Calculated on the basis of related figures in the *1982 Population Census of China.*

lier, this problem had already cropped up. The sudden increase of working-age population added to the pressure on providing employment and making arrangements for production. The sharp increase in the number of married couples created housing problems. And last but not least, the sharp increase in the number of old people in the coming years would add to the burden of the social welfare departments. Therefore, in making arrangements for the population in the days to come, it is necessary to work out short- and long-term plans. While controlling the birthrate, it is necessary to give consideration to the problem of an aging population. In this way, the Chinese population will after years of effort develop in accordance with the pattern of a stable population.

Three Factors Directly Affecting the Age Composition of the Population.   The changes in the level of childbirths, deaths, and migrations not only affect the total population but also the age composition of the population. From a long-term point of view and judging from most areas in the country, migration

has but little impact, and it is basically the changes in the level of childbirths and deaths that play the decisive role.

The effect of changes in the death rate on the age composition is manifested in the survival rate of the population of different age groups. If a decrease in the death rate in a certain period is mainly favorable to children, the proportion of the population in that age group will go up; and if it is favorable to old people, then the proportion of the population in the old-age groups will rise. However, when the childbearing rate is high, even a comparatively big change in the death rate will have only limited effect on the age composition of the population. It is only in certain specific periods when the death rate changes by a very big margin and the fertility rate remains basically unchanged that changes in the death rate will for a time play the leading role in affecting the age composition of the population.

In most cases, changes in the fertility level play a decisive role in affecting the age composition. And especially when the mortality rate drops to a low level and remains stable there, this decisive role becomes even more conspicuous. This is true with China.

From 1953 to 1964, the average annual birthrate was 31.62‰ and the average total fertility rate was 5.61. The median age of the total population went down from 22.7 years old in 1953 to 20.2 years old in 1964. Between 1964 and 1982, the average annual birthrate dropped to 27.25‰, and the average total childbearing rate was 4.39. The median age of the total population went up from 20.2 years old in 1964 to 22.9 years old in 1982. This shows that the high birthrate during the years between the 1953 and 1963 national censuses brought down the age median. (This was also because of the drop in the death rate during this period, and especially because the drop in the mortality of infants and babies was bigger than that of other age groups.) During the 1964–82 period, however, the drop in the birthrate led to a rise of the age median.

Changes in the fertility level also have a latent effect on the age composition of a population. After a high fertility level continues for a period of time and then drops by a big margin in a fairly short time, the proportion of the population of the middle age groups is bound to increase sharply in the following years. And if the fertility level continues to be at the low level for a long period of time, the proportion of the aged population will go up by a big margin when the population of the middle age groups, which is high in proportion, moves to the old age group, thereby leading to the serious aging of the population. It is imperative that China pay close attention to this question and make necessary and timely readjustments for its population plans.

The Trend of the Aging of China's Population. The aging of a population is a question of common concern the world over. In China, although the proportion of the aged (referring to people aged 60 and above) is at present not high (see Table 8-20), people in various circles attach great importance to forecasts on the trend of development of China's population in the future. In March 1982, the State Council approved the establishment of the "China Commit-

tee of the World Congress on the Aging Question," which was renamed the "China Aging Question National Committee" in October 1982.

The process of development of the aged population in China can be divided into two stages:

FROM 1953 TO 1964.   The rate of increase in the number of old people in China was rather slow, and in these 11 years there was only an increase of 716,000 people. The proportion of the aged in the total population was 6.08% in 1964, showing a slight drop compared with the 7.13% in 1953, and the growth rate of the aged was only 1.72% in 11 years. This was much lower than the growth rate of 19.22% for the country's total population in the same period.

FROM 1964 TO 1982.   The absolute number of the aged rose sharply, showing an increase of 34.38 million in 18 years. The growth rate was 81.37%, greatly exceeding the growth rate of 45.15% for the total population. The average annual growth rate of the aged was 3.36%, higher than the average annual growth rate of 2.09% for the total population. In this period we see that the older the population, the faster the growth rate was. Compared with 1964, the population of the 60–69 age group in 1982 rose by 65.91%; that of the 70–79 age group rose by 106.23%; and for the group aged 80 and above the increase was 178.61%. The average annual rate of increase was 2.85% for the 60–69 age group; 4.10% for the 70–79 age group; and 5.86% for those aged 80 and above.

Of the 29 provinces, municipalities, and autonomous regions on the Chinese mainland, there were in 1982 nine provinces and municipalities where the proportion of people aged 60 and above exceeded 8% of the total population. These provinces and municipalities were Shanghai, Jiangsu, Zhejiang, Shandong, Beijing, Tianjin, Hebei, Henan, and Guangdong.

According to the 1982 national census, there were in China 3,851 centenarians, of whom 1,135 were men and 2,716 were women; 3,592 were between 100 and 109 years old, of whom 991 were men and 2,601 were women; 225 were between 110 and 119 years old, of whom 126 were men and 99 were women; and 34 were 120 years old or over 120, of

Table 8-20.   Number of People Aged 60 and Above in 1953, 1964, and 1982

	1953	1964	1982
Total population	582,603,417	694,581,795	1,008,180,738
Number of people aged 60 and above	41,538,443	42,254,788	76,637,753
Percentage in the total population	7.13	6.08	7.60

Source: *Major Figures from China's Third Census*, China Statistics Publishing House, October 1982.

whom 18 were men and 16 were women. The oldest person during the census was 130 years old; he was called Kurbanyasen, a member of the Yingaleike production team of the Tashilik Commune in Xinhe County in the Xinjiang Uygur Autonomous Region.*

Among those over 100 years old, 1,510 were of the minority nationalities, accounting for 39.21%; 2,341 were of Han nationality, making up 60.79%. There were on the average 22.5 centenarians for every million people of the minority nationalities and 2.5 centenarians for every million people of Han nationality.

The number and the proportion of old people in the total population of the country will continue to grow in the future. According to forecasts, the proportion of people aged 65 and above will reach 7.2% of the total population by 2000 and the number of the aged will be over 280 million by 2040, making up 20.9% of the total population. That is to say, one out of every five people will then be an old person.†

Over the last 30 years and more, China has done a great deal of work for old people, such as the institution of a retirement system, the undertaking of social welfare and other benefits for the aged, medical and public health services, and cultural and physical education activities. Old people's study, daily life, and health are also well taken care of, thereby providing a secure and happy life for them. In caring for the old, China has adopted a three-in-one policy with Chinese characteristics, combining the efforts of the state, society, and family. With the constant increase in the number of old people, the work of making proper arrangements for them will become increasingly arduous, especially for those in the countryside. China will spare no efforts in caring for the old; its policy is that all old people will be given the support and medical care they need and opportunities will be created for them to continue to learn and accomplish something as they see fit. The welfare of old people is part of the economic growth and social development in China.

REGIONAL DIFFERENCE IN AGE COMPOSITION OF POPULATION

China has a vast territory, and its various regions differ greatly in historical background, natural environment, economic and social development, customs and habits, and distribution of nationalities. These differences affect to varying degrees the age composition of the population of these regions.

Differences Between the 29 Provinces, Municipalities, and Autonomous Regions. The differences in the age composition of the population in the 29 provinces, municipalities, and autonomous regions on the Chinese mainland have the following three major characteristics (see Table 8-21).

The age composition of the population in the interior* is younger than that in the coastal areas.†

Of the 18 provinces and autonomous regions in the interior, only the three provinces of Shanxi, Hubei, and Sichuan topped the nation's average level in median age, while in the other 15, the median age was lower than the nation's average level. These 15 were Inner Mongolia, Jilin, Heilongjiang, Anhui, Jiangxi, Henan, Hunan, Guizhou, Yunnan, Tibet, Shaanxi, Gansu, Qinghai, Ningxia, and Xinjiang.

The eight provinces and municipalities with the highest median age were all in the coastal areas. They were Shanghai, Beijing, Tianjin, Jiangsu, Hebei, Zhejiang, Liaoning, and Shandong. Generally speaking, these provinces and municipalities were comparatively advanced in cultural and economic development. For example, Jiangsu Province led all the provinces, municipalities, and autonomous regions in total output value of industry and agriculture in 1982, reaching 73.7 billion yuan. The per capita share of the total output value to industry and agriculture of Shanghai in 1982 was 5,719 yuan, which was the highest in the nation; in Tianjin the per capita share was 2,994 yuan, and in Beijing it was 2,716 yuan. The high median age in the eight coastal provinces and municipalities was attributable to the high proportion of urban population in their respective total populations. The proportion of urban population was 60.65% in Beijing, 66.23% in Tianjin, 53.30% in Shanghai, and 33.25% in Liaoning—all higher than the nation's average of 14.47%.

The median age of the five provinces and autonomous regions in northwest China was lower than the nation's average. Except Shaanxi, the median ages of the population in the other four (Gansu, Qinghai, Ningxia, and Xinjiang) were far below the

---

* There may be problems of accuracy in the age reporting of those who claim to be over 100 years old.
† "What Is the Trend of Development of the Aging Population in Our Country?" issued by the Demographic Department of the State Statistical Bureau of the People's Republic of China, *Guangming Ribao*, February 24, 1986, p. 2.

* Interior here refers to Shanxi, Inner Mongolia, Jilin, Heilongjiang, Anhui, Jiangxi, Henan, Hubei, Hunan, Sichuan, Guizhou, Yunnan, Tibet, Shaanxi, Gansu, Qinghai, Ningxia, and Xinjiang.
† Coastal areas refer to Beijing, Tianjin, Hebei, Liaoning, Shanghai, Jiangsu, Zhejiang, Fujian, Shandong, Guangdong, and Guangxi.

Table 8-21. Age Composition of Population in Mainland China (1982)

REGION	MEDIAN AGE	PROPORTION IN TOTAL POPULATION (%)			AGED-CHILD RATIO (%)	TOTAL DEPENDENCY RATIO (%)
		0–14	15–64	65+		
Mainland China	22.91	33.59	61.50	4.91	14.62	62.60
Beijing	27.20	22.38	71.97	5.65	25.22	38.95
Tianjin	26.67	24.18	70.24	5.58	23.07	42.37
Hebei	24.72	30.79	63.54	5.67	18.42	57.38
Shanxi	22.97	33.37	61.64	4.99	14.95	62.23
Inner Mongolia	21.11	35.52	60.87	3.61	10.17	64.28
Liaoning	24.60	28.71	66.48	4.81	16.74	50.42
Jilin	22.33	33.17	62.85	3.98	12.00	59.11
Heilongjiang	21.54	34.89	61.69	3.42	9.80	62.10
Shanghai	29.23	18.16	74.01	7.43	40.88	34.58
Jiangsu	25.53	28.98	65.56	5.55	19.14	52.67
Zhejiang	24.70	29.30	64.94	5.76	19.65	53.99
Anhui	20.17	36.15	59.77	4.08	11.30	67.31
Fujian	20.68	36.50	59.12	4.38	12.00	69.15
Jiangxi	19.70	38.80	56.70	4.50	11.61	76.37
Shandong	24.55	31.04	63.34	5.62	18.12	57.88
Henan	22.25	34.90	59.87	5.23	14.98	67.03
Hubei	23.05	32.72	62.28	5.00	15.27	60.57
Hunan	22.50	33.94	61.09	4.97	14.66	63.69
Guangdong	22.53	33.91	60.66	5.43	16.02	64.85
Guangxi	19.98	37.45	57.44	5.11	13.65	74.09
Sichuan	23.42	34.38	60.94	4.68	13.60	64.10
Guizhou	18.76	40.88	54.46	4.66	11.41	83.62
Yunnan	19.40	39.17	56.33	4.50	11.49	77.53
Tibet	21.45	36.61	58.79	4.60	12.58	70.10
Shaanxi	22.93	33.06	62.37	4.57	13.81	60.33
Gansu	20.10	36.32	60.19	3.49	9.61	66.14
Qinghai	18.54	40.56	56.75	2.69	.6.64	76.21
Ningxia	18.42	41.26	55.54	3.20	7.75	79.91
Xinjiang	19.54	39.56	56.76	3.68	9.31	76.18

Source: *Statistics Yearbook of China 1985*, China Statistics Publishing House, 1985, p. 202.

nation's average level. This was, on the whole, because of the backwardness of culture and economy in these regions.

According to the results of the 1982 census, the age composition of the population in the provinces and autonomous regions where large numbers of minority peoples live was comparatively young (see Table 8-22). Most of these provinces and autonomous regions are located in the interior.

Since the founding of New China, the provinces and autonomous regions where the minority peoples live in large numbers have made great achievements

Table 8-22. Proportion of Population of Minority Peoples in the Total Population of Seven Provinces and Autonomous Regions and Their Median Age (1982)

REGION	PROPORTION OF MINORITY PEOPLES IN THE TOTAL POPULATION (%)	MEDIAN AGE OF TOTAL POPULATION
Guangxi Zhuang Autonomous Region	38.26	19.98
Yunnan Province	31.71	19.40
Qinghai Province	39.42	18.54
Ningxia Hui Autonomous Region	31.94	18.42
Xinjiang Uygur Autonomous Region	59.61	19.54
Tibet Autonomous Region	95.10	21.45
Gansu Province	7.95	20.10

Sources: *Statistics Yearbook of China 1985*, China Statistics Publishing House, 1985, p. 202; *1982 Population Census of China*, China Statistics Publishing House, 1985, p. 218.

in economic and social development. But compared with the advanced provinces and regions, they still lag behind, and this invariably finds expression in matters related to population. Generally speaking, the fertility rate of the minority peoples is higher than that of the Han nationality and, therefore, the age composition is younger. Among the 15 major minority nationalities with a population of over one million each, the average median age is 19.42 years old, and that of the Hani people is the youngest, being 18.02 years old. Among these 15 minority nationalities, the number of people in the 0–4 age group makes up a high proportion in the total population. Except for the Korean and Manchu nationalities, the proportion of the population in the 0–14 age group of the other nationalities, is generally over 36%; that of Hani nationality ranks first, reaching 42.58%. It can thus be seen that the high fertility rate is a direct cause of the young age composition of the population of the minority nationalities.

Differences in the Age Composition of the Population in the Cities, Towns, and Counties. *   Following are three characteristics that describe the differences in the age composition of the population in the cities, towns, and counties in China:

First, the results of the 1982 census showed that the age of the city population was fairly high and that of the towns came next, while that of the counties was comparatively young (see Table 8-23). The median age of the city population was 26.03 years old; it was 25.57 years old for the towns and 21.05 years old for the counties.

The differences in the age composition of the city, town, and county population were the results of changes in the birthrate, deathrate, and migrations over a long period of time. At the same time, they were also the results of the different functions of

* City population does not include the population of counties under the jurisdiction of the cities, and county population does not include the population of towns under the counties.

each city, town, and county in the course of economic and social development.

Second, the proportion of the population in the 0–4, 5–9, 10–14, and 15–19 age groups in the total population of the counties was higher than that of the cities and towns.

The number of people of these age groups migrating between the cities, towns, and counties was few. Therefore, it basically showed the differences in fertility rate between the county population, on the one hand, and the city and town population, on the other. The general trend of the proportion of the population in the 20–24 to 55–59 age groups in the total population was that the proportion in the county population was lower than that of the cities and towns. But the general trend of the proportion of the population in the 60–64 age group and above was that the proportion in the county population was slightly higher than that of the city and town population (see Chart 8-3).

The above facts show that the proportion of people aged 19 and under and people over 60 was higher in the countryside than in the cities and towns. This calls for attention to the people in these two age groups in the countryside because they are the people who either need to be cared for and given an education or supported in old age. The whole society should show particular concern for them.

Third, the age composition of the population in some cities differed greatly from that of the counties. Following is a comparison between the population of the urban districts in Shanghai and that of the county population in the Ningxia Hui Autonomous Region (see Table 8-24 and Chart 8-4). The median age of the population of urban districts in Shanghai was 31.5 years old, while that of the counties in the Ningxia Hui Autonomous Region was 17.4 years old. The difference between the two was 14.1 years. This indicates two entirely different age composition patterns and the trend of development in China's counties and cities. The population of urban districts in Shanghai will grow increasingly old, whereas the

Table 8-23.   Proportion of Population in Three Age Groups in China's Cities, Towns, and Counties (1982)

AGE GROUP	CITY POPULATION (%)	TOWN POPULATION (%)	COUNTY POPULATION (%)
Total	100.0	100.0	100.0
0–14	26.0	28.3	35.4
15–64	69.3	67.5	59.6
65+	4.7	4.2	5.0

Source: *1982 Population Census of China*, China Statistics Publishing House, 1985, pp. 284, 294, 304.

Chart 8-3.   Age Composition of the Population in China's Cities, Towns, and Counties (1982)

Proportion (%)

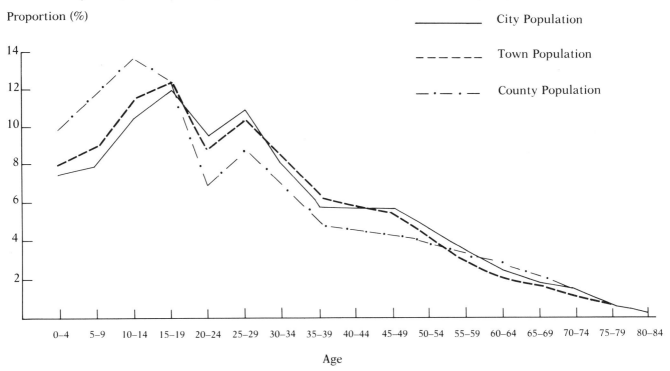

Source: *1982 Population Census of China*, China Statistics Publishing House, 1985.

Chart 8-4.   Comparison of the Age Composition of the Urban Population in Shanghai and the County Population in Ningxia in 1982

Proportion (%)

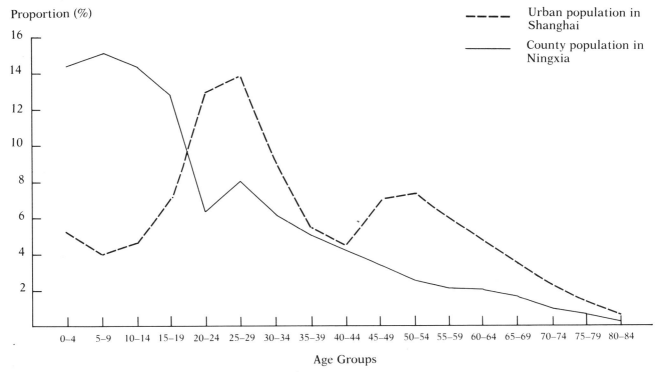

Sources: Calculated according to the age composition data from the *Shanghai 1982 Population Census of China* and the *Ningxia Hui Autonomous Region 1982 Population Census Data of China*.

Table 8-24. Comparison of the Age Composition of the Urban Population in Shanghai and the County Population in Ningxia (1982)

AGE GROUP	SHANGHAI URBAN DISTRICT POPULATION (%)	COUNTY POPULATION IN NINGXIA (%)	DIFFERENCE (ABSOLUTE VALUE) (%)
Total	100.00	100.00	
0–14	13.81	43.91	30.10
15–64	78.08	52.76	25.32
65+	8.11	3.33	4.78

Sources: Calculated according to the age composition data from the *Shanghai 1982 Population Census of China* and the *Ningxia Hui Autonomous Region 1982 Population Census Data of China.*

county population in Ningxia has the latent factor of a high birthrate in the future, and its population will therefore remain young.

The great difference between the age composition of the urban population in Shanghai and that of the county population in Ningxia was also the result of the difference in their childbearing rate and a reflection of their enormous difference in economic and social development.

Family planning was promoted in the early 1960s in Shanghai proper, and the fertility rate there has since continued to drop by a big margin. The proportion of the 0–14 age group population dropped from 43.05% in 1964 to 13.81% in 1982, a decrease of 68% in 18 years. This is inconceivable in other areas in China where economic and social development is comparatively slow. The proportion of the county population of the 0–14 age group in the Ningxia Hui Autonomous Region was 43.91% in 1982, close to the 1964 level in Shanghai's urban districts. Because the birthrate in Ningxia was still as high as 29.65‰ in 1981, the aforesaid great difference will continue for a period of time in the future. This also shows that it is difficult to change the age composition of the population in some areas, because such a change ultimately hinges on the economic and social structure of those areas as a whole.

CHAPTER NINE

MARRIAGE AND FAMILY

Marriage is a product of the evolution of human society at a certain stage. It is a social form of the union of two sexes and the basis for the building of a family and the reproduction of mankind. Besides being a unit of reproduction of mankind, the family is a social community based on marriages, blood relations, or adoption, composed generally of husband and wife, parents and children, brothers and sisters, and other close relatives. With the emergence of these phenomena, the multiplication of mankind is realized through certain forms of marriages and families. The nature and composition of the family and the ethics and views on childbirth corresponding to certain systems of marriage and family are major factors affecting the reproduction of mankind.

MARRIAGE
BRIEF SURVEY OF CHINA'S MARRIAGE SYSTEM

A marriage system is a social system directly connected with the mode of social production and is made up of various standards of action related to marriage. It generally takes the form of certain laws and is supplemented by ethical principles, customs, and traditions.

In the more than 2,000 years of feudal society in China, the marriage system was completely subordinate to the patriarchal clan system. Its chief characteristics were: there was no freedom of marriage for men or women and marriages were arbitrarily arranged by parents; the concept that men were superior to women held sway; the interests and rights of the children were disregarded; and marriage relations were under the trammels of political authority, theocratic authority, clan authority, and husband's authority. This feudal marriage system actually lasted thousands of years until the early days of the founding of the People's Republic of China, when arbitrary and mercenary marriages were still quite common. The people of the whole country, particularly the women, urgently demanded to be free from the shackles of the feudal marriage system so as to achieve happy marriages and build felicitous families.

In May 1950, the Marriage Law of the People's Republic of China was promulgated and put into force by the central people's government. The law put an end to the feudal marriage system characterized by marriages upon arbitrary decision by a third party, superiority of men over women, and disregard of children's interests; the law enforced the new democratic marriage system characterized by free choice of partners, monogamy, equal rights for both sexes, and protection of the lawful rights and interests of women and children. Later, stipulations and directives were issued by the government on several occasions to ensure the implementation of the marriage law. The enactment and implementation of these decrees and policies proclaimed the end of China's feudal marriage system and they have since brought about profound changes in China's marriage and family relations. According to the statistical data of 11 major cities in the first half of 1954, 97.5% of the marriages that year conformed to the requirements of the marriage law. Thirty years later, in September 1980, the law was revised on the basis of the practice and experience gained over the past three decades, and the new marriage law was put into effect in 1981. The new law retains many stipulations of the first law that have proved to be effective and includes new contents such as protection of the lawful rights of old people and the practice of planned parenthood. The new law has also changed the lawful age for marriage from 20 to 22 for men and from 18 to 20 for women. It also explicitly forbids marriages between men and women who are lineal relatives by blood or collateral relatives by blood (up to the third degree of relationship), stipulates the rights and duties of the husband and wife as well as the parents and children. In addition, the legal conditions for divorce are written into the new law.

It is thus evident that the present marriage system in China fully demonstrates that under socialism men and women are equal and that a new type of relationship exists between them. In this way, the age-old feudal marriage system, under which men were considered superior to women, was completely repudiated. It should be noted at the same time that marriage, as a social phenomenon, is interrelated with certain economic conditions. China is now a developing socialist country with a rather low level of productive forces, and its scientific, cultural, and educational undertakings are not developed. There still exist remnants of the old thoughts and ideology from the old society. Moreover, in Chinese society there are differences between the nature of work and the ownership of the means of production. Families are the cells of the society, and the level of the means of subsistence and consumption varies from family to family. All these impede to a certain degree the setting up of new types of marriage relations, leading to certain inequity between both sexes in marriage and family relations, interference in the freedom of marriage, or even arbitrary and mercenary marriages and bigamy in a disguised form. However, following the development of the economy, social progress, raising of the scientific, cultural, and educational level, and the subsequent changes in people's ideology and ethical standards, these irrational phenomena in marriages will gradually decrease, and the socialist marriage system that conforms to the present development of mankind will be steadily perfected.

In present-day Chinese society, freedom of marriage is on the increase. A man and a woman get to know each other, fall in love, and get married of their own will. Such marriages are, of course, protected by law. Taking the situation as a whole, however, such marriages are few in number today. In most cases, the man and woman get acquainted through the introduction of parents, relatives, friends, or colleagues, then the two decide on their own whether to get married or not. With the progress of society, young people will have more opportunities to get to know each other and there will be more cases of free marriages in the future.

MARITAL STATUS

Marital status can be classified as follows: unmarried, married, widowed, and divorced. Following is an analysis of marital status in China based on the 1982 census and other related materials.

Sex Composition of Marital Status. In 1982 the proportion of unmarried people constituted 28.57% of China's population aged 15 and over, which was much higher than in the past. Sample surveys conducted in some cities and counties in the 1940s showed that the percentage of unmarried was between 8.18 and 20.95%.* In the mid-1950s, the percentage of unmarried in Beijing was 19.36%.† The increase in the percentage of unmarried was mainly due to late marriages among the young people. This was a clear manifestation of the remarkable success achieved since the 1970s, following the promotion of family planning and implementation of the state policy advocating late marriages and late childbirths. Among the unmarried in 1982, 32.71% were men and 24.22% were women, with the male 8.49% higher than the female. The reasons for this were: First, among the population aged 15 and above, the ratio between men and women was 105:100, and men outnumbered women by 16.22 million. This being the case, it was therefore easier for women to get married. Second, the average age for first marriages was lower among women than among men.

In 1982, the proportion of men with spouses was 3.59% less than that of women. In absolute figures, men with spouses numbered nearly 1.61 million fewer than women. Under ordinary circumstances, the proportion of men with spouses is usually higher than that of women in many countries. In Canada, for instance, the proportion of men with spouses was 65.1%, while that of women was 64.1%. In the Federal Republic of Germany, the proportion in 1972 was 53.4% for men and 47.8% for women; the proportion in Denmark in 1976 was 47.4% for men and 46.5% for women.‡ In Japan, the proportion in 1980 was 67.7% for men and 64.1% for women.§ The abnormal phenomenon in China in 1982 was mainly due to the fact that the statistical data for the population aged 15 and above included the total number for the 29 provinces, municipalities, and autonomous regions but did not include soldiers of the People's Liberation Army in active service, the majority of whom were men, while their wives who did not stay

* Chen Da, *Population in Modern China*, Tianjin People's Publishing House, 1981.
† Based on a retrospective survey of 2,180 persons aged 15 and over made by the author in seven districts and counties in Beijing.
‡ *The Population of Canada, The Population of the Federal Republic of Germany*, and *The Population of Denmark*, C.I.C.R.E.D. Series.
§ *Population in Our Country, 1982*, by the Statistics Bureau of the Prime Minister's Office of Japan, quoted in *Population Research*, No. 3, 1984.

in the army were included in the civilian population of their respective localities and were classified as women with spouses. In the above-mentioned developed countries, the fact that the proportion of women with spouses was lower was also because the life span of women was longer than that of men.

Among the married couples in China in 1982, 7.16% lost their spouses, which was close to the 7.75%* of Beijing in the mid-1950s, but much lower than the level of some cities and counties in the 1940s, which ranged from 10.57 to 15.26%.† This shows that in the last 30 years and more, the Chinese people's health has improved markedly. Among the widowed the proportion of women was 5.55% higher than men. This is normal, because, generally speaking, the death rate of men is higher than that of women of the same age, and still higher than that of their wives who are younger than themselves.

In 1982 the proportion of divorced couples was higher than in the 1940s, but on the whole the proportion had not reached the level of the early and mid-1950s. (The reason for the high divorce rate in the 1950s was mainly due to the fact that the promulgation of the new marriage law enabled a number of women to free themselves from the bondage of irrational feudal and arbitrary marriages.)

In 1982, the proportion of divorced people constituted 0.59% of the total population aged 15 and above, 0.92% for divorced men and 0.25% for divorced women (see Table 9-1). Compared with the developed countries, this proportion was not high. In Canada, the 1971 census showed that the figure for men was 1% and for women was 1.3%.‡ In Japan in 1980, it was 1.2% for men and 2.5% for women.§

* Based on a retrospective survey of 2,180 people aged 15 and over in 1956 made by the author in seven districts and counties in Beijing.
† Chen Da, *Population in Modern China*, Tianjin People's Publishing House, 1981.
‡ *The Population of Canada*, C.I.C.R.E.D. Series.
§ *Population in Our Country, 1982*, by the Statistics Bureau of the Prime Minister's Office of Japan, quoted in *Population Research*, No. 3, 1984.

Age Composition in Marital Status. Of the various aspects of marital status, the age composition of unmarried people has always been a major point of attention. Table 9-2 shows that in 1982 the proportion of unmarried people aged 15–19 in China was as high as 97.38%. In other words, only 2.62% (1% of men and 4.38% of women) in this age group were married. More than half of the young women were married by ages 20–24: 25% of 20-year-old women and 79% of 24-year-old women were married. In the 25–29 age group, the proportion of unmarried people dropped by a big margin. At age 20, 7% of the men were married; at ages 24 and 29, the percentages were 49 and 86, respectively. Married men constituted 23.59%, that is, married men made up 76.41%. The proportion of ummarried women in this age group also dropped considerably, with married women making up 94.73%. In the 30–34 age group, unmarried men constituted only 8.84% and unmarried women 0.69%. These figures show that young men and women in China generally get married before 30, particularly women, and very few remain unmarried at an older age. (See Chart 9-1).

If we make a detailed study of the unmarried people of different ages in the 20–24 and 25–29 age groups, we can get a clear picture of the general trend in the change of the proportion of unmarried people and the difference in the marriage age of men and women (see Table 9-3). For example, 75.14% of the 20-year-old females and 76.14% of the 22-year-old males were unmarried, and 62.57% of the 21-year-old females and 63.44% of the 23-year-old males were unmarried. From these examples, we can see that if the percentage of unmarried men is to catch up with that of unmarried women, they must be 2 to 4 years older than women. With the increase in age, the gap will gradually widen to 3–4 years. The median of women's marriage age is around 22, while that of men is 24.

The unmarried status reflects that the difference between the percentage of unmarried men and that of unmarried women is by no means small. In the

Table 9-1   Marital Status of Chinese Population (1982)

UNMARRIED			WITH SPOUSES		
TOTAL	MALE	FEMALE	TOTAL	MALE	FEMALE
28.57	32.71	24.22	63.68	61.93	65.52

SPOUSES DECEASED			DIVORCED		
TOTAL	MALE	FEMALE	TOTAL	MALE	FEMALE
7.16	4.45	10.00	0.59	0.92	0.25

Source: *1982 Population Census of China*, China Statistics Publishing House, 1985.

Table 9-2 Marital Status of Different Age Groups (1982) (%)

AGE GROUP	UNMARRIED			WITH SPOUSES			SPOUSES DECEASED			DIVORCED		
	TOTAL	MALE	FEMALE	TOTAL	MALE	FEMALE	TOTAL	MALE	FEMALE	TOTAL	MALE	FEMALE
15–19	97.38	99.07	95.62	2.59	0.91	4.33	0.004	0.004	0.004	0.024	0.009	0.038
20–24	59.45	71.98	46.45	40.33	27.82	53.33	0.048	0.046	0.05	0.163	0.161	0.165
25–29	14.72	23.59	5.27	84.72	75.70	94.32	0.21	0.24	0.175	0.36	0.47	0.24
30–34	4.93	8.84	0.69	93.94	89.67	98.56	0.55	0.63	0.47	0.58	0.85	0.28
35–39	3.70	6.77	0.28	94.33	90.83	98.21	1.23	1.25	1.21	0.74	1.14	0.29
40–44	3.13	5.71	0.20	93.39	90.52	96.66	2.54	2.28	2.84	0.94	1.50	0.30
45–49	2.39	4.37	0.18	91.45	89.75	93.36	4.99	3.99	6.12	1.16	1.89	0.33
50–59	1.66	2.98	0.21	84.48	86.56	82.19	12.58	8.44	17.12	1.28	2.02	0.48
60–79	1.37	2.56	0.30	56.70	70.65	44.21	40.98	25.22	55.10	0.95	1.57	0.39
80+	1.11	2.63	0.29	17.72	37.32	7.17	80.80	59.23	92.41	0.37	0.82	0.13

Source: *1982 Population Census of China*, China Statistics Publishing House, 1985.

Chart 9-1.   Marital Status of Chinese Population (1982)

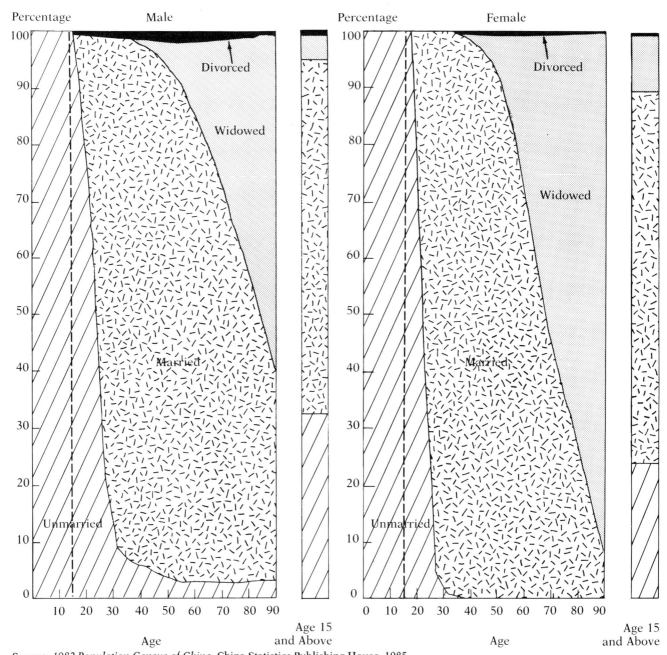

Source: *1982 Population Census of China,* China Statistics Publishing House, 1985.

35–39 age group, 6.77% of the men were unmarried, which was much higher than that of unmarried women of the same age. Among those over 50, the percentage of unmarried men was 2.78% and that of unmarried women was 0.26%. The reasons for this difference are: 1) before the founding of New China, in 1949, the laboring people lived in great poverty and could not afford to get married and support a family; 2) the male population at that time was slightly higher, so there were a number of them who could not get married.

In comparison with the 1971 figures for Canada, the percentage of unmarried men in China in 1982 was 1.1% higher, while the percentage of unmarried Chinese women was 0.8% lower. When compared with the 1980 figures for Japan, the percentage of

Table 9-3   Proportion of
Unmarried People in
the 20–29 Age Group (1982)(%)

AGE	MALE	FEMALE
20	93.38	75.14
21	87.13	62.57
22	76.14	48.61
23	63.44	33.22
24	51.00	20.96
25	38.42	12.05
26	28.66	6.83
27	21.05	3. 73
28	16.24	2.19
29	12.93	1.39

Source: *1982 Population Census of China*, China Statistics Publishing House, 1985.

both unmarried men and women in China was higher. But the actual situation of such differences between the various countries can be obtained only through a study of the different age groups.

The percentage of unmarried men younger than 24 in China was higher than that of Canada. However, beginning from the age of 25, the percentage of unmarried men in China started to decrease drastically, while that of Canada decreased at a slower pace. This shows that the marriage age for Chinese men was earlier and more concentrated, as most men got married before 30, while in Canada, 10.3% of the men in the 35–39 age group were still unmarried. In Canada, the percentage of unmarried men over 35 remained high, and the unmarried percentage was over 9% in most of the age groups over 35. As for those over 65, the percentage of unmarried men was as high as 10.6%. This indicates that there were many more lifetime bachelors in Canada than in China. In the case of unmarried women, the percentage was slightly higher in Canada, but this does not mean that Canadian women got married at a later age that Chinese women. On the contrary, the per-

centage of married Canadian women between 15 and 24 years old was higher than for their Chinese counterparts. But after 24, the drop in the proportion of unmarried women in Canada was far smaller than that of China. In the 25–29 age group, the percentage of unmarried women in China was 5.3%, while in Canada it was 15.4%. That shows that the marriage age of Chinese women was more concentrated than that of Canadian women, and the percentage of unmarried Canadian women older than the 30–34 age group remained at a fairly high level. The percentage for unmarried women over 65 in Canada was as high as 10.7%, while the proportion of unmarried Chinese women aged 60 and over 60 was less than 0.30%. As for Japan, because the proportion of unmarried Japanese people was on the whole lower than that of China, it would seem that Japanese young people got married at an earlier age than their Chinese counterparts. But actually, a survey of different age groups shows that the proportion of unmarried Japanese men and women from 15 to 39 was higher than that of China. This means that the average marriage age of Chinese youth was lower than the Japanese and the Chinese youth's marriage age more concentrated (see Table 9-4).

As shown in Table 9-2, in 1982 only 0.91% of the males and 4.33% of the females in the 15–19 age group had spouses. This shows that only a small number of women and very few men married at an early age. With the growing of age, the proportion of people having spouses also increased, reaching the peak at the 35–39 age group for men and the 30–34 age group for women. The reason is obvious: Most men and women of those two age groups had got married, and as they were in their prime, their death rate was lower than that of people of the higher age groups, and the rate of widowed was lower too. However, as they grew older, the proportion of people with spouses began to decrease with the increase of the proportion of the widowed.

Table 9-4   Percentage of Unmarried People in Different Age Groups in China, Canada, and Japan

AGE GROUP (MALE)	CHINA (1982)	CANADA (1971)	JAPAN (1980)	AGE GROUP (FEMALE)	CHINA (1982)	CANADA (1971)	JAPAN (1980)
Total	32.7	31.6	28.6	Total	24.2	25.0	20.9
15–19	99.1	98.4	99.6	15–19	95.6	92.5	99.0
20–24	72.0	67.6	91.5	20–24	46.5	43.5	77.9
25–29	23.6	25.6	54.8	25–29	5.3	15.4	23.9
30–34	8.8	13.3	21.5	30–34	0.7	9.1	9.1
35–39	6.8	10.3	8.7	35–39	0.3	7.3	5.6

Sources: For China, *1982 Population Census of China*, China Statistics Publishing House, 1985. The statistical data for Canada are from *The Population of Canada*, C.I.C.R.E.D. Series. The statistical data for Japan are from *Population in Our Country*, 1982, by the Statistics Bureau of the Prime Minister's Office of Japan, quoted in *Population Research*, No. 3, 1984.

Table 9-5 Proportion of Age-Specific First Married Among Women Aged 15–49 (1982)(%).

AGE GROUP	PROPORTION OF FIRST MARRIED	AGE GROUP	PROPORTION OF FIRST MARRIED	AGE GROUP	PROPORTION OF FIRST MARRIED	AGE GROUP	PROPORTION OF FIRST MARRIED
15	0.20	25	86.09	35	94.08	45	85.98
16	0.83	26	91.16	36	93.90	46	85.71
17	2.35	27	94.28	37	93.56	47	84.90
18	5.88	28	95.47	38	92.32	48	83.13
19	11.94	29	95.96	39	92.71	49	82.04
20	25.71	30	95.94	40	90.37	Total average	64.53
21	38.07	31	95.80	41	91.33		
22	49.76	32	95.11	42	89.54		
23	65.90	33	95.13	43	87.95		
24	78.38	34	94.65	44	88.45		

Source: Data from *One-Per-Thousand-Population Fertility Sampling Survey in China.* Supplied by the office of the relevant leading group under the State Family Planning Commission.

135

The above analysis brings into focus the following two features: 1) the percentage of people losing their spouses began to increase when they reached the age of 50, hitting 12.58% for the 50–59 age group and 43.61% for those over 60. But, both figures were lower than those of Beijing in the mid-1950s, which were 13.63% and 50.25%, respectively.* This was because the health and general physical conditions of the people had improved over the past 30-odd years. 2) While the proportion of widows in the general population is higher than that of widowers, the proportion of widowers is higher than that of widows in the 25–29, 30–34, and 35–39 age groups. The reason might be that women of these age groups were in their prime child-bearing period and the mortality rate of women before and after childbirth was higher than that of ordinary women. Another reason may be the high remarriage rate for widows; the census does not differentiate between first and second marriages.

The analysis also demonstrates that the main characteristic of cases of divorce in China is: The proportion of divorced people increases with the growth of age for both men and women. This is because the possibility of getting married again is in inverse ratio to the growth of age.

AVERAGE FIRST-MARRIAGE AGE FOR WOMEN AND RELEVANT CHANGES

First-marriage age means literally the age at which people get married for the first time. This age, especially for women, has a vital bearing on childbearing. The following is an analysis of the present situation of first marriages among Chinese women based on a one-thousandth sample survey of China's birthrate conducted by China's State Family Planning Commission in September 1982 in the country's 28 provinces, municipalities, and autonomous regions (not including Taiwan Province and the Tibet Autonomous Region).

Present Situation of First Marriages Among Women. The proportion of first marriages among women of childbearing age (15–49) is 64.53%, and that of older women (between 50 and 67) is 68.04%. For women of the 25–49 age group, the proportion of first marriages is over 80%, the highest being 95.96% for women aged 29. After that age, the proportion of first marriages among women begins to drop gradually

Table 9-6   Proportion of First Marriages Among Older Women Aged 50–57 (1982)(%)

AGE GROUP	PROPORTION OF FIRST MARRIED
50–54	77.46
55–59	70.19
60–64	59.46
65–67	52.68
Total average	68.04

Source: Data from *One-Per-Thousand-Population Fertility Sampling Survey in China.* Supplied by the office of the relevant leading group under the State Family Planning Commission.

along with the growth of age, while the proportion of the widowed, remarried, and divorced has increased slowly. But the proportion of first marriages still stands at 82.04% at the age of 49. Due to the same reasons, the proportion of first marriages among women over 50 continues to drop and at a faster rate than before (see Table 9-5 and Table 9-6).

In terms of first marriages for women of childbearing age, there are big differences between urban and rural areas (see Table 9-7). Major manifestations are as follows: First, the proportion of first marriages among women of childbearing age in the countryside is higher than in the cities; and second, the proportion of first marriages among these women in the countryside reaches its peak point at the 30–34 age group, while in the cities the peak point is the 35–39 age group. This shows that women in the countryside get married at an earlier age than those in the cities (see Table 9-7). A second reason may be that the

Table 9-7   Proportion of First Marriages Among Women of Childbearing Age (15–49) in China's Urban and Rural Areas (1982)(%)

AGE GROUP	URBAN AREAS	RURAL AREAS
15–19	0.57	5.11
20–24	26.90	59.95
25–29	81.81	94.87
30–34	93.97	95.64
35–39	94.89	93.09
40–44	93.04	88.69
45–49	89.55	83.00
Total	61.22	65.20

Source: Data from *One-Per-Thousand-Population Fertility Sampling Survey in China.* Supplied by the office of the relevant leading group under the State Family Planning Commission.

* Based on a retrospective survey of 2,180 people aged 15 and over in 1956 made by the author in seven districts and counties in Beijing.

mortality rate in rural areas is higher, causing widowhood to increase in those areas.

Change in average first-marriage age among women. The average first-marriage age among Chinese women has gone up significantly since the founding of New China. In the 10 years from 1940 to 1949, before liberation, the average first-marriage age was raised by only 0.36 year. In 1949, it was 18.57 years old, but by the first half of 1982 it had gone up to 22.66 years old for Chinese women, up 4.09 years in 30 years or an average of 1.24 years in every decade. This shows that it was only after the founding of New China that the average first-marriage age among women has been steadily raised as a result of the improvement of women's social status, the increase of opportunities for education and employment for them, and particularly the positive influence of the government population policy.

A stage-by-stage analysis will even more clearly show the change in the average first-marriage age among Chinese women over the past 30-odd years (see Tables 9-8 and 9-9).

In the 23 years from 1949 to 1972, the average first-marriage age among Chinese women had been raised at a steady pace by 2.35 years. A change took place in 1972. In the 1972–75 period, the average age for first marriages went up from 20.56 years old

Table 9-9 Average First-Marriage Age Among Chinese Women in 1940s, 1950s, 1960s, and 1970s

DECADE	NATIONAL AVERAGE	URBAN AREAS	RURAL AREAS
1940s	18.46	19.16	18.32
1950s	19.02	20.13	18.76
1960s	19.81	22.10	19.43
1970s	21.59	23.99	21.21

Source: Data from *One-Per-Thousand-Population Fertility Sampling Survey in China.* Supplied by the office of the relevant leading group under the State Family Planning Commission.

to 21.74 years old, or an increase of 1.18 years. The average age was raised by another 1.09 years from 1975 to 1978. By 1979, the average first-marriage age for women reached 23.12 years old, which was an all-time high in the 30-odd years after the founding of the People's Republic, and also the highest in China's history. Apart from political, economic, and cultural factors, the significant change in the average age for first marriages during this period was due to the population policy adopted by the Chinese government since the beginning of the 1970s, advocating late marriages, late childbirths, and giving birth to fewer but healthier babies.

Beginning in 1981, China put into effect the new Marriage Law, which appropriately raised the legal

Table 9-8 Average First-Marriage Age Among Chinese Women from 1940 to 1982

YEAR	NATIONAL AVERAGE	URBAN AREAS	RURAL AREAS	YEAR	NATIONAL AVERAGE	URBAN AREAS	RURAL AREAS
1940	18.21	18.73	18.12	1962	19.61	21.49	19.27
1941	18.21	18.88	18.09	1963	19.58	21.49	19.25
1942	18.34	18.78	18.27	1964	19.55	22.04	19.17
1943	18.41	19.39	18.22	1965	19.74	22.57	19.30
1944	18.46	19.17	18.32	1966	19.86	22.86	19.44
1945	18.60	19.35	18.45	1967	20.03	22.73	19.57
1946	18.69	19.57	18.50	1968	20.17	22.62	19.73
1947	18.53	19.21	18.40	1969	20.29	22.45	19.94
1948	18.59	19.39	18.42	1970	20.19	22.38	19.89
1949	18.57	19.16	18.44	1971	20.29	22.80	19.96
1950	18.68	19.41	18.52	1972	20.56	23.23	20.22
1951	18.69	19.43	18.54	1973	20.95	23.48	20.60
1952	18.94	19.75	18.76	1974	21.38	23.79	20.99
1953	18.94	19.85	18.71	1975	21.74	24.13	21.36
1954	19.00	20.12	18.72	1976	22.30	24.61	21.90
1955	19.07	20.28	18.81	1977	22.57	24.99	22.11
1956	19.19	20.51	18.87	1978	22.83	25.10	22.41
1957	19.23	20.40	18.90	1979	23.12	25.40	22.64
1958	19.15	20.77	18.78	1980	23.05	25.19	22.54
1959	19.35	20.81	19.01	1981	22.82	24.71	22.28
1960	19.57	21.25	19.24	1982	22.66	24.93	22.07
1961	19.70	21.46	19.40				

Source: Data from *One-Per-Thousand-Population Fertility Sampling Survey in China.* Supplied by the office of the relevant leading group under the State Family Planning Commission.

age for marriage. The law clearly stipulates, "No marriage should be contracted before the man has reached 22 years of age and the woman 20 years of age. Late marriage and late childbirth should be encouraged." Here, legal age for marriage means the lowest age for people to get married and does not mean that young men and women must get married at that age. It can be said that the new Marriage Law and the regulations on the age for marriage conform to both social needs and young people's physiological condition and their ability for economic independence. The Marriage Law has taken into consideration the actual conditions of the people in the cities and the acceptability by the country's 800 million peasants. Hence, it has been widely supported by the people since its promulgation. Many young people still follow the practice of late marriage and late childbirth* of their own accord after reaching the legal age for marriage. The result was that in the first half of 1982 the average first-marriage age of women still stood at 22.66 years old, a drop of only 0.46 year from that of 1979, but 2.66 years higher than the legal marriage age.

Although the average first-marriage age among Chinese women has been raised by a wide margin over the last three decades and more, it still lags behind that in some countries. For instance, according to data released by the Statistics Bureau of the Prime Minister's Office of Japan, the mean age at first marriage for Japanese women was 25.2 years old in 1980, as compared with 23.05 years old for Chinese women in the same year, which was just a little higher than 22.9 years old for Japanese women in 1950. In the 1961–69 period, the average first-marriage age for women in Sri Lanka went up from 22.7 years old to 23.5 years old,† which was not only higher than the average level of first-marriage age for Chinese women in the same period, but also higher than the average level for Chinese women in the latter half of the 1970s and the early 1980s. Since the beginning of the 1960s, the average first-marriage age among women in some developing countries in Southeast Asia, such as Singapore and the Philippines, has gone up to 23–24 years old. Women in Thailand and Malaysia have also approached this level.‡ The developing countries in Latin America

have the tradition of marrying at a late age. For instance, in 1971 the average first-marriage age for women in Cuba was 25.5 years old; in Mexico, it was 22.7 years old in 1973; in Argentina, it was 24.1 years old in 1970; and in Chile, it was 23.5 years old in 1972.* Although the average first-marriage age among women in some European and American countries has come down somewhat since World War II, in most of the countries it is still higher than that for Chinese women.

Difference in Average First-Marriage Age Among Women in China's Urban and Rural Areas. There is a big difference in the average first-marriage age for urban and rural women in China. In the 1940s, the average first-marriage age for women throughout China was 18.46 years old, and that for urban women was 0.84 year higher than that for rural women. In the 1950s, the national average was 19.02 years old, and that for urban women was higher by 1.37 years than rural women. By the 1960s, the national average had reached 19.81 years old, and the difference between urban and rural women had increased to 2.67 years. And in the 1970s, the national average first-marriage age for women went up to 21.59 years old, and that for women in the cities was 2.78 years higher than that for women in the countryside. This shows that while the average first-marriage age for women in the country as a whole kept rising, the increase in age for urban women was faster than that for rural women, and the difference also widened as time went by.

A year-by-year analysis will give a clearer picture. For instance, the average first-marriage age for Chinese women in the cities in 1949 was 19.16 years old and in 1955 it was 20.28 years old, an increase of 1.12 years in six years. As for rural women, the average age was 18.44 years old in 1949 and 19.44 years old in 1966—an increase of only one year in 17 years. In this period, the average first-marriage age for urban women had gone up to 22.86 years old, which means an increase of 2.58 years in the 11 years from 1955 to 1966. From 1966 to 1970, the average first-marriage age among rural young people showed a noticeable increase. In the cities, however, due to the serious anarchist tendency caused by the chaotic "cultural revolution," the average first-marriage age fell by 0.48 years. After 1970, it began to rise rapidly again thanks to the implementation of the state family planning policy. In a short period of three years, it

---

* Late marriage means young women and men get married at 24 and 25, respectively, in the countryside and at 24 and 26 in the cities. Late childbirth means women giving birth to children after age 25.
† *The Population of Sri Lanka*, C.I.C.R.E.D. Series.
‡ Wu Cangping and Hou Wenruo, *World Population*, China People's University Press, 1983.

* Lin Fude and Shen Qiuhua, *World Population and Economic Development*, China People's University Press, 1980.

rose by 1.1 years. By 1976, it further went up by 1.13 years and reached the peak of 25.40 years old by 1979, which means an increase of 3.02 years in nine years. During the same period, the average first-marriage age for rural women also went up rapidly, from 19.89 years old in 1970 to 20.99 years old in 1974, that is, an increase of 1.1 years in four years. In the following two years, the average first-marriage age for rural women again rose by 0.91 year to reach an all-time high of 22.64 years old in 1979, which means an increase of 2.75 years in nine years. With the promulgation and implementation of the new Marriage Law, the average first-marriage age for both urban and rural women began to drop. Comparing 1982 with 1980, the reduction for urban women was 0.26 year, and that for rural women was 0.47 year, with the latter obviously faster than the former.

Regional Differences in the Average First-Marriage Age. As China is a vast country with different climate and geological conditions, different customs and habits among the various nationalities, and, in particular, as the political, economic, cultural, and educational development is uneven in different regions, the average first-marriage age for women varies from place to place. An analysis of the situation in Liaoning, Inner Mongolia, Beijing, Jiangsu, Shanghai, Sichuan, and Hunan will show the regional differences in the average first-marriage age for Chinese women (see Table 9-10).

In static terms, of the four provinces, two municipalities, and one autonomous region shown in Table 9-10, Shanghai has the highest average first-marriage age for women, which was already more than one year higher than the national average in the 1940s and 1950s. In the 1960s and 1970s, Shanghai's average was over three years higher than the national average, and then two years higher. Next comes Beijing, where the average first-marriage age has been markedly higher than the national average since the 1960s. The average first-marriage age in coastal Liaoning and Jiangsu, both of which are comparatively developed in economy and culture, was also higher than the national average, but in Hunan, Inner Mongolia, and Sichuan, the average first-marriage age was lower than the national average. In terms of growth, from the 1950s to the early 1980s, Beijing witnessed the quickest rise in the average first-marriage age for women, a rise of 25.46%; next comes Inner Mongolia, with a rise of 24.26%. The rate of rise in the average first-marriage age was the lowest in Hunan and Sichuan, being 18.72% and 19.96%, respectively, both of which were lower than the national average of 20.08% during the same period.

Regional difference in the average first-marriage age among Chinese women is closely connected with the effectiveness of the implementation of the policy of late marriage and late childbirth in each region. The rate of late marriages in the aforesaid four provinces, two municipalities, and one autonomous region in 1983 was as follows: 86.3% for Jiangsu, 83.9% for Shanghai, 79.8% for Beijing, 67.5% for Liaoning, 63.8% for Inner Mongolia, 61.5% for Sichuan, and 50.8% for Hunan. Fundamentally speaking, these differences in late marriage rate reflected the varying levels of socioeconomic development in these regions.

FAMILY
CHINA'S FAMILIES AND HOUSEHOLDS

A family is an organizational form of social life based on marriage and blood relations. In modern Chinese society, marriage is a legal union and binding form of monogamy, and blood relations refer to the relationships between parents and their children and between brothers and sisters. In China, there is also the concept of "household." According to the Regula-

Table 9-10 Average First-Marriage Age for Women in Seven of China's Provinces, Municipalities, and Autonomous Regions

YEAR	NATIONAL AVERAGE	LIAONING	INNER MONGOLIA	BEIJING	JIANGSU	SHANGHAI	SICHUAN	HUNAN
1940–49	18.46	—	16.97	18.17	18.58	19.73	18.41	18.29
1950–59	19.02	19.90	17.89	19.76	19.04	20.79	18.64	18.64
1960–69	19.81	21.83	19.62	22.13	20.20	22.86	19.40	19.14
1970–79	21.59	23.59	20.54	24.20	22.24	25.00	21.08	21.16
1980–82*	22.84	24.54	22.23	24.79	23.15	25.49	22.36	22.13

* For Beijing the 1980–83 figure is used, and for Shanghai and Liaoning the 1980–81 figures are used in this table.
Source: Data from *One-Per-Thousand-Population Fertility Sampling Survey in China.* Supplied by the office of the relevant leading group under the State Family Planning Commission.

tions of the People's Republic of China Concerning Household Registration, a household is made up of a person in charge of the house and those living with the said person who is the head of the household; a person living as a single also makes up a household. Those living in the dormitories of government offices, public organizations, schools, enterprises, and other undertakings together make up one household or they may register as separate households. This kind of household is, in concept, a collective household. A household composed of people linked by marriage, blood relations, or adoption is called a family household. It can be seen, therefore, that China's household refers mainly to a group of persons distinguished by their place of residence; in concept, it is different from and at the same time connected with the family.

In most years, no distinction is made in statistics between family households and collective households. Therefore, the study of China's family households in this chapter can only be based on the total number of households (including both family households and collective households). By using this method of calculation, it is inevitable that the number and average size will be slightly bigger than that of family households. In Beijing, for example, the average size of the households calculated according to the total number of households was 0.17 person bigger in 1949 than the size calculated according to the actual number of family households; the size was 0.86 person bigger in 1955, 0.24 person bigger in 1969, 0.48 person bigger in 1978, and 0.23 person bigger in 1982. According to China's third census, taken in 1982, the average size of the households calculated according to the total number of households was 4.54 persons, while the average size of the households calculated according to the total number of family households was 4.41 persons, a difference of 0.13 person.

Another point that merits attention is that the total number of family households in China both in its regular household registration and in its 1982 census was slightly higher than the actual number. Therefore, the average number of persons in a household thus calculated was slightly smaller than the actual number. The reason was that in some cities and towns preferential treatment was given to members of collective households in the supply of staple and nonstaple food, with the result that some family households registered their job-holding members who actually lived with them as members of the collective households of the units in which they worked. In addition, in the border areas be-

tween the cities and countryside, some family households had both job-holders in the cities and peasants working in the field, and they might have two household registers because of the difference in the supply of staple and nonstaple food. In view of this, the Census Office under the State Council and the Census Department of the State Statistical Bureau double-checked the size of 19,922 family households in the three municipalities of Beijing, Shanghai, and Tianjin and six provinces after the national census in 1982. They found that there were 2.86% more members in an average family household than the results obtained in the 1982 census. Basing their calculations on this coefficient, they readjusted the average size of family households in 1982 to 4.43 persons, up 0.02 person or 0.11 person fewer than that of an average family household calculated according to the total number of households.

After readjustment, there was only a slight difference in the average size of family households calculated in two different ways—according to the number of family households or according to the total number of households. The following is an analysis of the number, size, and composition of China's family households based on the data obtained for China's total number of households.

NUMBER AND SIZE OF FAMILY HOUSEHOLDS
General Trend of the Number and Average Size of Family Households. Under Kuomintang rule in old China, the nation lacked both reliable demographic data and household data. According to official household data and scholars' investigations at that time, it might be approximately ascertained that the average size of a Chinese household in the 1930s and 1940s was around 5.3 persons.*

Since the founding of the People's Republic of China, the tremendous changes in the mode of production and the considerable growth of its population have brought about a great change in the number of family households and the average size of family households (see Table 9-11). Compared with 1947, the total number of households in 1953 had increased by 54.8%, and the average size of the households had been reduced from 5.35 persons to 4.33 persons, a drop of 19.07%. The basic reasons for these changes were: In the early postliberation years, the birthrate still remained at the high level of the

* Ma Xia, "An Analysis of the Size and Composition of Chinese Family Households," quoted in *Population Research*, No. 3, 1984.

Table 9-11   Changes in the Total Number of Households and Average Size of a Household

YEAR	TOTAL NUMBER OF HOUSEHOLDS (10,000)	AVERAGE NUMBER OF PERSONS PER HOUSEHOLD	YEAR	TOTAL NUMBER OF HOUSEHOLDS (10,000)	AVERAGE NUMBER OF PERSONS PER HOUSEHOLD
1953	13,411	4.33	1971	17,508	4.84
1954	13,572	4.45	1972	18,222	4.76
1956	14,021	4.47	1973	18,555	4.78
1957	14,431	4.48	1974	18,906	4.78
1959	14,848	4.60	1976	19,787	4.71
1961	15,307	4.30	1979	20,986	4.63
1962	15,533	4.33	1980	21,396	4.59
1963	15,637	4.42	1981	22,057	4.52
1964	15,759	4.47	1982	22,116	4.54
1966	16,098	4.61	1983	23,000	4.44
1969	17,072	4.71	1984	23,476	4.39

Source: Gu Jiantang, *A Tentative Analysis of the Number and Size of China's Family Households, Population and Economics*, No. 6, 1986, pp. 30–35.

past (the birthrate was 37‰ from 1950 to 1953), while on the other hand, with the completion of democratic reforms, the restoration of the national economy, and the improvement of the people's livelihood, the death rate had dropped to 18‰ in 1950 and to 17‰ in 1952. It was under these circumstances that China's total population grew rapidly (increasing by 27% from 1947 to 1953*), culminating in a considerable increase in the total number of households. At the same time, influenced by various reforms introduced under the new system, various types of families in the country split into smaller ones, with the result that the average size of the households had been reduced considerably while the total number of households had further increased.

In the 31 years from 1953 to 1984, tremendous changes took place in Chinese society. Owing to the great differences in social, political, and economic development in the various periods, there were fluctuations in the population and changes in the total number of households and their average size.

• A baby boom from the early postliberation years to the mid-1950s. During this stage, the total number of households in China increased 10.20 million from 134.11 million in 1953 to 144.31 million in 1957. This was a 7.61% increase and the annual growth rate was 1.85%. In the same period, the average size of the households increased by 0.15 person.

Major reasons contributing to the considerable increase in the total number of households and the slight expansion of the size of a household were: This

* Taking China's population as 531.0 million in 1947 and 587.96 million in 1953.

stage witnessed the first baby boom after the founding of New China: the birthrate fluctuated between 31.9‰ and 38‰, and the death rate continued to drop. The natural population growth rate increased rapidly, with the result that the nation's total population increased by 11.22% or at an annual rate of 2.09%, a rate higher than that of the total number of households for the same period. This shows that the total number of households had increased because of the growth of the population, the drop in the number of families with several generations living under the same roof, and the rapid setting up of small families, but the splitting of big families into smaller ones was slower than the growth of the population. The consequence was that while the total number of households increased rapidly, the average size of the households increased only slightly.

• A low birthrate from the late 1950s to the early 1960s. During this period, the total number of households increased by 6.85 million from 148.48 million in 1959 to 155.33 million in 1962, an increase of 4.61% or an annual growth rate of 1.51%. At the same time, however, the average size of the households decreased by 0.27 person.

The main factors accounting for the increase in the total number of households and the reduction in the size of the households were: The country was confronted with temporary yet serious economic difficulties and the birthrate dropped markedly. It plummeted to 24.8‰ in 1959 and further down to 18.1‰ in 1961, the lowest since the founding of New China, in 1949. At the same time, the death rate rose, resulting in a 1.40% reduction in the total population in the 1959–62 period. In order to get over the difficulties during those years, people reduced the size of their families and big families split into smaller ones at an accelerated speed. Thus while the total population decreased, the total number of households increased.

• A second baby boom from the mid-1960s to the early 1970s. There emerged a second baby boom in China in the 1963–72 period, during which the total number of households increased by 25.85 million, an increase of 16.53%, or an annual growth rate of 1.71%. In the same period, the average size of the households increased by 0.34 person.

The basic reasons for these increases were: After the nation overcame the economic difficulties, there emerged a "compensatory" high birthrate. On top of this, the chaotic "cultural revolution" broke out and lasted 10 years. During this period, childbirth got out of control and a second baby boom emerged, which lasted much longer than the first one in the 1950s. The population increased by 28.32% and the average annual growth rate was 2.81%, both greater than the increase in the total number of households. Together with the increase in the total number of households, the average size of the households also expanded. In 1971, for example, the average size was 4.84 persons, a size seldom seen since the founding of New China in 1949.

• A low birthrate since the mid-1970s. During the period of low birthrate after the mid-1970s, the total number of households increased from 185.55 million in 1973 to 234.76 million in 1984, an increase of 49.21 million or 26.52%, the average annual growth rate being 2.16%. At the same time, the average size of the households was reduced by 0.39 person.

The major reason for the rapid increase in the total number of households during this stage was that those born during the first baby boom of the 1950s came of marriage age, leading to a high rate of marriage. Though the nation adopted the family planning policy in the early 1970s and the natural growth rate of China's population began to drop rapidly (it stood at 20.9‰ in 1973, 11.6‰ in 1979, and 11.5‰ in 1983) to bring about a second low birthrate since the founding of New China in 1949, the base of China's population was already large, so that in absolute numbers the population still grew rapidly. Thus the total number of households increased while the average size of the households shrank, because big families split at a faster pace than the growth rate of the population.

As mentioned before, in the 30-odd years since the founding of New China (except for a few years), the total number of households increased with the increase of the population. The average size of the households by and large increased during the 1953–

71 period, with 1971 as the peak year. After 1971, the number of small families increased and the average size of households began to shrink. Even so, the average size was slightly bigger than that of 1953.

Internationally, the average size of households varied greatly from country to country. Generally speaking, countries with a low fertility rate have small families, while those with a high fertility rate have big families. Comparatively, the average size of Chinese households is smaller than that of most of the developing countries. (For example, the size of a household in Pakistan was on the average 5.7 persons in 1968. In Syria it was 5.9 persons in 1970; in Brazil it was 5.1 persons in 1970; and in Mexico it was 4.9 persons in 1970.) But household size was larger than in the developed countries. (For example, it was 3.5 persons in Canada in 1971, 3.1 persons in the United States in 1970, 3.7 persons in the Soviet Union in 1970, and 2.7 persons in the Federal Republic of Germany in 1970.*)

Difference Between the Size of Urban and Rural Family Households. There is a conspicuous difference between the average size of urban family households and that of rural households in China (see Table 9-12). This difference changed in different periods.

First, throughout the 1953–64 period, the average size of family households in the cities and towns was bigger than that of rural households and the national average.

Second, since the 1970s, the average size of rural family households has become bigger than that of urban households and the national average.

Third, in the 1953–64 period, the average size of urban family households now expanded and now shrank, but the general trend was one of expanding by 4.10% or an annual growth rate of 0.37%. With the exception of a few years, the average size of rural family households also became larger by 2.09% or an annual growth rate of 0.19%, both lower than in the urban areas.

Fourth, with the exception of a few years, the average size of family households both in the cities and countryside gradually decreased from the 1970s. By 1984 the size of urban family households had decreased by 14.26%, the average annual rate of decrease being 1.18%, and the size of rural family households had shrunk by 7.82%, the average annual rate of decrease being 0.62%. In the last decade or so,

* Wu Cangping and Hou Wenruo, *World Population*, China People's University Press, 1983

Table 9-12   Average Size of Family Households in Urban and Rural Areas

YEAR	NATIONAL AVERAGE	URBAN AVERAGE	RURAL AVERAGE	YEAR	NATIONAL AVERAGE	URBAN AVERAGE	RURAL AVERAGE
1953	4.33	4.88	4.30	1973	4.78	4.67	4.80
1954	4.45	4.94	4.40	1974	4.78	4.63	4.80
1956	4.49	4.83	4.43	1976	4.71	4.23	4.79
1959	4.60	5.01	4.51	1979	4.63	4.36	4.67
1961	4.30	4.93	4.20	1981	4.52	4.17	4.58
1964	4.47	5.08	4.39	1982	4.41	3.84	4.57
1971	4.84	4.70	4.86	1983	4.44	4.05	4.53
1972	4.76	4.70	4.77	1984	4.39	4.03	4.48

Source: Gu Jiantang, *A Tentative Analysis of the Number and Size of China's Family Households, Population and Economics*, No. 6, 1986, pp. 30–35.

the average size of urban family households became smaller by a bigger margin and at a faster pace than that of rural households.

The difference between the average size of urban and rural family households points up an unusual phenomenon: From the early postliberation years to the 1960s, the average size of rural family households was always smaller than that of their urban counterparts. In countries where cities and countryside differ vastly in economic and cultural development, the average size of rural households is invariably larger than that of urban ones. In the Soviet Union, for example, the size of a rural family in 1979 was 3.8 persons as against 3.3 in an urban family.* In preliberation China, according to statistics released in 1928 and 1947 by the department of statistics of Kuomintang government's Ministry of Interior Affairs, the average size of most urban family households was smaller than their rural counterpart in the same province.† The drastic change in the average size of China's rural families within such a short span of time after liberation may be attributed to the following factors:

First, with the birth of New China and socioeconomic development, more and more rural people have gradually turned to nonagricultural work and have in this process changed their place of residence and become urban citizens.

Second, the birthrate in both urban and rural areas across the country was quite high in the early postliberation years, but because of lower mortality rate resulting from better economic and public health conditions, the people in the cities enjoyed a higher natural growth rate than those in the rural

areas during the entire 1950s. This situation lasted until 1963 when the urban population growth rate stood at 37.81‰ and that of the rural population was 28.1‰. A higher natural growth rate resulted in a big increase in the total number of households in the cities. Moreover, big urban families did not split into smaller families as fast as those in the rural areas. Hence the average size of urban family households was larger than that of rural households.

Third, tremendous social changes took place after the founding of New China. In the rural areas land reform was carried out, followed by the movements to set up mutual-aid teams, cooperatives, and people's communes, all of which inevitably led to the disintegration of large numbers of corporate families and an increase in the number of smaller families, most being nuclear families. During the late 1950s and early 1960s when the nation suffered severe economic difficulties, the going was tougher in the countryside than in the cities, and to tide over the difficulties, rural families further reduced their size. Table 9-12 shows that in the 1959–61 period, the average size of urban families shrank by 0.08 person while that of rural families was reduced by 0.31 person.

The foregoing analysis shows that changes in the natural growth rate of the population and the tremendous influence of social, political, and economic reforms were the basic factors accounting for the fact that from the early 1950s to the mid-1960s the average size of rural families was smaller than that of urban families.

After the mid-1960s, especially from the 1970s, the situation changed drastically. The birthrate in the cities declined, which resulted in a lower natural growth rate. In the rural areas, though the birthrate dropped just as quickly as in the cities, and was in fact slightly higher, the mortality rate plummeted at a speed almost double that of the cities. (During the

* Wu Cangping and Hou Wenruo, *World Population*, China People's University Press, 1983.
† Ma Xia, "An Analysis of the Size and Composition of Chinese Households," *Population Research*, No. 3, 1984.

1964–83 period, the birthrate and mortality rate in the countryside were reduced by 50.61 and 36.81%, respectively, as compared with 50.31 and 18.57% in cities. Thus the natural growth rate increased much faster in the rural areas than in the cities. In 1971, for example, the natural population growth rate was 15.95‰ in the cities and 24.29‰ in the countryside; in 1979, it was 8.60‰ and 12.04‰; and in 1983, it was 10.07‰ and 12.20‰, respectively. Under these circumstances, the average size of rural family households gradually outgrew that of urban households beginning from the mid-1960s.

Regional Difference in the Average Size of Family Households.   The vast difference in the economic and cultural development of the various regions, each with its own religions and traditional folkways, has led to a difference in the average size of family households. Following is a comparison between the various provinces, municipalities, and autonomous regions in 1954, 1972, and 1984 (see Table 9-13).

The table shows that in those three decades, the number of family members increased with each passing year in Jiangxi, Guangxi, Guizhou, and Tibet, with Jiangxi leading in the rate of growth, reaching 28.94%. The average size of families was reduced in Beijing, Tianjin, Shanghai, Inner Mongolia, Liaoning, Gansu, Ningxia, and Sichuan, and the rate of reduction in Beijing—27.57%—was the highest. During this period, the average size of households in 17 provinces and autonomous regions showed a tendency of growth first, followed by a reduction. In Xinjiang, which was an exception, the households became smaller at first and then increased in size. The table also shows that the size of families in 1984 was larger than in 1954 in Shanxi, Anhui, Fujian, Henan, Hubei, Hunan, Jiangxi, Guangdong, Guangxi, Guizhou, and Yunnan, and the difference was the biggest in Jiangxi: in 1984 the average family had 1.12 persons more than in 1954. In the other 16 provinces, municipalities, and autonomous regions the opposite was the case. For example, in Beijing an average family in 1984 had 1.37 persons fewer than in 1954, while in Liaoning and Shanghai an average family in 1984 had 1.21 persons and 1.16 persons fewer, respectively, than in 1954.

Table 9-13 also shows that in 1984 Shanghai's average family size was the smallest, with 3.54 persons, followed by Beijing (3.6 persons) and Tianjin (3.8 persons), Zhejiang (3.84 persons), Jiangsu (3.86 persons), and Liaoning (3.97 persons)—all fewer than 4 persons. Heading the list with the largest size of families was Tibet (5.57 persons), followed by

Table 9-13   Average Size of Family Households in China's Provinces, Municipalities, and Autonomous Regions (Unit: person)

REGION	1954	1972	1984
National average	4.45	4.76	4.39
Beijing	4.97	4.49	3.60
Tianjin	4.69	4.42	3.80
Hebei	4.48	4.64	4.15
Shanxi	4.05	4.38	4.18
Inner Mongolia	4.52	4.46	4.41
Liaoning	5.18	5.01	3.97
Jilin	5.13	5.30	4.28
Heilongjiang	4.97	5.29	4.37
Shanghai	4.70	4.07	3.54
Jiangsu	4.31	4.35	3.86
Zhejiang	4.03	4.50	3.84
Anhui	4.40	4.63	4.49
Fujian	4.23	5.15	4.80
Jiangxi	3.87	4.90	4.99
Shandong	4.50	4.64	4.18
Henan	4.61	5.03	4.68
Hubei	4.12	4.95	4.56
Hunan	4.06	4.45	4.28
Guangdong	4.09	4.85	4.77
Guangxi	4.47	5.02	5.18
Sichuan	4.57	4.55	4.24
Guizhou	4.53	4.89	4.92
Yunnan	4.74	5.22	5.18
Tibet		5.22	5.57
Shaanxi	4.79	5.20	4.53
Gansu	5.59	5.50	5.05
Qinghai	5.51	5.64	5.26
Ningxia		5.41	5.17
Xinjiang	4.39	4.07	4.35
Rehe*	5.07		
Xikang*	4.62		

* No longer an independent province.
Source: Gu Jiantang, *A Tentative Analysis of the Number and Size of China's Family Households, Population and Economics*, No. 6, 1986, pp. 30–35.

Qinghai (5.26 persons), Yunnan and Guangxi (both 5.18 persons), Ningxia (5.17 persons), and Gansu (5.05 persons). In the other 17 provinces and autonomous regions, an average family had 4 to 5 members.

If we classify the average size of families in the different regions in China, then in Tibet, Qinghai, Yunnan, Guangxi, Ningxia, and Gansu—regions located in the northwest and southwest, inhabited by minority nationalities and handicapped by a slow economic and cultural development—the average size was the largest; in inland China and a few coastal provinces, such as Jiangxi, Guizhou, Fujian, Guangdong, Henan, and Hubei, an average family had 4.56–4.99 persons; in Hebei, Shanxi, Shandong, Sichuan, Hunan, Jilin, Heilongjiang, Inner Mongolia, Anhui, and Xinjiang the average size was comparatively small, ranging between 4.15 and 4.49 members, and all except Xinjiang showed a tendency of reduction in size between 1972 and 1984. In Shanghai, Beijing, and Tianjin, where the economy and culture are developed, and in the three coastal provinces of Zhejiang, Jiangsu, and Liaoning, the average family size was not only the smallest but was also shrinking the fastest. This analysis shows that changes in the family size are closely connected with the level of development, the growth of population (including changes in the natural population growth, migration, family planning, and composition of families) and the traditional customs and religion of the regions concerned.

Composition of Families of Different Sizes.   In order to make an in-depth study of the size of families, it is necessary to understand the composition of families of different sizes. According to the results of the 1982 census in China, most families have four members, followed by five- and three-member families; families with eight or more people and one-member families are the fewest in number. A comparison with the situation in the 1930s shows that the percentage of families with three, four, five, and six people in present-day China is roughly the same as in the 1930s; the number of seven-member families has decreased, and the number of families with eight or more members shows a conspicuous drop, but one- and two-member families have increased markedly (see Table 9-14). This shows that over the past five decades the average size of Chinese families has become smaller, the percentage of big families has dropped markedly, and the number of small families is steadily growing. These changes are in conformity with the tremendous changes that have taken place politically, economically, and culturally in Chinese society over the last 50 years; they also conform with the general trend in the change in the size of families in other parts of the world (see Table 9-15).

Compared with some other countries in the world, the percentage of one-, two- and three-member families in China is higher than in most of the developing countries but lower than in the developed countries; the percentage of families with six, seven, eight, and more members is lower in China than in most of the developing countries but higher than in the developed countries; and the percentage of four- and five-member families is higher than in the developing countries and most of the developed countries. As the size of families is closely connected with the level of fertility, the above facts show that the birthrate in China is now lower than in many of the

developing countries but higher than in the developed countries.

TYPES OF FAMILIES

Modern families can generally be divided into four categories: 1) nuclear families, which are composed of father, mother, and their unmarried chilren; these also include broken families in which the father or mother has died or they have divorced but with children living in the house; 2) extended families, consisting of the father and mother, a son and daughter-in-law; 3) corporate families, comprising the father and mother and several married children; 4) single-member families and others. Nuclear families are the most stable, and extended and corporate families, known also as big families, are of an unstable type. Extended families are less stable than nuclear families, but more stable than corporate families.

The type of family is a major factor affecting the family's size. For more than half a century the size of families in China has been gradually reduced, and this has been a process closely linked with the changes in the types of families during those years. According to a sample survey conducted by the Population Research Centre of the Chinese Academy of Social Sciences in seven provinces, municipalities, and autonomous regions, the percentage of nuclear families in the rural areas increased from 30% in 1940 to 36% in 1981; the percentage of extended families increased from 43% to 55%; the percentage of corporate families dropped from 23% to 6%; and the percentage of other types of families increased from 3% to 4%.* A survey of marriage and childbirth in urban families conducted in Tianjin by the Research Institute of Sociology under the Chinese Academy of Social Sciences showed that the number of nuclear families was growing with the passage of time, and that women in the 1970s had 35.9% more opportunities than women in the 1940s to build nuclear families.†

Statistics also showed that tremendous changes in the makeup of the different types of Chinese families had taken place not only just before and after the founding of the People's Republic but also in the three decades that followed. A retrospective survey of 1,000 families in Beijing showed that the percent-

---

* Chen Yuguang and Zhang Zehou, "On the Composition of Chinese Families," *Population and Economics*, No. 4, 1983.
† Pan Yunkang and Pan Naigu, "A Tentative Analysis of China's Urban Families and Their Composition," *Tianjin Social Sciences*, No. 3, 1982.

Table 9-14 Chinese Family Size in 1931 and 1982 (%)

FAMILY SIZE

YEAR	1 MEMBER	2 MEMBERS	3 MEMBERS	4 MEMBERS	5 MEMBERS	6 MEMBERS	7 MEMBERS	8 MEMBERS OR MORE	TOTAL
1931	2.50	8.30	15.40	19.00	17.90	13.00	8.80	15.10	100.0
1982	7.97	10.08	16.05	19.54	18.35	13.11	7.95	6.94	100.0

Sources: Figures for 1931 are based on the data collected from 22 provinces by Professor Buck of the University of Nanjing, quoted from "An Analysis of the Size and Composition of Chinese Family Households," by Ma Kia, published in *Population Research*, No. 3, 1984. Figures for 1982 are based on *1982 Population Census of China*, China Statistics Publishing House, 1985.

Table 9-15 Family Size in 12 Countries (%)

FAMILY SIZE

COUNTRY	YEAR	1 MEMBER	2 MEMBERS	3 MEMBERS	4 MEMBERS	5 MEMBERS	6 MEMBERS	7 MEMBERS	8 MEMBERS OR MORE	TOTAL
Iran	1966	5.5	11.6	13.5	15.2	15.4	13.9	10.6	14.3	100.0
Singapore	1970	13.2	8.6	10.4	12.1	11.8	10.9	9.4	23.6	100.0
Thailand	1970	3.2	6.9	10.9	13.8	14.8	14.4	12.3	23.7	100.0
Morocco	1971	10.7	10.4	10.5	10.9	11.3	11.0	10.2	25.0	100.0
Mexico	1970	7.5	14.6	14.4	13.6	12.3	11.0	8.6	18.0	100.0
Chile	1970	5.6	11.1	13.9	15.8	14.9	12.1	8.9	17.7	100.0
Japan	1970	13.1	15.0	19.1	24.9	14.1	8.2	3.5	2.1	100.0
USA	1970	17.5	29.6	17.2	15.4	9.8	5.3	2.7	2.5	100.0
France	1968	20.3	26.9	18.6	15.0	9.2	4.9	2.5	2.6	100.0
Hungary	1970	17.5	25.7	23.9	18.9	8.5	3.4	1.2	0.9	100.0
Sweden	1970	25.3	29.6	19.4	16.3	6.5	2.0	0.6	0.3	100.0
Soviet Union	1970	25.4*		26.2	24.1	12.6	5.9	2.8	3.0	100.0

* The percentages of one- and two-member households are combined for the Soviet Union.
Source: Lin Fude and Shen Qiuhua, *Development of World Population and Economy*, China People's University Press, 1980.

age of nuclear families increased from 58.9% in 1956 to 69.5% in 1982; the percentage of extended families rose from 14.9 to 15.8%, the percentage of corporate families dropped from 19.6 to 4.5%, and the percentage of single-member families increased from 6.6 to 10.2%.*

A comprehensive survey of the different types of families was first made in China in the 1982 census. Families were divided into seven types on the basis of traditional classifications and in line with China's own characteristics. The seven types were families composed of a couple, families consisting of two generations, families consisting of three or more generations, families consisting of one generation and other relatives and nonrelatives, families consisting of two generations and other relatives and nonrelatives, families consisting of three or more generations and other relatives and nonrelatives, and single-member families. Of these types of families, those consisting of two generations, i.e., nuclear families consisting of father, mother, and their unmarried children, accounted for the largest proportion of all families in modern China. If we add to this the nuclear families consisting only of husband and wife, then the two together accounted for 69.5% of all families. This was followed by families with three or more generations, i.e., extended families, which made up 17.13%. Corporate families—families consisting of one generation and other relatives and nonrelatives and families consisting of two or three generations and other relatives and nonrelatives—combined to make up 5.39% of all families. Single-member families accounted for 7.97% (see Table 9-16).

Profound changes have taken place in the composition of different types of families in China over the last three decades and more. Such changes are inseparably linked with the tremendous changes in Chinese society in those years, and have deep economic and social roots.

First, let us look at the economic causes of these changes. In old China, rural population accounted for more than 90% of the nation's total. The overwhelming majority made a living by tilling the land rented from landlords or by farming their own small plots. Owing to the low level of the productive forces, many peasant families could manage to make ends meet only when members worked in concerted ef-

* Based on data collected from a retrospective survey of 1,000 households in 1956 made by the author in seven districts and counties in Beijing.

Table 9-16   Types of Chinese Families (1982)

TYPE	%
Husband-and-wife families	4.78
Two-generation families	64.72
Families with three or more generations	17.13
Single-generation families with other relatives and nonrelatives	1.02
Double-generation families with other relatives and nonrelatives	2.74
Families with three or more generations and other relatives and nonrelatives	1.63
Single-member families	7.97
Total	100.0

Source: *1982 Population Census of China*, China Statistics Publishing House, 1985.

forts according to a certain division of labor. That was why big families existed in the rural areas, for they were suited to the low level of the productive forces and the self-sufficient natural economy at that time. After liberation, the private ownership of land was abolished, agricultural collectivization was introduced, and family members were engaged mainly in collective productive labor. With growth of the productive forces and improvement in the people's livelihood, self-sufficiency in consumer goods gradually gave way to commodity supplies, thereby eliminating the basis of natural economy on which big families relied for existence.

Second, let us look at the social roots of the changes. The feudal-patriarchal system, which was prevalent in old China, consituted the foundation for big families, in which several generations lived under the same roof. At that time a big family population was regarded as a sign of prosperity and a hallmark of prestige and power on the social ladder.

The fundamental change of the social system after liberation, the rapid development of the economy and culture, and the resultant changes in the people's psychology and traditional concepts have changed the relationships between family members and shaken the once dominant patriarchal rule to its foundations. In contemporary Chinese society, the people are more and more in favor of small, quiet families rather than big families that are often plagued by complex relations, misunderstandings, and disharmony over petty matters. In China today, there are still multigenerational households for the following reasons: poor living conditions, the need for mutual support financially and in daily life between two generations, and the carrying forward of the fine tradition of respecting the old and loving the young.

There are vast differences in the types of families in countries around the world. This is because of the differences in social and economic conditions, in marriage and family relations, and in fertility, mortality rate, and the makeup of age groups and sexes. Generally speaking, the proportion of nuclear families and single-member families in the total number of families in China is smaller than that of the developed countries. (The proportion of nuclear families was 80% in the Soviet Union in 1979, and the proportion of single-member families was 23% in the United States in the late 1970s.* On the other hand, the proportion of extended families and corporate families in China is higher than that of the developed countries. (In the Federal Republic of Germany, extended families made up 6.6% of all families in the 1970s,[†] and in the Soviet Union, corporate families accounted for 3.7% of all families in the 1970s.[‡]

* Wu Cangping and Hou Wenruo, *World Population*, China People's University Press, 1983.
† Ibid.
‡ *Handbook on Population of Various Countries in the World*, Sichuan People's Publishing House, 1982.

CHAPTER TEN

WORKING POPULATION

Working population constitutes the most important part of the entire population. The activities of this particular portion of the population are vital to the whole and exert a direct influence on socioeconomic activities. Working population covers a wide scope and includes labor resources, work-age population, labor force, and employed and unemployed population. These terms, which are interrelated and at the same time distinct from each other in theory and in practice, all belong to the category of working population. This chapter will mainly deal with the characteristics and changes of the work-age and employed population since the establishment of New China by using the data collected from the censuses and routine statistics.

SIZE AND COMPOSITION OF WORK-AGE POPULATION

By work-age population we mean that portion of people who should work because of their age. Working age is often clearly defined: in China, for a long period of time the minimum age has been 16 and the maximum age has been 60 for men and 55 for women (the legal age for retirement). In international practice working age is considered to be from 15 to 64. These two norms will be used alternately in this chapter according to the needs and availability of related data when analyzing China's work-age population.

SIZE OF WORK-AGE POPULATION AND ITS TREND OF DEVELOPMENT

The size of work-age population is determined by the size of the total population and the proportion of the former in the total population. China is the most populous country in the world and the proportion of its work-age population (15–64) is high. Consequently, China's work-age population is the world's largest (see Table 10-1).

Generally speaking, the proportion of work-age population is less than 60% of the total population in developing countries and over 60% in developed countries. For instance, in 1983, work-age population was 57% in India, 59% in Thailand, 57% in Egypt, and 56% in Peru, while in Britain it was 65%, in Japan it was 68%, in the United States it was 67%, and in the Soviet Union it was 66%.* The proportion of China in 1982 was significantly higher than that of most developing countries but lower than that of the developed countries.

* World Bank, *World Development Report, 1985,* Chinese edition, China Financial and Economic Publishing House, pp. 214–215.

Table 10-1   China's Work-Age Population (15-64)

YEAR	TOTAL POPULATION (10,000)	WORK-AGE POPULATION (10,000)	PROPORTION OF WORK-AGE POPULATION IN TOTAL POPULATION (%)
1953	56,745	33,649	59.3
1964	69,458	38,445	55.3
1982	100,394	61,738	61.5

Sources: Data for 1953 and 1964 are quoted from *Major Figures from China's Third Census,* China Statistics Publishing House, 1982. Data for 1982 are taken from *1982 Population Census of China,* China Statistics Publishing House, 1985.

China's work-age population is not only large but is growing rapidly. From 1953 to 1982, its average yearly increase rate was 2.11%, while the rate for the total population was 1.99%. The reason that the growth rate of work-age population was higher than that of the total population was that the growth rate of China's total population gradually slowed down as a result of the family planning program, which started in the 1970s. During this period, however, more and more young people had reached working age. In 1953, 9.89 million people reached the legal working age of 16. This figure increased to 13.04 million in 1964, 16.31 million in 1975, 23.54 million in 1978, and 25.68 million in 1982.

According to an analysis of the age composition and the death rate of different age brackets in 1982, China's work-age population will register a net increase of about 200 million from 1982 to 1998, averaging 12.69 million a year or an annual increase rate of 1.96%, according to the Chinese age norm. The increase will be about 206 million according to international age norms, averaging 13.75 million a year or an annual increase rate of 1.94%. With the employed population making up 93.57% of the total work-age population in 1982, the former will reach 711 million by 1998 according to the Chinese age norm, averaging an increase of 11.86 million a year. In other words, if the employment rate remains unchanged,

an average of 12 million additional people will have to be given jobs every year* (see Table 10-2).

If Chinese women have an average of 1.7 babies after 1998, by 2006 the proportion of work-age population in the total population will reach a peak of 65.4% according to the Chinese legal working age. It will then gradually decrease, and by 2020 the work-age population will be about 763.25 million, or 59.5% of the total population at that time.[†]

SEX AND AGE COMPOSITION OF WORK-AGE POPULATION

The sex and age composition of the work-age population has a significant bearing on the volume of labor resources and, consequently, on economic development. As regards sex composition, its influence finds expression in the following ways. First, owing to physiological differnces, some types of work are not suitable for women and other types are not suitable for men. Therefore, the difference in sex proportion in the work-age population will lead to differences in the actual volume of labor resources. Second, owing

---

* Pan Jiyi and Guo Shenyang, "Prospects for Shifts of China's Rural Labour Force," *Population Research*, No. 2, 1986, p. 17.
† Cheng Yuqin, "Hundred-Year Forecast on China's Population," *Encyclopaedic Knowledge*, China Encyclopaedia Publishing House, No. 8, 1983.

Table 10-2   Forecast on China's Work-Age Population (1983–1998) (unit: 10,000)

YEAR	CHINESE NORM			INTERNATIONAL NORM (15–64)		
	MALE (16–59)	FEMALE (16–54)	TOTAL	MALE	FEMALE	TOTAL
1983	30,471.7	25,721.1	57,192.8	32.840.3	30,641.2	63,481.5
1984	31,326.2	27,483.6	58,809.8	33,917.2	31,676.6	65,593.8
1985	32,333.4	28,433.6	60,767.0	34,870.9	32,596.7	67,467.6
1986	33,238.6	29.270.1	62,508.7	35,865.8	33,553.0	69,418.8
1987	34,193.8	30,161.4	64,355.2	36,733.6	34,390.9	71,124.5
1988	35,030.3	30,928.5	65,958.8	37,598.2	35,230.5	72,828.7
1989	35,819.3	31,655.3	67,474.9	38,374.3	35,987.4	74,361.7
1990	36,560.7	32.326.1	68,886.8	39.022.2	36,625.6	75,647.8
1991	37,152.9	32,890.3	70,043.2	39,604.1	37,205.6	76,809.7
1992	37,686.3	33,375.6	71,061.9	40,125.3	37,731.3	77,856.6
1993	38,152.2	33,817.5	71,969.7	40,568.6	38,185.5	78,754.1
1994	38,539.2	34,224.8	72,764.0	41,069.0	38,688.6	79,757.6
1995	38,975.3	34,682.2	73,657.5	41,470.6	39.098.6	80,569.2
1996	39,353.8	35,070.4	74,424.2	41,875.4	39,476.1	81,311.5
1997	39,666.4	35,384.9	75,051.3	42,353.8	39,992.6	82,346.4
1998	40,148.0	35,852.5	76,000.6	—	—	—

Source: Pan Jiyi and Guo Shenyang, "Prospects for Shifts of China's Rural Labour Force," *Population Research*, No. 2, 1986.

to social and historical factors, the proportion of women taking part in social labor is, to varying degrees, lower than that of men. The difference in the sex proportion, therefore will result in differences in the actual volume of labor resources being employed.

As regards age composition, its effects on economic development are as follows. Younger people in the work-age population are strong in physique, quick at learning new techniques and new knowledge, capable of undertaking heavy labor, and easily adaptable to the needs of new trades. But they are comparatively deficient in work experience and proficiency. Older people are experienced in production, proficient in work, and well-versed in specialized knowledge. But they are less capable of coping with production developments and are not suitable for work that requires a quick reaction and physical strength. Consequently, a lopsided age composition, either too old or too young, will result in labor shortage in some trades and departments and excessive labor force in others. This will directly affect production and economic development.

According to data obtained from China's three censuses, males outnumber females in the work-age population (15–64), and the ratio between them is about the same as that in the total population. According to the age limit stipulated in China's legislation on labor, the male work-age population is even larger that that of females (see Table 10-3). Therefore, the volume of labor resources available and the possibility of their utilization is much greater than statistics have shown.

The basic situation in the age composition of China's work-age population shows that the proportion of younger people (15–44) had risen from 73.3% in 1953 to 74.6% in 1964 and 75.7% in 1982, while the proportion of older people had dropped (see Table 10-4). This kind of age composition is typical of developing countries and is in sharp contrast to that of

Table 10-4 Age Composition of China's Work-Age Population (15–64) (%)

AGE	YEAR		
	1953	1964	1982
15–19	15.3	16.2	20.3
20–24	13.8	13.2	12.0
25–29	12.5	13.1	15.0
30–34	11.3	12.1	11.8
35–39	11.0	10.7	8.8
40–44	9.4	9.3	7.8
45–49	8.5	8.0	7.7
50–54	7.2	6.9	6.6
55–59	6.1	5.9	5.5
60–64	4.9	4.6	4.4
Total	100	100	100

Sources: Data for 1953 and 1964 are quoted from *Major Figures from China's Third Census*, China Statistics Publishing House, 1982. Data for 1982 are taken from *1982 Population Census of China*, China Statistics Publishing House, 1985.

the developed countries where the proportion of older people in the work-age population is increasing and labor force is comparatively insufficient (see Table 10-5).

Compared with other countries, China's work-age population belongs to the young and vigorous type, with good prospects for development. For this reason, the society has to intensify training and education and create more job opportunities.

GEOGRAPHICAL DISTRIBUTION OF WORK-AGE POPULATION

The geographical distribution of population is an expression of the population process in space. Its basic features vary with the population process and the change in the factors affecting this process. The geographical distribution (referring only to regional differences in the size of population) of work-age population, which is the major part of the population, is

Table 10-3 Sex Composition and Sex Ratio of China's Work-Age Population

YEAR	CHINESE NORM			INTERNATIONAL NORM (15–64)		
	MALE (%) (16–59)	FEMALE (%) (16–54)	SEX RATIO	MALE (%)	FEMALE (%)	SEX RATIO
1953	53.0	47.0	112.9	51.3	48.7	105.1
1964	53.6	46.4	115.5	51.6	48.4	106.5
1982	53.4	46.6	114.5	51.8	48.2	107.3

Sources: Data for 1953 and 1964 are quoted from *Major Figures from China's Third Census*, China Statistics Publishing House, 1982. Data for 1982 are taken from *1982 Population Census of China*, China Statistics Publishing House, 1985.

Table 10-5   Age Composition of the World's Work-Age Population
(1975) (%)

	WORK-AGE POPULATION	AGE 15–44	AGE 45–64
World	100	74.1	25.9
Developed regions	100	67.7	32.3
Underdeveloped regions	100	76.7	23.2
China*	100	75.7	24.2

* 1982 figures.

Sources: The world figures are quoted from *Demography*, China People's
University Press, 1981, p. 41. Figures for China are quoted from *1982 Population
Census of China*, China Statistics Publishing House, 1985.

restricted by the geographical distribution of the entire population. We shall now deal with the geographical distribution of China's work-age population from two aspects—urban-rural distribution and regional distribution.

Changes in Urban-Rural Distribution. According to the statistics of the 1964 and 1982 censuses, the urban-rural distribution of China's work-age population underwent great changes between 1964 and 1982. The urban work-age population multiplied 2.7 times, with an annual increase rate of 5.67%, and its proportion in the total work-age population of the country was on the increase. However, the rural work-age population increased by only 43.3%, or an annual increase rate of 2.02%, and its proportion in the total work-age population of the country was decreasing (see Table 10-6).

Population distribution is a socioeconomic phenomenon. Changes in geographical distribution of the population are always closely related with the development of the productive forces and other social and historical factors. The causes for the changes in China's urban-rural distribution are: 1) With the socioeconomic development after the founding of New China, the tendency for the agricultural population to shift to nonagricultural population has increased and more and more work-age people have

moved from the countryside to urban areas. 2) Since 1964, the birthrate has fallen sharply in the cities. As a result, the proportion of youngsters has decreased too, and that of work-age people has increased. However, the birthrate in the countryside has decreased at a slower pace than in the cities; hence the slow drop in the proportion of youngsters and the slow rise in the proportion of work-age people. It can be expected that in the course of China's modernization, these trends will intensify and further affect the distribution of China's urban and rural population.

Changes in Regional Distribution. The regional distribution of China's work-age population is very uneven. The fundamental cause for this is the great difference in the size of the population in the various regions, resulting from the differences in natural environment, level of the productive forces, and natural changes of the population and migration, as well as from social, economic, and historical factors. For the convenience of comparison, we shall look into the characteristics of the regional distribution of China's work-age population in 1953, 1964, and 1984 by dividing, in the traditional way, the 29 provinces, autonomous regions, and municipalities on the Chinese mainland into six big regions (see Table 10-7).

The East China region (including the Shanghai municipality and Jiangsu, Zhejiang, Anhui, Fujian,

Table 10-6   Urban-Rural Distribution of China's Work-Age Population (1964 and 1982)

	URBAN WORK-AGE POPULATION			RURAL WORK-AGE POPULATION		
YEAR	SIZE (10,000)	PROPORTION IN THE NATION'S WORK-AGE POPULATION (%)	PROPORTION IN THE POPULATION OF CITIES AND TOWNS (%)	SIZE (10,000)	PROPORTION IN THE NATION'S WORK-AGE POPULATION (%)	PROPORTION IN THE RURAL POPULATION (%)
1964	5,257	13.7	53.7	33,188	86.3	55.6
1982	14,186	23.0	68.7	47,552	77.0	59.6

Sources: Data for 1964 are quoted from *Major Figures from China's Third Census*, China Statistics Publishing House, 1982. Data for 1982 are taken from *1982 Population Census of China*, China Statistics Publishing House, 1985.

Table 10-7   Regional Distribution of China's Work-Age Population*

1953		1964		1982	
SIZE (10,000)	PERCENTAGE IN NATION'S WORK-AGE POPULATION	SIZE (10,000)	PERCENTAGE IN NATION'S WORK-AGE POPULATION	SIZE (10,000)	PERCENTAGE IN NATION'S WORK-AGE POPULATION
North China Region					
3,230	10.8	4,020	11.8	6,581	11.9
East China Region					
9,377	31.3	10,277	30.1	16,404	29.8
Southwest China Region					
4,800	16.0	5,491	16.1	8,523	15.5
Northeast China Region					
2,417	8.1	2,897	8.5	5,273	9.6
Central-South China Region					
8,366	27.9	9,166	26.8	14,574	26.5
Northwest China Region					
1,808	6.0	2,298	6.7	3,732	6.8

* Age 16–59 for males, and age 16–54 for females.
Sources: Data for 1953 and 1964 are quoted from *Major Figures from China's Third Census*, China Statistics Publishing House, 1982.
Data for 1982 are taken from *1982 Population Census of China*, China Statistics Publishing House, 1985.

Jiangxi, and Shandong provinces), with the least amount of land had the largest work-age population. Next came the Central-South China region (including Henan, Hubei, Hunan, and Guangdong provinces, and the Guangxi Zhuang Autonomous Region) and the Southwest China region (including Sichuan, Guizhou, and Yunnan provinces and the Tibet Autonomous Region). Th North China region (including Beijing and Tianjin municipalities, Hebei and Shanxi Provinces, and Inner Mongolian Autonomous Region) and the Northeast China region (including Liaoning, Jilin and Heilongjiang provinces) were placed fourth and fifth, respectively. The Northwest China region (including Shaanxi, Gansu, and Qinghai provinces, and the Ningxia Hui Autonomous Region and Xinjiang Uygur Autonomous Region), which is sparsely populated, possesses the greatest amount of land of all six regions, covering 32.84% of China's territory, but the smallest work-age population, which was 37.32 million in 1982, or 6.8% of China's total population.

The trend of development indicated that the proportion of work-age population in North China and Northeast China was rising, while that of East China, Central-South China, and Southwest China was falling. Changes in Northwest China were not significant. The trend of development also found manifestation in the annual increase rate. Between 1953 and 1964, Northwest China had the highest increase rate of work-age population (2.2%), followed by North China (2%), Northeast China (1.66%), and

Southwest China (1.23%). The increase rate for East China and Central-South China was only 0.83%. From 1964 to 1982, the increase rates all went up markedly, with Northeast China the highest (3.38%). The increase rates in other regions were all over 2%: North China 2.78%, Northwest China 2.73%, East China 2.63%, Central-South China 2.61%, and Southwest China 2.47%

EMPLOYMENT AND LEVEL OF EMPLOYMENT OF THE WORKING POPULATION

Employment is an importat issue in a country's economic and social development. China is a socialist country, and under socialism the antagonism between capital and wage labor has been eliminated. But owing to the low level of development of the productive forces over the years resulting from certain unavoidable historical and present-day limitations, plus the mistakes and lack of practical experience in socialist construction, the supply of labor force outstrips the demand in certain periods. In the cities it finds expression in a part of the labor force waiting for jobs, and in the rural areas it takes the form of surplus labor. In the last few years, however, with the institution of economic reforms and the continual growth of the economy in the cities and countryside, this labor force is gradually being transferred to industry and the service industry.

EMPLOYMENT OF THE WORKING POPULATION

Serious unemployment, left over from old China, was the first thing New China had to tackle in solving the problem of unemployment. When New China was founded, there were about 4 million unemployed workers and intellectuals in the cities. In the course of restoring and developing the national economy, the Chinese government and trade unions adopted a series of measures to help these people to find work in a comparatively short period. These measures included allocating funds for public welfare undertakings and city construction projects, and for setting up collectively owned production units and opening various kinds of short-term training classes to help the unemployed acquire certain skills. From 1949 to 1966, jobs were found almost every year for junior and senior middle school graduates who could not continue their studies. In general, proper arrangements were made and these people were given jobs soon after graduation, and there was practically no question of people waiting for employment. In the 10-year turmoil of the "cultural revolution" (1966–76), the national economy suffered greatly and many undertakings were unable to take on new job seekers, thereby affecting the normal placement of workers. During this period, while 17 million urban educated youths were encouraged to go and settle in the countryside, 13 million peasants were recruited to work in the cities. This flow and counterflow of labor force gave rise to confusion in job allocation. After the "cultural revolution," when the country still had difficulty with its economy, the state adopted the principle of combining official job allocations with allowing people to find their own jobs to solve the unemployment problem. Great successes were achieved. Data from the state statistical departments showed that in the cities and towns 5 million people were given jobs in 1977, 5.444 million in 1978, 9.026 million in 1979, 9 million in 1980, 8.2 million in 1981, 6.65 million in 1982, 6.283 million in 1983, 6.733 million in 1984, and an estimate of 7.45 million in 1985, totalling 63.786 million people in those nine years, averaging 7.087 million a year.

In the last few years, while the state found employment for the people in the cities and towns, a large number of people waiting for jobs, with the support of local governments at various levels, raised funds by themselves and set up private businesses according to the policies laid down by the government. These individual businesses are now a supplement to China's socialist economy, and they not only help revitalize the market in the cities and countryside but also solve the question of employment for a large number of people. Figures from the State Industrial and Commercial Administration Bureau show that in 1985 the number of individual industrial and commercial households increased by 25.5% over 1984 and the number of employed went up by 34.8%. By the end of 1985 there were 11.68 million licensed private industrial and commercial households which employed 17.56 million people, or 3 million more than the number of workers in the commercial departments throughout the country.[*]

The facts mentioned above show that employment is not now a serious question in China's cities and towns. However, nearly 80% of China's population and the great majority of its labor power lived in rural areas in 1982. Moreover, the rural areas have more surplus labor force than the urban areas. On top of this, the work-age population in the rural areas increases faster than the nation's total work-age population. It is estimated that, calculated according to Chinese age norms (16–59 years old for men and 16–54 for women), the net increase of work-age population in the rural areas from 1982 to 1998 will be 181 million, averaging 11.31 million a year, or an annual increase rate of 2.24%. According to the international age norms (15–64), the net increase by 1997 will be 179 million, averaging 11.96 million a year, or an annual increase rate of 2.16%.[†] It is clear, therefore, that China's major labor resources in the future are in its rural areas. According to Chinese age norms, of the net increase in the nation's work-age population in the 16 years from 1982 to 1997, that of the rural areas will account for 89.16%.[‡] Such a huge increase of labor force will inevitably aggravate the existing contradiction between a large population and a limited amount of arable land, thus putting new pressure on the work of providing employment. This being the case, it is imperative to plan well, find the way out for rural surplus labor, and gradually transfer agricultural labor to nonagricultural fields. This is not only an urgent question that must be solved but also one of long-term strategic importance. The main principles China has adopted to solve this question follow:

• Energetically developing rural household economy. Developing the rural household economy is in keeping with the institution of the household contract responsibility system in China's rural areas

---

[*] *Renmin Ribao*, February 23, 1986.
[†] Pan Jiyi and Guo Shenyang, "Prospects for Shifts of China's Rural Labour Force," *Population Research*, No. 2, 1986, p. 18.
[‡] Ibid.

today. Its organizational form is specialized households of various kinds. Statistics show that there are 15.637 million specialized households (including key households) in the rural areas at present, accounting for 9.4% of the total number of rural households in the country.* Owing to the limitations of techniques, funds, and low educational level, these households mostly engage in labor-intensive production and their business scope is confined to agriculture. But the trend is that with the rapid development of the rural economy, these specialized households are gradually moving from farming and poultry raising to industry, commerce, transportation, construction, and the service trades. This shows that the rural household economy will absorb a large amount of surplus labor in the countryside.

• Vigorously developing rural industry and sidelines. In the last few years, while readjusting the makeup of farm production, China has drawn lessons from concentrating only on grain production and put forward the basic guiding principle of "never slackening grain production and actively developing a diversified economy." Following this principle, China has encouraged grain production and at the same time actively developed a diversified economy that includes the production of cash crops, the expansion of forestry, animal husbandry, and fishery, and the development of industry, construction, transportation, and service trade in the rural areas. All these activities have resulted in a big increase in grain production and an all-round development of the rural economy; a way out for the large amount of rural surplus labor has been found. With the diversification of the economy, the rural enterprises run by the townships have played a big role in developing the economy and in providing jobs for rural surplus labor. And to develop these rural enterprises has become a must if China's rural economy is to flourish.

The development of rural township enterprises has bright prospects. They have the following strong points: 1) They may engage in various kinds of production such as the food industry, fodder industry, building materials industry, transportation, and service trades. At present, some of these rural enterprises and their products account for a large proportion of the nation's total. In 1984, garments produced by these enterprises accounted for about half of the nation's total, and the output value of the building materials they produced made up 53% of the nation's total.* 2) The output value of the rural enterprises is considerable and has become an important new source of income for the state. In 1984 the total output value of these enterprises reached 170.9 billion yuan, which was equivalent to the nation's total product of society in 1964 and one-sixth of the nation's total industrial and agricultural output value in 1984. The total output value of rural enterprises in 1985 increased to 230–240 billion yuan, equivalent to one-fifth of the nation's total industrial and agricultural output value in the same year. From 1979 to 1984, they handed over to the state a total of 27.7 billion yuan in taxes, averaging an annual increase of 23.7%. Their exports earned US $3.3 billion (not including gold) in 1984, and in 1985 they paid to the state 12 billion yuan in taxes, 30% more than in 1984. Also in 1985 their exports brought in a big increase in foreign exchange compared with 1984.[†] 3) These rural enterprises helped solve the employment question. In 1984, for instance, they employed a total of 52 million people and in 1985 they employed 60 million.[‡]

Rural enterprises have changed the traditional distribution of China's industry and agriculture and have become an important component of the nation's industry as a whole. What is important is that with their development, they will absorb more and more labor force. According to estimates made by departments concerned, by the year 2000 these rural enterprises are expected to accommodate 180 million people, or 40% of the rural labor force. Thus the rural enterprises have now become a major outlet for the large numbers of surplus laborers in the rural areas.

• Actively developing and building small cities and towns. To develop and build small cities and towns in a planned way and to change the agricultural population into a nonagricultural population is of great importance to improving the distribution of the productive forces, readjusting the distribution of urban and rural population, and absorbing surplus labor in the rural areas.

Small cities and towns in China refer to county seats and market towns in the rural areas. At present, there are about 3,200 county seats in China; with regard to market towns, historically about 5,300 were formally established according to regulations,

---

* Xu Tianqi and Ye Zhendong, "The Inevitable Trend and Major Ways of Shift of China's Labour Force," *Population Research*, No. 5, 1985, p. 19.

* *Renmin Ribao*, December 7, 1985.
† *Renmin Ribao*, December 7 and 30, 1985 and January 13, 1986.
‡ *Renmin Ribao*, December 7 and 31, 1985.

and now most of them are the locations of the township governments. As economic and cultural centers of their own localities, they generally have a good economic foundation and are situated at intersections of communication lines, thereby linking industrial and agricultural areas as well as rural and urban economies. In the next few years, if each market town can absorb an average of 2,000 able-bodied peasants, a way out will be provided for 120 million rural laborers. At present, the makeup of Chinese cities is irrational, as by the end of 1985 43% of the urban population lived in extra-large and large cities, which are overpopulated, and there is no more room for rural surplus labor. It is therefore necessary to develop and build small cities and towns while developing rural industry, sidelines, and rural enterprises in order to help the agricultural population become nonagricultural in their own localities.

In a word, only when we draw up comprehensive short- and long-term plans in light of China's actual conditions and with due consideration for the characteristics of China's population and economic development can we handle correctly the relationships between the employment of work-age population and economic growth and enable our national economy to develop in a steady and sustained way.

SIZE OF EMPLOYED POPULATION AND LEVEL OF EMPLOYMENT

By employed population we mean those who engage in social labor and get remunerations for their work or earnings from their trade. Thus all work-age people doing work and getting remunerations in this was fall uner this category whether they work in state-owned or collectively owned enterprises or engage in private business in either urban or rural areas.

Data show that the proportion of employed people in the total population of China has been increasing over the last three decades. In 1949 the proportion was 33.4% and in 1984 it reached 46%, which is clearly above the level in most developing countries and is approaching that of the developed countries. The number of employed increased from 180.82 million in 1949 to 475.97 million in 1984, registering a 2.63-fold increase and an average annual growth rate of 2.8% (see Table 10-8).

Now we shall examine the level of employment in China today according to the proportion of employed people in different age groups and sexes and in different cities, counties, and towns.

The Proportion of Employed People of Different Age Groups. According to the data of the 1982 census

Table 10-8   China's Employed Population (1949–1984)

YEAR	NUMBER OF EMPLOYED (MILLION)	PROPORTION IN CHINA'S TOTAL POPULATION (%)
1949	180.82	33.4
1952	207.29	36.1
1953	213.64	36.3
1954	218.32	36.2
1955	223.28	36.3
1956	230.18	36.6
1957	237.71	36.8
1958	266.00	40.3
1959	261.73	38.9
1960	258.80	39.1
1961	255.90	38.9
1962	259.10	38.5
1963	266.40	38.5
1964	277.36	39.3
1965	286.70	39.5
1966	298.05	40.0
1967	308.14	40.4
1968	319.15	40.6
1969	332.25	41.2
1970	344.32	41.5
1971	356.20	41.8
1972	358.54	41.1
1973	366.52	41.1
1974	373.69	41.1
1975	381.68	41.3
1976	388.34	41.4
1977	393.77	41.5
1978	398.56	41.4
1979	405.81	41.6
1980	418.96	42.5
1981	432.80	43.3
1982	447.06	44.0
1983	460.04	44.9
1984	475.97	46.0

Source: *Statistics Yearbook of China 1985*, China Statistics Publishing House, 1985.

collected by computers, there were 521.505 million employed people 15 years and above. Basing our calculations on this figure, the proportion of employed people in the total population of 15 and above was 78.2%, higher than in the developed countries. (The figures here vary slightly from those in Table 10-8 because different bases were used.) In the 15–64 age group, there were 513.625 million employed people, and the proportion was 83.2%. This was also higher than that of the developed countries. According to the Chinese work-age norms (16–59 for men and 16–54 for women), in 1982 there were 482.01 million employed people in China, and the proportion was 87.5%. Of the total number of people in this age group, some were studying while others were unable to work because of physical deficiencies. That the proportion of employed people was so high even under these circumstances showed that the great majority of work-age people in China were employed and that China's rich labor resources were brought into full use. However, it also reflected that China lagged behind in secondary and higher education.

The Proportion of Employed People of Different Sexes and Age Groups. The proportion of employed people of different sexes and age groups (see Table 10-9) show the following characteristics:

• Of the employed in various age groups, the proportion of those in the advanced age groups (over 50) was the smallest while the proportion of employed people in the prime (20–49) was the largest. The proportion of employed in the 30–34 age bracket was as high as 94% and that of the 20–44 age group was over 90%.

• The proportion of employed in the 15–19 age group was 74.12%. This was higher than that of many other countries. In the United States the proportion of employed in the 16–19 age group was 47% in 1979, and in Japan that of the 15–19 age group was only 19.4% in 1980. The proportion of employed people in the 15–24 age group in China was as high as 81.3%. This was not only higher than that in the developed countries but also a little higher than that in some developing countries.

• In the 15–19 age group, the proportion of employed women was higher than that of men. But in the other age groups, the proportion of employed men was markedly higher, and the difference between the two sexes became greater with the advance of age.

The characteristics mentioned above show that people in the advanced age groups gradually drop out of the ranks of the employed as they grow older and become the nonemployed. This is a normal phenomenon.

The great majority of China's young people are now working. This shows that the Chinese government has achieved success in the last few years in providing more job opportunities for the people. But an inevitable result of young people taking up jobs at an early age is that they have to discontinue their schooling. The causes of this phenomenon, in addition to the slow development of secondary education and insufficient opportunities for school-age youngsters to go to school, are the employment policy of "low wage system and high employment rate" followed by the government for a long time in the past, the system of letting children take up their parents' work after the parents retire practiced in some places a few years ago, and the shortsightedness of some parents of caring only about immediate economic benefits and letting their children go to work at an early age. Social productive labor and especially agricultural production in China today does not need a high education or advanced skills. This makes it easy for young people to find work, and thus the proportion of employed young men and women is high. As a result, the great majority of young people can do only manual labor, and though the employment rate is high, productivity is low. From a long-term point of view, this unreasonable employment structure will hold back the progress of China's industrial makeup.

In the 15–19 age bracket, the employment rate of women is higher than that of men. This shows that a considerable number of young women have discontinued their schooling because they take part in work at too early an age. Thus, as far as women are concerned, equality in employment has in fact covered up the inequality in schooling. This is even more serious in rural areas. For instance, according to statistics, girl students in junior middle schools in the villages account for only 36.5% of the total number of students, and in the senior middle school, girl students make up only 31.1%. To provide more schooling opportunities for young girls, especially those in the rural areas, is therefore an issue that merits special attention and needs to be solved.

Proportion of Employed People in Cities, Towns, and Counties. An analysis of the employed population

Table 10-9 Proportions of Employed People of Different Sexes and Ages (15–64) (%)

AGE GROUP	TOTAL	MEN	WOMEN	AGE GROUP	TOTAL	MEN	WOMEN
15–19	74.12	70.54	77.82	40–44	91.49	98.63	83.34
20–24	93.30	96.16	90.34	45–49	84.79	97.47	70.57
25–29	93.84	98.59	88.77	50–54	72.27	91.42	50.90
30–34	94.00	98.82	88.77	55–59	58.72	82.95	32.87
35–39	93.94	98.86	88.46	60–64	40.31	63.67	16.87

Source: *1982 Population Census of China*, China Statistics Publishing House, 1985.

Table 10-10   Proportion of Employed People in China's Cities, Towns, and Counties (1982) (%)

	PROPORTION OF EMPLOYED PEOPLE IN THE TOTAL POPULATION	PROPORTION OF EMPLOYED PEOPLE 15 YEARS AND ABOVE IN THE TOTAL POPULATION
Nation's total	51.94	78.22
Cities	56.28	76.06
Towns	53.36	74.44
Counties	51.05	79.00

Source: *1982 Population Census of China*, China Statistics Publishing House, 1985.

in China's cities, towns, and counties will show the great differences in the level of employment (see Table 10-10).

In 1982 the proportion of employed people in the total population of the cities and towns in China was 4.34% and 1.42% higher, respectively, than the nation's average, while that of the counties was 0.89% lower than the nation's average. This was because the counties had a population of 797.6 million, or 79.45% of the nation's total population, and among them people of the 0–14 age bracket made up 35.38%. But the people living in cities and towns made up 20.55% of the nation's total, of whom people of the 0–14 age group made up 26.69%, both lower than those of the counties. Thus in calculating the proportion of employed people in the total population, the numerator did not include the people under 15 years old while the denominator did; the inevitable result was that the proportion of employed people in the total population of the counties was smaller than that of the cities and towns. Another reason was that manpower in the rural areas was more fully used than in the urban areas, and more young people of the 15–24 age group in the countryside joined the work force while their schooling rate was low.

TRADES AND PROFESSIONS OF EMPLOYED PEOPLE

Trade means the work units of the laborers or the departments of economic activities to which they belong, classified according to their nature in the national economic activities. These trades are interrelated and react on each other to form an economic structure compatible with a certain level of the productive forces and certain relations of production, thereby enabling the national economy to become an organic whole. The various trades in the national economy generally fall into two categories: material production and nonmaterial production. The pro-

ductivity of material production, especially the high or low productivity of agricultural production, has a great bearing on the proportion of employed people in the material and nonmaterial production fields. It is necessary to understand and study the trade composition of employed people in order to know the characteristics and existing problems of socioeconomic development, analyze the economic structure of the country and its various localities, and thereby readjust in good time the speed of economic development.

By profession or occupation we mean the actual work one does. In the same department there may be people of different professions. According to their characteristics, workers may be divided into two major categories: manual workers and white-collar workers. The profession or occupation of the employed people reflects the level of social, economic, scientific, and technical development. Therefore, analyzing the number of people with different technical skills and their distribution in the different trades will help determine labor force planning and improve the occupation composition of the labor force.

THE PROPORTION OF PEOPLE IN DIFFERENT TRADES

The 1982 census in China classified trades into 15 kinds, which fall under two big categories—material production and nonmaterial production. Material production departments include agriculture, forestry, animal husbandry and fishery, mining and lumbering, the production and supply of electric power, gas and tap water, manufacturing, geological survey and prospecting, building industry, communications and transportation, post and telecommunication, commerce, catering trade, and the supply, marketing, and storage of materials. According to data from the censuses, the population employed in these departments came to 492.044 million, accounting for 94.35% of the total population of the employed. Nonmaterial production departments include residence management, administration of public utilities and service trade for the residents, public health, physical culture, and social welfare undertakings, educational, cultural, and art undertakings, scientific research and comprehensive technical services, finance, insurance, state organs, political parties and mass organizations, and others. The number of people employed in these departments was 29.457 million, or 5.65% of the total population of the employed.

The fairly high proportion of the Chinese population employed in the material production departments and the low proportion in the nonmaterial production departments are manifestations of the underdevelopment of China's economy. Take some developed countries in the world for example. The high proportion of the employed population in the material production departments was no more than 73.7% (Japan in 1978) and the low proportion was 59.2% (United States in 1977). The proportion was 64.8% for France and 70.1% for the Federal Republic of Germany in 1978, all much lower than that of China. At the same time, the proportion of the population employed in the nonmaterial production departments in these countries was much higher than that of China. For example, it was 40.8% in the United States (1977), 26.3% in Japan (1978), 29.9% in the Federal Republic of Germany (1978), and 35.2% in France (1978).*

Chinese statistical data over the years show that since the founding of New China, in 1949 (with the exception of a few years), the proportion of the employed in the material production departments was more than 96% from 1952 to 1977, while that of the nonmaterial production departmens was lower than 4% throughout. It was only after 1978 that the proportion of the employed in the material production departments gradually decreased and that of the nonmaterial production departments gradually went up (see Table 10-11).

The data also showed that while the proportion of the employed population in these two big departments changed slowly in the 1952–83 period, the composition of the employed population in the various trades and occupations also underwent some changes (see Table 10-12). The trend and characteristics of the changes are as follows:

First, although the proportion of the employed population in agriculture, animal husbandry, for-

estry, and fishery dropped each year, the number of people employed in these departments still accounted for the great majority of the population of the employed. According to the 1982 census data, of the employed population in agriculture, animal husbandry, forestry, and fishery 97.6% were in agriculture, and of the people employed in agriculture, 91.4% were engaged in the cultivation of food crops. This shows that China has a long way to go in order to achieve modernization in agriculture. Meanwhile, the proportion of the employed population in industry, by and large, gradually went up each year, with a growth rate of 159.6%. The growth rate of the employed population in the building industry and in resources prospecting was 138.5%, and that of transport, post, and telecommunication departments was 97.56%.

Second, the proportion of the employed population in commerce, catering and service trades, and materials supply and marketing departments fluctuated. In the 1950s and 1960s it dropped, and toward the end of the 1970s it began to go up slowly. Compared with 1952, it increased by 33.67% in 1983. According to the 1982 census, the number of people employed in these departments accounted for less than 4% of the total population of the employed in the various trades. All this indicated that in the economic construction in the past, there were disparities and contradictions between the development of production and the improvement of the people's living standard.

Third, although the proportion of the employed in scientific research, culture and education, health and social welfare undertakings showed a yearly increase, the growth rate was small and could not meet the needs of the expanding economic construction in the country.

A look at the situation of various countries in the world will show that most people in many developing countries are engaged in agriculture (primary industry) and that a comparatively small number of people are engaged in the manufacturing and construction industries (secondary industry) and in various kinds of service trades (tertiary industry) including commerce, transportation and telecommunications, finance and insurance, as well as mass organizations, social and individual service trades. But in many developed countries, more people are engaged in the manufacturing and construction industries and in various kinds of service trades, while only a small number of people are engaged in agriculture. If the trade composition of China is classified according to the above-mentioned standard,

---

* *Economic Statistics of the Capitalist Countries*, Shanghai People's Publishing House, 1983, p. 135.

Table 10-11   Proportion of the Employed Population in Material Production and Nonmaterial Production Departments in China

YEAR	NUMBER OF PEOPLE EMPLOYED IN MATERIAL PRODUCTION DEPARTMENTS (10,000)	PROPORTION IN THE TOTAL POPULATION OF THE EMPLOYED* (%)	NUMBER OF PEOPLE EMPLOYED IN NONMATERIAL PRODUCTION DEPARTMENTS (10,000)	PROPORTION IN THE TOTAL POPULATION OF THE EMPLOYED* (%)
1952	20,126.9	97.09	602.2	2.91
1953	20,714.6	96.96	648.9	3.04
1954	21,189.2	97.05	643.2	2.95
1955	21,660.1	97.01	667.1	2.99
1956	22,317.6	96.96	700.4	3.03
1957	23,035.9	96.91	735.2	3.09
1958	25,853.2	97.19	747.6	2.81
1959	25,300.9	96.67	871.7	3.33
1960	24,874.4	96.12	1,005.0	3.88
1961	24,547.2	95.93	1,042.6	4.07
1962	24,987.4	96.44	922.1	3.66
1963	25,673.0	96.37	967.4	3.63
1964	26,693.8	96.24	1,041.9	3.76
1965	27,570.0	96.16	1,100.0	3.84
1966	28,708.0	96.32	1,097.0	3.68
1967	29,703.0	96.39	1,111.0	3.61
1968	30,782.0	96.45	1,133.0	3.55
1969	32,119.0	96.67	1,106.0	3.33
1970	33,318.0	96.76	1,114.0	3.24
1971	34,438.8	96.68	1,181.5	3.32
1972	34,608.0	96.52	1,246.0	3.48
1973	35,397.3	96.58	1,254.6	3.42
1974	36,056.0	96.49	1,312.6	3.51
1975	36,784.8	96.38	1,383.0	3.62
1976	37,361.2	96.21	1,472.9	3.79
1977	37,839.0	96.09	1,538.5	3.91
1978	38,176.0	95.78	1,680.8	4.22
1979	38,773.3	95.55	1,807.4	4.45
1980	39,970.0	95.40	1,926.5	4.60
1981	41,245.5	95.30	2,035.0	4.70
1982	42,575.6	95.23	2,130.7	4.77
1983	43,822.5	95.26	2,181.3	4.74

* For total population of the employed, see Table 10-8.
Source: *Statistics Yearbook of China 1984*, China Statistics Publishing House, 1984, pp. 107, 114, 119, 122.

then the proportion of its population engaging in the primary sector exceeds that of many developing countries, while the proportion of its population in the secondary sector, and especially in the tertiary sector, is lower than that of some developing countries (see Table 10-13).

It should be pointed out that, apart from its direct relations with the living standard of the people, the tertiary sector is also an indispensable and vital sector in the construction and development of a country. To develop the tertiary sector is an objective requirement for achieving the socialization and modernization of production and management in a country. It can be expected that in the course of modernizing China's industry, agriculture, national de-

fense, science, and technology, the proportion of the population employed in the tertiary sector will increase rapidly.

THE PROPORTION OF PEOPLE IN VARIOUS PROFESSIONS

The 1982 census in China classified the employed population under eight professional categories according to the nature of their work. They were: specialized personnel and technicians of various trades; leading members of state organs, Party and mass organizations, enterprises, and undertakings; office workers and other related personnel; commercial workers; service workers; workers in agriculture,

Table 10-12 Changes in the Trade Composition of China's Employed Population

TRADE	1952 NUMBER OF PEOPLE (10,000)	1952 PERCENTAGE	1957 NUMBER OF PEOPLE (10,000)	1957 PERCENTAGE	1965 NUMBER OF PEOPLE (10,000)	1965 PERCENTAGE	1978 NUMBER OF PEOPLE (10,000)	1978 PERCENTAGE	1982 NUMBER OF PEOPLE (10,000)	1982 PERCENTAGE	1983 NUMBER OF PEOPLE (10,000)	1983 PERCENTAGE
Agriculture, animal husbandry, forestry, and fishery	18,243	88.01	20,566	86.52	23,585	82.26	30,342	76.13	33,278	74.44	34,258	74.47
Industry	893	4.31	1,086	4.57	1,782	6.22	4,259	10.69	5,051	11.30	5,150	11.19
Building industry and resources prospecting	188	0.91	291	1.22	482	1.68	837	2.10	961	2.15	998	2.17
Agriculture, forestry, water conservancy, and meteorology	24	0.12	112	0.47	495	1.73	893	2.24	860	1.92	865	1.88
Transport, post, and telecommunications	169	0.82	292	1.23	428	1.49	655	1.64	735	1.64	745	1.62
Commerce, catering and service trades, materials supply, and marketing	610	2.94	689	2.90	798	2.78	1,190	2.99	1,690	3.78	1,806	3.93
Scientific research, culture, and education, health and social welfare undertakings	296	1.43	392	1.65	656	2.29	1,069	2.68	1,288	2.88	1,312	2.85
Government organs and mass organizations	259	1.25	279	1.17	293	1.02	431	1.08	577	1.29	591	1.28
Others	47	0.23	64	0.27	151	0.53	180	0.45	266	0.59	279	0.61
Total	20,729	100.0	23,771	100.0	28,670	100.0	39,856	100.0	44,706	100.0	46,004	100.0

Source: *Statistics Yearbook of China 1984*, China Statistics Publishing House, 1984, pp. 107, 113, 122.

Table 10-13   Comparison of the Employed Population in the Three Industries of Various Countries (%)

COUNTRY	YEAR OF SURVEY	TOTAL	PRIMARY INDUSTRY	SECONDARY INDUSTRY	TERTIARY INDUSTRY	OTHERS
China	1982	100.0	73.7	16.0	10.3	—
India	1971	100.0	72.1	11.5	15.7	0.7
Philippines	1970	100.0	56.3	17.3	24.7	1.7
Thailand	1970	100.0	79.2	5.9	14.0	0.9
Mexico	1970	100.0	39.4	22.9	31.9	5.8
Japan	1975	100.0	13.8	34.7	51.2	0.3
Federal Republic of Germany	1970	100.0	7.5	48.1	44.4	—
Britain	1971	100.0	2.6	44.5	52.1	0.8
United States	1970	100.0	3.9	34.1	62.0	—

Sources: Figures for China are from *Population of China*, China Statistics Publishing House, 1985. Other figures are from Shen Yimin, *World Censuses and Population in the Last 30 Years*, Qunzhong Publishing House, 1983, p. 265.

forestry, animal husbandry, and fishery; productive laborers, transport workers, and other related personnel; and other laborers.

Following are the characteristics of the profession or occupation composition of the employed population:

First, the proportion of manual workers was high. If the commercial and service workers were not included, the total number of manual workers directly engaged in agriculture, forestry, animal husbandry, and fishery and the productive enterprises and transportation accounted for 87.96% of the total population of the employed, and those engaged in agriculture, forestry, animal husbandry, and fishery made up nearly 72%. And of the number of workers in agriculture, forestry, animal husbandry, and fishery, agricultural workers accounted for 69.04%, or 78.49% of the industrial and agricultural workers who directly took part in physical labor, totalling 360.06 million. This shows that China now still relies on the great majority of its workers to solve the question of supplying grain, cotton, vegetables, and other daily necessities. And this points up the urgent need to further raise the labor productivity of China's agriculture.

What merits attention is the high proportion of workers in China's agriculture, forestry, animal husbandry, and fishery, which is a conspicuous phenomenon even among the developing countries. Available statistics show that only in a few countries does the proportion of workers in these fields exceed 70% of the total population engaged in various economic activities. In Bangladesh the proportion of such workers was 79.1% in 1974; it was 72% in India in 1971; 94.4% in Nepal in 1971; 79.4% in Thailand in 1970; and 73.7% in Cameroon in 1976. The figures for Indonesia, the Philippines, Sri Lanka, and South Korea were all less than 60%.* As for the developed countries, the total number of workers directly engaged in agriculture and industry was less than 50% of the total population engaged in economic activities; and of this number, the proportion of those engaged in agriculture, forestry, animal husbandry, and fishery was only 2.8% in the United States in 1978 and 11.3% in Japan in 1978.[†]

Second, the proportion of white-collar workers was low; specialized personnel and technicians in various fields, government functionaries, office workers, and other related personnel totalled 26.45 million, or 7.93% of the total population of the employed. Of this number, the specialized personnel and technicians in various fields made up only 5.07%. Although this was a little higher than in some developing countries, it was markedly lower than in the developed countries. The proportion of specialized personnel and technicians in the economic activities was, for example, 7.2% in Japan and 14.3 and 15.5%, respectively, in the United States and France in 1978.[‡] The proportion of the above-mentioned specialized personnel in China consisted mainly of teachers, people engaged in economic affairs, and medical and public health personnel, accounting for 82.82% of the total number of specialized personnel and technicians in various fields, while the proportion of scientific research personnel, engineers and technicians, and technical personnel engaged in agriculture and forestry was small, totalling only 11.57%.

* Shen Yimin, *World Censuses and Population in the Last 30 Years*, Qunzhong Publishing Hose, 1983, pp. 358–361.
† *Economic Statistics of the Capitalist Countries*, Shanghai People's Publishing House, 1983, p. 136.
‡ *Economic Statistics of the Capitalist Countries*, Shanghai People's Publishing House, 1983, p. 136.

After the founding of the People's Republic of China, in 1949, along with the development of socialist construction and education, those who have received a higher or secondary education have doubled or redoubled. But, because we had a poor foundation to start with and as a result of the suspension and destruction wrought on scientific research and education by the "cultural revolution," the specialized personnel and technicians in various fields now available cannot, either in number or in quality, meet the needs of China's modernization drive. To vigorously develop education by various means, raise the scientific and cultural level of the whole nation, and train qualified personnel in various scientific fields are major tasks the country has to tackle for a long period of time in the future.

Third, the proportion of workers in the service trades was small. According to the 1982 census, the number of personnel working in commerce and service trades totalled 20.92 million in the whole country, accounting for 2.03% of China's total population, or 4.01% of the total population of the employed. It is quite obvious that this proportion was too small. Compared with other countries in the world, the proportion of Chinese workers in the service trades was not only lower than in the developed countries but also lower than in most developing countries.* And of the number of workers in the service trades, the proportion of those working in restaurants, hotels and guest houses, cinemas and theaters, stadiums, public bathrooms, childcare establishments, environmental sanitation departments, and those on trains and buses, ships and planes, etc., was quite low, accounting for only 2.21% of the total population of the employed. Even in the cities, the proportion of workers in this category accounted for only 6.85% of the employed population or 3.85% of the total population in the urban areas, and the proportion of such workers was 7.07% of the employed population and 3.77% of the total population of the market towns. In the vast rural areas, the proportion was 0.89% and 0.45%, respectively.

This much too low proportion of workers in China's service trades shows that for a long time there have existed serious disproportions in the occupation composition and personnel composition that are incompatible with the actual needs of day-to-day life. In 1957, the total number of workers in commerce and the catering and serivce trades was 8.955 million. The figure dropped to 7.073 million in

1965, and went up again to 9.378 million in 1978. The increase in those 21 years was only 4.72%,* while in the corresponding period the population had increased by 48.89% in the country. It was only toward the end of the 1970s and at the beginning of the 1980s that the number of people working in commerce and service trades began to increase markedly. By the end of 1983, people in this category reached 22.268 million, which was 2.37 times that of 1978.† While continuously and rationally readjusting the economic structure in the future, we should, in a planned and proportionate way, increase the proportion of people working in commerce and service trades of various economic types, so as to gradually enable this category to be in consonance with the economic life of the nation and the improvement of the living standard of the whole people.

THE DISTRIBUTION OF PEOPLE OF DIFFERENT OCCUPATIONS IN DIFFERENT TRADES

An analysis of the distribution of people of different occupations in different trades (see Table 10-14) showed that the social division of labor was still not developed in China and that the level of specialization in the service trades was not high. The concrete manifestations were: The enterprises and undertakings of the various trades at the grass-roots level were very often big and all-embracing or small and all-embracing, and many industrial enterprises had their own schools, hospitals, canteens, and residential quarters ensuring the daily needs of their workers and staff members. As a result, almost every trade and profession had its own doctors, teachers, shop assistants, chefs, cooks, barbers, and child-care workers, etcetera. According to the 1982 census, about 4% of the people engaged in teaching were in the industrial departments; about 14.6% of the people engaged in commerce were in the industrial departments and only 78.7% of them were actually working in the commercial departments. As to medical and health workers and technicians, 33.9% were in medical and health units of other trades (of which 9.7% were in the industrial departments and 17.8% were in the agricultural, animal husbandry, forestry, and fishery departments), and only 66.10% of them were actually working in the medical and health departments. Of the personnel working in the service trades, chefs and cooks accounted for 26.52%, but

---

* Shen Yimin: *World Censuses and Population in the Last 30 Years*, Qunzhong Publishing House, 1983, pp. 358–362.

* *Statistics Yearbook of China 1984*, China Statistics Publishing House, 1984, p. 375.
† Ibid.

Table 10-14   Percentage of People of Different Occupations in Different Trades in China (1982)

TRADE OR PROFESSION	AGRICULTURE, ANIMAL HUSBANDRY, FORESTRY, AND FISHERY	INDUSTRY	GEOLOGICAL PROSPECTING AND GENERAL SURVEYING	CONSTRUCTION INDUSTRY	COMMUNICATION AND TRANSPORTATION, POST AND TELECOMMUNICATION	COMMERCE, CATERING, TRADE, MATERIALS SUPPLY, MARKETING, AND STORAGE	RESIDENTIAL QUARTERS AND PUBLIC UTILITIES ADMINISTRATION, SERVICES FOR RESIDENTS
Specialized personnel and technicians in various fields	10.42	17.50	0.66	2.91	2.31	4.97	0.71
Leading member of state organs, Party and mass organizations, enterprises and undertakings	5.47	32.87	0.52	3.70	4.48	12.47	1.08
Office workers and other related personnel	3.87	23.59	0.73	3.58	11.02	9.66	1.29
Commercial workers	2.09	14.64	0.11	0.76	0.73	78.73	0.45
Workers in service trades	5.87	35.54	0.57	3.53	6.97	19.73	12.33
Workers in agriculture, forestry, animal husbandry, and fishery	99.60	0.19	0.003	0.015	0.057	0.027	0.021
Production enterprises and transportation workers and other related personnel	7.10	67.43	0.56	10.94	7.38	3.25	0.64
Other workers	4.25	54.28	0.83	7.51	4.94	6.32	1.14

Table 10-14 (Continued)

TRADE OR PROFESSION	HEALTH, PHYSICAL CULTURE, AND SOCIAL WELFARE	EDUCATION, CULTURE, AND ART	SCIENTIFIC RESEARCH AND COMPREHENSIVE TECHNOLOGICAL SERVICES	FINANCE AND INSURANCE	GOVERNMENT ORGANS, POLITICAL PARTIES, AND MASS ORGANIZATIONS	OTHERS	TOTAL
Specialized personnel and technicians in various fields	12.31	36.57	2.11	2.79	6.64	0.11	100.0
Leading member of state organs, Party and mass organizations, enterprises and undertakings	2.11	10.11	0.97	2.12	24.02	0.09	100.0
Office workers and other related personnel	1.23	4.23	0.99	0.88	38.56	0.37	100.0
Commercial workers	0.19	0.42	0.12	0.02	1.64	0.10	100.0
Workers in service trades	3.30	6.93	0.51	0.26	4.13	0.33	100.0
Workers in agriculture, forestry, animal husbandry, and fishery	0.005	0.014	0.025	—	0.026	0.009	100.0
Production enterprises and transportation workers and other related personnel	0.19	0.83	0.39	0.02	1.11	0.16	100.0
Other workers	2.16	3.03	2.24	0.97	8.42	3.91	100.0

Source: *1982 Population Census of China*, China Statistics Publishing House, 1985.

only 21.46% of them were actually working in the commercial and catering trades, while those working in other departments accounted for 78.54%. Of this percentage, those working in the industrial departments made up 33.15%, far exceeding the proportion of those working in the commercial and catering trades. Among the attendants in the restaurants, hotels, and guest houses, cinemas and theaters, stadiums and bathhouses as well as barbers. ticket sellers, and environmental sanitation workers, only 16.18% worked in the housing administration and public utilities departments and the service trades for the neighborhood residents. Those working in the commercial departments, catering trade, materials supply, marketing, and storage departments also made up only 19.74%, while those working in the manufacturing departments accounted for more than 27.29%. These figures show that at the present stage the distribution of people of different occupations in different trades is irrational, and the level of socialization of the service trades is especially low. Full attention should therefore be paid to readjusting the distribution of people of different occupations in different trades in the light of China's actual conditions so as to bring into play the advantages of the country's enormous labor resources.

SEX AND AGE COMPOSITION OF EMPLOYED POPULATION

The sex composition of the employed population reflects the differences in the size and proportion of the male and female labor force of a country, and the age composition of the employed population shows whether the type of a country's labor force is young, middle-aged, or old. A study of the sex and age composition of the employed population is of extreme importance in understanding the basic structure of a country's labor force and, on this basis, in formulating a series of appropriate plans for the development of its economy and utilization of its labor force.

SEX COMPOSITION OF EMPLOYED POPULATION

According to the computerized data of China's 1982 census, of the employed population over 15 years old, 293.66 million, or 56.3% were men, and 227.84 million, or 43.7%, were women. The male employed population made up 56.9% of the nation's total male population, and the female employed population accounted for 46.6% of the country's total female population. These basic data show that in China women

enjoy the same right as men to participate in labor, and the proportion of employed females is quite high, but the proportion of employed men is higher than that of women. Now we shall examine the sex composition of China's employed population in different trades and occupations.

According to data from the 1982 census, the proportion of employed men was higher than that of women in most trades. The proportion of the male employed population in all six major trades was over 70%. Of these six trades, one requires heavy manual labor and mainly involves outdoor and field work. Limited by their physiology, very few women do such work. In the building industry, for instance, the proportion of men workers accounted for 81.13%, while that of women made up only 18.87%; in mining and lumbering, men workers made up 80.64%, and women 19.36%. In other departments, such as geological prospecting and general survey, communications and transportation, post and telecommunications, and the production and supply of electricity, gas, and tap water, the difference between the proportion of men and that of women was quite big. In government organs, Party and mass organizations, the proportion of men was as high as 79.55%, and women made up only 20.45%. This was unreasonable, because physiologically women were quite suitable for work in these organizations. The main reason why men outnumbered women was that the cultural and educational level of most women was lower than that of men. Another reason was that women had fewer chances than men to work in these organizations because they were burdened with household chores and because there were remnants of the concept that men were superior to women. The situation in many other countries is just the opposite. There are more women than men working in these organizations and in the social and private service trades. According to data from censuses in 55 countries, there were 21 countries where the number of women working in these organizations was greater than that of men. For instance, the number of women working in these departments accounted for 71.5% in the Philippines in 1970; 54.7% in Bulgaria in 1975; 68.5% in Sweden in 1975; 55.2% in Brazil in 1970; and 60.4% in the United States in 1970.* However, in ordinary production departments, where the work was suited to the physiological characteristics of women, the situation in China was the same as in many other countries, and the proportion of women

---

* Shen Yimin, *World Censuses and Population in the Last 30 Years,* Qunzhong Publishing House, 1983, pp. 267–343.

Table 10-15 Occupations of Women in Selected Countries (%)

OCCUPATION	CHINA (1982)	INDIA (1974)	INDONESIA (1971)	JAPAN (1975)	THAILAND (1970)	PHILIPPINES (1970)	FRANCE (1975)	USA (1970)
Specialized personnel and technicians	38.27	17.74	31.06	39.29	41.25	56.79	44.37	40.10
Administrative workers	10.38	1.70	19.36	5.25	7.14	28.52	16.36	16.57
Office workers	24.47	4.01	11.23	49.90	32.80	37.92	66.63	73.46
Service workers	47.93	16.65	42.76	54.08	48.87	66.04	66.72	55.20
Commercial workers	45.86	6.14	43.87	39.40	55.28	56.89	49.65	38.54
Workers in agriculture, animal husbandry, forestry, fishery, and hunting	46.79	19.89	32.30	49.07	49.72	19.58	29.09	9.54
Workers in production and transportation departments	35.42	8.41	31.36	24.30	28.80	33.07	17.43	17.98

Sources: Figures for China, *1982 Population Census of China*, China Statistics Publishing House, 1985. Figures for other countries are quoted from Shen Yimin, *World Censuses and Population in the Last 30 Years*, Qunzhong Publishing House, 1983, pp. 366–424.

workers was rather high. For instance, in commerce, catering trade, the supply, marketing, and storage of materials, the manufacturing industry, housing management, public utilities administration, and neighborhood services, male workers accounted for about 55% and female workers about 45%. In public health, physical culture, and social welfare undertakings, the proportion between men and women was nearly the same — 51.87% for men and 48.13% for women. In agriculture, animal husbandry, forestry, and fishery, women accounted for 46.24% and men 53.76%. Such a proportion was quite normal.

The proportion of male population employed in various trades was higher than the proportion of females, and the difference between the proportion of men and women leading members was especially big in government organs, Party and mass organizations, enterprises and undertakings. Men working in these units made up 89.62% while women only 10.38%. Among the office workers and other related personnel, men accounted for 75.53% and women only 24.47%. Among the service and commercial workers and those working in agriculture, animal husbandry, forestry, and fishery, the proportion of men and women workers was fairly close; in these predominantly manual labor and service units, women workers accounted for more than 45%.

The difference in the sex composition of China's employed population in the different professions shows that for a long time in the past Chinese women had fewer chances than men to receive an education, their cultural level was lower, and so they had less freedom than men to choose work or to shift from one job to another. As a result, the proportion of Chinese women employed in administrative and office work or as specialized technicians was lower than their counterparts in the developed countries and, in some cases, even lower than in some developing countries. On the other hand, the proportion of Chinese women working in agriculture, animal husbandry, forestry, and fishery and in production and transportation departments was higher than that of their counterparts in the developed countries and in some developing countries (see Table 10-15).

AGE COMPOSITION OF EMPLOYED POPULATION

The age composition of China's employed population is young (see Table 10-17) because the general age structure of the population is quite young. According to the computerized data of the 1982 census, China's employed population in the 15–29 age group accounted for 48.51% ; for the 30–44 age

Table 10-16   Age Composition of Employed Population in China, Japan, and the United States (%)

AGE GROUP	CHINA (1982)	JAPAN (1975)	USA (1970)
15–19*	18.09	3.25	7.94
20–24	13.51	12.02	12.95
25–34	30.26	26.26	20.77
35–44	18.55	23.86	20.35
45–54	13.57	19.14	20.33
55–64	6.03	10.57	13.73
65+	—	4.91	3.93
Total	100.0	100.0	100.0

* 14–19 for the United States.

Sources: Figures for China, *1982 Population Census of China,* China Statistics Publishing House, 1985. Japan and the United States are quoted from Shen Yimin's *World Censuses and Population in the Last 30 Years,* Qunzhong Publishing House, 1983, pp. 368, 369, 424.

group it was 31.90%, and for the 45–64 age group it was 19.60%. In the developed countries, the employed population over 45 years old generally makes up about one-third of the total. For instance, in Japan the proportion in this age group accounted for 34.62% in 1975, and in the United States it was 37.99% in 1970 (see Table 10-16).

Chinese workers in material production departments are generally young. For instance, as shown in Table 10-17, those aged between 15 and 29 working in agriculture, animal husbandry, forestry, and fishery accounted for 48.02%; those of the same age group working in the building industry accounted for 52.86%; in the manufacturing industry, 51.94%; in electricity, gas, and tap water production and supply departments, 46.49%; in commerce, catering trade, in materials supply, marketing, and storage departments, 45.29%. In nonmaterial production departments, the proportion of workers in the 15–29 age group working in financial and insurance establishments was the highest (48.38%); the second highest proportion was 43.34% for those working in housing management, public utilities departments, and neighborhood services; those working in educational, cultural, and art institutions accounted for 39.98%; and the proportion of those working in other trades was below 44%. The proportion of those engaged in scientific research and comprehensive technical services was 32.58%; and in public health, physical culture, and social welfare undertakings, it was 38.97%. The proportion of young people working in government organs, political parties, and mass organizations was the lowest, being only 29.81%.

As regards occupation, Chinese manual workers are generally young, while white-collar workers are

Table 10-17   Age Composition of Chinese People Employed in Different Trades (1982) (%)

TRADE	AGE GROUP						TOTAL
	15–19	20–24	25–29	30–34	35–54	55+	
Agriculture, animal hus-bandry, forestry, and fishery	20.00	12.25	15.77	12.74	30.84	8.4	100.0
Mining and lumbering	10.69	15.09	19.37	15.89	36.45	2.5	100.0
Electricity, gas and tap water production and supply departments	8.69	16.59	21.21	15.19	35.73	2.59	100.0
Manufacturing industry	14.56	17.64	19.74	14.72	29.71	3.62	100.0
Geological prospecting and general surveying	7.40	16.07	18.62	14.60	41.60	1.70	100.0
Building industry	14.68	17.95	20.23	14.04	29.57	3.54	100.0
Communications and trans-portation, post and tele-communications	8.76	15.53	19.88	14.66	36.14	5.04	100.0
Commercial, catering trade, materials supply, marketing and storage departments	11.21	16.39	17.69	13.09	33.13	8.49	100.0
Housing management, public utilities, neighborhood services	10.79	15.68	16.87	11.73	33.28	11.65	100.0
Public health, physical culture, and social welfare undertakings	5.79	12.76	20.42	14.35	40.27	6.41	100.0
Education, culture, and arts	5.68	14.19	20.11	15.02	40.51	4.49	100.0
Scientific research, compre-hensive technical services	4.94	11.04	16.60	11.69	51.05	4.69	100.0
Financial and insurance departments	13.86	20.31	14.21	8.16	38.36	5.10	100.0
Government organs, Party and mass organizations	5.36	10.40	14.05	12.47	49.86	7.87	100.0
Others	12.37	15.17	16.11	14.23	34.27	7.85	100.0

Source: *1982 Population Census of China*, China Statistics Publishing House, 1985.

older in age. For instance, workers between 15 and 34 years old in agriculture, animal husbandry, forestry, and fishery accounted for 60.87%; those of the 35–54 age group made up 30.69%, and those aged 55 or older made up 8.45%. Among workers in production, transportation, and other related departments, those of the 15–34 age group accounted for 70.47%; those of the 35–54 age group, 26.61%; and those aged 55 or older, only 2.91%, the average age being 31.19—the youngest in the eight major categories of occupations. In comparison, specialized personnel and technicians in the various trades in the 15–34 age group accounted for 53.40% of the white-collar workers; those of the 35–54 age group made up 42.69%; and those aged 55 and older made up only 3.92%. The average age of leading members in government organs, Party and mass organizations, enterprises, and undertakings was the highest; those of the 15–34 age group accounted for only 14.30%, those of the 35–54 age group made up 73.59%, and

those aged 55 and older accounted for 12.10% (see Table 10-18).

Compared with developed countries such as the United States and the Federal Republic of Germany, the age composition of the employed population of China is younger, and this is especially the case with manual workers. However, the proportion of Chinese administrative and managerial personnel from 15 to 34 years old obviously is lower than that of their counterparts in the United States and the Federal Republic of Germany, the latter two being higher by 10.13% and 10.42%, respectively (see Table 10-19).

It should be noted, however, that the high age composition of administrative and managerial personnel in China was based on the census conducted in July 1982. In the last few years, the Chinese government has placed special emphasis on the need to promote younger cadres to leading posts. In response to this, many leading cadres advanced in age have, from the central down to the local levels,

Table 10-18   Age Composition of Chinese Workers in Various Occupations (1982) (%)

OCCUPATION	AGE GROUP						TOTAL
	15–19	20–24	25–29	30–34	35–54	55+	
Specialized personnel and technicians	4.99	13.26	19.78	15.37	42.69	3.92	100.0
Leading members of government organs, Party and mass organizations, enterprises, and undertakings	0.09	0.94	4.68	8.59	73.59	12.10	100.0
Office workers and other related prsonnel	5.35	12.29	17.32	15.33	44.98	4.72	100.0
Commercial workers	11.91	16.66	18.47	13.86	30.61	8.48	100.0
Service workers	10.31	12.77	14.64	11.97	37.22	13.09	100.0
Workers in agriculture, animal husbandry, forestry, and fishery	20.21	12.23	15.74	12.69	30.69	8.45	100.0
Workers in production, transportation, and related departments	15.49	19.08	20.99	14.91	26.61	2.91	100.0
Others	33.22	23.62	15.21	8.42	15.92	3.60	100.0

Source: *1982 Population Census of China*, China Statistics Publishing House, 1985.

stepped down and made way for a large number of young and middle-aged cadres in their prime who have been promoted to the leading bodies at various levels. Statistics show that by the end of 1985, the number of cadres and workers who had retired throughout the country totalled 16.37 million, or more than 10% of the nation's total number of people employed.* This figure, to a certain extent, shows that the age composition of administrative and man-

* *Renmin Ribao*, May 11, 1986.

agerial personnel in China today has changed considerably from what it was during the 1982 census. The average age now has decreased greatly.

SCIENTIFIC AND EDUCATIONAL LEVEL OF THE EMPLOYED POPULATION

The scientific and educational level is an important aspect in making a comprehensive assessment of the employed population of a country. This is particu-

Table 10-19   Age Composition of the Employed in China, the United States, and Federal Republic of Germany (%)

OCCUPATION	CHINA (1982)			USA (1970)			FED. REP. GERMANY (1970)		
	15–34	35–54	55+	14–34	35–54	55+	15–34	35–54	55+
Specialized and technical workers	53.40	42.69	93.2	43.49	41.58	14.93	44.75	38.78	16.47
Administrative personnel	14.30	73.59	12.10	24.43	52.58	22.99	24.71	50.28	25.00
Office workers	50.29	44.98	4.72	48.27	37.77	13.96	49.77	36.14	14.09
Workers in agriculture, animal husbandry, forestry, fishery, and hunting	60.87	30.69	8.45	30.67	38.05	31.28	26.11	41.03	32.86
Production and transportation workers	70.47	26.61	2.91	40.41	42.68	16.91	45.86	39.28	14.86

Sources: Figures for China, *1982 Population Census of China*, China Statistics Publishing House, 1985. Figures for the Federal Republic of Germany and the United States are quoted from Shen Yimin, *World Censuses and Population in the Last 30 Years*, Qunzhong Publishing House, 1983, pp. 392, 424.

larly important today when science and technology are developing rapidly and production conditions and techniques as well as managerial expertise are being modernized day by day.

EDUCATIONAL LEVEL OF THE EMPLOYED POPULATION

China's 1982 census showed that the educational level of its employed population was comparatively low. Of the total number of employed, only 0.87% had a college education, 10.54% a senior middle school education, and 26% a junior middle school education (the three altogether making up 37.41%), while 34.38% had only a primary school education and 28.20% were illiterates or semi-illiterates (the two combined to make up 62.58%). Such an educational level is incompatible with the heavy tasks of modernization. It also shows that even though rapid progress has been made in education since the founding of the People's Republic, and the number of people who have received a higher education or secondary specialized education has increased many times,* China has as yet been unable to fundamentally change the low educational level of its employed population.

EDUCATIONAL LEVEL OF PEOPLE IN VARIOUS TRADES AND OCCUPATIONS

The educational level of the employed population in China's material production departments is very low, and that of people working in agriculture, animal husbandry, forestry, and fishery is the lowest. Those with a senior middle school education accounted for only 5.47%; only about 30 out of every 10,000 had a college education, and the rate of illiteracy was 35.90%. At the present stage manual labor still holds the dominant position in China's agriculture and the level of mechanization is very low. In industries such as mining, power, and manufacturing industries, workers with a senior middle school education accounted for 21.94%, and the educa-

tional level of those working in the power, gas, and tap water industries was the highest, with 32.53% having received a senior middle school or higher education. This was followed by the manufacturing industry, with 22.32% of its workers having received a senior middle school or higher education. The educational level of those working in the mining and lumbering industries was rather low, with only 17.37% having received a senior middle school or higher education and illiterates and semi-illiterates making up 11.43%. In the building industry and in communications and transportation, post and telecommunications, commerce, catering trade, materials supply, marketing and storage departments, the workers' educational level was also low. The rate of illiteracy and semi-illiteracy of those working in communications and transportation, post and telecommunications was 9.08%. Among the materials production departments, those working in geological prospecting and general surveying had the highest educational level, with 6.68% having received a college education and 27.16% having had a senior middle school education. Specialized and technical personnel in this field of work accounted for a fairly high proportion — 21.15%. In the nonmaterials production departments, with the exception of housing management, public utilities management, and neighborhood services where the educational level of the workers, was low, the educational level of workers in other trades was generally high (see Table 10-20).

As regards occupation, it goes without saying that the educational level of white-collar workers is higher than that of manual workers (see Table 10-21). Among Chinese white-collar workers, those with the highest educational level were specialized and technical personnel, especially those engaged in scientific research (those having a college education making up 77.10%). Among Chinese manual laborers, those with a relatively high educational level were the commercial workers. Among them, those with a senior middle school education accounted for 23.57%. Workers in production, transportation, and related departments who had a senior middle school education made up 19.12%. The educational level of those working in agriculture, animal husbandry, forestry, and fishery was the lowest. Among them, those with a senior middle school or higher educational level accounted for only 5.20%; the rate of illiteracy and semi-illiteracy was 36.53%, and the rate of illiteracy and semi-illiteracy among workers in animal husbandry was 52.39%, while those having had a senior middle school education accounted for only 2.04%.

---

* In the 1949–83 period, the number of graduates from institutes of higher learning in China totalled 4,110,200 (22.2 times the accumulative total of 185,000 before liberation), of whom 1,163,900 were graduates from 1979 to 1983, accounting for 28.32% of the total number of college graduates after liberation. The number of graduates from secondary technical schools from 1949 to 1983 totalled 7,223,600 (13.2 times the accumulative total of 546,700 before liberation), of whom 2,017,100 were graduates from 1979 to 1983, accounting for 27.92% of the total number of graduates from secondary technical schools after liberation. (See *Statistics Yearbook of China, 1984*, China Statistics Publishing House, 1984, p. 492.)

Table 10-20   Educational Level of Chinese Workers in Various Trades (1982) (%)

TRADE	UNIVERSITY GRADUATES	UNIVERSITY STUDENTS	SENIOR MIDDLE SCHOOL	JUNIOR MIDDLE SCHOOL	PRIMARY SCHOOL	ILLITERATE AND SEMI-ILLITERATE	TOTAL
Agriculture, animal husbandry, forestry, and fishery	0.03	0.007	5.43	21.47	37.16	35.90	100.0
Mining and lumbering	1.01	0.06	16.30	36.05	35.15	11.43	100.0
Electricity, gas and tap water production and supply	2.70	0.21	29.62	42.29	22.46	2.72	100.0
Manufacturing industry	1.44	0.13	20.75	40.37	29.77	7.53	100.0
Geological prospecting and general surveying	6.47	0.21	27.16	36.70	26.48	2.99	100.0
Building industry	1.70	0.12	17.77	40.11	33.45	6.86	100.0
Communications and transportation, post and telecomunications	0.95	0.09	20.73	38.36	30.79	9.08	100.0
Commerce, catering trade, supply, marketing and storage of materials	0.57	0.10	23.44	41.72	27.14	7.03	100.0
Housing management, public utilities, and neighborhood services	0.54	0.09	19.04	35.76	30.98	13.58	100.0
Public health, physical culture, and social welfare undertakings	9.04	0.34	37.28	35.97	15.96	1.41	100.0
Education, culture and arts	11.47	0.73	51.75	28.40	6.43	1.22	100.0
Scientific research and comprehensive technical services	28.25	0.83	30.10	26.74	13.13	0.95	100.0
Financial and insurance businesses	1.67	0.28	45.41	37.62	14.34	0.68	100.0
Government organs, Party and mass organizations	6.43	0.41	31.50	41.36	17.76	2.53	100.0
Others	1.86	0.22	20.60	33.35	30.60	13.37	100.0

Source: *1982 Population Census of China*, China Statistics Publishing House, 1985.

It should be noted that in the last few years the Chinese government has taken a series of effective and far-sighted measures and policies to speed up the development of higher education (the number of students studying in institutes of higher learning increased from 1.14 million in 1980 to 1.7 million in 1985), readjust the structure of secondary education, promote vocational and technical education, popularize primary education, and develop various forms of education for adults. All this has gradually raised the education level of China's employed population. The government also plans, during the Seventh Five-Year Plan period (1986-90), to attach strategic importance to making progress in science and technology and to development of intellectual resources so as to promote the advancement of science and education in a still better way. The government has pointed out explicitly: "It is our consistent long-term strategy to attach great importance to education. We have to improve elementary education, energetically promote nine-year compulsory education as well as vocational and technical training, and continue to consolidate and improve higher education and adult education. We should establish a system

Table 10-21   Educational Level of Chinese Workers in Various Occupations (1982) (%)

OCCUPATION	UNIVERSITY GRADUATES	UNIVERSITY STUDENTS	SENIOR MIDDLE SCHOOL	JUNIOR MIDDLE SCHOOL	PRIMARY SCHOOL	ILLITERATE AND SEMI-ILLITERATE	TOTAL
Specialized and technical personnel	12.45	0.60	44.45	32.49	10.01	—	100.0
Leading members of government organs, Party and mass organizations, enterprises, and undertakings	5.85	0.57	21.87	42.78	26.96	1.97	100.0
Office workers and other related personnel	3.80	0.37	32.70	43.75	18.21	1.17	100.0
Commercial workers	0.23	0.07	23.27	42.24	27.81	6.38	100.0
Service workers	0.08	0.04	13.96	31.17	36.95	17.81	100.0
Workers in agriculture, animal husbandry, forestry, and fishery	0.009	0.005	5.19	21.12	37.16	36.53	100.0
Workers in production, transportation, and other related departments	0.13	0.05	18.94	40.29	32.16	8.43	100.0
Others	6.63	0.52	35.29	38.16	14.65	4.75	100.0

Source: *1982 Population Census of China*, China Statistics Publishing House, 1985.

for offering advanced studies to scientific and technological workers," adding that local governments at all levels should encourage state enterprises, collectives, and other sectors of the society to sponsor different types of educational programs.* All these principles and measures of long-term and strategic significance will exert positive and important influence on fundamentally improving the educational level of the whole nation and thereby raise the educational level of China's employed population.

* Zhao Ziyang: "Report on the Seventh Five-Year Plan," *Renmin Ribao*, April 14, 1986.

CHAPTER ELEVEN

POPULATION OF MINORITY NATIONALITIES

China is a unified multinational country. In jointly creating the long history of the Chinese nation and its brilliant culture, all the nationalities in the country have made great contributions. But owing to the fact that the feudal ruling class throughout the ages and the reactionary Kuomintang regime had adopted the policy of discrimination against the minority peoples, the population problem of the minority nationalities had been neglected for thousands of years and no investigations whatever had been made. Only since the birth of New China has the population problem of the minority peoples been given due attention and serious study.

NATIONALITY COMPOSITION OF THE CHINESE POPULATION AND GROWTH OF POPULATION OF THE MINORITY PEOPLES

After liberation, the Communist Party of China and the People's Government adopted the policies of national equality, national unity, and joint prosperity for all the nationalities, and worked persistently to identify and confirm the various nationalities and their component parts. As a result, the number of minority nationalities has increased gradually. During China's first census, in 1953, 41 minority nationalities were identified and confirmed; the number rose to 53 during the second census, in 1964.

In 1965 and 1979, the government identified and confirmed the Loba and Jinuo peoples as independent nationalities. Thus, by 1982, when the third national census was conducted, the total number of minority nationalities in China had increased to 55. With the increase in the number of minority nationalities in the country and the fast growth of their population, the nationality composition of China's population has undergone corresponding changes too.

INCREASE OF POPULATION OF MINORITY NATIONALITIES AND CHANGES IN THE NATIONALITY COMPOSITION OF CHINA'S POPULATION

After liberation, and particularly after 1964, the population of the various minority nationalities increased at a fast pace, and its proportion in the total population of the country has become larger (see Table 11-1). But as the speed of population growth of the various minority nationalities varies, their proportion in the nation's total population varies too (see Table 11-2).

The population growth of China's minority nationalities after the founding of New China has the following characteristics:

• The population of various minority nationalities has increased gradually—from a slow to a fast pace, and the population of some minority nationalities has grown from a negative rate to a high rate. During the 1953 and 1964 censuses, with the exception of a few minority nationalities whose annual increase rate was over 2%, most of the other minority nationalities had a low growth rate of less than 1%. And the population of 10 minority nationalities including Tibetans, Kazakhs, and Russians even showed a negative growth. From 1964 to the 1982 census, however, not only had all the nationalities eliminated a negative population growth rate but switched to having a high rate of growth. For instance, there were 30 minority nationalities whose average annual population growth rate was 2–3%. These included the Hui, Tibetan, Uygur, Yi, Zhuang, Bouyei, Manchu, Yao, and Bai nationalities. Those with an average annual growth rate of 3.1–4.0% included the Mongolian,

Table 11-1 Changes in Population Growth of China's Nationalities*

NATIONALITY	1953		1964		1982		INCREASE OF POPULATION 1953–64 (%)		INCREASE OF POPULATION 1964–82 (%)	
	POPULATION (10,000)	PROPORTION IN NATION'S TOTAL (%)	POPULATION (10,000)	PROPORTION IN NATION'S TOTAL (%)	POPULATION (10,000)	PROPORTION IN NATION'S TOTAL (%)	PERCENT INCREASE	AVERAGE ANNUAL INCREASE	PERCENT INCREASE	AVERAGE ANNUAL INCREASE
Total of 29 provinces, municipalities, and autonomous regions	58,060.34	100.00	69,122.01	100.00	100,391.39	100.00	19.05	1.60	45.24	2.10
Han nationality	54,528.30	93.92	65,129.64	94.22	93,667.48	93.30	19.44	1.63	43.82	2.04
Minority nationalities	3,532.04	6.08	3,992.37	5.78	6,723.90	6.70	13.03	1.12	68.40	2.94

* Not including servicemen.

Source: Based on *1982 Population Census of China*, China Statistics Publishing House, 1985, pp. 18, 536.

Miao, Kazakh, and nine other nationalities. Those with an average annual growth rate of 4.1–5.0% included the Tu, Qiang, Russian, and Heche nationalities. If the population of the above-mentioned 46 nationalities goes on increasing at their present rate, it would take only 16–28 years to double their population. Those nationalities that need the shortest time to have their population doubled include the Russian (16 years), Heche (17 years), Qiang (17 years), Tu (17 years), Salar (18 years), and Dongxiang (19 years). Those with an average annual population growth rate of over 5.1% included four nationalities: Gaoshan, Tujia, Xibe, and Jing. Among them, the Gaoshan and Tujia nationalities have the highest annual population growth rate, reaching 8.7% and 9.8%, respectively. Only the Korean nationality had a lower growth rate, but it was still at a medium rate of 1.5% and will take 47 years to have its population doubled.

• Nationalities with a population of more than one million each have increased in number. There were 20 during the years from 1953 to 1964, but 15 in 1982.

• The proportion of the population of most minority nationalities in the nation's total has undergone great changes. The proportion of the population of minorities nationalities with more than one million people each in the nation's total dropped from 4.92% in 1953 to 4.75% in 1964; but it went up quickly to 6.01% in 1982. The proportion of the population of some nationalities in the nation's total was found to have experienced a high-low-high process during the three censuses. In 1982, some minority nationalities, including the Uygurs, Yis, and Tibetans, still had not reached their 1953 level, while some others such as Miao, Manchu, Bouyei, Bai, Kazakh, Lisu, Va, and Dongxiang had reached or exceeded their 1953 level.

• During the three census years, the proportion of the population of some nationalities in the nation's total population was found to be on the rise. They included the Zhuang, Hui, Mongolian, Yao, and Hani nationalities.

• During the three census years, the proportion of some other nationalities in the nation's total population was found to remain unchanged. They included the Dai, Naxi, and Khalkhas nationalities.

AN ANALYSIS OF CAUSES OF CHANGES IN POPULATION GROWTH OF MINORITY NATIONALITIES

Factors contributing to the increase of population of the minority nationalities are many. They include the following:

1. The fast growth of the population of minority nationalities is determined by numerous factors such as the mode of social production, social progress, economic development, government policy of encouraging childbirths, and improvement of medical service and health work. After liberation, areas inhabited by minority nationalities successively carried out democratic and social reforms. In areas where the Mongolians, Zhuangs, and Huis lived in compact communities, democratic reforms were carried out in the early 1950s. This, during the first census, in 1953, they had already attained a high population growth rate, while the Yis and Tibetans still maintained a low growth rate, for in their areas democratic reforms were implemented at a later date. Thanks to social reforms and efforts made by the Communist Party of China and the People's Government to help the minority peoples speed up their economic and cultural development, the industrial and agricultural output value of these minority areas registered an average annual increase of 6.9%* during the 1953–82 period, and the material and cultural well-being of the people there improved steadily. This constituted the basis for the improved health and survival of the minority peoples and the increase in their population.

With regard to the question of childbirths, since liberation the central authorities have adopted special policies for the minority nationalities and encouraged them to increase their population. In September 1980, the Central Committee of the Chinese Communist Party issued an Open Letter to All the Party Members and Communist Youth League Members on the Question of Controlling the Chinese Population Growth. The open letter stressed that a lenient policy be adopted toward the minority nationalities.

The government has also shown great concern for the development of medical and health work in the minority areas (see Table 11-3). Besides actively developing medical and health services in those areas, the government has often organized mobile medical teams from the big cities to work in the minority areas and help cure and prevent various kinds of diseases. This has in a very short period of time brought fundamental changes to the situation in which the minority areas suffered from a dearth of doctors and medicine and, at the same time, prevented and cured acute infections and endemic dis-

* *Statistics Yearbook of China 1983*, China Statistics Publishing House, p. 34.

Table 11-2 Changes in Population Growth of China's Various Nationalities

NATIONALITY	1953 POPULATION (10,000)	1953 PROPORTION IN NATION'S TOTAL (%)	1964 POPULATION (10,000)	1964 PROPORTION IN NATION'S TOTAL (%)	1982 POPULATION (10,000)	1982 PROPORTION IN NATION'S TOTAL (%)	INCREASE OF POPULATION 1953–64 (%) PROPORTION	INCREASE OF POPULATION 1953–64 (%) AVERAGE ANNUAL INCREASE	INCREASE OF POPULATION 1964–82 (%) PROPORTION	INCREASE OF POPULATION 1964–82 (%) AVERAGE ANNUAL INCREASE
Total of 29 provinces, municipalities, and autonomous regions	58,060.34	100.00	69,122.01	100.00	100,391.39	100.00	19.05	1.60	45.24	2.10
Han	54,528.30	93.92	65,129.64	94.22	93,667.49	93.30	19.44	1.63	43.82	2.04
Zhuang	661.11	1.14	838.61	1.21	1,338.31	1.33	26.85	2.19	59.59	2.63
Hui	355.93	0.61	447.31	0.65	722.84	0.72	25.67	2.10	61.60	2.70
Uygur	364.01	0.63	399.63	0.58	596.35	0.59	9.79	0.85	49.23	2.24
Yi	325.43	0.56	338.10	0.49	545.36	0.54	3.89	0.35	61.30	2.69
Miao	251.13	0.43	278.21	0.40	502.12	0.50	10.78	0.94	80.48	3.33
Tibetan	277.56	0.48	250.12	0.36	384.29	0.39	−9.89	−0.09	53.64	2.41
Mongolian	146.29	0.25	196.58	0.28	341.14	0.34	34.38	2.72	73.54	3.11
Manchu	241.89	0.42	269.57	0.39	430.50	0.43	11.44	0.99	59.70	2.63
Bouyei	124.78	0.21	134.81	0.20	211.93	0.21	8.04	0.71	57.21	2.55
Korean	112.04	0.19	133.96	0.19	176.52	0.18	19.56	1.64	31.67	1.54
Yao	66.59	0.11	85.73	0.12	141.20	0.14	28.74	2.32	64.70	2.81
Dong	71.28	0.12	83.61	0.12	142.64	0.14	17.30	1.46	70.60	3.01
Hani	48.12	0.08	62.87	0.09	105.88	0.11	30.65	2.46	68.41	2.94
Bai[1]	66.71	0.11	70.66	0.10	113.11	0.11	5.92	0.52	60.07	2.65
Tujia	—*		52.48	0.08	283.68	0.28	—		440.55	9.83
Kazakh	50.94	0.09	49.16	0.07	90.75	0.09	−3.49	−0.32	84.60	3.46
Dai	47.90	0.08	53.54	0.08	83.95	0.08	11.77	1.02	56.80	2.53
Li	36.09	0.06	43.88	0.06	88.71	0.08	21.58	1.79	102.26	3.99
Lisu	31.75	0.05	27.06	0.04	48.19	0.05	−14.77	−1.44	78.09	3.26
She	—		23.42	0.03	27.20	0.04	—		58.84	2.60
Lahu	13.91	0.02	19.12	0.03	30.43	0.03	37.46	2.93	59.05	2.61
Gaoshan	0.03		0.04		0.17		11.25	0.97	350.82	8.73
Loba					0.11				—	
Monba			0.38		0.11				−70.07*	−0.65*
Va	28.62	0.05	20.03	0.03	29.86	0.03	−30.01	−3.19	49.09	2.24
Shui[2]	13.36	0.02	15.61	0.02	28.69	0.03	16.84	0.87	83.79	3.44
Naxi	14.35	0.02	15.68	0.02	25.16	0.02	9.27	0.81	60.46	2.66
Dongxiang	15.58	0.03	14.74	0.02	27.95	0.03	−5.39	−0.50	89.62	3.62
Tu[3]	5.33	···	7.73	0.01	15.96	0.02	45.03	3.44	106.47	4.11
Jingpo	10.19	0.02	5.78	0.01	9.30	0.01	−43.28	−5.02	61.02	2.68
Khalkhas	7.09	0.01	7.02	0.01	11.34	0.01	−0.99	−0.09	62.54	2.70
Qiang	3.57	···*	4.91	0.01	10.28	0.01	37.54	2.94	109.28	4.19
Daut	—		6.34	0.01	9.41	0.01	—		48.42	2.22
Mulao	—		5.28	0.01	9.04	0.01	—		71.20	3.03

180

Table 11-2 (Continued)

NATIONALITY	1953		1964		1982		INCREASE OF POPULATION 1953–64 (%)		INCREASE OF POPULATION 1964–82 (%)	
	POPULATION (10,000)	PROPORTION IN NATION'S TOTAL (%)	POPULATION (10,000)	PROPORTION IN NATION'S TOTAL (%)	POPULATION (10,000)	PROPORTION IN NATION'S TOTAL (%)	PROPORTION	AVERAGE ANNUAL INCREASE	PROPORTION	AVERAGE ANNUAL INCREASE
Bulang	—	—	3.94	0.01	5.85	0.01	—	—	48.37	2.22
Salar	3.07	...	3.47	0.01	6.91	0.01	13.03	1.12	99.35	3.90
Xibe	1.90	...	3.34	...	8.37	0.01	75.79	5.26	150.90	5.24
Maonan	—	—	2.24	...	3.82	...	—	—	70.54	3.01
Gelao	—	—	2.69	...	5.42	0.01	—	—	101.49	3.97
Pumi	—	—	1.43	...	2.42	...	—	—	69.23	2.97
Tajik	1.45	...	1.62	...	2.66	...	11.72	1.01	64.20	2.79
Nu	—	—	1.50	...	2.29	...	—	—	52.67	2.38
Achang	—	—	1.20	...	2.04	...	—	—	69.89	2.99
Ewenki[4]	0.50	...	0.97	...	1.94	...	94.00	6.21	100.00	3.93
Deang[5]	—	—	0.73	...	1.23	...	—	—	69.33	2.97
Jinuo	—	—	—	—	1.20	...	—	—	—	—
Yugur	0.39	...	0.57	...	1.06	...	46.15	3.51	84.87	3.47
Uzbek	1.36	...	0.77	...	1.22	...	−43.38	−5.04	58.44	2.69
Jing	—	—	0.43	...	1.31	...	—	—	204.65	6.38
Drung	—	—	0.31	...	0.46	...	—	—	48.39	2.22
Oroqen	0.23	...	0.27	...	0.41	...	17.39	1.47	52.53	2.37
Tartar	0.69	...	0.23	...	0.41	...	−66.67	−9.50	79.90	3.32
Heche	—	—	0.07	...	0.15	...	—	—	107.38	4.14
Russian	2.26	...	0.13	...	0.29	...	−94.24	−22.86	119.98	4.48
Baoan	0.50	...	0.51	...	0.90	...	2.00	0.18	75.94	3.19
Nongren[6]	19.57*	0.03	—	—	—	—	—	—	—	—
Sharen[7]	11.24	0.02	—	—	—	—	—	—	—	—
Yakute[8]	0.0003	...	—	—	—	—	—	—	—	—
Others	101.73	0.18	3.24	0.01	87.92	0.09	−96.82	—	2612.66	—
Chinese citizens of foreign origin	0.10	...	0.74	...	0.48	...	—	—	—	—

Notes: The population of the whole country and the population of the various minority nationalities do not include servicemen. The population of the minority nationalities includes those which have not yet been identified and confirmed:

[1] Bai was called Minjia during the 1953 census.

[2] Shui was called Shujia during the 1953 census.

[3] Tu was called Turen (Qinghai) during the 1953 census.

[4] Ewenki was called Sulun during the 1953 census.

[5] Deang was called Benglong before 1985.

[6,7] Nongren and Sharen were incorporated into Zhuang nationality in accordance with the need of nationality identification and their own will.

[8] Yakute was incorporated into Ewenki nationality in accordance with the need of nationality identification and its own will.

*: no figures available; . . . : less than 0.01.

Sources: 1982 Population Census of China, China Statistics Publishing House, 1985, pp. 18–21; Human Geography, People's Education Publishing House, 1986, pp. 206–207.

Table 11-3   Development of Medical and Health Work in Minority Areas

	1952	1957	1965	1978	1983	INCREASE 1952–83 (%)
Number of medical and health establishments	1,176	13,819	25,306	23,934	28,800	2,350
Number of beds in hospitals and sanatoriums	5,711	26,470	93,229	224,409	273,033	4,680
Number of medical workers (10,000)	1.79	6.56	15.69	27.94	38.77	2,070

Source: *Statistics Yearbook of China, 1984*, China Statistics Publishing House, 1984, p. 41.

eases such as smallpox, dysentery, measles, typhoid, and syphilis. This has greatly improved the physical quality of the minority peoples and rapidly reduced their mortality rate.

2. The natural population growth of the minority peoples has increased rapidly since liberation as a result of the social, economic, medical, and public health development. Although detailed data on the natural growth changes of the population of the minority nationalities in the whole country are lacking, materials available through routine statistics suffice to show the tendency of natural changes in their population (see Table 11-4).

3. The accuracy of population data and changes in international migration affected the growth of the population of the minority nationalities.

Table 11-2 shows some seemingly abnormal negative or high population growth of a number of national minorities between 1953 and 1964. This was directly connected with the accuracy of population data and changes in international migration.

For a variety of reasons, the 1953 census was not directly conducted in some minority areas, especially those on the cold highlands and in inaccessible regions. Consequently, some data were collected at seminars in which representatives of the upper strata of the minority peoples participated, while others were calculations made on the basis of original statistics and by collecting and sorting out relevant data. By the time of the 1964 census, the population of some minority nationalities in the border regions of Tibet and Yunnan was determined partly through a general survey and partly through calculations. However, generally speaking, the 1964 data were far more accurate than those of 1953. Owing to the fact that the 1953 figures for a number of national minorities were either too big or too small, their population growth rate and respective proportion in the nation's total population so obtained were good only for reference.

In addition, many nationalities in the border regions of Yunnan, Tibet, and Xinjiang live on both sides of the national boundaries, where international migrations have never ceased. For instance, some Russians in Xinjiang have moved back to the Soviet Union, and some have moved overseas to settle in Australia, Canada, and other countries. This affected, to a certain extent, the population growth rate of these nationalities.

4. The work of nationality identification has had its effect on the changes in the population of the minority nationalities.

The in-depth implementation of the government's nationality policies after liberation has promoted the rapid growth of the population of a number of minority nationalities. An increasing number of people of minority nationalities were identified as work in this field progressed. Consequently, the population of the minority nationalities increased. Coupled with this, the preferential treatment given by the government has also played an active part in increasing their population. The 1981 government decision on "Restoring and Correcting the Nationality Status" encouraged many minority people who had concealed their status to revert to their original nationality. The decision stipulated, "Minority people who, no matter when or why, were unable to correctly make known their real nationality should, upon application, be restored to their original nationality status." It was estimated that such "returnees" made up about half of the population increase in the 1978–82 period. Table 11-2 shows that the average annual population growth rate of the Tujia, Russian, Jing, and Gelao peoples was very high, and of the newly added number of people, the "returnees" occupied an even higher proportion.

At the same time, frequent contacts between people of different nationalities and harmonious relations between them led to an increasing number of intermarriages between the minority peoples

Table 11-4 Tendency of Natural Changes in the Population of Selected Minority Areas

YEAR	NATURAL CHANGES OF POPULATION	XIN BARAG YOUQI IN INNER MONGOLIA (MONGOLIAN)	LANCANG LAHU AUTONOMOUS COUNTY IN YUNNAN (LAHU)	FANGCHEN NATIONALITIES AUTONOMOUS COUNTY IN GUANGXI (ZHUANG, YAO, LI, JING AND HAN)	GUANGXI JINXIU YAO NATIONALITY AUTONOMOUS COUNTY IN GUANGXI (YAO)	JIANCHUAN COUNTY IN YUNNAN (BAI)
1949	Birthrate	6.5	22.2	21.0	—	—
	Mortality rate	9.5	13.6	17.4[4]	—	—
	Natural growth rate	−3.0	8.6	3.6	—	—
1954	Birthrate	17.1	23.8	35.1	39.6	—
	Mortality rate	8.2	11.1[1]	13.5	21.5	—
	Natural growth rate	8.9	12.8	21.6	18.1	—
1964	Birthrate	21.1	41.4	38.7	42.2	25.3
	Mortality rate	4.8	20.4	8.8	10.5	8.1
	Natural growth rate	16.3	21.0	29.9	31.8	17.2
1972	Birthrate	33.8	30.1	30.0	32.6	36.7
	Mortality rate	7.9	10.3[2]	5.8	8.7	9.4
	Natural growth rate	25.9	19.8	23.2	23.9	27.3
1978	Birthrate	28.3	30.2	26.8	23.4	26.5
	Mortality rate	6.1	9.3	4.4	6.5	8.8
	Natural growth rate	14.2	20.9	22.3	16.9	17.7
1980	Birthrate	28.5	—	24.7	18.9	18.2
	Mortality rate	6.5	—	4.4	6.0	7.6
	Natural growth rate	22.0	—	20.6	13.0	10.6
1981	Birthrate	25.5	28.8	31.2	25.1	18.9
	Mortality rate	10.0	10.1[3]	4.8	6.8	8.4
	Natural growth rate	15.5	18.7	26.5	18.3	10.5

Notes: [1] 1953 figure.

[2] 1970 figure.

[3] 1982 figure.

[4] 1950 figure.

[5] 1966 figure.

Sources: Statistical data from the regions concerned.

Table 11-4 *(Continued)*

YEAR	NATURAL CHANGES OF POPULATION	MEIGU COUNTY IN SICHUAN (YI)	ABA COUNTY IN SICHUAN (TIBETAN)	MAOWEN QIANG AUTONOMOUS COUNTY IN SICHUAN (QIANG)	CEHENG COUNTY IN GUIZHOU (BOUYEI)	TIBET AUTONOMOUS REGION (TIBETAN)
1949	Birthrate	36.0	11.4	26.5	—	—
	Mortality rate	29.1[4]	10.3[4]	12.4	—	—
	Natural growth rate	6.9	1.1	14.1	—	—
1954	Birthrate	—	—	—	—	—
	Mortality rate	—	—	—	—	—
	Natural growth rate	—	—	—	—	—
1964	Birthrate	33.0	16.8	29.5	—	15.2
	Mortality rate	20.7	9.1	10.2	—	6.3[5]
	Natural growth rate	12.3	7.7	19.3	—	8.9
1972	Birthrate	—	—	—	37.6	26.9
	Mortality rate	—	—	—	12.7	11.2
	Natural growth rate	—	—	—	24.9	15.7
1978	Birthrate	—	—	—	30.8	22.9
	Mortality rate	—	—	—	10.6	8.7
	Natural growth rate	—	—	—	20.2	14.2
1980	Birthrate	—	—	—	26.8	23.0
	Mortality rate	—	—	—	10.8	8.2
	Natural growth rate	—	—	—	16.0	14.8
1981	Birthrate	46.2	34.6	34.8	38.0	31.1
	Mortality rate	18.0	14.0	9.4	13.2	8.4
	Natural growth rate	28.2	20.6	25.4	24.8	22.7

and the Hans. This was another noteworthy factor accounting for the rapid increase of the population of the minority nationalities, because in most cases the children of these families chose the minority nationality status, which entitled them to preferential treatment. According to statistics, of the 101 children of Hui-Han families living in the Niujie and Tangfang neighborhoods of Xuanwu District in Beijing, 81, or 80.2% of the total, chose the Hui nationality status. In the Beimujiayu Hui Nationality Township in Miyun County on the outskirts of Beijing, of the 19 children born of intermarriages, 17, or 89.5%, opted for Hui status. In the Tanying Manchu-Mongolian Nationalities Township of the same county, 232, or 73.9%, of a total of 314 offspring of Manchu-Han families registered as Manchu people, and 33, or 94.3%, of the 35 children from Mongolian-Han families chose Mongolian status. In the Beijing Central Institute for Nationalities, 64, or 97%, of the 66 children of parents of Han and minority nationalities applied for minority nationality status. It is obvious, therefore, that intermarriages between people of different ethnic groups have contributed to the accelerated population growth of the minority peoples.

FERTILITY RATE AND PATTERN OF MINORITY NATIONALITIES
FERTILITY RATE OF MINORITY WOMEN FROM 1940S TO EARLY 1960S

The trend of changes in the fertility rate from the 1940s to the early 1960s can be discerned by examining the lifelong childbearing rate of minority women aged 50–67 in 1982 (see Table 11-5).

Women of the 65–67 and 60–64 age groups were 27–34 years old at the founding of New China in 1949. Their peak fertility period was in the 1940s and early 1950s. Their lifelong fertility rate might be taken to represent the fertility level of those years. The following two characteristics should be noted:

First, the lifelong fertility rate of minority women was lower than that of Han women.

Second, the lifelong childbearing rate of minority women of the 65–67 age bracket was higher than that of minority women of the 60–64 age bracket.

In 1982, women of the 50–54 and 55–59 age groups were 17–26 years old at the time of the founding of New China, and they were in their peak fertility period in the 1950s and early 1960s. Therefore, their lifelong fertility rate was representative of the fertility level of this period. Their fertility rate was characterized by three significant points:

First, the fertility rate of women of these two age groups, whether Hans or national minorities, was higher that that of women in the over 60 age groups.

Second, the fertility level of minority women was beginning to overtake that of Han women.

Third, the fertility rate of women of the Han and minority nationalities in the 50–54 group had surpassed that of the 55–59 group.

WIDENING OF DIFERENCE IN TOTAL CHILDBIRTHS BETWEEN WOMEN OF HAN AND MINORITY NATIONALITIES AFTER MID-1960S

Drastic changes in the fertility rate of minority women occurred between the mid-1960s and 1981 (see Chart 11-1). Major manifestations were:

First, the total fertility rate of minority women reached a peak (6.72) after 1964. The 1968 peak value came to 7.02. By 1977 it dropped to below 5.0, and hit the lowest point of 4.01 in 1980, but rose again in 1981 to 4.49. The drop was due to family planning practiced in some cities and in areas inhabited by both Han and minority peoples. In areas where family planning had not yet begun, the minority peoples were so impressed by the benefits brought by planned parenthood to the Han families and their children that they started to control childbirth on their own.

Second, as Chart 11-1 shows, the gap between the aggregate fertility rate of minority women and that of Han women was widening. It indicated that the drop in the case of the former was much slower than in the case of the latter.

Table 11-5   Live Births by Women of Han and Minority Nationalities Aged 50–67 (1982)

AGE GROUP		50–54	55–59	60–64	65–67
Average number of live births	Minority nationalities	5.84	5.66	4.26	5.04
	Han people	5.58	5.48	5.30	5.17

Source: Hu Xuehui, *A Brief Analysis of Marriages and Fertility Rate of China's Minority Women* (p. 69), published in a collection of theses read at the International Forum on a One-Thousandth Sample Survey of China's Birthrate.

Chart 11-1   Changes in the Total Fertility Rate of
Minority and Han Women

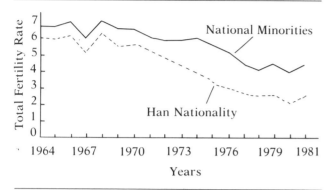

Source: *One-Per-Thousand-Population Fertility Sampling Survey
in China*, China Population Information Centre, 1986, pp.
219–222.

DIFFERENCES IN FERTILITY RATE BETWEEN WOMEN IN DIFFERENT MINORITY AREAS

The 1982 census revealed that in the autonomous prefectures and counties where people of minority nationalities lived in compact communities, both the fertility rate of women and the total fertility rate were high in 1981. However, there were differences between the various regions (see Table 11-6).

Jianchuan County in Yunnan Province, inhabited by the Bai nationality, had the lowest aggregate fertility rate. Yet it was over 50% above the birth replacement level. In 57.1% of the areas listed in the table, the aggregate childbearing rate was around 6.0. Before liberation, the aggregate fertility rate of the Tibetans and Mongolians living on the Qinghai-Tibet plateau was low (around 3.0), but it has now increased to double and treble the birth replacement level. This is a reflection of the effect of economic development, social progress, and sound nationality policies on population growth. It is also a turning point and a new starting point in the demographic history of the Tibetan and Mongolian nationalities. The Uygurs and Huis have a tradition of marrying at an early age and having many children. But even before practicing family planning, their total fertility rate was lower than that of the Tibetans and Mongolians, and much lower than that of the Yis. The aggregate fertility rate in Meigu and Putog counties in the Liangshan Yi Autonomous Prefecture of Sichuan Province was 7.68 and 8.12, respectively. These were the highest among China's nationalities, and they were even higher than that of the three highest countries in 1981 — Libya (7.4), Bahrain (7.4), and Kenya (8.1).

DIFFERENCE IN TOTAL FERTILITY RATE BETWEEN MINORITY WOMEN IN CITIES AND COUNTRYSIDE

There were significant differences in the aggregate fertility rate between minority women living in the cities and those in the countryside in the years 1964–81 (see Chart 11-2). Major indications were as follows:

First, the aggregate fertility rate of rural women was always higher than that of urban women. The latter's aggregate fertility rate had dropped to below the birth replacement level in 1975, while that of women in the countryside was still more than double the birth replacement level in 1981.

Second, the drop of aggregate fertility rate in the cities was greater and speedier than the drop in the countryside. Between 1964 and 1981, the urban aggregate fertility rate fell from 3.99 to 1.38, a drop of 65.4%. However, the drop in the countryside in the same period was from 6.88 to 4.70, or 31.7%. This was partly attributable to the family planning program, which was first carried out in the cities. But, more importantly, it was due to the fact that urban minority people had a higher level of education, better jobs, and more family income. In the city of Urumqi, capital of the Xinjiang Uygur Autonomous Region, and Moyu County where the inhabitants were chiefly Uygurs, the aggregate fertility rate of Uygur women came down gradually in the years 1968–83 when family planning had not been promoted on a large scale (see Table 11-7). For the Uygur women in Urumqi, the drop was 47.2%, while that of Moyu County was only 26.8%.

Chart 11-2   Changes in Total Fertility Rate Among Rural
and Urban Minority Women (1964–1981)

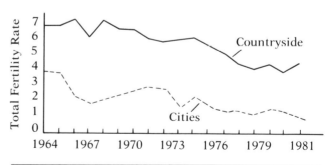

Source: *One-Per-Thousand-Population Fertility Sampling Survey
in China*, China Population Information Centre, 1986, pp.
223–230.

Table 11-6   Fertility Rate of Women in Selected Minority Areas (1981)

| AREA | NATIONALITY COMPOSITION OF POPULATION (%) | | CHILDBIRTH RATE OF WOMEN OF CHILD-BEARING AGE (‰) | AGGREGATE CHILDBEARING RATE |
	HAN	MINORITIES		
Yushu Tibetan Autonomous Prefecture in Qinghai	4.41	Tibetan (95.30)	170.44	6.36
Henan Mongolian Autonomous County in Qinghai	6.01	Mongolian (87.82)	183.63	6.26
Garze County in Sichuan	5.88	Tibetan (94.00)	130.79	4.68
Serxu County in Sichuan	3.12	Tibetan (96.86)	171.11	6.24
Maowen Qiang Autonomous County in Sichuan	18.67	Qiang (78.64)	155.52	5.34
Meigu County in Sichuan	3.90	Yi (96.00)	203.49	7.68
Putog County in Sichuan	8.70	Yi (91.10)	211.79	8.12
Jianchuan County in Yunnan	4.86	Bai (90.50)	90.01	3.27
Fugong County in Yunnan	1.93	Lisu (73.60)	190.36	6.75
Cangyuan Va Autonomous County in Yunnan	7.32	Va (84.30)	158.01	5.51
Luchun County in Yunnan	4.68	Hani (83.50) Yi (5.87)	141.48	4.10
Gongshan Drung-Nu Autonomous County in Yunnan	4.83	Drung (14.4) Nu (19.7) Lisu (52.5)	157.98	5.72
Sandu Shui Autonomous County in Guizhou	7.69	Shui (60.80)	169.98	6.63
Taijiang County in Guizhou	6.06	Miao (93.62)	162.87	6.23
Ceheng County in Guizhou	22.85	Bouyei (73.10)	162.89	5.99
Jingxi County in Guangxi	0.59	Zhuang (99.30)	117.11	4.34
Tiandeng County in Guangxi	1.07	Zhuang (98.80)	107.60	3.83
Jingyuan County in Ningxia	3.36	Hui (96.63)	172.44	6.35
Jiashi County in Xinjiang	1.09	Uygur (98.83)	187.00	5.92
Shache County in Xinjiang	3.50	Uygur (95.40)	169.61	5.50
Taxkorgan Tajik Autonomous County in Xinjiang	3.95	Tajik (81.10)	207.36	6.98

Source: Statistical data from the 1982 census in regions concerned.

Table 11-7   Changes in Total Fertility Rate of Uygur Women in Urumqi and Moyu County (1968–1983)

AREA	1968	1972	1976	1983
Urumqi (Uygurs)	5.3	4.9	3.2	2.8
Moyu County	7.1	6.6	6.0	5.2

Source: *Population Trends*, No. 1, 1986, p. 34, China Population Information Centre.

CHILDBIRTH PATTERN IN MOST MINORITY AREAS—SPONTANEOUS BIRTH TYPE

According to a one-thousandth sample survey of China's birthrate in 1982, the childbirth pattern of different age groups of women of Han nationality in 1981 had switched to a new, controlled type, that is, a pattern of "narrow, high and low curves." The childbirth pattern of the minority women was entirely different. It was one of a "broad, slow and high" spontaneous curve (see Chart 11-3).

The following three characteristics should be noted:

First, the fertility peak value of the five age groups averaged 0.272, about 30% higher than that of Han nationality; the extent of the 0.1 fertility rate spanned four age groups—20–24, 25–29, 30–34, and 35–39. It was evidently wider than that of Han

Chart 11-3 Fertility Rate of Han and Minority Women of Different Age Groups (1981)

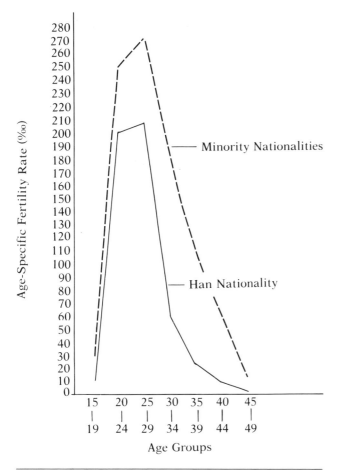

Source: Based on Tables 6 and 17, *1984 Handbook on China's Population*, China Population Information Centre, pp. 354, 380.

nationality and the direct result was a rise in the general fertility rate and total fertility rate.

Second, although the childbearing rate of the 40–44 and 45–49 age groups was lower than that of the above four age groups, it still exceeded by far the fertility rate of women of Han nationality.

Third, the fertility rate of women of the 15–19 age group was 0.028, which was 2.7 times that of women of Han nationality. This showed that the proportion of early marriages and childbirths was still quite high.

Charts 11-4, 11-5, 11-6 show the fertility pattern of women of 16 minority nationalities in 16 areas inhabited by minority peoples. It can be seen from these patterns that, except the Tujia Autonomous County in Shizhu of Sichuan Province and the Jianchuan County of the Bai Autonomous Prefecture in Dali of Yunnan Province, the remaining 14 minority areas showed a spontaneous birth pattern of "broad, slow and high" curves. Their common feature was that the 20–24, 25–29, 30–34, 35–39, and 40–44 age groups had an age-specific fertility rate of 0.1 or above. (A 15–19 age group was added in the Henan Mongolian Autonomous County in Qinghai Province.) In some areas inhabited by minority nationalities such as Yushu Tibetan Autonomous Prefecture in Qinghai, the Taxkorgan Tajik Autonomous County in Xinjiang, and Putog County in the Liangshan Yi Autonomous Prefecture of Sichuan Province, the fertility rate of women of the 45–49 age group was fairly high, reaching 0.051, 0.063, and 0.063, respectively.

The fertility pattern in the Tujia Autonomous County in Shizhu of Sichuan Province and Jianchuan County (Bai nationality) in Yunnan Province had switched to one of a "narrow, steep and low" curve like that of women of Han nationality. The width of the 0.1 fertility rate in Shizhu County was concentrated in the 20–24 and 25–29 age groups and the fertility peak value was as high as 0.318 in the second age group; however, the total fertility rate had dropped to 3.19. The width of the 0.1 fertility rate in Jianchuan County was concentrated in the 20–24, 25–29, and 30–34 age groups. Its fertility peak value of 0.276 was in the 25–29 age group and its total fertility rate had dropped to 3.27. The switch of the childbirth pattern and the dip in the total childbearing rate in Shizhu County were mainly due to the fact that, before the founding of the Tujia Autonomous County in October 1984, the policy of family planning was implemented, just as in areas inhabited by the Han people. When the 1982 census was conducted, only 21 people in that county registered as of

Chart 11-4   Fertility Rate of Women of Different Age Groups in Five Minority Areas in 1981

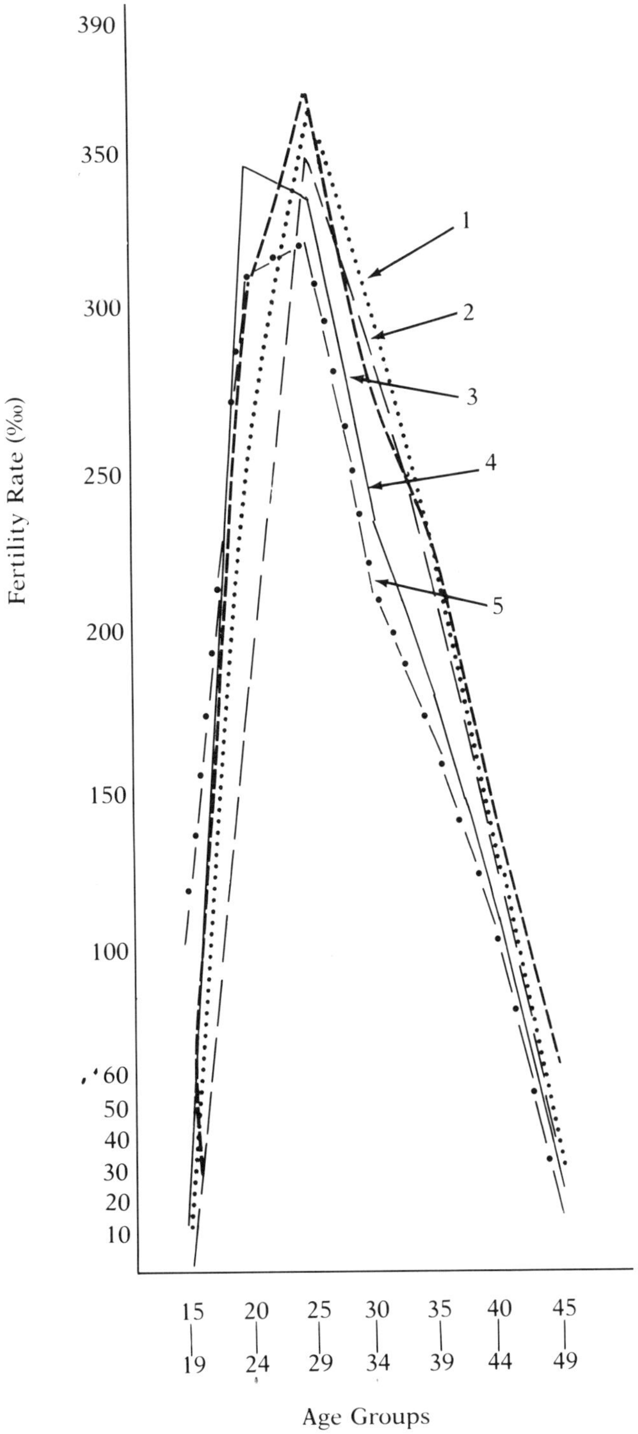

Chart 11-5   Fertility Rate of Women of Different Age Groups in Five Minority Areas (1981)

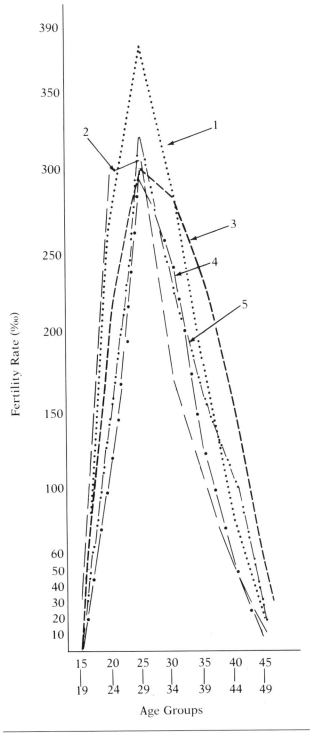

(1) Sandu Shui Autonomous County in Guizhou.
(2) Ceheng County in Guizhou (Bouyei nationality).
(3) Taxkorgan Tajik Autonomous County in Xinjiang.
(4) Jingyuan County in Ningxia (Hui nationality).
(5) Henan Mongolian Autonomous County in Qinghai.

(1) Taijiang County in Guizhou (Miao nationality).
(2) Luchun County in Yunnan (Hani nationality).
(3) Yushu Tibetan Autonomous Prefecture in Qinghai.
(4) Jingxi County in Guangxi (Zhuang nationality).
(5) Maowen Qiang Autonomous County in Sichuan.

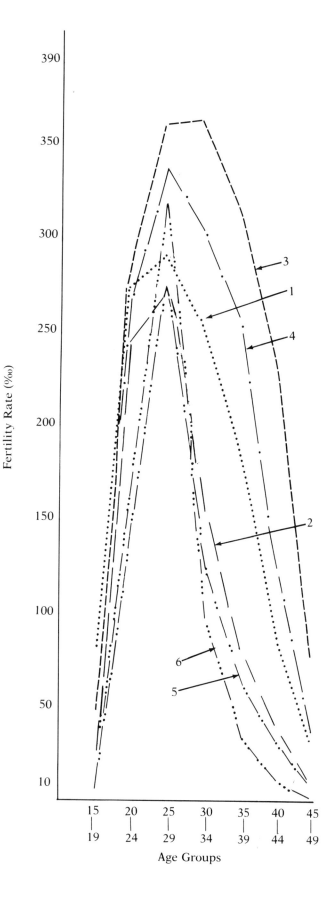

Chart 11-6   Fertility Rate of Women of Different Age Groups in Six Minority Areas (1981)

(1) Jiashi County in Xinjiang (Uygur nationality).
(2) Jinxiu Yao Autonomous County in Guangxi.
(3) Putog County in Sichuan (Yi nationality).
(4) Fugong County in Yunnan (Lisu nationality).
(5) Jianchuan County in Yunnan (Bai nationality).
(6) Shizhu Tujia Autonomous County in Sichuan.
Source: Statistical data for the three charts are from the 1982 census in the regions concerned.

Tujia nationality. The change in the childbirth pattern in Jianchuan County was because its economy and culture were fairly developed and family planning was carried out at an early date.

IMPACT OF INFANT MORTALITY RATE ON FERTILITY RATE IN MINORITY AREAS

Since liberation, the social and economic development as well as improvement in transportation, medical, and public health conditions in the various minority nationality areas have been uneven. This has resulted in a difference in the death rate, especially the infant mortality rate, in those regions. Generally speaking, the infant mortality rate of the minority nationality areas is higher than the nation's average level (with the exception of Jiandeng and Jingxi Counties in Guangxi), and in some areas it is much higher than the nation's average level (see Table 11-8).

The high infant mortality rate will surely be a feedback to the compensatory childbirths, which becomes one of the important reasons for the high childbearing rate in some minority nationality areas. Therefore, it is an urgent task for the government to promote social and economic development, raise the material and cultural well-being, and improve the medical and public health conditions and maternity and child care of the minority peoples in these areas. It is also a fundamental way to change the childbirth pattern and rationally control the population growth rate there.

DISTRIBUTION OF THE POPULATION OF MINORITY NATIONALITIES

Owing to historical reasons, the population of the minority nationalities is generally concentrated in areas where they live in compact communities. While people of Han nationality are mainly concentrated in the southeastern and central parts of China,

Table 11-8   Infant Mortality Rate of Various Minority Areas (1981)

MINORITY AREAS	INFANT MORTALITY RATE (‰)	MINORITY AREAS	INFANT MORTALITY RATE (‰)
Whole country	33.4	Ceheng County in Guizhou (Bouyei)	102.0
Tiandeng County in Guangxi (Zhang)	26.6	Taijiang County in Guizhou (Miao)	104.1
Jingxi County in Guangxi (Zhuang)	27.6	Sandu Shui Autonomous County in Guizhou	65.6
Jinxiu Yao Autonomous County in Guangxi	40.3	Garze County in Sichuan (Tibetan)	97.1
Drung and Nu Autonomous County in Yunnan	75.9	Aba County in Sichuan (Tibetan)	161.2
Jianchuan County in Yunnan (Bai)	54.4	Yushu Tibetan Autonomous Prefecture in Qinghai	116.2
Fugong County in Yunnan (Lisu)	142.4	Henan Mongolian Autonomous County in Qinghai	146.0
Luchun County in Yunnan (Hani)	122.3	Keping County in Xinjiang (Uygur)	131.4
Cangyuan Va Autonomous County in Yunnan	130.5	Taxkorgan Tajik Autonomous County in Xinjiang	93.1
Tongxin County in Ningxia (Hui)	60.9	Xinbaerhuzuo Banner in Inner Mongolia	58.6
Jingyuan County in Ningxia (Hui)	66.7	Maowen Qiang Autonomous County in Sichuan	75.9
Meigu County in Sichuan (Yi)	113.4		
Putog County in Sichuan (Yi)	155.8		

Source: From the data on the 1982 census in the regions concerned. Formula for calculation:

$$\text{Infant mortality rate} = \frac{\text{Number of infants of the 0 age group who died that year}}{\text{Number of infants who survived in the same year}} \times 1000‰.$$

the minority peoples live mainly in the border regions and the vast areas of China's western provinces and autonomous regions (see Table 11-9).

CHARACTERISTICS OF THE DISTRIBUTION OF MINORITY NATIONALITIES

Following are the characteristics of the distribution of population of the minority nationalities:

• The population of the minority nationalities is distributed over a vast area. Although the population of China's minority nationalities is only 60 to 70 million, or 6.7% of the nation's total, it is distributed over a vast area, and minority people live in almost every county and city throughout the country. The autonomous regions for the various national minorities are also widely distributed. By the end of 1984, there were five autonomous regions, 31 autonomous prefectures, and 81 autonomous counties, covering an area of 6.1 million square kilometers, or about 64% of the nation's total territory.

• The population of the minority nationalities is unevenly distributed in the various provinces, munici-

palities, and autonomous regions. According to the 1982 census, major indications of the uneven distribution were as follows: First, the Guangxi Zhuang Autonomous Region and Yunnan Province were the areas with the most population of the minority nationalities—13.936 million and 10.319 million, respectively, or 20.7% and 15.3% of the total population of the minority nationalities in the country. Shanghai and Jiangsu Province were the places with the least population of the minority nationalities, and they had only 49,000 and 22,000 people, respectively, or 0.07 and 0.03% of the total population of the minority nationalities. Second, there were 27.77 million people of the minority nationalities living in the five autonomous regions, accounting for 41.3% of the total population of the minority nationalities in the country. Of these five autonomous regions, the absolute number and the percentage of the minority peoples in each also differed greatly. For instance, the Guangxi Zhuang Autonomous Region had the most population as well as the highest proportion of minority peoples in the country, while in the Ningxia Hui Autonomous Region, there were only 1.244 million minority peoples, accounting for only 1.85% of

Table 11-9　Regional Distribution of the Population of Minority Nationalities in China

NATIONALITY	MAJOR AREAS OF RESIDENCE	DISTRIBUTION OF THE POPULATION OF THE MINORITY NATIONALITY (%)	
		1964	1982
Mongolian	Inner Mongolia	70.43	72.97
	Liaoning	14.49	12.55
	Xinjiang, Jilin, and Heilongjiang	9.10	8.99
Hui	Ningxia	14.46	17.09
	Gansu	13.26	13.24
	Henan, Qinghai, Xinjiang and Yunnan	28.84	31.40
Tibetan	Tibet	48.32	45.86
	Sichuan	24.25	23.96
	Qinghai	16.90	19.59
	Gansu and Yunnan	10.31	10.41
Uygur	Xinjiang	99.88	99.87
Miao	Guizhou	56.76	51.43
	Hunan	15.42	15.16
	Yunnan	15.39	14.98
	Sichuan, Guangxi and Hubei	11.27	17.36
Yi	Yunnan	63.44	61.48
	Sichuan	26.18	27.99
	Guizhou	10.20	10.35
Zhuang	Guangxi	90.23	92.09
	Yunnan	6.73	6.68
Bouyei	Guizhou	99.04	99.03
Korean	Jilin	64.69	62.55
	Heilongjiang	22.96	24.45
	Liaoning	10.94	11.23
Manchu	Liaoning	45.74	46.25
	Heilongjiang	22.90	21.22
	Jilin	12.54	12.06
	Hebei, Inner Mongolia and Beijing	16.55	17.14
Dong	Guizhou	56.91	59.67
	Hunan	26.31	22.34
	Guangxi	16.68	16.10
Yao	Guangxi	60.97	61.18
	Hunan	20.23	20.03
	Yunnan and Guangdong	16.28	17.30
Bai	Yunnan	99.63	99.04
Tujia	Hubei	22.04	52.44
	Hunan	75.62	26.26
	Sichuan	2.15	21.09
Hani	Yunnan	99.97	99.96
Kazakh	Xinjiang	99.49	99.54
Dai	Yunnan	99.79	99.56

Table 11-9   *(Continued)*

NATIONALITY	MAJOR AREAS OF RESIDENCE	DISTRIBUTION OF THE POPULATION OF THE MINORITY NATIONALITY (%)	
		1964	1982
Li	Guangdong	99.83	91.40
Lisu	Yunnan	97.09	97.09
Va	Yunnan	99.98	99.97
She	Fujian	54.96	56.70
	Zhejiang	42.95	39.86
Gaoshan	Fujian	22.95	25.52
	Sichuan	10.38	20.91
Lahu	Yunnan	99.99	99.96
Shui	Guizhou	98.07	95.09
Dongxiang	Gansu	93.91	85.10
	Xinjiang	5.68	14.43
Naxi	Yunnan	98.06	93.93
Jingpo	Yunnan	99.06	99.89
Khalkhas	Xinjiang	99.18	99.10
Tu	Qinghai	89.59	80.93
	Guizhou and Gansu	10.06	16.34
Mulao	Guangxi	99.54	98.32
Daur	Inner Mongolia	54.65	62.29
	Heilongjiang	40.74	32.13
Qiang	Sichuan	99.54	99.75
Bulang	Yunnan	99.99	99.75
Salar	Qinghai	85.96	88.21
	Gansu	9.79	7.40
Maonan	Guangxi	99.80	99.41
Gelao	Guizhou	97.73	95.12
Xibe	Liaoning	45.24	59.03
	Xinjiang	51.48	32.72
Achang	Yunnan	99.99	99.86
Pumi	Yunnan	99.97	99.60
Tajik	Xinjiang	99.97	99.90
Uzbek	Xinjiang	99.56	99.80
Russian	Xinjiang	89.92	96.29
Ewenki	Inner Mongolia	93.56	93.71
Deang	Yunnan	99.88	99.81
Baoan	Gansu	98.63	92.29
Yugur	Gansu	98.39	96.77
Jing	Guanxi	96.46	75.25
	Guizhou	—	10.86
Tartar	Xinjiang	99.43	98.93
Drung	Yunnan	99.84	99.27
Oroqen	Inner Mongolia	44.41	49.70
	Heilongjiang	54.93	48.79
Hezhe	Heilongjiang	97.21	90.82
Monba	Tibet	99.45	95.96
Loba	Tibet	—	95.12
Jinuo	Yunnan	—	99.93
Nu	Yunnan	99.96	99.74

Source: 1964 figures are based on the *Statistical Data on the Second Census of the People's Republic of China* (III: "Population of China's Nationalities," p. 243), issued by the Office of the Central Census Leading Group in October 1964.

the total population of China's minority nationalities. Third, the proportion of minority peoples in the population of the provinces, municipalities, and autonomous regions where they lived also varied greatly. For instance, the total number of Tibetan, Monba, Loba, and Hui peoples accounted for 95.2% of the total population of the Tibet Autonomous Region, while the population of the minority nationalities accounted for only 0.1% of the total population of Jiangxi Province. Fourth, the situation in the large regions also showed that the population distribution was uneven. The population of the minority peoples in northwest China (20.257 million) and its proportion (30.1%) in the total population of the minority nationalities in the country were both the highest, while the population of the minority peoples in east China (1.261 million) and its proportion (1.9%) in the total population of the minority nationalities were the lowest. Fifth, the population distribution of the minority nationalities differed greatly between the border areas and the inland provinces. The number of minority peoples in Liaoning, Jilin, Heilongjiang, Inner Mongolia, Gansu, Xinjiang, Tibet, Yunnan, Guangxi, and Guangdong totalled 45.801 million, accounting for 68.1% of the total population of the minority nationalities in the country, while those in Shaanxi, Shanxi, Henan, Hebei, Hubei, Hunan, Jiangxi, Anhui, and Sichuan Provinces totalled 8.869 million, accounting for only 13.2% of the total population of China's minority nationalities. Sixth, the nationality composition also differed greatly in the various provinces, municipalities, and autonomous regions. The Ningxia Hui Autonomous Region and the municipality of Tianjin had the fewest number of nationalities in 1982—29 and 28, respectively, while there were 54 nationalities in Beijing and 50 nationalities in Sichuan Province.

• The population density is low and varies greatly in the minority nationality regions. When the national census was taken in 1982, the total population in China's national autonomous areas (including five autonomous regions, 30 autonomous prefectures, and 72 autonomous counties and banners) was 120.071 million,* making up 11.96% of China's total population, averaging 20 people per square kilometer, which was only one-fifth of the nation's average density of 105 people per square kilometer. The population density in the various national autonomous areas also differed greatly. First of all, there were great differences in the population density and growth speed between the five autonomous regions (see Table 11-10). The population density increased very quickly in the Xinjiang Uygur Autonomous Region and the Inner Mongolian Autonomous Region, while in the Tibet Autonomous Region the increase was the slowest. This was closely connected with the natural population growth and migrations.

Second, the difference in the population density of the various autonomous prefectures was also great, and the difference between the 30 autonomous prefectures set up before 1982 was even greater. Only seven prefectures had an average density of more than 100 people per square kilometer, and of these seven, the Linxia Hui Autonomous prefecture in Gansu Province had the highest density, with 171 people per square kilometer. Eleven autonomous prefectures had a density of fewer than 10 people per square kilometer, and the one with the lowest population density was the Haixi Mongolian, Tibetan, and Kazakh Autonomous Prefecture in

* *Statistical Yearbook of China, 1983,* China Statistics Publishing House, p. 31.

Table 11-10   Changes in Population Density in Five Autonomous Regions
(Persons per sq km)

REGION	1953	1964	1982	INCREASE FROM 1953 TO 1982 (%)
Xinjiang Uygur Autonomous Region	3	5	8	166.7
Tibet Autonomous Region	1	1	1.6	60.0
Ningxia Hui Autonomous Region	—	32	59	—
Guangxi Zhuang Autonomous Region	85	101	158	85.9
Inner Mongolian Autonomous Region	6	10	16	166.7

Source: *1982 Population Census of China,* China Statistics Publishing House, 1985, pp. 16, 537.

Qinghai, averaging only 0.8 person per square kilometer. The highest value of difference in the population density between the various autonomous prefectures was 213-fold. Last, the difference in the population density between the various autonomous counties and banners was even more striking. Of the 72 autonomous counties (banners) set up before 1982, 24 had an average density of more than 100 people per square kilometer. Of these, the one with the highest population density was the Dachang Hui Autonomous County in Hebei Province, with 497 people per square kilometer. There were 13 autonomous counties (banners) in the country that had fewer than 10 people per square kilometer. Of these, the one with the lowest population density was the Aksay Kazakh Autonomous County in Gansu Province, with only 0.2 person per square kilometer. The highest value of difference in the population density between the various autonomous counties (banners) was 2,484-fold.

• The phenomena of various nationalities living together in large numbers or in compact communities are very common. After long years of exchanges, migrations, and development, the people of China's various nationalities have gradually formed large or small compact communities, but the phenomena of various minority nationalities living together or scattered is also conspicuous. Data from the 1982 national census showed that a total of 17.158 million people of the minority nationalities (25.5% of the total population of minority peoples) lived scattered in various parts of the country. Even in the national autonomous areas, the population of the minority peoples only made up on the average 41.7% of the total population of those areas, while the remaining 58.3% were people of Han nationality. In China there is no autonomous region, prefecture, or county (banner) where only people of a single nationality live.

To help meet the needs of socialist economic and cultural construction and to learn from and to help each other, people of Han nationality have constantly moved to areas inhabited by the minority peoples. On the other hand, people of minority nationalities have also moved to administrative districts (2,375) at the city and county levels (see Table 11-11). Among them, the Mongolian people have migrated at the fastest speed. Between 1964 and 1982, they moved, on the average, to 30 administrative districts a year, and by 1982 the distribution of the Mongolian population covered 78.7% of these administrative districts throughout the country. The Zhuang people had, on the average, moved annually to 25 of these

administrative districts, and by 1982 the distribution of the Zhuang population covered 80.5% of the administrative districts in the whole country. As for the Hui people, they did not migrate as rapidly and had, on the average, moved to only 10 of these administrative districts a year. But the scope of distribution of the Hui population covered 97.3% of the administrative districts.

CAUSES AFFECTING DISTRIBUTION OF POPULATION OF MINORITY PEOPLES

The distribution of the population of the minority nationalities as it is today is the result of multifarious causes throughout the ages. There have been social, historical, political, economic, and cultural factors, in addition to natural conditions, and all these have very often exerted their influence simultaneously. Of course, certain factors have played a more direct or striking role on certain nationalities at a certain period of time.

Social, Historical, and Political Factors. The fact that China's minority peoples live mainly in the border regions and mountainous areas, on the plateau and grasslands, and close to the deserts and semideserts is attributable to many factors. Apart from the fact that some minority nationalities are natives of those places, born and bred there, they were in the past discriminated against, oppressed and driven by the reactionary ruling classes to out-of-the-way places. Though the people of many minority nationalities had moved to the interior and lived scattered among the Han people, they sort of vanished later or their numbers were greatly reduced. This was perhaps because, on the one hand, they were oppressed and discriminated against and many of them were forced to conceal their real nationality and professed themselves to be Han people instead. On the other hand, perhaps they were influenced by the advanced production techniques and culture of the Han and other nationalities, and as differences between the various nationalities gradually vanished, they were merged into or were assimilated by the other nationalities.

The phenomena of various nationalities living together in large numbers or in compact communities are the results of constant migrations and interflow before settling down in various places. After the Qin and Han Dynasties (221 B.C.–A.D. 220), large numbers of minority peoples moved to the interior and lived together with the Han people. On the other hand, a still greater number of Han people moved to

Table 11-11   Changes in Distribution of Minority Peoples in Administrative Districts at City and County Levels

| NATIONALITY | NUMBER OF CITIES AND COUNTIES WITH MINORITY PEOPLE | | INCREASE FROM 1964 TO 1982 | |
	1964	1982	NUMBER OF CITIES AND COUNTIES	%
Mongolian	1,327	1,868	541	40.8
Hui	2,125	2,310	185	8.7
Tibetan	765	1,133	368	48.1
Uygur	297	478	181	60.9
Miao	1,212	1,575	359	29.6
Yi	677	1,046	369	54.5
Zhuang	1,467	1,912	445	30.3
Bouyei	285	812	527	184.9
Korean	744	1,023	279	37.5
Manchu	1,790	2,092	282	16.9
Dong	384	999	615	160.2
Yao	484	797	313	62.7
Bai	490	804	314	145.1
Tujia	328	821	493	150.3
Hani	118	343	225	190.7
Kazakh	112	151	39	34.8
Dai	196	411	215	115.2
Li	206	486	280	135.9
Lisu	101	215	114	112.9
Va	70	134	64	91.4
She	167	375	208	124.6
Gaoshan	138	327	189	136.9
Lahu	65	138	73	112.3
Shui	168	374	206	122.6
Dongxiang	112	206	94	83.9
Naxi	238	379	141	59.2
Jingpo	45	67	22	48.9
Khalkhas	91	107	16	17.6
Tu	82	460	378	461.0
Daur	194	338	144	74.2
Mulao	97	194	97	100.0
Qiang	91	178	87	95.6
Bulang	37	65	28	75.7
Salar	116	144	28	24.1
Maonan	46	132	86	186.9
Gelao	60	115	55	91.7
Xibe	202	457	255	126.2
Achang	18	43	25	138.9
Tajik	37	38	1	2.7
Pumi	27	96	69	255.6
Nu	22	54	32	145.5
Uzbek	85	89	4	4.7
Russian	101	138	37	36.6
Ewenki	58	103	45	77.6
Deang	18	39	21	116.7
Baoan	36	76	40	111.1
Yugur	29	81	52	179.3
Jing	49	232	183	373.5
Tartar	66	62	−4	−6.1
Drung	15	45	30	200.0
Oroqen	53	93	40	75.5
Hezhe	17	53	36	211.8
Monba	7	40	33	471.4
Loba	—	33	—	—
Jinuo	—	25	—	—

Sources: The 1964 figures are based on the *Statistical Data on the Second Census of the People's Republic of China* (III: "Population of China's Nationalities," pp. 253–423), issued by the Office of the Central Census Leading Group in October 1964. The 1982 figures are based on the *Manually Collected Data on the Third National Census* (Vol. IV, "Population of China's Nationalities," pp. 12–334), issued by the Census Office of the State Council in June 1983.

China's northeast, Inner Mongolia, northwest, the Yangtze basin, and areas in south China where they settled in regions inhabited by minority peoples. There they propagated and gradually increased in number. When the ruling class of some nationalities established political power on a national scale, the people of that nationality therefore had the conditions to move and settle in the interior provinces.

Another historical cause was that the ruling class conscripted the people of various nationalities into expeditionary forces, forcing them to fight and settle in remote areas. For example, in the fourth year of the reign of Emperor Tai Zu of the Ming Dynasty, in 1372, the emperor had a battalion of Uygur soldiers led by Habashi transferred to Taoyuan County in central China's Hunan Province and stationed there. After the collapse of the Ming Dynasty, these soldiers continued to make their homes in Changde and Taoyuan in Hunan. That was how 4,000 people in Hunan registered as Uygur nationality during the 1982 national census. Again for example, in the twenty-ninth year of the reign of Emperor Qian Long of the Qing Dynasty in 1764, the Qing government selected 1,000 soldiers of Xibe nationality and their family members totalling 2,200 people from Shengjing (present-day Shenyang), Liaoyang, Fenghuang, and 10 other cities to form 19 Zalan contingents to take up garrison duty in northwest China's Xinjiang. This is the historical reason that a number of people of Xibe nationality live in Xinjiang today. When the Mongol troops conquered many countries in Europe and Asia, the Mongol rulers conscripted local people of various nationalities, totalling two to three million, to form the so-called Western Army. One of the contingents was called the "Hui Hui Army." This army fought together with the Mongol troops from northwest to north China, and then to southwest and southeast China. During the war years, they fought battles, and in normal times, they settled in the various regions where they later took up permanent residence.

After liberation, the Chinese government implemented the policy of national equality and unity and joint prosperity among all the nationalities in the country. As the work of identification of nationalities progressed, a number of hitherto unidentified nationalities have been recognized and confirmed. As a result, many people who had for one reason or another professed themselves to be people of Han nationality have reverted to their original nationality status. In addition, to help speed up the exploitation of resources and the development of economy and culture in the areas inhabited by the minority nationalities, cadres, technicians, industrial, and agricul-

tural workers of various nationalities have increased their exchanges and mutual help. Running training classes and other activities has helped to change the nationality composition of the various provinces, municipalities, autonomous regions, perfectures, and counties (banners). All these have resulted in a growing number of places where people of various nationalities live together in large numbers or in compact communities.

Economic and Technical Factors. The level of economic and technical development and high or low economic incomes have not only affected the size of the population of various nationalities but also their population distribution. In those minority areas where farming and animal husbandry are still at a primitive stage or are of a low level, using age-old traditional methods, the people can barely make a living because of the low labor productivity. Hence their low natural population growth and population density.

Since the founding of New China, in 1949, the economic and technical improvement and the changes in the economic activities have served as the material foundation for the people of various nationalities to increase the size and density of their population. The Xinjiang Uygur Autonomous Region, for example, before liberation had only a dozen or so small factories with obsolete equipment; the region even had to ship in matches and nails from the inland provinces. But in 1983, Xinjiang had 4,200 enterprises including 54 large and medium-sized ones. The area under cultivation in the region had expanded from 20 million *mu* before liberation to 48 million *mu*. In the Inner Mongolian Autonomous Region, there were only 700 small workshops in 1947, but by 1984 the region had 7,300 enterprises including 83 large and medium-sized ones. Economic growth in these regions has greatly increased their population density. The reason is simple. The exploitation of natural resources and the development of production depend on the number of able-bodied people, and the increase in the amount of products and social incomes can in turn support a larger population.

The trade and occupation composition of the population also affects the distribution of the population. People of Hui nationality, for instance, apart from taking part in agricultural production, are engaged in handicraft industry and commerce. This is a major reason that most of them live in cities and market towns. And what is more, the possibility and frequency of migrations and interflows of these people are far greater than for those who engage in farm-

Table 11-12 Age Structure of the Population of China's Minority Nationalities (%)

NATIONALITY	0–14 YEARS OLD	15–64 YEARS OLD	65 AND OVER	COMPARISON BETWEEN OLD AND YOUNG $\frac{65\ \text{AND OVER}}{0-14}\times100$	DEPENDENCY RATIO $\frac{(0-14)\ 65\ \text{AND OVER}}{15-64}\times100$	CHILD DEPENDENCY RATIO $\frac{0-14}{15-64}$	AGED DEPENDENCY RATIO $\frac{65\ \text{AND ABOVE}}{15-64}\times100$	AGE MEDIAN (YEARS OLD)
China	33.59	61.50	4.91	14.62	62.60	54.62	7.98	22.70
Han people	33.19	61.87	4.94	14.88	61.63	53.64	7.99	22.90
Minority peoples	39.16	56.46	4.38	11.18	77.12	69.36	7.76	19.40
Mongolian	39.43	57.18	3.39	8.60	74.89	68.96	5.93	19.00
Hui	35.29	60.53	4.18	11.84	65.21	58.30	6.91	18.69
Tibetan	39.66	55.55	4.79	12.08	80.02	71.40	8.62	19.83
Uygur	40.34	54.45	5.21	12.92	83.65	74.08	9.57	20.59
Miao	42.38	53.45	4.17	9.84	87.09	79.29	7.80	18.77
Yi	42.33	53.77	3.90	9.21	85.97	78.72	7.25	18.85
Zhuang	38.86	56.97	4.17	10.73	75.53	68.21	7.32	19.45
Bouyei	39.69	55.22	5.09	12.82	81.10	71.88	9.22	19.39
Korean	28.33	67.55	4.12	14.54	48.04	41.94	6.10	24.33
Manchu	33.94	61.49	4.57	13.46	62.63	55.20	7.43	21.27
Dong	38.64	56.82	4.54	11.45	75.99	68.00	7.99	19.39
Yao	40.39	55.17	4.44	10.99	81.26	73.21	8.05	18.87
Bai	38.78	56.74	4.48	11.55	76.24	68.35	7.89	19.44
Tujia	37.52	57.85	4.63	12.34	72.86	64.86	8.00	19.66
Hani	42.58	53.97	3.45	8.10	85.29	78.90	6.39	18.02
Kazakh	47.35	49.68	2.97	6.27	101.29	95.31	5.98	16.20
Dai	37.40	58.24	4.36	11.68	71.71	64.22	7.49	19.69
Li	44.18	51.83	3.99	9.03	92.94	85.24	7.70	17.31
Lisu	41.64	54.39	3.97	9.53	83.86	76.56	7.30	18.64
Va	42.02	54.88	3.10	7.38	82.22	76.57	5.65	18.38
She	36.07	58.27	5.66	15.69	71.61	61.90	9.71	21.39
Gaoshan	27.21	70.06	2.73	10.03	42.74	38.64	3.90	22.12
Lahu	40.77	55.77	3.46	8.49	79.30	73.10	6.20	18.86
Shui	42.65	52.99	4.36	10.22	88.72	80.49	8.23	18.10
Dongxiang	40.63	55.94	3.43	8.44	78.76	72.63	6.13	18.39
Naxi	36.73	58.05	5.22	14.21	72.26	63.27	8.99	20.66
Jingpo	43.22	52.48	4.30	9.95	90.55	82.36	8.19	18.11

198

Table 11-12 (*Continued*)

NATIONALITY	0–14 YEARS OLD	15–64 YEARS OLD	65 AND OVER	COMPARISON BETWEEN OLD AND YOUNG $\frac{65\ \text{AND OVER}}{0-14} \times 100$	DEPENDENCY RATIO $\frac{(0-14)\ 65\ \text{AND OVER}}{15-64} \times 100$	CHILD DEPENDENCY RATIO $\frac{0-14}{15-64}$	AGED DEPENDENCY RATIO $\frac{65\ \text{AND ABOVE}}{15-64} \times 100$	AGE MEDIAN (YEARS OLD)
Khalkhas	44.17	51.31	4.52	10.23	94.89	86.08	8.81	17.80
Tu	43.42	53.54	3.04	7.00	86.78	81.10	5.68	17.44
Daur	37.76	62.24	3.60	9.53	66.45	60.67	5.78	19.70
Mulao	39.26	55.73	5.01	12.76	79.44	70.45	8.99	19.05
Qiang	44.29	51.98	3.73	8.42	92.38	85.20	7.18	17.55
Bulang	41.15	54.89	3.96	9.62	82.18	74.97	7.21	18.81
Salar	46.98	49.87	3.15	6.70	100.52	94.20	6.32	16.31
Maonan	40.09	55.37	4.54	11.32	80.60	72.40	8.20	18.72
Gelao	45.53	49.87	4.60	10.10	100.52	91.30	9.22	16.93
Xibe	37.59	58.29	4.12	10.96	71.56	64.49	7.07	19.52
Achang	40.99	54.49	4.52	11.03	83.52	75.22	8.30	18.84
Pumi	41.45	54.18	4.37	10.54	84.57	76.50	8.07	18.56
Tajik	41.83	52.91	5.26	12.74	89.00	79.06	9.94	19.46
Nu	42.74	52.97	4.29	10.04	88.79	80.69	8.10	18.26
Uzbek	40.30	56.30	3.40	8.44	77.62	71.58	6.04	18.84
Russian	30.58	59.89	9.53	31.16	66.97	51.06	15.91	24.32
Ewenki	43.67	53.88	2.45	5.61	85.60	81.05	4.55	17.13
Deang*	41.59	54.22	4.19	10.07	84.44	76.71	7.73	18.57
Baoan	37.10	59.41	3.49	9.41	68.32	62.45	5.87	19.69
Yugur	42.25	55.02	2.73	6.46	81.75	76.79	4.96	17.67
Jing	36.50	59.29	4.21	11.53	68.66	61.56	7.10	20.46
Tartar	44.83	51.73	3.44	7.67	93.41	86.66	6.65	17.19
Drung	41.23	53.98	4.79	11.62	85.25	76.38	8.87	18.89
Oroqen	41.80	54.77	3.43	8.21	82.58	76.32	6.26	17.92
Hezhe	39.36	57.95	2.69	5.45	72.56	67.92	4.64	17.19
Monba	33.51	62.02	4.47	13.34	61.24	54.03	7.21	17.43
Loba	37.05	57.88	5.07	13.68	72.77	64.01	8.76	21.67
Jinuo	38.95	56.85	4.20	10.78	75.90	68.51	7.39	19.38

* Deang was formerly called Benglong.

Source: Based on *1982 Population Census of China*, China Statistics Publishing House, 1985, pp. 232–239.

ing and animal husbandry. Although the Hui people never established national or regional political power, the wide distribution of their population outstrips that of the Mongolian and Manchu nationalities, which had set up political power on a national scale. After the founding of New China, favored by the environment of national equality and unity and joint prosperity, the Hui people have spread even more rapidly to all parts of the country, living together with the people of Han and other nationalities in practically all the administrative districts at the city and county levels. This phenomenon is directly linked with the trades and occupations in which they are engaged.

Natural and Environmental Factors. Natural environment is the basic living space for people and also the source of all the means of production and means of livelihood created by humans. Natural environment favorable for people to live and work, such as a favorable climate, sufficient water resources, fertile soil, vast plains, and rich natural resources, brings the greatest profits to production activities. Therefore, the size and density of the population in these areas will increase. Of course, people have undergone several developmental stages—from passively submitting to the vagaries of nature to adaptation to nature, and making use of and transforming nature. Though natural environment is not the only factor determining the distribution of population, it is still the foundation on which people live and work because of the limitations in the development of the productive forces. For example, the size and density of the population of the Guangxi Zhuang Autonomous Region are bigger than those of the Tibet Autonomous Region. This is because Guangxi is situated in the hilly areas with a high temperature and abundant rainfall that are conducive to agricultural production. With its increase in grain output, the land can support more and more people, and population density is also being continuously raised. In contrast to this, Tibet is located on the "roof of the world" with a high elevation, low temperature, thin air, and scarce rainfall. The harsh natural environment is an important reason that Tibet has a low population density and its population growth has stagnated for a long period of time.

AGE AND SEX STRUCTURE OF THE POPULATION OF MINORITY NATIONALITIES
AGE STRUCTURE

Since liberation, and especially after the mid-1960s, the reproduction pattern of the population of China's

minority nationalities has changed to one of high birthrate, low mortality rate, and high natural population growth. This and the influence of economic, social, religious, and marriage factors as well as the customs and habits in the minority areas have resulted in some characteristics of the age composition of the population of the minority nationalities.

Young Population Pattern. In 1982 the age structure of China's population as a whole and of Han nationality was in a stage of transition from a young to an adult pattern, but that of most minority nationalities still belonged to the young pattern (see Table 11-12). Among the 55 minority nationalities, the Koreans and Russians belonged to the adult pattern, and the Uygur, Gaoshan, Manchu, She, Naxi, Jing, and Loba nationalities were in the transition stage from the young to the adult pattern. The remaining 46 minority nationalities all belonged to the young population pattern. They accounted for 83.6% of the minority peoples, and among them 13 minority nationalities had a very young age structure. These 13 were the Monba, Oroqen, Tartar, Yugur, Ewenki, Qiang, Tujia, Khalkhas, Li, Gelao, Salar, Kazakh, and Hezhe nationalities. The children aged 0–14 of the majority of these nationalities made up more than 40% (47.3% for the Kazakh and 47% for the Salar peoples), and their old people (65 and over) made up less than 4% (2.4% for the Hezhe, 2.7% for the Ewenki, and 2.4% for the Yugur peoples), while the age median was in all cases below 18 years. For the Salar and Kazakh peoples, it was only 16.3 and 16.2 years old, which meant that over half of the population of these two nationalities were born after 1966. Because of the young age structure, the dependency ratio of most of these 13 nationalities was over 80%, and the highest was over 100% for the Gelao, Salar, and Kazakh nationalities. The high dependency ratio, especially the high children's dependency ratio, led directly to a drop in the income accumulation rate and a rise in the consumption rate, thereby impeding the economic and social development of these minority nationality areas.

Because of the young age composition, the number of people who will join the ranks of the working population in the coming years will also increase (see Table 11-13).

With the exception of the Korean nationality, the population of the 0–14 age group of all the other nationalities was more than double that of the 30–44 age group, the highest being that of the Salar and Dongxiang nationalities, reaching 220% and 260%, respectively. While this shows that the labor resources in these minority nationality areas will become increasingly abundant and that they will pro-

Table 11-13   Trend of Growth of Working-Age Population of Some Nationalities in 1982 and Future Years

| NATIONALITY | 1982 | | | COMPARATIVE SIZE OF POPULATION GROUPS (1):(2):(3) |
	30–44 YEARS OLD (10,000) (1)	15–29 YEARS OLD (10,000) (2)	0–14 YEARS OLD (10,000) (3)	
Mongolian	48.8	106.1	134.5	1:2.17:2.76
Hui	125.4	209.0	265.1	1:1.67:2.14
Tibetan	64.7	92.8	152.6	1:1.43:2.36
Uygur	94.1	156.7	240.6	1:1.67:2.56
Miao	81.5	123.4	212.8	1:1.51:2.61
Yi	85.8	135.7	230.1	1:1.58:2.68
Zhuang	213.3	362.1	520.1	1:1.70:2.44
Bouyei	35.7	52.4	84.1	1:1.47:2.36
Korean	33.7	59.4	50.1	1:1.76:1.49
Dong	24.5	36.6	55.1	1:1.49:2.25
Yao	21.7	38.1	57.0	1:1.76:2.63
Bai	17.4	30.2	43.9	1:1.76:2.52
Hani	16.1	27.9	45.1	1:1.73:2.80
Kazakh	11.9	24.6	43.0	1:2.07:3.60
Qiang	1.7	2.5	4.6	1:1.47:2.71
Shui	4.5	6.9	12.2	1:1.53:2.71
Dongxiang	4.8	7.7	11.4	1:1.60:3.20
Tu	2.4	4.3	6.9	1:1.79:2.88
Salar	1.0	1.6	3.2	1:1.60:2.38
Xibe	1.3	2.6	3.1	1:2.00:2.38
Oroqen	0.06	0.13	0.17	1:2.17:2.89
Hezhe	0.0218	0.0467	0.0586	1:2.14:2.63

Source: Based on *1982 Population of China*, China Statistics Publishing House, 1985, pp. 232–239.

vide sufficient reserve labor force for socialist modernization, it portends that there will be pressure in providing them with sufficient job and schooling opportunities.

Some Comparisons With the Nation's Average Level. As the collected data on the 1982 age composition of the population of China's various minority nationalities did not include detailed data for the different ages or five-year age groups, it is therefore possible only to select the related materials from some minority regions and compare them with the nation's average level (see Table 11-14), so as to show roughly the characteristics of the age composition and trends of change in the population of the minority peoples.

First, with regard to the proportion of the 0 age group (baby group) in the total population, only that of Jianchuan County in Sichuan Province was lower than the nation's average level; the proportion in all other minority nationality areas was higher than the nation's average level. In addition, the difference between the various regions was also great. This was mainly due to the difference between childbearing rate and mortality rate.

Second, the proportion of the population of the 1–3 age group (toddlers), 4–5 age group (preschool age group), and 7–12 age group (primary school age group) in the various minority nationality areas was higher than the nation's average level. But such difference will gradually decrease with the increase of age. As the childbearing rate of women in various age groups in the minority nationality regions was constantly on the increase while the infant mortality rate steadily decreased, the proportion of children in the 1–6 age group was higher for most groups than that of the 7–12 age group. This was just opposite to the trend of change in the country as a whole.

Third, as regards the proportion of the 15–25 age group (youth group) in the total population, only that of the Cangyuan Va Autonomous County in Yunnan Province and the Jinxiu Yao Autonomous County in Guangxi was slightly higher than the nation's average, and the proportion in all other minority areas was lower than the nation's average. This meant that when the people in that age group were born, the childbearing level in those areas was generally lower than the level of the country as a whole, while the mortality rate was higher than the nation's level.

Fourth, the proportion of women of the 15–49 childbearing age group in the minority areas was lower than the nation's average level. This indicated that since 1964 the increase in the size and the speed of population growth in the minority areas was not

Table 11-14 Population Composition According to Age Groups in Some Minority Areas

AREA	0 YEAR OLD	1–3 YEARS OLD	4–6 YEARS OLD	7–12 YEARS OLD	15–25 YEARS OLD	15–49 YEARS OLD (FEMALE)	0–14 YEARS OLD (FEMALE)
Whole country	2.07	5.50	5.82	14.93	21.78	24.74	16.27
Tibet Autonomous Region	2.78	7.38	7.07	14.57	20.66	24.14	18.15
Yushu Tibetan Autonomous Prefecture in Qinghai	3.29	9.06	9.52	17.91	15.45	21.39	21.59
Henan Mongolian Autonomous County in Qinghai	3.20	9.65	8.93	18.30	17.24	20.19	22.07
Jiashi County in Xinjiang (Uygur)	3.65	8.42	8.12	16.01	19.25	21.61	19.72
Taxkorgan Tajik Autonomous County in Xinjiang	3.59	10.12	9.32	16.01	19.69	21.51	21.36
Jinyuan County in Ningxia (Hui)	3.73	10.21	9.75	17.56	18.37	20.92	22.52
Meigu County in Sichuan (Yi)	4.15	9.88	8.65	16.53	16.32	21.58	22.10
Putog County in Sichuan (Yi)	4.11	9.63	8.58	15.49	16.76	22.43	21.52
Shiqu County in Sichuan (Tibetan)	3.27	8.70	9.08	16.27	15.93	20.89	20.89
Maowen Qiang Autonomous County in Sichuan	3.02	8.39	8.77	17.27	18.26	21.37	20.71
Taijiang County in Guizhou (Miao)	3.60	8.00	9.84	18.58	16.74	21.32	22.42
Ceheng County in Guizhou (Bouyei)	3.35	7.92	8.74	16.33	19.70	22.35	20.47
Sandu Shui Autonomous County in Guizhou	3.37	8.60	8.40	16.90	18.22	21.76	20.88
Gongshan Drung and Nu Autonomous County in Yunnan	4.01	8.80	8.93	15.31	20.37	23.10	20.66
Fugong County in Yunnan (Lisu)	4.18	9.77	9.40	16.41	19.73	21.96	21.76
Jianchuan County in Yunnan (Bai)	2.03	6.26	8.44	16.99	20.23	23.54	19.43
Cangyuan Va Autonomous County in Yunnan	3.54	7.96	8.45	16.10	22.06	23.78	20.17
Tiandeng County in Guangxi (Zhuang)	2.77	6.99	7.46	15.48	20.21	23.82	17.48
Jinxiu Yao Autonomous County in Guangxi	2.62	6.36	6.99	16.72	21.81	22.42	18.28
Luchun County in Yunnan (Hani)	2.88	7.81	8.99	17.48	21.50	21.20	21.07

Source: Based on the data from the 1982 national census in the regions concerned.

due to a large increase in the number of childbearing women but was due mainly to the increase in the childbearing rate of women living in those areas and the increase in the survival rate of the infants.

Fifth, the proportion of girls in the 0–14 age group in the total population of the minority areas was higher than the nation's average level. Because girls in that age group would be the future childbearing population, their high proportion in the total population meant that the various minority nationality areas would enter a peak childbearing period in the future.

SEX STRUCTURE

Sex Structure of the Total Population of the Minority Peoples.   Data from the 1982 census showed that the sex ratio of the total population of the minority peoples was lower than that of the whole country and of

the Han nationality (see Table 11-15). Of the 67.239 million people of the minority nationalities in the country, the number of men was about 34.217 million and that of women was 33.022 million. There were 1.195 million more men than women.

There were differences between the sex structures of the population of various minority nationalities. But nationalities with more men than women accounted for 72.7%. (There were more men than women in 40 of the 55 minority nationalities in China.) The sex ratio of the Manchu, She, Gaoshan, Xibe, and Uzbek nationalities exceeded 110 males per 100 females. Minority nationalities with more women than men accounted for 18.2% of the total, including the Tibetan, Korean, Dai, Jingpo, Achang, Russian, Jing, Drung, Loba, and Jinuo nationalities. The sex ratio of the Russian nationality was as low as 64.2 males per 100 females. This was perhaps due to the fact that more men than women had moved

Table 11-15   Sex Structure of the Population of China's Various Nationalities, 1982 (Civilian Population Only)

NATIONALITY	SEX STRUCTURE		SEX RATIO (FEMALE = 100)	NATIONALITY	SEX STRUCTURE		SEX RATIO (FEMALE = 100)
	MALE	FEMALE			MALE	FEMALE	
Whole country	51.3	48.7	105.3	Jingpo	48.1	51.9	92.7
Han	51.4	48.6	105.6	Jingpo	48.1	51.	92.7
Minority				Khalkhas	51.1	48.9	104.5
nationalities	50.9	49.1	103.7	Tu	51.5	48.5	106.2
Mongolian	51.4	48.6	105.6	Daur	51.4	48.6	105.6
Hui	50.8	49.2	103.3	Mulao	50.9	49.1	103.7
Tibetan	48.9	51.1	95.7	Qiang	50.4	49.6	101.6
Uygur	51.3	48.7	105.3	Bulang	50.4	49.6	101.6
Miao	51.3	48.7	105.3	Salar	50.3	49.7	101.2
Yi	50.5	49.5	102.0	Maonan	51.6	48.4	106.6
Zhuang	50.4	49.6	101.6	Gelao	52.2	47.8	109.2
Bouyei	50.4	49.6	101.6	Xibe	53.0	47.0	112.8
Korean	49.5	50.5	98.0	Achang	49.6	50.4	98.4
Manchu	53.4	46.6	114.6	Pumi	50.5	49.5	102.0
Dong	52.1	47.9	108.8	Tajik	51.3	48.7	105.3
Yao	51.3	48.7	105.3	Nu	51.1	48.9	104.5
Bai	50.1	49.9	100.4	Uzbek	52.5	47.5	110.5
Tujia	52.1	47.9	108.8	Russian	39.1	60.9	64.2
Hani	50.5	49.5	102.0	Ewenki	51.1	48.9	104.5
Kazakh	51.5	48.5	106.2	Benglong*	50.0	50.0	100.0
Dai	49.6	50.4	98.4	Baoan	51.2	48.8	104.9
Li	50.3	49.7	101.2	Yugur	50.1	49.9	100.4
Lisu	50.3	49.7	101.2	Jing	47.1	52.9	89.0
Va	50.2	49.8	100.8	Tartar	51.8	48.2	107.5
She	52.9	47.1	112.3	Drung	48.7	51.3	94.9
Gaoshan	53.7	46.3	116.0	Oroqen	50.8	49.2	103.3
Lahu	50.4	49.6	101.6	Hezhe	51.2	48.8	104.9
Shui	51.1	48.9	104.5	Monba	51.0	49.0	104.1
Dongxiang	51.3	48.7	105.3	Loba	47.0	53.0	88.7
Naxi	50.2	49.8	100.8	Jinuo	49.7	50.3	98.8

* Benglong was renamed Deang nationality in 1985.

Source: Based on *1982 Population Census of China*, China Statistics Publishing House, 1985, pp. 18–21.

Table 11-16 Sex Ratio of Different Age Groups in Selected Minority Regions (1982) (FEMALE = 100)

MINORITY REGION	TOTAL	0	0–4	5–9	10–14	15–19	20–24	25–29	30–34	35–39	40–44	45–49	50–54	55–59	60–64	65+
China	105.5	107.6	107.1	106.2	106.0	103.6	103.8	106.5	108.3	111.3	114.2	112.3	111.6	106.7	100.4	79.8
Tibet Autonomous Region	97.8	99.4	101.9	102.1	101.0	100.2	100.0	103.3	102.6	99.5	100.9	98.7	92.2	88.1	62.4	65.1
Yushu Tibetan Autonomous Prefecture in Qinghai	92.5	99.6	101.1	103.1	98.2	106.6	105.7	102.3	101.4	101.9	88.4	75.9	70.5	58.3	53.3	38.3
Henan Mongolian Autonomous County in Qinghai	99.1	96.7	111.4	106.1	105.6	103.4	107.9	112.2	105.6	101.9	88.3	100.7	92.6	74.3	62.5	47.6
Jiashi County in Xinjiang (Uygur)	106.4	99.8	100.7	102.4	105.7	120.3	95.1	96.0	110.7	110.3	107.8	117.0	103.1	127.9	102.7	123.4
Taxkorgan Tajik Autonomous County in Xinjiang	106.4	110.2	105.0	101.6	105.6	119.1	109.4	92.9	99.1	97.2	100.0	108.7	123.6	134.4	98.5	130.8
Shache County in Xinjiang (Uygur)	104.7	98.8	100.3	101.9	106.3	97.0	96.9	94.1	109.2	103.5	111.2	107.3	109.4	126.8	118.3	130.2
Jingyuan County in Ningxia (Hui)	107.6	105.7	104.3	106.1	107.2	104.5	110.0	110.9	116.4	97.5	111.6	116.3	119.2	114.8	98.3	114.0
Meigu County in Sichuan (Yi)	101.9	99.6	100.5	102.4	103.3	108.8	106.8	104.6	104.1	109.7	103.7	105.3	106.0	93.8	95.6	85.1
Maowen Qiang Autonomous County in Sichuan	105.5	107.5	102.1	107.2	107.1	105.6	103.9	105.9	115.2	102.8	108.5	118.6	108.3	106.5	104.7	86.4
Taijiang County in Geizhou (Miao)	105.0	97.1	101.9	104.4	105.9	104.5	99.1	108.2	111.4	106.8	108.9	112.4	125.4	111.6	102.0	78.9
Ceheng County in Geizhou (Bouyei)	100.4	103.6	101.4	103.3	103.4	100.0	101.3	100.2	104.7	109.0	103.2	105.4	100.7	94.4	85.6	75.7
Sandu Shui Autonomous County in Guizhou	103.1	103.5	104.9	103.8	103.5	100.9	101.3	105.3	106.4	105.0	107.7	110.7	109.3	107.9	94.1	77.9
Gongshan Drung and Nu Autonomous County in Yunnan	100.8	109.8	96.9	103.9	110.0	99.2	108.0	97.6	95.6	97.4	96.1	112.8	105.3	87.9	84.1	96.1
Mongolians in Inner Mongolia	105.9	—	101.2	101.4	103.4	102.5	102.6	107.2	103.4	110.2	109.7	115.3	122.9	119.8	126.2	137.7
Fugong County in Yunnan (Lisu)	102.3	97.2	102.2	105.4	109.0	106.5	99.3	95.1	100.1	96.6	99.2	105.7	92.1	104.7	89.0	103.9
Jianchuan County in Yunnan (Bai)	96.2	98.4	102.6	102.4	103.2	98.3	92.9	99.1	99.0	94.4	89.2	90.1	91.9	87.6	81.7	69.5
Luchun County in Yunnan (Hani)	105.0	107.4	102.6	104.1	103.6	102.2	104.7	103.5	123.0	122.8	116.1	114.4	112.1	105.3	89.7	67.2
Cangyuan Va Autonomous County in Yunnan	102.6	100.1	100.4	106.6	104.8	103.4	94.5	94.7	103.9	98.1	101.2	112.5	104.3	117.2	108.3	101.0
Tiandeng County in Guangxi (Zhuang)	99.9	103.4	105.6	105.0	105.4	101.5	100.3	104.3	102.3	98.8	94.1	97.6	95.1	94.7	87.5	73.3
Jinxiu Yao Autonomous County in Guangxi	110.4	109.5	107.2	112.8	111.8	112.0	117.1	108.1	119.5	109.7	103.8	117.8	117.9	111.1	108.5	85.4
Putog County in Sichuan (Yi)	102.3	100.2	99.6	100.5	97.7	102.0	104.1	100.0	105.4	107.0	118.2	110.0	109.5	96.8	84.6	86.7
Shiqu County in Sichuan (Tibetan)	97.9	100.2	99.9	104.7	101.2	105.4	109.6	111.7	103.0	98.6	102.0	93.1	98.4	80.8	74.6	56.8

Source: Based on data from the 1982 census in the areas concerned.

abroad. The proportion between men and women in the population of the Bai, Va, Naxi, Deang, and Yugur nationalities was basically the same.

The Sex Structure of the Population of Different Age Groups in Some Minority Areas. For lack of data on the sex structure of the population of different age groups of the minority nationalities in the 1982 census, we can only select the related data of some nationality areas in examining the sex composition of the population of different age groups (see Table 11-16). From the table two salient features can be discerned.

First, the difference in the sex ratio of babies in the 0 age group was very conspicuous. For example, the sex ratio of babies in areas inhabited by the Tibetans, Uygurs, Mongolians, Yis, Miaos, Lisus, and Bais was all below 100, while that of areas inhabited by the Tajik, Drung, Nu, and Yao peoples was between 109 and 110. Whether such differences were the result of natural causes or other factors remains to be clarified through further investigation and study.

Second, the sex ratio of the older age groups in some minority areas was unusually high. Generally speaking, in various countries across the world there are more women than men among the old people. This is also true in China and most of its minority areas, as can be seen from Table 11-6. But the sex ratio of people in the 30–34 and older groups in Jiashi and Shache Counties in Xinjiang was pretty high, with that of the over 65 age group reaching 123 and over 130, respectively. The sex ratio in the 35–39 and older age groups among the Mongolian people in Inner Mongolia was over 110, while that of the 65 plus age group was as high as 138. In other places, such as the Taxkorgan Tajik Autonomous County in Xinjiang and the Jingyuan County in Ningxia, the sex ratio of the old people was also high. This shows that in these areas the mortality rate of old women was higher than that of old men. This was probably because in these regions women's status in the family and in society was low, and because they had weak constitutions resulting from overwork and too many childbirths. Sex-selective migration or choice of minority status may also cause a high sex ratio.

POPULATION PYRAMIDS IN SOME MINORITY REGIONS

The term population pyramid vividly illustrates the population situation in the minority regions. Due to the lack of data on the sex and age composition of the minority peoples, we can only select the related materials of a few representative minority regions to illustrate their population pyramids (see Chart 11-7).

These population pyramids have the following characteristics:

1. All the population pyramids have a broad base, but the apex is not pointed. This shows that all these regions have a high birthrate, low mortality rate, and a long life span on the average. Their population belongs to the type whose size keeps increasing.

2. These pyramids become broader and broader layer by layer from top to bottom. With the exception of Tiandeng County in Guangxi where each half of the pyramid's base made up a little over 6% of the county's total population, all the others made up more than 7%, and that of Taijiang County in Guizhou, the Gongshan Drung and Nu Autonomous County in Yunnan, Fugong County in Yunnan, Jingyuan County in Ningxia, and Meigu County in Sichuan all made up more than 8%. This shows that in recent years the birthrate of various minority nationalities has been increasing while their mortality rate has dropped. It also shows that in the future their population will grow on a larger scale and at a faster pace.

3. The population pyramids in some minority areas have three visibly shrinking layers, that is, the 55–59-year-old layer representing the population born between 1923 and 1927, the 20–24-year-old layer representing the population born between 1958 and 1962, and the 0–4-year-old layer representing the population born between 1978 and 1982. The shrinking of the first two layers obviously was due to the decrease of birthrate and increase of mortality rate resulting from certain causes, while the contraction of the third layer was due to the promotion of family planning, which led to a sharp fall in birthrate and a drop in mortality rate.

4. The population pyramids of the Mongolian, Daur, and Ewenki nationalities in Inner Mongolia have their own peculiarities. Before family planning was promoted, contraction had begun at the last two layers close to the base. This showed that the proportion of children in these two age groups had decreased. And the population pyramids of the Ewenki and Daur nationalities beginning from the 35–39-year-old layer to the top, showed irregularities, sometimes shrinking and sometimes expanding. This indicated that the population of these age

Chart 11-7   Population Pyramids of Some Minority
Regions

Population Pyramid of Jianchuan County in Yunnan
(July 1, 1982)

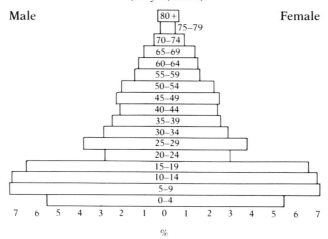

Population Pyramid of Fugong County in Yunnan
(July 1, 1982)

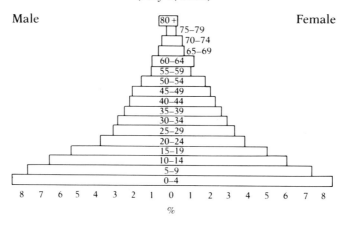

Population Pyramid of the Henan Mongolian Autonomous
County in Qinghai
(July 1, 1982)

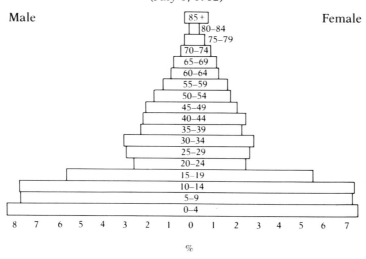

All the data used for the population pyramids are based on the
1982 census in the regions concerned.

Chart 11-7   *(Continued)*

Population Pyramid of the Yushu Tibetan Autonomous County of Qinghai
(July 1, 1982)

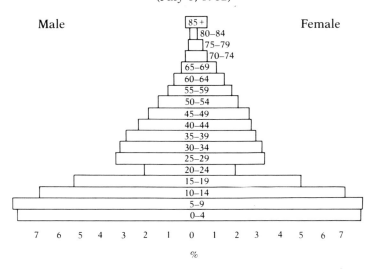

Population Pyramid of Ewenkis in Inner Mongolia
(July 1, 1982)

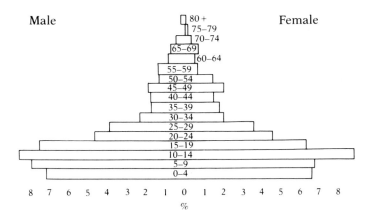

Population Pyramid of the Cangyuan Va Autonomous County in Yunnan
(July 1, 1982)

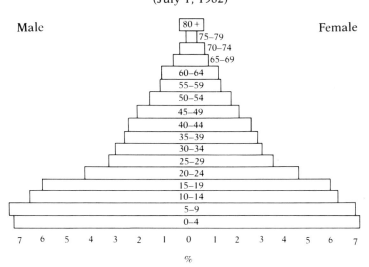

Chart 11-7 *(Continued)*

Population Pyramid of the Mongolian in Inner Mongolia
(July 1, 1982)

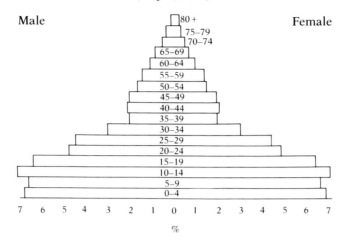

Population Pyramid of Luchun County in Yunnan
(July 1, 1982)

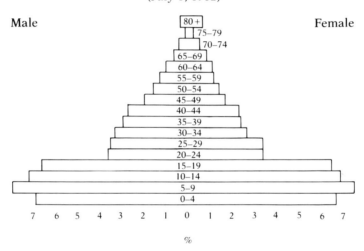

Population Pyramid of Taijiang County in Guizhou
(July 1, 1982)

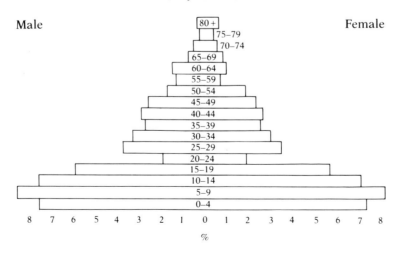

Chart 11-7 *(Continued)*

Population Pyramid of Tiandeng County of Guangxi
(July 1, 1982)

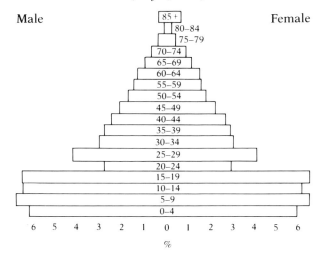

Population Pyramid of Meigu County in Sichuan
(July 1, 1982)

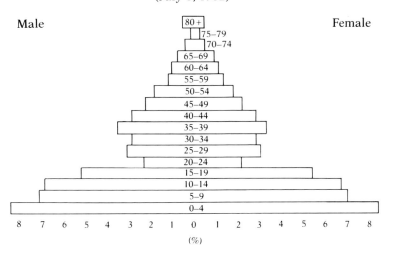

Population Pyramid of Naqu in Tibet
(July 1, 1982)

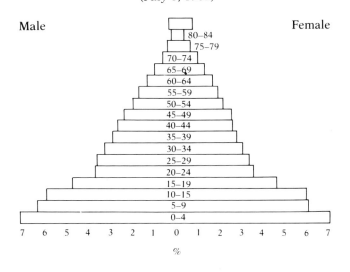

Chart 11-7 *(Continued)*

Population Pyramid of Ceheng County in Guizhou
(July 1, 1982)

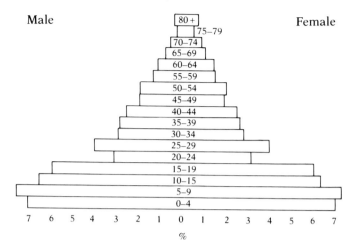

Population Pyramid of Jiashi County in Xinjiang
(July 1, 1982)

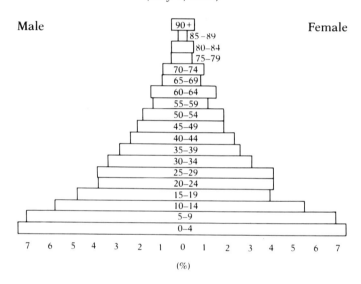

Population Pyramid of Jingyuan County in Ningxia
(July 1, 1982)

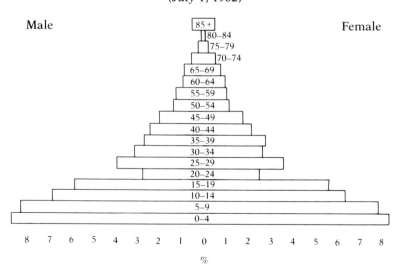

Chart 11-7   *(Continued)*

Population Pyramid of the Gongshan Drung and Nu Autonomous County In Yunnan
(July 1, 1982)

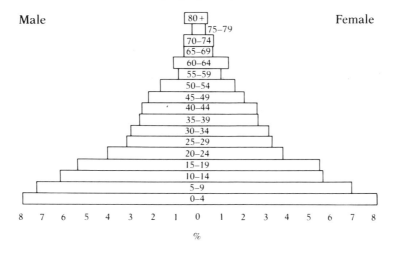

Population Pyramid of Daurs in Inner Mongolia
(July 1, 1982)

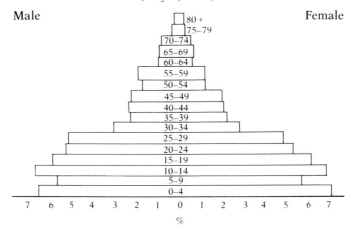

groups was in an unstable state, now increasing and now stagnating or decreasing.

5. The sex ratio in most of the population pyramids was normal. But the population pyramids of the Mongolian and Daur peoples in Inner Mongolia and the population pyramids of Jingyuan County in Ningxia and Jiashi County in Xinjiang showed that in the older age groups there were more men than women.

CHAPTER TWELVE
CHINA'S POPULATION POLICY AND FAMILY PLANNING

The view a country adopts toward the social phenomenon of population, the trend it selects for its population development, and the methods it follows to solve its population problems—all these constitute that country's principles and policy on population. Population policy serves the politics and economy of a country and is therefore an important part of its social, political, and economic policies.

China's population policy is the principle and methods by which the state gives guidance to its population growth and solves its population problems. It is set forth in accordance with the law of population growth under socialism and China's specific conditions. It embodies the will and interests of the people at large and serves China's socialist cause. The major thrust of China's population policy is to control the size and raise the quality of the population. Of course, population policy in a broad sense involves many aspects of the process of population, social, and economic development. But given China's specific conditions, even in its broad sense population policy centers on controlling the size of the population and improving its quality.

CHINA'S NEED TO CONTROL POPULATION GROWTH AND PRACTICE FAMILY PLANNING

Article 25 of the Constitution of the People's Republic of China stipulates: "The state promotes family planning so that population growth may fit the plans for economic and social development." This is China's strategic principle on population and development. This strategic principle and a series of related policies are adopted according to China's actual conditions, and they reflect the objective need for coordinated development between the population, natural resources, society, and economy, as well as the need to constantly improve the standards of the people's material and cultural well-being.

POPULATION GROWTH AND NATURAL RESOURCES AND ENVIRONMENT

Natural resources and environment are the material basis on which people live and multiply. With the constant growth of the population, the capability to exploit these resources increases and so does the consumption of these resources. The relationship between population on the one hand and natural resources and environment on the other has aroused increasing concern. Because of the overquick growth of the population in the past 30-odd years since the founding of the People's Republic in 1949, it has become an outstanding problem and is today a major factor affecting China's social development.

- Energy. China is one of the countries in the world with the richest energy resources. Its coal reserves account for more than 10% of the world's total, and its water power resources top the world. It also has very rich oil reserves. If these resources are converted into standard coal, then in absolute amount China can be considered a very rich country in energy resources. But China's energy consumption also tops the list due to its large population. In terms of exploitable deposits, its average per capita amount of energy resources is only half of that of the world. China's energy output has increased very quickly since the founding of the People's Republic. Compared with 1949, its coal output in 1983 had increased 22.3-fold from 32 million tons to 715 million tons; crude oil increased 884-fold from 120,000 tons to 106.07 million tons; and electricity generated went up 81.7-fold from 4.3 billion kwh to 351.4 billion kwh. But because of the overquick increase of

213

the population, per capita energy consumption at present is only 0.6 ton of standard coal (not including biological energy consumed in the countryside), less than one-third of the world's average (about 1.96 tons in 1980). This is the first point that should be mentioned. The second point is that the rural population is large and has grown rapidly. Because of the serious energy shortage, the rural population consumes crop stalks and firewood in large quantities, and this has caused damage to the ecological balance in some places. Third, energy resources are not evenly distributed, with most of the coal and oil reserves in northeast, north, and northwest China, while the bulk of water power resources is concentrated in southwest China (accounting for 67.8% of the nation's total). Since these energy reserves are mostly far from the densely populated consuming areas, they pose great difficulty for development and transportation and for an even distribution in the building of industries. The aforesaid situation shows that over-rapid population growth has brought great pressure on energy supply, and to make China's population growth commensurate with the availability of energy resources, it is extremely important to step up energy production and to control the population growth.

• Land and grain production. China is one of the largest countries in the world, with favorable natural conditions on its 9.6 million kilometers of land. In absolute figures, the country's land resources are enormous, but its average per capita amount of land is far less than the world's average — its average per capita amount of land is only 30% of the world's average; cultivated land, only 27%; usable grassland, 31%, and afforested land, 12% (see Table 12-1).

The area under cultivation in China accounts for 10.3% of the nation's total area, higher than in the rest of the world. But the average per capita amount of land for the agricultural population or able-bodied peasants is far lower than the world's average level. Because of the development of industry, transport, and other undertakings and the growth of the population over the past 30-odd years, both China's total area of cultivated land and its average per capita amount of cultivated land have decreased year by year (see Table 12-2).

With regard to grain output, China has made rapid progress since liberation, in 1949. Compared with other countries, China's total grain output and rate of increase lead the world. In 1978, total grain output was 56.2% more than that of 1957. During the same period, however, its population increased 48.2%. Because of the population growth and the rise of industrial grain consumption, the average increase of grain for each person was only 16.5 kilograms, or a mere 5.5% increase. Although China's grain production has witnessed a fairly rapid increase since the beginning of the 1980s, the relationship between grain output and population growth is still an extremely important question affecting the country's overall situation.

• Forests — important biological resources. Due to the limitations of natural conditions and long years of indiscriminate cutting, China's area covered by forests is relatively small. Now, the country has only 122 million hectares of forests, accounting for 12.7% of the nation's total area (or 3% of the world's total forest area of 4 billion hectares). The average for each person is only 0.3 acre, equivalent to only 12% of the world's per capita average of 2.54 acres. At

Table 12-1   Land Resources of China, the World, and Selected Countries[1]

		WORLD	CHINA	USA	USSR	INDIA
Land resources (million hectares)	Total area	13,400	960	930	2,240	328
	Cultivated land	1,326	99	186	227	166
	Grassland[2]	3,150	224	215	372	13
	Afforested land	4,056	122	305	92	67
	Uncultivated land and area unable to be cultivated	—	517	229	721	81
Average per capita amount (acres)	Land area	8.12	2.46	10.74	20.83	—
	Cultivated land	0.90	0.25	2.10	2.12	064
	Grassland	1.87	0.57	2.41	3.48	0.05
	Afforested land	2.54	0.30	3.39	8.56	0.26

[1] Figures in the table for China are from 1979, and figures for the world and selected countries are from 1978.
[2] Area of grassland refers to usable area.
Source: *Population Handbook,* edited by Liu Hongkang, compiled and published by the Chengdu Family Planning and Education Sub-Centre, 1984.

Table 12-2 Changes in the Area of Cultivated Land in China

YEAR	TOTAL CULTIVATED AREA (1,000 HECTARES)	AVERAGE PER CAPITA AMOUNT (ACRE)	PER CAPITA AVERAGE FOR AGRICULTURAL POPULATION (ACRE)	PER CAPITA AVERAGE FOR ABLE-BODIED PEASANTS (ACRE)
1949	97,881	0.44	0.54	—
1952	107,919	0.46	0.54	1.53
1957	111,830	0.42	0.51	1.43
1962	102,903	0.38	0.45	1.19
1965	103,594	0.35	0.42	1.09
1970	101,135	0.30	0.36	0.89
1975	99,708	0.27	0.31	0.83
1977	99,247	0.26	0.30	0.83
1978	99,389	0.25	0.31	0.82

Source: *Population Handbook,* edited by Liu Hongkang, compiled and published by the Chengdu Family Planning and Education Sub-Centre, 1984.

present, China has an accumulated total of 8.656 billion cubic meters of timber, less than 9 cubic meters per person, equivalent to only one-ninth of the world's per capita average. Insufficient forest resources and their gradual decline have not only produced serious effects on economic development and people's lives but have also directly affected environmental protection and given rise to a series of problems related to ecological balance. The reduction in the area of forests and the growth of the population inevitably require that China pay special attention to controlling its overquick population growth, while making energetic efforts to afforest the land and protect the forest resources.

POPULATION GROWTH AND SOCIOECONOMIC DEVELOPMENT

While population growth reflects economic development, it is also restricted by such development. For its part, population growth also affects economic development, playing the role of promoting or prolonging it. It is an objective requirement of social progress that population growth must keep pace with economic development. Although China has made much headway in industrial and agricultural production over the more than three decades since the founding of New China, its national economic level is still low when compared with that of the developed countries; the improvement of the people's living standards has been slow and the country as a whole has not yet got rid of its backwardness. The reasons for this are many. But the overrapid population growth over the years, which is not in harmony with the economic and social development, is an important one. This is mainly manifested in the following aspects.

First, China's gross industrial and agricultural output value increased 21-fold from 1949, when the People's Republic was founded, to 1983, and its national income went up 9-fold from 1952 to 1983. But, as the population nearly doubled during the same period, the country's per-capita national income multiplied 4.4 times. During the 1957–81 period, the total amount of consumption fund for the people's livelihood went up by 390%, while the average per-capita amount of consumption increased by only 190%. From 1953 to 1978, the total amount of consumption fund increased by 280%. But as the population also increased by 66% in the same period, the average per-capita amount of consumption only went up by 130%, with about 58% of the yearly increased sum being spent by the newly added population (see Table 12-3).

Second, rapid population growth has created great problems for employment. During the 1951–70 period, China's average annual natural population growth was 25‰ and it was 33.3‰ in the highest year. The natural population growth determines the rate of increase of the labor force. When population increases quickly, labor force follows suit. Hence the difficulty in providing jobs for the newly added labor force. Since the latter half of the 1970s, in particular, about 20 million people seek employment every year. Of this number, 3 to 5 million are in the cities and towns, and this makes it all the more difficult to realize full employment. At present, the newly added labor force in the cities and towns every year is about three times that of each year of the First (1953–57) and Second Five-Year Plan (1958–62) period. Such a rapid increase of workers exceeds the growth of newly added fixed assets. On the one hand, it has resulted in more people awaiting employment in the cities and towns. On the other, it has led to overstaff-

Table 12-3   China's Major Economic Figures Since 1949

	1949	1952	1965	1978	1981	1983
Year-end population (thousand)	541,670	574,820	725,380	962,590	1,000,720	1,024,950
Gross industrial and agricultural output value (million yuan)	46,600	81,000	223,500	563,400	758,000	920,900
Gross output value of society (million yuan)	55,700	101,500	269,500	684,600	907,100	1,105,200
National income (million yuan)	35,800	58,900	138,700	301,000	394,000	467,300
Per capita national income (yuan)	66	104	194	315	396	458

Source: *Statistics Yearbook of China 1984,* China Statistics Publishing House, 1984.

ing in many units, making it impossible to bring into full play the role of human resources and therefore disadvantageous to raising labor productivity. In the more than 30 years since the founding of the People's Republic, the number of workers and staff in state-owned units has increased by more than 66 million, an annual increase of about 2.3 million, but in 10 of these years labor productivity has dropped. Though a downturn in production and slow development are important reasons, the overquick increase in labor force is also a factor that should not be neglected.

Surplus labor in the countryside is also serious. In terms of able-bodied people, total labor force in the counryside has gone up from more than 200 million to more than 300 million today. and it will continue to increase for some years in the future. The average per capita amount of cultivated land for able-bodied peasants had decreased from 1.53 acres in 1952 to 0.83 acre in 1977, which was much lower than the world's average. Now, the per capita average is only about 0.82 acre, which is not enough for cultivation by manual labor and draft animals, still less by making use of farm machinery.

The above-mentioned situation shows that while making efforts to develop production, readjust and reform its economy, China must reduce its rapid population growth so as to alleviate the pressure of newly added labor force every year on its limited resources.

Third, over-rapid population growth makes it difficult for educational and cultural development to keep pace with population. Statistics show that every year China has to spend about half of its newly increased income to support its newly added population, which runs to tens of millions. Under such circumstances, how can the state appropriate sufficient funds for educational and cultural undertakings? According to the third census, in 1982, for every 100,000 people in China there were only 599 people

with a college education, 6,622 senior middle school students, 17,758 junior middle school students, and 35,377 primary school pupils, and there were as many as 230 million illiterate and semi-illiterate people in the country. At present, about 6% of school-age children cannot enter primary schools; 12% of primary school pupils cannot enter junior middle schools; 50% of junior middle school students cannot go to senior middle schools; and 75% of senior middle school graduates cannot get admittance into institutions of higher learning. The fact that eductional undertakings cannot keep pace with population growth directly affects the quality of the labor force. At present, people who have received a junior middle school or primary school education account for more than 80% of China's workers and staff; those having acquired a senior middle school education account for only 10%; and those having received a college education account for only 4%. In addition, there are 5% illiterate people. This has led to the situation in which we find, on the one hand, the over-rapid increase of labor force far exceeds the actual needs, and on the other, there is a serious shortage of people with special knowledge and professional skills urgently needed for modernized production. This situation cannot possibly be changed when the population increases at a rapid pace. Therefore, China must take all necessary measures to control the overquick growth of its population while developing its economy and educational and cultural undertakings.

Fourth, the incompatibility of the overquick population growth with the speed of socialist expanded production has affected the accumulation of funds needed for the modernization drive. During the 1949–77 period, China spent an estimated 1,330 billion yuan to cover the basic living expenses for bringing up 600 million newborn babies during this period, a sum equivalent to 31% of the total national income for the same period. Of the total living expenses, 30%, or about 400 billion yuan, were borne by the state and the collectives, equivalent to one-third of the total accumulated funds of the same period. If 200 million fewer babies were born after liberation, families would have spent almost 300 billion yuan less on bringing them up, and the state and the collectives, too, would have reduced expenses for this purpose by 140 billion yuan. And if these living expenses were used as accumulation funds, the total amount of accumulation funds would have increased by more than 10%.

In short, overquick growth of the population has brought serious difficulties to China's socialist modernization, an objective fact of the last 30-odd years that must not be ignored. In order to solve this problem, apart from developing the productive forces, the most important thing is to control the growth of the population, practice family planning, and take serious measures to bring population growth into the orbit of planned and proportionate development of the national economy.

HISTORICAL CHANGES IN CHINA'S POPULATION POLICY AND FAMILY PLANNING

Over the last 30 years and more, after the founding of the People's Republic, China's population policy and family planning work have undergone a process of probing before defining and gradually improving them. This process can roughly be divided into the following four stages.

1. From the founding of New China to the end of the 1950s. This was a period during which a call was initially issued for birth control and checking population growth. In the early period after the establishment of the People's Republic, agrarian reform was carried out in the countryside, the problem of unemployment was basically solved in the cities, the national economy was restored, and the broad masses of people were freed from the serious threat of poverty, starvation, and death. With the fundamental change of the social and economic conditions, the nation's mortality rate dropped remarkably while birthrate remained at a fairly high level. As a result, China's population grew rapidly.

In the first four years after the birth of New China, the country's population rose from 541.67 million in 1949 to 587.96 million in 1953, a net increase of 46 million people. This rapid growth of the population attracted the attention of the state leaders and authorities. They gradually came to realize the need to encourage birth control in the interests of the nation and families as well as in the interests of women and children.

In 1953, the Government Administration Council approved the measures concerning contraception and induced abortion submitted by the Ministry of Public Health. In December 1954, the Central Government held a forum on birth control in Beijing, at which Comrade Liu Shaoqi explicitly pointed out, "What we must affirm here is that the Party is in favor of birth control; appropriate measures should be taken to encourage birth control and we should not oppose it." After the forum, the government designated the departments concerned to organize research groups on birth control and to work out methods for publicizing this work. In March 1955, the Party Central Committee issued the Directive on Controlling Population, calling on the Ministry of Public Health to help the people to practice birth control and to revise the relevant provisions on contraception and induced abortion. In 1956 in the National Program for Agricultural Development (Draft) drawn up under his guidance, Comrade Mao Zedong pointed out, "Except for areas inhabited by minority nationalities, we should publicize and promote birth control in all densely populated areas and encourage bearing and raising children in a planned way." In his Report on the Proposals for the Second Five-Year Plan for the Development of the National Economy, delivered on September 27, 1956, Comrade Zhou Enlai also pointed out, "To protect women and children and bring up and educate our younger generation in a way conducive to the health and prosperity of the nation, we agree that due measures of birth control are desirable." At the Supreme State Conference held in February 1957, Comrade Mao Zedong issued the call, "Mankind should control itself and ensure a planned growth." At the Third Plenary Session of the Eighth Party Central Committee in October that same year, he again pointed out, "It won't do for mankind to practice absolute anarchism in matters of child-birth, it should practice planned parenthood." At that time, the noted Chinese economist Ma Yinchu and other scholars also set forth their views and proposals on controlling population growth. During this period, various views and ideas concerning China's population policy were voiced. It was under these circumstances that birth control was advocated in a number of large and medium-sized cities, and newspapers and magazines began publicizing it.

Beginning in the second half of 1957, however, due to the influence of the "leftist" ideology that lopsidedly stressed the role of people as producers, the continuous growth of population was seen as the law governing population growth in socialist countries, while the correct view on birth control was criticized as the Malthusian theory on population. Thus the birth control program that was being advocated could not actually check the rapid growth of the population throughout the country. In the 1950–57 period, China's population grew by 105 million, the average annual rate of increase being 22.4‰, making it the first peak period of population growth after the founding of New China. During this period, the people's living standards were steadily raised, medical and health conditions improved year after year, and many diseases that seriously endangered the people's lives were brought under control. These factors led to a big drop in mortality rate. (According to a survey of some counties and cities in 16 provinces and autonomous regions, the death rate fell from 25‰ in the preliberation years to 10.8‰ in 1957; during the same period, infant mortality dropped from 200‰ to 70.9‰.) However, population growth actually remained out of control, and more than 20 million babies were born annually, with the total childbearing rate reaching six births per woman and a birthrate above 30‰. In short, this period witnessed a change from a population pattern of high birth and high death rate and slow population growth before the founding of New China to one of high birthrate, low death rate, and overquick growth of population.

2. From the late 1950s to the late 1960s. This was a period in which the Party and government again focused their attention on controlling population growth and formally launched family planning work; it was also a period that witnessed serious relapses. After a period of economic difficulties and negative population growth in the late 1950s and early 1960s, there began in 1962, when the economy took a turn for the better, the quick emergence of a compensatory childbirth upsurge in China. As a result, the imbalance and contradiction between the overquick population growth and social and economic development, which existed in the previous stage, surfaced once again. Under such circumstances, at the end of 1962 the Party Central Cimmittee and the State Council jointly issued the Directive on Conscientiously carrying out Family Planning, which called for "birth control in cities and densely populated countryside and for appropriately controlling the natural growth rate of the population, so that

child-birth will change gradually from an unplanned to a planned state. This is an established policy in China's socialist construction." Since then, family planning has formally become an established Chinese policy. In October 1963, the Party Central Committee approved and transmitted the State Council's decision taken at the Second Urban Work Conference, which required that "both the central and local departments should set up family planning committees to give concrete guidance to this work." The decision also called for energetic efforts to carry out family planning work, strengthen technical guidance, and organize scientific research and manufacture and supply of contraceptives and medicines. At the same time, the departments concerned were required to revise appropriately those provisions that were disadvantageous to family planning and to encourage late marriage.

In 1964, the State Council decided to set up a special office in charge of family planning work, and similar special organizations were also established one after another in various places. In 1965, the Party and government put forward a series of specific policies and measures for controlling population growth. These included encouraging the manufacture of oral contraceptives, issuing contraceptives free of charge, improving birth-control technology, integrating health work with family planning work, strengthening the publicity, education, and technical guidance on family planning, paying equal attention to planned parenthood, improvement of living standards, and reasonable arrangement of labor force. The Party and government also set the target of population growth and concrete demands regarding the number of births, "One is enough, two is just good, three is too many." During this period, family planning was first tried out in the cities under the guidance of the Party and government, and then gradually spread to the countryside. As a result, the birthrate and natural population growth rate in many big and medium-sized cities dropped to some extent in the 1963–66 period. Of course, because family planning was not earnestly carried out in the vast countryside, the birthrate and natural population growth rate of the country as a whole remained very high.

However, like work in other fields, family planning, which had just been launched in a vigorous way in the cities and was in urgent need of being publicized in the vast countryside, was seriously disrupted during the "cultural revolution," which started in 1966. Family planning organizations at all levels were disbanded and various correct policies and systems were undermined. During the "cultural revolution," although Comrades Mao Zedong and Zhou Enlai issued several directives on checking the population growth, and the people, too, had the desire for birth conrol, China's population growth was, on the whole, out of control. This was due to the severe damage brought about by the "left" ideology of the "cultural revolution" which prevailed throughout the country for many years. Thus the 1962–70 period again witnessed a second upsurge in China's population growth. These nine years saw a net increase of 160 million people throughout the country, an average annual growth rate of 2.6%, with the childbearing rate reaching 5.91 children per woman. As a result of the "cultural revolution," the national economy stagnated and even retrogressed, while the population grew rapidly again. This presented serious difficulties to the state and brought tremendous pressure on the society.

3. From the early 1970s to the late 1970s. This was a period in which China's rapid population growth was being controlled step by step. After 1971, Comrade Zhou Enlai gave personal guidance to the family planning program, and many places and departments did a great deal of work after surmounting numerous difficulties and overcoming all sorts of interferences. Beginning in 1973, the target of national population growth was incorporated into the state plan for economic development. Family planning organizations at national and local levels were restored and strengthened and the family planning program spread nationwide. Birthrate in China began to drop.

Since the downfall of the gang of four, in 1976, family planning has registered new achievements in an even broader area in China. These achievements mainly include the following:

• The Marxist theory on population has been disseminated widely among the people, study classes and discussion meetings on population theory have been held across the country, and erroneous views on some major questions regarding population have been corrected. All these have helped lay the ideological and theoretical foundation for formulating and implementing China's population policy.

• The Constitution amended at the First Session of the Fifth National People's Congress in 1978 explicitly stipulates that "the state advocates and encourages family planning," and makes family planning a basic right and duty of the citizens. At that time, the state also isued the call that for each couple it is "best to have one child and at most two." Policies and

provisions disadvantageous to family planning have been revised, and policies and stipulations conducive to controlling the growth of population have been formulated.

• Family planning institutions at all levels have been reorganized and strengthened, and the experiences gained in family planning work over the years have been summed up.

• The ranks of scientific and technical personnel engaged in the work of family planning have been strengthened and the research, production, and supply of contraceptives have been improved.

• The government has instituted the system of awarding couples with only one child, and called for the strengthening of social insurance and the improvement of maternity and child care and welfare for old people so as to consolidate the achievements gained in family planning.

The implementation of these measures resulted in a gradual drop of the birthrate from 33.43‰ to 17.82‰ during the 1970–79 period, and the total fertility rate also decreased from 5.44 to 2.75 during the same period. If 1970 was taken as the base and calculation was done in accordance with the total fertility rate, than about 100 million fewer babies were born during those nine years. In short, the entire 1970s (especially in the years after the gang of four was smashed) was a period in which the overquick growth of China's population was brought gradually under control.

4. From 1979 to the present. This was a period in which China's policies on population and family planning were laid down and perfected. As to how to solve the population question, China has had both positive and negative experiences over the past 30-odd years, and it was only after the Third Plenary Session of the 11th Party Central Committee, held in December 1979, that a correct answer was found ideologically as well as in policy and practice. The goal was set to keep the population within 1.2 billion by the end of this century and more specific principles and policies have been worked out, thus creating a new situation in China's family planning program.

• In September 1980, the Party Central Committee and the State Council jointly issued an Open Letter to All the Communist Party Members and Communist Youth League Members Regarding the Control of China's Population Growth, which ideologically and theoretically explained the urgency and importance of family planning and issued the call encouraging every couple to have only one child.

• In September 1980, the Third Session of the Fifth National People's Congress adopted the new Marriage Law, which stipulates, "Both husband and wife have the duty to practice family planning," and "late marriage and late childbearing should be encouraged." The Marriage Law also emphasized the need to bear and raise healthy children.

• In his Report on Government Work delivered at the Fourth Session of the Fifth National People's Congress in November 1981, Premier Zhao Ziyang clearly pointed out, "It is our policy to control population growth while raising the quality of the population." In his report entitled "Create New Situation in All Fields of Socialist Modernization," made at the 12th National Congress of the Communist Party of China in September 1982, Party General Secretary Hu Yaobang pointed out, "Population has always been an extremely important issue in China's economic and social development. Family planning is a basic policy of our state."

• The new Constitution adopted at the Fifth Session of the Fifth National People's Congress in December 1982 stipulates, "The state promotes family planning so that population growth may fit the plan for economic and social development," and "both husband and wife have the duty to practice family planning." The Constitution also stipulates that the State Council and people's governements at or above the county level should, within the limit of their power as prescribed in the law, lead and handle family planning programs.

• The Sixth Five-Year Plan (1981–85) for economic and social development clearly stated, "Strictly control the growth of population, properly arrange the employment of urban labor force and, on the basis of production development and the raising of labor productivity, enable urban and rural people's material and cultural life to further improve."

• In order to encourage every couple to have only one child and quickly reduce the rate of population growth, the state adopted during this period a series of specific policies ensuring the well-being of only children and their families. These included preferential treatment for only children in enrolling in nurseries and schools, in medical care, employment, urban housing, and the distribution of land for rural housing.

In 1984, the Party Central Committee approved and transmited the State Family Planning Committee's Party group's Report on the Work of Family Planning. Proceeding from the general goals and general tasks of China's socialist modernization, the report realistically and profoundly summed up and analyzed the practical experience gained in promoting family planning. It emphasized that the family planning policy should be reasonable so that it is supported by the masses and easy for the cadres to carry out their work. The report called for further improvement of the policy on family planning and the style of work on the part of the cadres, so that population growth is effectively brought under control and closer relations between the Party and the masses are forged, thereby promoting stability and unity. This important document has greatly boosted efforts to create a new situation in the country's family planning program.

Practice has shown that family planning has gradually embarked on the road of sound development in China. Altogether 86% of couples of childbearing age have taken various contraceptive measures for planned parenthood. Population growth control has increasingly become a conscious action of the people.

CONCRETE REQUIREMENTS OF CHINA'S POPULATION POLICY AND BASIC METHODS OF PROMOTING FAMILY PLANNING
CONCRETE REQUIREMENTS

China's population policy is to "control population growth and raise the quality of the population." The concrete requirements are: late marriage, late childbearing, giving birth to fewer babies, bearing and raising healthy children.

• Late marriage. This means, on the basis of the lawful marriage age, postponing the actual marriage age. The Marriage Law adopted at the Third Session of the Fifth National People's Congress on September 10, 1980, stipulates that the minimum marriage age is 22 for men and 20 for women. If, on the basis of these minimum marriage ages, young men and women further postpone their marriage for two or three years, they are regarded as getting married at a late age. Marriage and childbearing generally are closely related. The aim of advocating late marriage is to slow down and regulate the rate of present and future population growth, promote social and economic development, and raise the people's living standards. Also, late marriage is helpful to the healthy growth of young people and conducive to the modernization drive.

• Late childbearing. This means postponing the birth of married women's first child and prolonging the birth interval between the first and second child. Late marriage and late childbearing supplement each other and play an equally important role in controlling the rapidly growing population. Of course, late childbearing, like late marriage, does not mean the later the better. Generally speaking, giving birth to a child after marrying at a late age is regarded as late childbearing. When a woman over 24 gives birth to her first child, she is considered to have met the requirements of late childbearing. If she wants to have a second child, it is encouraged that she have it four years later.

• Fewer babies. This is the core of the population policy as well as the key to controlling the overrapid growth of the population. At present and for a period of time to come, to have fewer babies means encouraging each couple to have only one child. But this does not mean that all women of childbearing age have to give birth to only one child. In concrete terms, this means that in the case of state cadres, workers and staff members, and residents of the cities and towns, every couple is to have only one child, except those who, because of special reasons, may after approval by related departments have a second child. In the countryside, it is also advocated that every couple should have only one child; for those who have real difficulties and wish to have a second child, arrangements will be made according to a plan after their applications have been approved. But under no circumstances should there be a third child. For the minority peoples, family planning is also advocated, but the requirements are more flexible in practice. China's current population policy stems from its specific conditions and serves its goals set for economic and social development and population growth by the end of this century. It therefore conforms to the fundamental interests of the people. According to statistics, by the end of 1984 the total population of the 29 provinces, autonomous regions, and municipalities on the mainland reached 1,030.51 million. To realize the goal of keeping China's population at around 1.2 billion by the end of this century, the birthrate must be kept under effective control in the remaining more than a dozen years.

According to a national one-per-thousand fertility rate sample survey conducted in 1982, in the 10 years from 1983 to 1992, an average of more than 12 million couples of young people will enter the marriage and childbearing age every year; and from 1993 to 2000 there will be about 10 to 11 million such young couples every year. So, a total of 200 million young couples will enter the marriage and childbearing age by the end of the century. If the total fertility rate of the nation's women of childbearing age develops at different levels in the next dozen years, then different results will be obtained (see Table 12-4).

Therefore, it is obvious that advocating "one couple, one child" is entirely necessary in order to realize China's goals for population growth and for its social and economic development.

To encourage each couple to have one child does not mean that all couples should have one child only, which is neither possible nor necessary. To encourage each couple to have one child is a necessary measure taken for the present stage because of China's large population, its rapid growth, young age composition, and long high-birthrate period. This policy may change at the opportune time. When

Table 12-4 A Forecast of China's Population Growth Under Four Different Scenarios

	SCENARIO	A	B	C	D
1985	Total fertility rate	2.4	2.3	2.2	2.2
	Total population (million)	1,049	1,048	1,047	1,047
1990	Total fertility rate	2.4	2.0	1.7	1.7
	Total population (million)	1,121	1,113	1,106	1,106
1995	Total fertility rate	2.4	2.0	1.5	1.5
	Total population (million)	1,208	1,179	1,148	1,148
2000	Total fertility rate	2.4	2.0	1.5	2.0
	Total population (million)	1,300	1,250	1,192	1,192
	Peak year for total population	2081	2033	2017	2051
	Total population (million)	2,070	1,443	1,236	1,268

China's population situation changes in the years to come, the state will take adequate measures to make necessary amendments to its population policy.

• Giving birth to healthy babies. This means giving birth to babies with a sound mind and a sound body, which is the prerequisite to raising the quality of the population. Only by having such babies can physically and intellectually outstanding individuals multiply.

Genetic factors have an important bearing on healthy babies and they directly affect the quality of babies. People with hereditary diseases are not only carriers but also disseminators of morbid genes. Hereditary diseases can be passed on to the second and third generation, thus making the pathological defects more and more serious and widespread.

In order to raise the quality of the Chinese people and bring up a healthy posterity and to consolidate the achievements of the family planning program, the state has made giving birth to healthy babies an important component of China's population policy and, proceeding from the country's actual conditions, has adopted a series of measures for its realization. For instance, China's Marriage Law forbids marriages between "lineal relatives by blood or collateral relatives by blood (up to the third degree of relationship)," and marriages in which "one party is suffering from leprosy, a cure not having been effected, or from any disease which is regarded by medical science as rendering a person unfit for marriage." To implement these regulations, medical departments conduct prenatal examinations for pregnant women; they have also established genetics consultation clinics and prenatal clinics, which give timely advice to mothers to halt their pregnancies if the fetuses have hereditary or congenital diseases. In addition, maternity and child care has been strengthened, new methods for midwifery and puerperal care have been popularized, and efforts have been made in the research of eugenics and in the training of special personnel in this field.

• Raising healthy children. This means to protect the children and enable them to grow up healthy. This not only helps consolidate the achievements in giving birth to fewer but healthy babies, but will further raise the quality of the population. Therefore, it is also an important part of China's population policy. Children are the future of the state and the hope of the nation. Both the state and parents hope that every newborn baby will grow up healthy and that the younger generation will from childhood receive sound, scientific care and education, so that they will become useful people needed in the country's socialist modernization drive.

To attain the goal of raising healthy children, the state has adopted a series of necessary measures. First, maternity and child care has been constantly strengthened and improved, babies and children are given regular physical checkups, and scientific knowledge on baby care has been publicized. Second, efforts have been made to run well nurseries and kindergartens and cultivate among the children sound moral qualities and good habits. At the same time, attention has been paid to mobilize the task of bringing up children in a healthy way. Third, active efforts have been made to cure and give a good education to physically handicapped and mentally retarded children.

BASIC WAYS OF PROMOTING FAMILY PLANNING

In carrying out family planning and controlling population growth, China's basic methods and experiences are as follows:

1. Uphold the principle of combining state guidance with the voluntariness of the people. This means the state takes into consideration the long-term interests of the whole people, sets forth the principles and enacts appropriate laws, makes forecasts, and draws up population growth plans. The state also provides the necessary conditions in terms of materials, funds, and personnel for promoting family planning. Publicity and education on family planning are conducted among the people, and technical guidance on birth control is provided. In other words, the state adopts various practical measures in legislation, policy, planning, and education to help the people realize their own long-term interests and those of the state so that they will practice family planning conscientiously. Here, it should be stressed that family planning policy should be reasonable and should be supported by the people, so that it can be easily implemented by those engaged in the work. With regard to the methods to be followed, attention should be paid that everything should proceed from the actual conditions and different methods should be applied to different situations, i.e., giving guidance to different cases according to their merits and avoiding "tackling all things in the same way." In short, it is necessary to organically combine the state's practical and realistic guidance with enhancing the people's understanding and consciousness; coercion in any form must be opposed.

2. Incorporate the population plan into the state's general plan for economic and social develop-

ment. In drawing up and implementing the population plan, the various localities should adopt the method of "from bottom to top and from top to bottom" to combine the efforts both "at the top and at the bottom." This is to say, all grass-roots units — villages, urban neighborhoods, factories, and mines — and provincial, autonomous regional, and municipal authorities must, with due consideration to their own population, economic situation, and natural resources, draw up their own population plans that will effectively control population growth and at the same time conform to the local conditions and the wishes of the people. The state will then collate the plans submitted by various localities, make an overall balance, and put forward different demands and measures for different regions according to their concrete conditions while leaving some leeway. It should be pointed out in particular that a plan must be made public as soon as it is adopted. The aim is to put the plan on the basis of popular support, so that it will be fulfilled through the people's conscious implementation.

3. Promote family planning in a sustained and thoroughgoing way. To do so, China has over a long period upheld three key factors — stressing education and publicity work, encouraging contraception and birth control, and doing the work regularly. Education and publicity are the central link in family planning and constitute the fundamental way to change the people's traditional views on childbearing. Family planning committees at all levels throughout the country have special departments and personnel in charge of education and publicity on family planning. The grass-roots units, too, have full-time or part-time personnel in charge of this work. In this way a nationwide network is formed, and effective ways welcomed by the people are adopted. For instance, during prenatal examinations and registrations for marriages, young couples and newlyweds are given necessary informations on late marriage, late childbearing, and giving birth to fewer but healthier babies. The people at large are organized to make calculations and comparisons between their local population, land and natural resources, grain output, and income, so as to let them educate themselves on the importance of family planning and controlling population growth. In addition, education on family planning is combined in various ways with the country's efforts to promote socialist culture and ethics. The purpose is to enable the people to consciously get rid of old concepts on childbearing. In the middle schools, population theory and related subjects are also being gradually introduced.

The use of contraception, another key link in family planning, encourages birth conrol through various methods, so as to better protect the health of women of childbearing age. With regard to contraceptive methods, due attention is given to the physical condition of the people concerned, and comprehensive birth control measures are adopted.

Another key link is to do the work regularly. It means carrying out family planning education and publicity work in a sustained way and drawing up necessary working rules. The purpose is to consolidate and expand the achievements made in family planning work through regular and meticulous education.

In promoting family planning, many places have done their best to send contraceptives, necessary information, and medical service to the doorsteps of families concerned. People engaged in the work have also energetically publicized knowledge on population theory, birth control, giving birth to fewer babies, and bringing them up in a healthy way. In addition, grass-roots medical institutions and organizations in charge of family planning have extended all possible help to cure women of sterility and to run nurseries and kindergartens as well as old people's homes and other social welfare and insurance facilities.

4. Establish and improve organizations with competent personnel in charge of family planning. Such organizations have been set up at the central, provincial, and county levels. In addition, factories and mines, urban neighborhoods, and rural villages have full-time staff members supervising the work. With regard to publicity, the state has set up a family planning publicity center and a training center as well, and some provinces and counties also have established publicity organizations giving guidance to this work. In the field of scientific research, the state and some provinces have established research institutes, and the counties have set up technical guidance stations. Hospitals at and above the county level have family planning clinics, and those in rural villages and small towns have established family planning groups. All these together form a nationwide network incorporating family planning guidance, publicity, and technical service.

With the development of a family planning program, related associations have been set up throughout the country. These people's organizations, along with population research institutes, constitute a social force in promoting family planning.

In recent years, Chinese departments in charge of population and family planing have established and developed friendly cooperation with international organizations and with their counterparts in a number of countries. Fruitful results have been obtained through such cooperation and exchanges, and they have played a positive role in promoting family planning work in China.

CHINA'S ACHIEVEMENTS IN FAMILY PLANNING AND REGIONAL DIFFERENCES
ACHIEVEMENTS

Since the 1970s, especially since the Third Plenary Session of the 11th Party Central Committee in December 1978, China has made remarkable progress in family planning, in controlling population growth, and in raising the quality of the population.

First, China has within a comparatively short period of time brought about a noticeable reduction in the birthrate, mortality rate, and natural growth rate of its population. There has also been a fairly big increase in life expectancy. From 1970 to 1984, the country's birthrate went down from 33.43‰ to 17.50‰, mortality rate dropped from 20‰ in the early postliberation years to around 7‰ in the 1970s (this level has thenceforth been maintained), and the natural population growth declined from 25.83‰ to 10.81‰. In 1981, the country's average life expect-

ancy increased to 67.88 years — 66.47 years for men and 69.35 years for women. A comparison between the four years from 1979 to 1982 and the eight years from 1971 to 1978 shows that the average annual number of births decreased from 22 million to 19 million, which means the average annual population growth dropped from 18.71‰ to 13.44‰. The pattern of reproduction of China's population has moved to one of low birthrate, low mortality rate, and low natural population growth rate.

Second, the fertility rate of Chinese women has dropped to a low level. The reduction in birthrate stems mainly from the reduction in the fertility rate of women. China's total fertility rate was 5.81 in the 1950s, 5.68 in the 1960s, and 4.01 in the 1970s, and it further dropped to 2.1 in 1983 (see Chart 12-1). Such a fertility rate was the lowest ever recorded in China's history.

Third, the number of people responding to the call for family planning has been increasing, and more and more couples of childbearing age have voluntarily taken various measures of birth control. In the last few years, as an increasing number of people have come to a better understanding of the Party's policy and principles and the advantages of family planning, great changes have taken place in their views and practice concerning childbearing. By 1984, about 86% of the married couples in China

Chart 12-1   Changes in China's Total Fertility Rate (1970–1983)

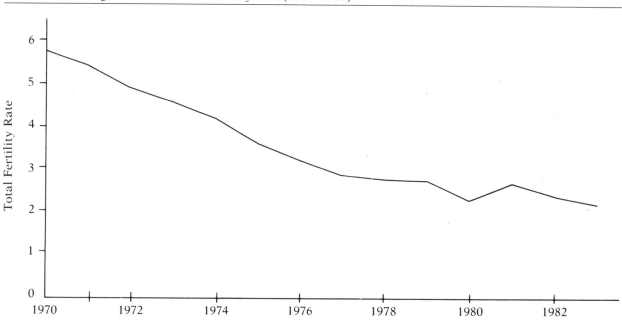

Source: *One-Per-Thousand-Population Fertility Sampling Survey in China*, special issue of *Population and Economy*, 1983.

Chart 12-2   Changes in the Average Age of Marriage for Women Since 1970

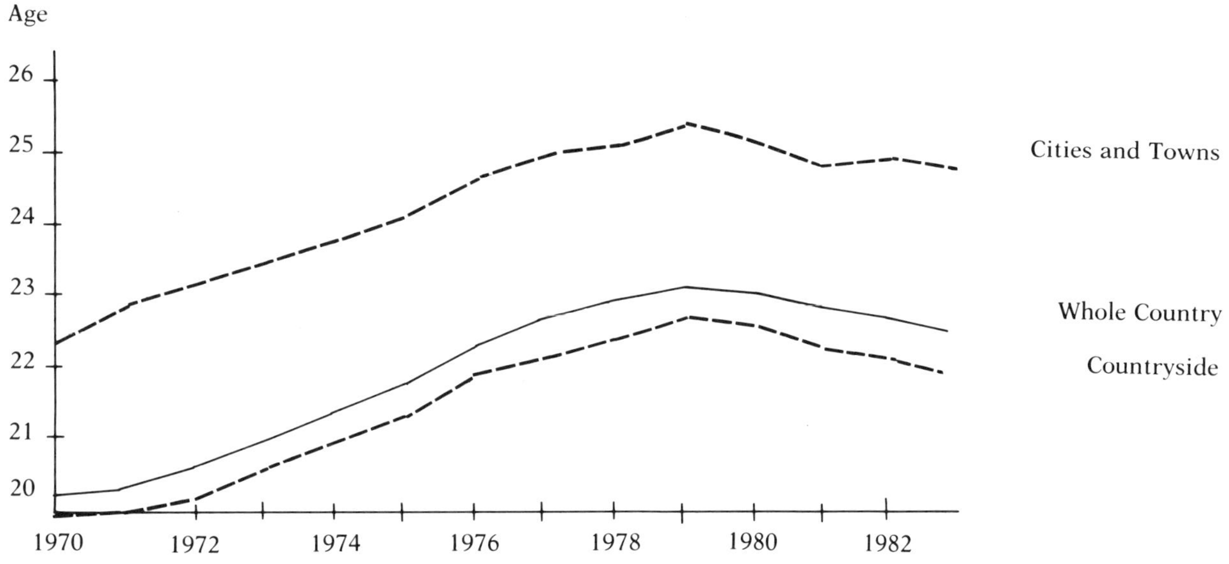

Source: *One-Per-Thousand-Population Fertility Sampling Survey in China*, Special issue of *Population and Economy*, 1983.

had taken contraceptive measures, three times as many as in 1971.

Fourth, the average age of marriage for Chinese women has gone up, while the average childbearing age has come down. This shows that most Chinese women have practiced late marriage, late childbearing, and giving birth to fewer babies. In the 1970s, the average age of marriage for women was 19.81 years old and in 1983 it went up to 22.31 (see Chart 12-2). Prior to 1970, Chinese women's average childbearing age remained at around 30. It has come down noticeably since the beginning of the 1970s—from 29.8 years old in 1970 to 27.2 years old in 1981. For more than four decades, 90% of Chinese women gave birth to children between ages 15 and 39. Since 1970, this has gradually dropped to between 15 and 34, a reduction of five years in more than a decade's time.

Fifth, the number of people responding to the call "one couple, one child" is increasing annually in China. As a result, since 1970 the rate of babies born has undergone remarkable changes (see Table 12-5).

Especially since 1979, when the call "one couple, one child" was widely publicized, the number of people receiving single-child certificates has been increasing annually. By the end of 1984, the number had reached 27.9 million.

Sixth, initial results have been achieved in giving birth to and raising healthy children in China, and the quality of the population has improved. China's Constitution explicitly stipulates, "Marriage, the family and mother and child are protected by the state." The Marriage Law has a clause prohibiting marriage between people who are lineal relatives by blood. Public health and science and technology de-

Table 12-5   Parity Distribution of Births in Selected Years (1970–1983)

YEAR	NUMBER OF BABIES BORN	FIRST CHILD		SECOND CHILD		THIRD OR HIGHER-ORDER CHILD	
		NUMBER	%	NUMBER	%	NUMBER	%
1970	29,295	6,073	20.73	4,998	17.06	18,224	62.21
1977	19,997	6,171	30.86	4,918	24.59	8,908	44.55
1981	21,342	9,938	46.57	5,411	25.35	5,993	28.08
1983	17,089	9,633	56.37	4,200	24.58	3,256	19.05

Source: *One-Per-Thousand-Population Fertility Sampling Survey in China*, Special issue of *Population and Economy*, 1983.

partments have begun the study of eugenics, widely publicized knowledge on contraception and the bearing and raising of healthy children, provided consultation service and antenatal diagnoses, as well as improved maternity and child care. According to statistics based on a survey by public health departments, in 1954 (based on a survey of 50,000 people in 14 provinces) infant death rate was 138.5‰; by 1981 (based on census) the figure dropped to 34.68‰. In 1975, the number of newborn babies who died of diseases accounted for 2.65% of the total number of babies who died; by 1984 the figure had fallen to 2.37%. The number of babies delivered by new methods rose from 88.5% in 1977 to 94.4% in 1984. The physical condition of children improved remarkably. Take seven-year-old children, for example. Compared with 1975, in 1979 boys were taller by 0.6 cm and girls taller by 1.1 cm; the weight of boys increased by 0.3 kg and that of girls increased by 0.2 kg; the chest measurement of boys increased by 0.6 cm and that of girls increased by 0.3 cm. Children's education and maternity and child care also made considerable progress. The number of children in kindergarten was 11.51 million in 1980 and 12.95 million in 1984. There were 2,610 maternity and child care centers (stations) across the country in 1980, and the number rose to 2,716 in 1984. The achievements gained in the work of giving birth to and raising healthy children showed that China's family planning policy and its implementation conformed both to the needs of social development and to the wishes of the people all over the country.

REGIONAL DIFFERENCES IN
FAMILY PLANNING WORK

Because of China's large population, vast territory, and different natural, historical, economic, and cultural conditions in different places, the achievements of the family planning program also vary from place to place in degree and in manifestation.

• Differences between cities and countryside. Over the last 30 years, the birthrate in the countryside was on the whole higher than that in the cities. During the 1949–83 period, birthrate in the cities averaged 25.6‰, and in the years 1971–82 the average was 15.96‰, as against 28.34‰ and 24.02‰, respectively, for the corresponding periods in the countryside. In 1983, the planned birthrate in the cities throughout the country was 86.3%, while in the countryside it was only 71.7%. In 1981, the total fertility rate of urban women of childbearing age was 1.39 while in the countryside it was 2.91. Although rural family planning work has made remarkable

progress since the 1970s, it still lags behind that of the cities. The primary reason for this lies in economic differences. The costs of raising a newborn baby in the city are 60–70% higher than in the countryside. In addition, because of the low level of the productive forces and the lack of social insurance in the countryside, it is unavoidable that the peasants should cherish the idea of raising children to support them in their old age. This prompts them, to a great extent, to have more children and at an early age. The second reason is the difference in education and culture. The cultural and educational level in cities is generally higher than in the countryside, and cultural level has profound influence on people's concepts concerning the bearing and raising of children. It can be said that with the raising of the people's cultural level, their concept on having children (especially on having several children) will change (see Table 12-6).

It is clear from Table 12-6 that the fertility rate of women with a university education generally was only 41.99‰, whereas that of women with a primary school education was more than double, reaching as high as 87.39‰, and the fertility rate of illiterate and semi-illiterate women was even higher. The third reason that rural family planning lags behind that of the cities is that the cities started practicing family planning earlier than the countryside. In large and medium-sized cities, birth control was promoted as early as the 1950s, and in the 1960s family planning was promoted in an all-round way. In the countryside, however, it was not until the mid-1970s that family planning was promoted in earnest. Hence the difference in the length of time in actively promoting family planning.

• Difference between areas inhabited by people of Han nationality and by minority nationalities. In the old society, the population of the minority nationalities of China grew very slowly, and in some cases the population decreased drastically. Since the founding of New China, as a result of the implementation of the correct nationality policy of the Party and government, the population of minority nationalities has increased rapidly. With the exception of a very few minority nationalities, the population of the overwhelming majority of minority peoples has increased at a rate faster than that of the Hans. Among the minority nationalities, especially among those whose population is comparatively large and dense and has grown at a fast rate, family planning is gradually promoted so that they can further develop their economy, improve their material and cultural well-being, and protect the health of women and children.

Table 12-6   Female Fertility by Educational Level (1981)

| CULTURAL LEVEL | GENERAL FERTILITY RATE (PER 1,000 WOMEN OF CHILDBEARING AGE) | PERCENTAGE OF CHILDREN BORN | | AVERAGE NUMBER OF CHILDREN BORN |
		FIRST CHILD	HIGHER-ORDER CHILD	
With education	76.64	57.77	17.96	1.72
University education	41.99	88.55	1.23	1.13
Senior middle school education	64.62	81.86	3.14	1.23
Junior middle school education	68.30	70.39	9.15	1.44
Primary school education	87.39	44.35	26.75	2.02
Illiterate or semi-illiterate	95.47	32.10	40.19	2.44

Source: *One-Per-Thousand-Population Fertility Sampling Survey in China,* Special issue of *Population and Economy,* 1983.

Of course, while formulating the family planning policy for the minority peoples, the state generally adopts more flexible methods for these regions than for the areas inhabited by the people of Han nationality. This is why the differences in the results of family planning between the two are quite distinct.

• Differences between various provinces and autonomous regions. In 1984, the total fertility rate of women of childbearing age in the three municipalities of Beijing, Tianjin, and Shanghai and in the three northeast provinces and Jiangsu Province all dropped to below 1.5; the total fertility rate for the women in Shandong, Shanxi, Zhejiang, and Shaanxi Provinces fell to below 2, and that in other provinces and regions is above 3.

According to a one-per-thousand fertility rate sample survey in 1981, there are six provinces and autonomous regions where the birth of three babies or more accounted for more than 40% of the babies born in that year; 15 provinces and autonomous regions where the birth of three babies or more accounted for 20–40%; three provinces where the birth of three babies or more accounted for 10–20% and four provinces where the birth of three babies or more accounted for less than 10%. In 1981, the birth of several babies averaged 28.09%. Of the 28 provinces, autonomous regions, and municipalities where a sample survey was conducted, there were 12 where the birth of several babies was higher than this average and 16 where the average was lower. The highest rate of birth of several babies was 62%, and the lowest was 1.07%. Generally speaking, the differences in the results of family planning work in differ-

ent provinces and autonomous regions mainly reflect the differences in their economic, cultural, and educational levels and in the length of time of active promotion of this work. In addition, such differences are not only found in different provinces and autonomous regions but can often be found in different parts of a province or even a county. This phenomenon is also mainly caused by the aforementioned differences.

China's population policy has been laid down and the family planning program is being promoted in a sound way. This is a policy of strategic importance and a great social engineering project as well. Its formulation and evolution are, in the final analysis, determined by the objective needs of China's social and economic development and serve the general tasks and goals of the nation's modernization drive. It therefore represents the fundamental interests of the people and is increasingly becoming the conscious action of tens of millions of Chinese people. Although China is currently facing a baby boom resulting from the growth of the population in the 1960s, and although the tasks of controlling population growth and family planning are arduous, the whole nation is paying greater attention than ever before to this important work and regards the raising of social results as the sole guideline. China will continue to exercise strict control over its population growth, improve the quality of the population, make greater efforts, and take more effective measures for the realization of the goal of keeping the nation's total population within 1.2 billion by the end of the century, thereby bringing about a still better population composition for the next century.

INDEX